coming home:

ART & THE GREAT HUNGER

EDITED BY NIAMH O'SULLIVAN

■ IRELAND'S GREAT HUNGER MUSEUM/QUINNIPIAC UNIVERSITY PRESS ■

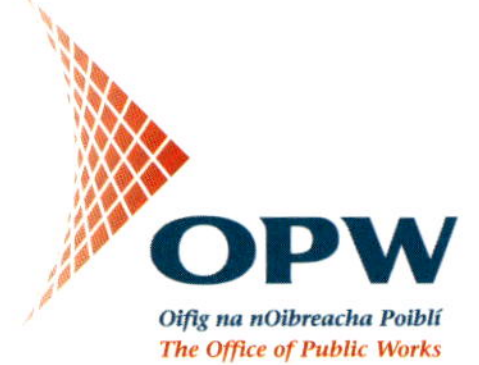
OPW
Oifig na nOibreacha Poiblí
The Office of Public Works

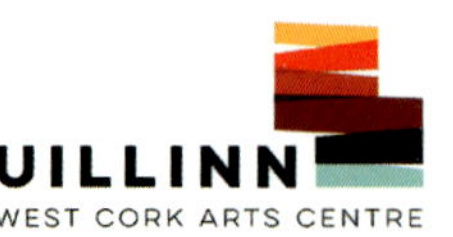
UILLINN
WEST CORK ARTS CENTRE

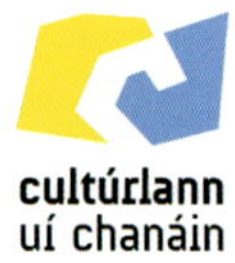
cultúrlann
uí chanáin

Exhibition dates & venues:

8 March–30 June 2018
The Coach House
Dublin Castle

20 July–13 October 2018
Uillinn: West Cork Arts Centre
Skibbereen

18 January–16 March 2019
Cultúrlann Uí Chanáin
Derry

Curator: Niamh O'Sullivan
Project Manager: Claire Puzarne

Contents:

Preface:

MICHAEL D. HIGGINS
UACHTARÁN NA hÉIREANN/ PRESIDENT OF IRELAND

I am delighted to have this opportunity to contribute to the catalogue of the powerful and moving Famine-related art collection from Ireland's Great Hunger Museum at Quinnipiac University.

For a very long time it was something to which we could not give a name. It was something with which we were not able to engage. It was something that generated a great silence. There can be no doubting, however, that *An Gorta Mór* was a defining moment in the history of modern Ireland and a turning point in the history of our people. The exodus from our shores during that period was unprecedented in Irish history, and our rising population fell by 2.5 million as a result of death and mass emigration.

It was, indeed, to be a significant indication of what was to become a regular pattern of emigration from Irish shores; a pattern shaded by a great sense of displacement and loss that entered, and remained within, our national psyche. The Irish sense of "family" emerged as something emotionally rooted, a refuge in a treacherous sea of breakdown and dispersal; and our sense of place was darkened by a parallel sense of loss and dislocation. This complex relationship between home and the "elsewhere" became a defining element in Irish culture, with migration remaining an important part of our national experience; and one that has continued to play a significant role in defining us as a society and as a people. Perhaps the scholarship in the social sciences has not given as much attention to the transience of the migratory experience as the literary accounts have.

Today we are fortunate to have a great body of scholarship that adds to our understanding of that tragic chapter of our history and provides us with material for reflection, understanding, and, indeed, resolution. Through such new and informed historiographies we have now been enabled to take some instructive lessons and draw some new conclusions as we craft a future that will continue to be informed and shaped by the historical narrative of this island.

Today, we can take a long view of *An Gorta Mór* – described by some historians as the greatest human tragedy of the nineteenth century – comparing it to the experience of other famines and beginning to discern some patterns.

Famine is never simply an accident of nature or a series of mistakes. Neither is it some form of fate or providence that is beyond human control. *An Gorta Mór* took place in the context of empire and against a background of landownership dominated by a powerful minority. Below that elite, in 1841, forty-five per cent of the landholdings were under five acres. In the west seventy-five per cent of those who scratched a living from the land lived on holdings, where they had them, with a valuation of less than £4.

It was such inequity, embedded into the fabric of a nation under colonial power, that created the social vulnerability that became the Great Irish Famine. It was a vulnerability that stemmed from the reliance of the vast majority of Ireland's population on a single variety of a single form of food – the Lumper potato.

Such vulnerability would be exacerbated by new assumptions that came to dominate political and, it was claimed, moral thinking. The new citizen of the post-Industrial Revolution period was to be thrifty, industrious, and motivated by individual welfare. Avoiding the creation of dependency became the primary goal of an imperial elite, even in the midst of the greatest loss of life – one which would end up with over one million Irish dying of hunger and related diseases, and 1.5 million fleeing from a country with no hope.

Across the many decades that now separate us from that great tragedy, it is imperative that we consider the Irish Famine against the background of the economic assumptions that served as context to it. The notion that one could change the moral character of the peasantry, and do so in conditions of poverty, was not the only assumption to come into play. The model of agricultural production that was assumed to have a future was that of commercialized agriculture, leading to massive evictions of the smaller farmers in order to clear the land for such production.

Today we have the capacity to anticipate the threat of famine and to take measures to avoid it. Yet we continue to allow people across our world to live in conditions of extreme but avoidable hunger. The moral challenge to our humanity has not changed: we continue to face the question of whether we should adjust our populations to an abstracted economic ideology, or use the best of our reason to craft economic and social models that can anticipate the needs and care for the peoples who share this fragile planet. How we answer that question is vital to our shared future and to the society we wish to craft together.

In Ireland we retain an instinctive compassion born out of our own pain and despair, and have become a people with a reputation for great generosity of spirit; a people willing to rise to the call and work with those who now face hunger in their lands, in their houses, and within their families. We are a people whose relationship with our diaspora remains deep and profound. At its heart lies a sense of inclusivity and of the coming together of Irish people, wherever they may be in the world, in a spirit of support and solidarity. It is a support and solidarity we must continue to extend to all global citizens as we commit to leading the way in the difficult but not insurmountable battle against the scourge of food shortage and famine in our world today.

Foreword:

JOHN L. LAHEY
PRESIDENT, QUINNIPIAC UNIVERSITY & CHAIRMAN OF THE BOARD OF IRELAND'S GREAT HUNGER MUSEUM

The scale of the Famine, and the horror of it, were unprecedented. It permeated everything, the traces of which remain to this day. But the visual dimensions of the loss of life and the erosions of language and culture remained unaddressed until Quinnipiac University opened Ireland's Great Hunger Museum in 2012, to considerable acclaim.

In 1997, during the one-hundred-and-fiftieth anniversary of the Great Hunger, I had the honor to serve as grand marshal of the New York City St Patrick's Day Parade. I made the Famine the theme of the parade. As I delivered speeches, the late Murray Lender, a Quinnipiac University alumnus and vice-chairman of our Board of Trustees, heard about the catastrophe for the first time, and was struck by its devastating effect on Ireland and its people. Murray grasped the importance of educating people about its causes and consequences. His vision, and the generous financial support of both Murray and his brother, Marvin, led to the creation of the Lender Family Special Collection Room in the Arnold Bernhard Library on our Mount Carmel Campus. This initial collection of art, research, and educational materials grew over a twenty-year period, with the advice of Conor Kenny of Kenny's Galway.

From its gestation, and since its opening five years ago, Ireland's Great Hunger Museum has become the world's largest collection of Famine-related art. The mission of the museum is to place the visual at the center of Great Hunger scholarship. University museums, with their capacity to draw on a wide range of academic disciplines, are ideally placed to generate new knowledge, connect disparate areas of scholarship, and form new ways of understanding. In the museum we engage with scholars across a broad interdisciplinary spectrum, on both sides of the Atlantic, to bring the collection to life, explore its legacies, and make meaningful connections between Ireland and its diaspora today.

Prior to the opening of the museum we appointed Professor Emerita Niamh O'Sullivan as consultant curator, and she continues to advise on the curation and developmental aspects of the museum and on its publications program. As we deepened our commitment to the Great Hunger project, we established Ireland's Great Hunger Institute, under the directorship of Professor Christine Kinealy, now a professor at Quinnipiac University. The combination of the museum and the institute enables us to enrich our educational programming and cater to all levels of education and interest.

As a largely invisible trauma whose consequences were intrinsic to the subsequent development of Ireland - no less than the United States - the museum collects and displays images and supporting documentation that address both the lacunae and interconnections in representations of the Great Hunger in Irish and diasporic history, culture, and memory. Our museum publications program, *Famine Folios*, makes available new research in Famine studies by internationally established scholars in history, art history, cultural theory, media history, political economy, literature, architecture, philosophy, and music. This multi-award-winning initiative was devised to augment the museum experience, and is part of its commitment to scholarship and education. The *Folios* - beautifully illustrated with works from the museum and related collections - ensure that audiences have access to the latest scholarship as it pertains to both the historical and contemporary dimensions of the collection. Spanning 170 years, the collection features work by many leading Irish and Irish-American artists, and, importantly, includes works that break new ground both stylistically and thematically, as may be seen in the catalogue. The catalogue includes essays by Niamh O'Sullivan, Ciarán Reilly, Laurence Geary, and Breandán Mac Suibhne. We greatly appreciate them sharing their knowledge and scholarship with us.

Now, mindful of the suffering of so many, a large number of whom nonetheless went on to contribute so much to America, Quinnipiac University brings its collection home, to share with the people of Ireland. *Coming Home: Art and the Great Hunger* is an important act of cultural reconnection with Ireland's past and living diaspora, and is a major cultural, educational, and tourist event of local, national, and international interest.

The exhibition is managed by Claire Puzarne, assistant director of the museum, and curated by Niamh O'Sullivan. I want to thank them, and Ryan Mahoney, our new executive director, as well as my own museum board at Quinnipiac: Lynn Bushnell, Jean Husted, Mark Varholak, Pat Healy, and Niamh O'Sullivan. *Coming Home: Art and the Great Hunger* will tour three venues: Dublin Castle; Uillinn: West Cork Arts Centre, Skibbereen; and Cultúrlann Uí Chanáin, Derry, and we are grateful to the boards and staff of the associated institutions for their interest and cooperation. The exhibition is accompanied by a rich contextual program of lectures, readings, and performances, and we are very appreciative of the many other cultural institutions that are organizing complementary programs.

We have received invaluable financial assistance and support in kind from the Department of Foreign Affairs and Trade, the Department of Culture, Heritage and the Gaeltacht, the Department of Education and Skills, and from The Ireland Funds; we thank them wholeheartedly.

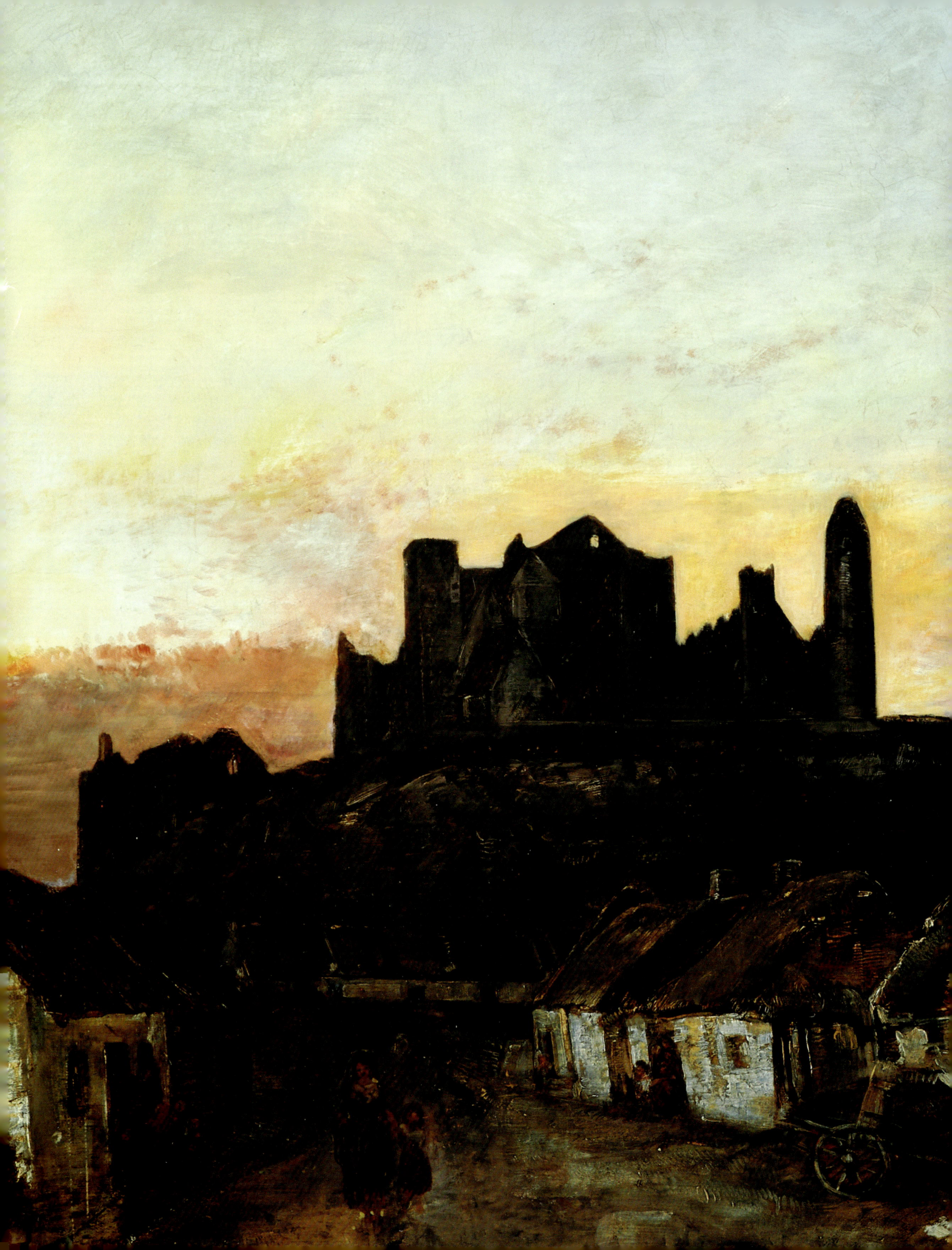

"In the land of the dead": ART & THE GREAT HUNGER

NIAMH O'SULLIVAN

Henry Mark Anthony's painting *Sunset* (*c.* 1847, IGHM) **[Figure 1]** contrasts two visions of Ireland in the mid-nineteenth century, as the majestic ruins of the Rock of Cashel tower over the more recent ruins of a society on the verge of collapse. For Thomas Davis, Ireland's antiquities bore witness to a glorious past, their very survival testifying to the endurance of that civilization. The abject poverty of the countryside in which the ruins stood, however, showed the condition into which that civilization had sunk, and the need to breathe a new spirit into the nation: "his roof rotten, his chimney one hole, his window another", Davis wrote of the Irish peasant, "even his hovel has not the security of the wild beast's den".[1] This is the vista in the foreground of Anthony's painting.

The romantic splendor of the medieval Rock of Cashel is raised almost in hope above the village, but in everyday life Davis noted that the credo of the peasant amounted to "hope on earth, agitation – his hope hereafter, the Lord God".[2] Thomas Davis did not live to see the horrors of the Great Hunger: by a tragic irony, the edition of the *Nation* newspaper, edged in black, that announced his early death in September 1845 also carried the first reports of potato blight in the countryside. In the decades that followed, another vision of hope presented itself to the Irish poor: emigration and a new life in the United States, Britain, or Australia.

Ireland's Great Hunger Museum (IGHM) is home to a wide range of images that chart the vast upheavals of nineteenth-century Ireland. It is worth noting at the outset, however, that many of the most salient changes did not lend themselves to visual representation, nor was a repertoire of styles and genres available to capture the extremes of Irish experience. "The truth is too strong for fiction", Maria Edgeworth commented on her writing late in life, "and on all sides pulls it asunder".[3] In Anthony's painting we can see some of the pressures placed on conventional art by the forces that brought devastation to both country and city in Ireland. Artists tended to fall back on more acceptable themes, or to draw on stock images relating to Irish scenery and character (the two, notably, conjoined for all practical purposes), but it is precisely against this backdrop that such works

1 (Henry) Mark Anthony, *Sunset* **[detail]**

as do break new ground – as in Daniel Macdonald's depictions of social life before and during the Great Famine – are thrown into relief.

As the calamitous events of the 1840s receded from living memory, they passed not so much into history as into a fraught silence, though the persistence of poverty, land agitation, and, above all, the American diaspora acted as reminders that the political conditions of the catastrophe were still in place. With the founding of the Irish state, to some extent a veil was drawn over the horror, but the 1945 centenary saw the first attempts to bring the Famine back into the visual imagination, through an exhibition staged in the National College of Art. It was not until the last decades of the twentieth century, particularly the one-hundred-and-fiftieth-anniversary commemorations from 1995, that the image finally caught up with history, resulting in many of the modern works exhibited here. One hundred years earlier, in 1885, a leader of the Métis people of Canada, Louis Riel – who had an Irish background – lamented their loss of culture, and predicted: "My people will sleep for 100 years, but when they awake it will be the artists who give them back their spirit."[4] The same can be said of the Famine in Ireland. Tracing the history of visual representations had to await the centennial and one-hundred-and-fiftieth-anniversary commemorations. The establishment of Ireland's Great Hunger Museum is part of this ongoing process.

The pall of death, emigration, and destitution, the erosion of language and culture, and, not least, the guilt of survivors meant the burden of representation passed from one generation to the next. The conflict between the need to remember and yet the need to forget resulted in what many perceive as a Great Silence, However, the traditional practice of history – concerned with great deeds by great men rather than voices from below – may provide a truer explanation of why the Famine, with a few notable exceptions, was not central to narratives of the nation. There are photographs of Young Ireland leaders but none of the Great Famine. The need to come to terms with the presence of the past is a relatively recent concept, as is the idea that art has a role to play in that endeavor. As time passes, remembrance becomes more elusive. David Rieff suggests that "the essence of historical remembrance consists of identification and psychological proximity rather than historical accuracy, let alone historical nuance and depth".[5] In the case of post-Famine generations, the opportunity to represent it aesthetically had to await changes in visual styles that could absorb unsettling historical subject matter, as art itself moved beyond representation to grasp forces released by the shock of modernity.

As we grow more distant in time, we can better face the past, but perhaps understand it less. In the face of mass social suffering, Primo Levi's suggestion that a "decanting" of experience, whereby "historical events acquire their chiaroscuro and perspective only some decades after their conclusion", may help to explain the profusion of writing about, and memorializing of, the Famine since the sesquicentenary.[6] The impossibility of giving voice to those who experienced the Famine, the paucity of material traces, and the scarcity of contemporary images create challenges and interpretative opportunities that, arguably, artists are uniquely equipped to meet.

■ ■ ■

In 1790 the population of Ireland was approximately four million; it increased at an unprecedented rate to more than 8.1 million by 1841. By 1891 it had dropped to 4.7 million. Over a million died during the Great Hunger, and both during and in the immediate aftermath approximately 1.5 million emigrated, followed by up to two million further emigrations to the end of the nineteenth century. Over a fifty-year period, almost half of the population disappeared. The effects of the catastrophe extended far beyond the immediate and direct losses, and are still evident around the world today: Ireland's diaspora is now estimated at around seventy million.

In the nineteenth century, the majority of people in Ireland were employed on land owned by a tiny minority of landlords. Following the Act of Union in 1800, a succession of crises resulted in a perpetual state of emergency during the early decades: the fallout from the 1798 Rebellion; bitter sectarianism over Catholic Emancipation; the Tithe War; class conflict; high food prices and low wages exacerbated by the post-Napoleonic Wars economic crash; a series of shorter but nonetheless deadly famines in 1817 and 1822; and an outbreak of cholera in 1832. From 1700 until the Great Famine there had been twenty-seven total or partial failures of the potato crop. The 1741 "Arctic Famine" killed a greater percentage of the population and in a shorter period of time than the 1845–52 Great Hunger, but this latter famine was remarkable for its longevity. The calamity of the mid-nineteenth century is best understood as arising from a steady process of disintegration rather than as a seven-year event – an outcome of systematic neglect by government. Appalling living conditions were the breeding ground for the single greatest loss of life in Europe between the Napoleonic Wars and the First World War. It occasioned some of most searing accounts of living conditions, but its visual history is more complicated.

As conditions deteriorated, there was comment from afar, even in the late eighteenth century. Benjamin Franklin contrasted the lives of landlords "living in the highest affluence and magnificence" with tenants "living in the most sordid wretchedness, in dirty hovels of mud and straw, and clothed only in rags",[7] Of landlords, Arthur Young reported in the 1770s:

Nothing satisfies him but an unlimited submission. Disrespect or anything tending towards sauciness he may punish with his cane or his horsewhip with the most perfect security ... many of their cottars [sic] *would think themselves honoured by having their wives or daughters sent for to the bed of their master; a mark of slavery that proves the oppression under which such people must live.*[8]

Visiting Ireland on the eve of the Famine, Frederick Douglass saw much to remind him in Ireland of his former life: "[O]f all places to witness human misery, ignorance, degradation, filth and wretchedness, an Irish hut is pre-eminent"; the Irish peasant, he believed, lived "in much the same degradation as the American slaves".[9] *The Times*, in keeping with colonial stereotypes, tended to blame the victims: "a wretched, indolent, half-starved tribe of savages ... [who] have never approached the standard of the civilized world" (January 4, 1847). Cottierism – potato cultivation on poor, rented plots, and occasional labor for low wages on larger estates – kept the Irish peasant in a continual subsistence crisis and on the verge of starvation.

Cyclical shortages caused immense hardship but were rarely sequential, allowing for some recovery before the next; hence the devastating potato blight of 1845 was first seen as a temporary shortage. The expectation was that the 1846 harvest would be a bumper one, but there were complete failures in 1846 and 1848, and extensive failures in the next five years produced cumulative effects. Prior to 1845, Irish peasants were among the healthiest in Europe; by 1850 the least. As the Famine entered its second year, the *Nation* lamented that

a cry of Famine, wilder and more fearful than ever, is rising from every parish and county in the land ... Last year government had to bethink themselves how to provide against a very general deficiency; this year they will have to consider how a starving nation is to be fed. (August 15, 1846)

The Duke of Cambridge had the answer: "rotten potatoes and sea-weed, or even grass, properly mixed, afford ... a very wholesome and nutritious food ... all knew that Irishmen could live upon anything and there was plenty grass in the field though the potato crop should fail."[10]

While there are a small number of contemporary paintings of conditions during the Famine period, Daniel Macdonald's *Irish Peasant Family Discovering the Blight of Their Store* (1847, NFC, UCD) **[see Figure 44]** is unique in that it confronts the blight itself. The panic that had set in by 1847 explains the heightened pitch of the painting. Victorian painting was hierarchical in subject matter, technically controlled, restrained in sentiment, and respectful of propriety. Given Macdonald's acknowledged graphic and painterly skill, the *terribilità* of the work was not the result of an inability to control medium or message, but an innovative attempt, without resorting to melodrama, to depict the "invisible" horror of an impending calamity. The shock value of the painting was such that, with a single exception, it was critically ignored when exhibited at the British Institution in 1847. Its sole reviewer, in the *Art Union* (edited by the Irishman Samuel Carter Hall), noted the "power manifested in the conception of this picture", adding that it was "not exaggerated" (March 1, 1847). The subject matter *was* ominous – the scene may seem overwrought, but is not travestied – and there were no visual precedents. In the painting the diseased potatoes are strewn, the slane is cast down, the sun is setting, and the storm closing in.[11] There is almost a sense of otherworldly keening in the air, recalling Thomas Davis's words a short time earlier: "Think of the long,

long patience of the people ... their huts, their hunger, their disease ... Oh! How they cross us like Banshees when we would range free on the mountain."[12]

■ ■ ■

If famine presented difficulties for representation, how did people around the world learn of the appalling conditions in Ireland? The Great Hunger coincided with the birth of mass-produced, illustrated newspapers, and here we find a limited visual record, which has in turn passed into the popular archive. In the face of the devastation such illustrations may come across as ineffectual, but by looking at how images worked in the new visual economies of the mid-nineteenth century, we can see a radical shift in visualization, as it attempted to address untold horrors. However timid, the scenes of Irish distress in the illustrated press were as shocking to the Victorians as contemporary famine scenes in Africa or India on our television and social-media screens are to us today.

Though the first decade of the new medium of photography coincided with the Great Famine, due largely to the unwieldy nature of the apparatus and the expense involved, no known photographs exist of the calamity. Early practitioners were landed gentry; they were uninterested in exposing the immorality of a system that kept the peasantry in its place to their own advantage. As Justin Carville suggests, photographs of living conditions were not taken as "the philosophical and ethical concept of documentary" had not "entered the cultural lexicon of photography among the Anglo-Irish".[13] That is not to say that the concept of the image as evidence did not exist, for as the illustrated periodicals showed, pictorial verisimilitude assumed documentary authority.[14] Founded in 1842, the *Illustrated London News* (*ILN*) led the way on both sides of the Atlantic. With sixteen pages and thirty-two engravings per issue, it was selling 100,000 copies by 1850. For every purchaser there were an average thirty readers, which suggests that three million people learned what they knew of the suffering in Ireland from its pages. These weeklies had huge international reach, and the Famine was one of the first global calamities to feature in the popular press.[15]

Many illustrators were primarily artists, but as illustrators they had to learn how to represent factually rather than compose imaginatively, as a fine artist might have done. But representations of the calamity needed to be framed in such a way as to attract audiences without disturbing them. Success with diverse publics lay in the symbiotic relationship between image and text - albeit one that shifted depending on the issue - and from one illustrator to another. There are inherent ambivalences in images that allow them to be digestible to audiences of contrasting backgrounds; thus, illustrated newspapers were read differently in Ireland and England. British newspapers were generally not sympathetic to the Irish, and their artists tended to toe the line. But for balance, and for their knowledge, some employed Irish illustrators and reporters. For native illustrators, such as the artist James Mahony, the desire to convey the reality was balanced by the requirements to visually contain the horror and avoid compromising the humanity of the victims.

Mahony "saw the dying, the living, and the dead, lying indiscriminately upon the same floor, without anything between them and the cold earth, save a few miserable rags upon them." The story of a family struggling to a graveyard and literally entombing themselves in a small shed "surrounded by a rampart of human bones" was beyond even *his* visual powers, and he would have thought it indecent to try. "In this horrible den, in the midst of a mass of human putrefaction, six individuals, males and females, labouring under most malignant fever, were huddled together, as closely as were the dead in the graves around." He "had immediately to draw back, so intolerable was the effluvium". Mahony's pictorial devices of the closed door and the back view of the victims occlude the effects of famine on starving, fevered bodies, and allows death to take place, if not with dignity, at least in privacy. By closing the door visually, spectators can only imagine the nightmare within. The eloquence of the image lies in its restraint (*ILN*, "The Hut or Watch-house in the Old Chapel Yard", February 13, 1847) **[Figure 2]**.

Unlike paintings, illustrations were thought to provide mimetic records of events, but these engravings have distinctive technical and aesthetic characteristics that render them far from a true picture. Constructed as they are by a chain of hands, the opportunities for insinuation were rife. From the original sketch by the artist in the field, through the elaboration of the sketch by the home-based illustrator on wood panels in the office, and the dividing of the image into blocks for engraving, the process of production offered many opportunities for manipulation, if only to accord with the house style.

In sending artists and correspondents to Ireland, these weeklies claimed "authenticity", but the truth is that pictorial newspaper content is never unmediated. The written accounts and the visual renditions vary wildly, the former predominantly condemnatory of a peasantry in the grip of primitivism, the latter representing an increasingly enfeebled people. However, the complexity of Famine narratives did not allow for the compression of cause and effect into a single image; the Famine was irreducible to a single "truth", and its representation beyond the skills of any one artist.

The contrast between the written accounts of starvation and the anatomical solidity of the illustrated victims is striking. Descriptions of malnutrition – with attendant tooth loss, swollen joints, distended stomachs, and bursting blood vessels – leading to disease and death were all but unrepresentable. Drawing starving bodies challenged not only the skills of artists but the conceptual frames of reference of the time. And it was not just the physical aspects that posed a challenge: Dr Daniel Donovan, medical officer of the Skibbereen Poor Law Union, described mothers snatching food from their starving children; knew a son who killed his father for a potato; and saw parents look on the putrid bodies of their offspring without evincing emotion. At the extreme he recounted how a fourteen-year-old boy slit the throats of two children for food. Elsewhere, there are accounts of cannibalism, one involving a family so hungry that the mother ate the flesh of the leg of her dead son. No such transgressions were illustrated; indeed, few of them were written about.[16]

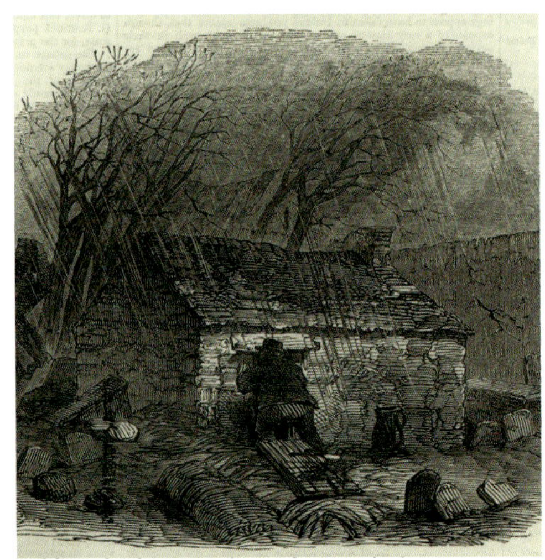

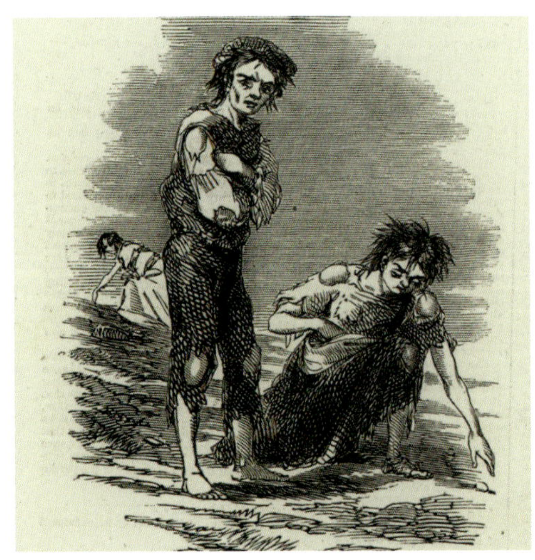

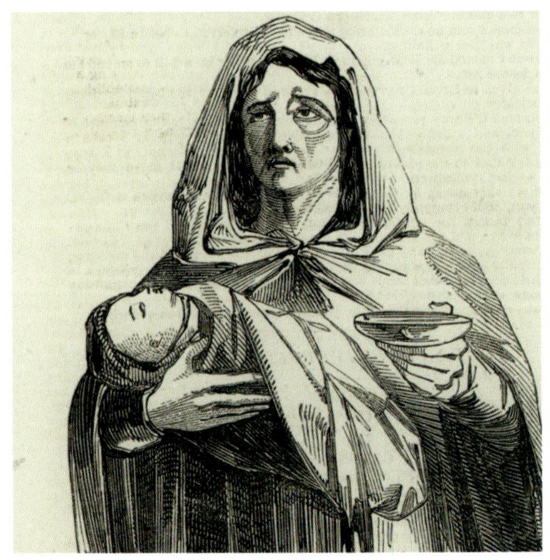

Even in illustration form, there are few images of the effects of starvation and disease on the human body.[17] In locking eyes with the spectator, the traumatized boy in "Boy and Girl at Cahera" (*ILN*, February 20, 1847) **[Figure 3]** compels us to imagine what the child sees, as he looks back at us. Malnourishment is evident in his thin, spiky hair, but we are left to complete the bigger picture from the compressed image. These orphans are delineated as individuals, but the vignette treatment suggests that they are representative of a class. His huddled arms suggest cold and hunger, but could also connote resentment. Scrounging for a morsel to eat, as they do, "like dogs after truffles", could also be subjected to different readings (*ILN*, December 22, 1849). Famine illustrations betimes evoked sympathy, guilt, embarrassment, and revulsion, encouraged charity, indicted government and landlords, engendered fear of contagion and retaliation, or reinforced negative stereotypes.

In "Woman Begging at Clonakilty" (*ILN* February 13, 1847) **[Figure 4]**, the gaunt mother also looks the viewer in the eye. The lower half of the figure bleeds out, a metaphor for the Famine as a whole. The text tells us she was carrying in her arms "the corpse of a fine child" and "making the most distressing appeal ... for aid to enable her to purchase a coffin and bury her dear little baby". In their near nakedness, "Bridget O'Donnel and Children" (*ILN*, December 22, 1849) **[Figure 5]** are more shocking than the woman from Clonakilty, whose shawl shrouds her hunger and modesty. The rags expose Mrs O'Donnel's skeletal body, reiterating the description of "half-clad spectres" in the accompanying article. With her distended stomach and concave chest, she was far from the Victorian feminine ideal, but a cast-off from a kingdom that prided itself on its social advances and progress.

Most master illustrators were classically trained in accordance with preset methods: they learned by drawing parts of Greek and Roman casts, before progressing to the human form. Upon progressing to the human body, they continued to see it through the lens of the antique; consequently, they had little experience of looking directly at unfiltered images of trauma, distress, or poverty. "Attack on a Potatoe [*sic*] Store" (*ILN*, June 25, 1842) **[Figure 6]** was the very first newspaper illustration of a scene in Ireland. It draws on the repertoire of fine art to convey its message. The diagonal thrust and the use of *repoussoir* figures to concentrate the action in the center creates a vortex of violence that intensifies the narrative. The brutish protagonists, in thrall to popery (note the crucifix worn by the woman in the center), define the prejudices in play. From the outset, in coupling hunger and violence it implicated the Irish in their own degradation.

■ ■ ■

In early 1847 a man called Leahey died in Mienies, County Cork. His wife and children remained with his corpse "until the putrescent exhalations from the body drove them from their companionship with the dead". Several days later loud snarling was heard; on entering, the gnawed and mangled skeleton of Leahey was found. The man's mother - having gone out to beg for money for a coffin in which to bury him - on her return found the dogs eating her son (*ILN*, February 20, 1847) **[Figure 7]**. The hooded child and crouching

2 "The Hut or Watch-house in the Old Chapel Yard"
3 "Boy and Girl at Cahera"
4 "Woman Begging at Clonakilty"
5 "Bridget O'Donnel and Children"
6 "Attack on a Potatoe [*sic*] Store"
7 "Village of Mienies"

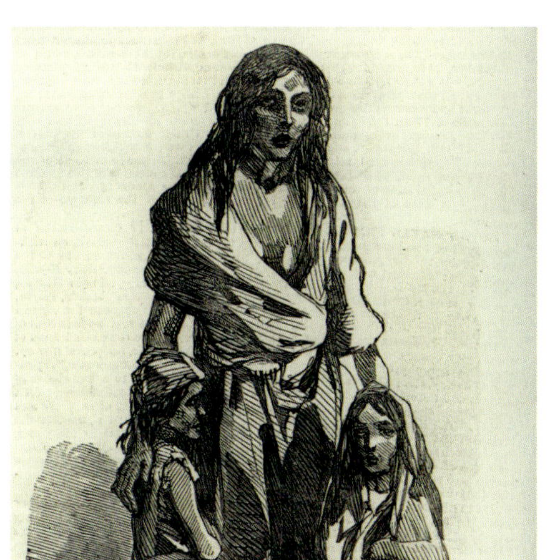

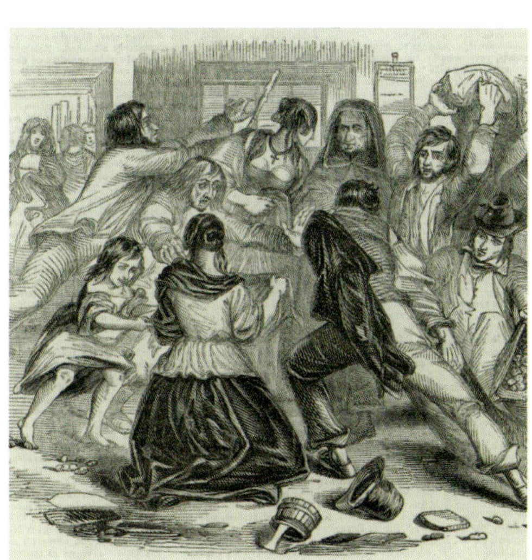

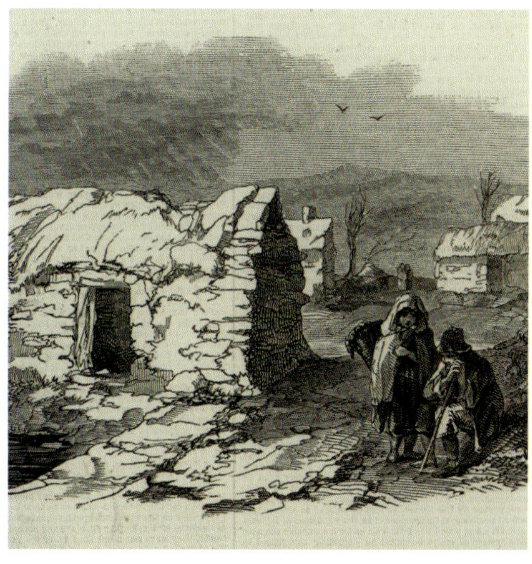

figure, the darkened door, and the open cesspit hint at the horror, but again Mahony leaves the abomination within to our imagination.

In 1847, coincidentally the peak of the Famine, Édouard Manet called on painters to paint what they *see,* not what they *know*. Although the hierarchy of genres, with history painting at the apex, did not allow ordinary people serious treatment in art, in 1848 – the year of revolutions in Europe – the call for political representation *for* and *of* the people led Gustave Courbet to break the mold. Notwithstanding French realists bringing peasants into the studio, the *reality* of peasant experience concentrated on the everyday rather than the extremes, with the result that even realism was incapable of pictorializing an epic catastrophe such as the Famine. Empathy from afar was difficult to manage aesthetically, the Famine's effects being so far beyond human imagination.

The iconography of atrocity raises far-reaching aesthetic and ethical considerations. Its precedents are found in history painting – mythological slayings, religious crusades, and the great battles of empire – made at a remove from time and place. History painting was intended to commemorate the past, not provide a documentary account of the events or ideas they represent. With few exceptions, depicting atrocity in the time of its occurrence is largely unknown before the late eighteenth century. In representing the near contemporary *Death of General Wolfe* (1770, National Gallery of Canada), Benjamin West flaunted history painting, and sent shock waves through the academy, but even then followed classical decorum. Jacques-Louis David's *Death of Marat* (1793, Musées Royaux des Beaux-Arts, Brussels) was arguably the first convincing image of death; for his *Raft of the Medusa* (1818–19, Musée du Louvre) **[Figure 10]**, Théodore Géricault visited a morgue to ensure accurate portrayal of his corpses; while Courbet's *Burial at Ornans* (1849–50, Musée d'Orsay) **[Figure 8]** in a sense marked the burial of history painting itself. But the artist with the most penetrating eye for atrocity was Goya **[Figure 9]**. In his Napoleonic invasion paintings and his Peninsular War series, Goya depicted murder, torture, and rape. The second part of *Los Desastres de la Guerra* focused on the famine that ravaged Madrid between 1811 and 1812. In the seventeen famine plates (nos 48–64), Goya's visual rhetoric, in which the narrative is implicit rather than explicit, communicates unrepresentability per se. Given their dates, *Los Desastres* (1810–20) might have provided iconographic antecedents of Great Hunger imagery, but they were not published until 1863, denying Famine artists a model they so badly needed.

If Goya's caption "I saw it" implicates the artist, *seeing* the artwork implicates the viewer. Responsibility to bear witness thus includes the observer, in what Susan Sontag calls co-spectatorship.[18] The resistance of the authorities to alleviating famine distress is beyond comprehension, but it is also hard to understand the passivity of those who read the accounts and saw the imagery, even in the relatively sanitized pictorial press.[19] One inquest recounted the death of a mother and her three children in a dyke, the hand of one child and the foot of another "devoured by rats". In Schull a dead woman was found with her dead infant at her breast, the child having bitten off a nipple trying to squeeze a drop of milk from her dying body. Accounts of families struggling to cemeteries to bury themselves, because there would be no one left to do it for them when

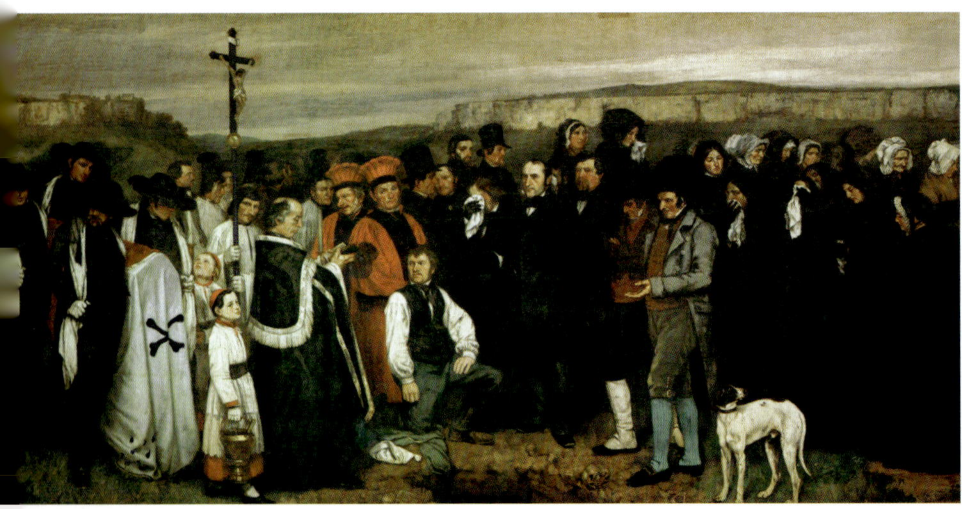

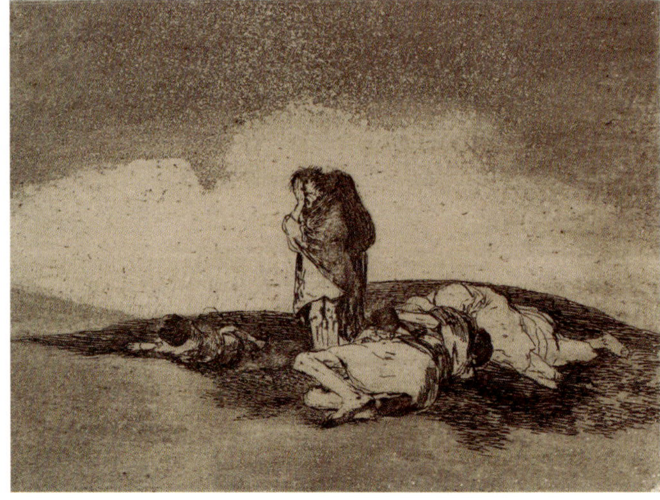

they were gone, defied representation. Those who had any such experience, in person or by proxy, would have considered it improper to turn it into art. And, of course, the moral, social, and cultural obstacles to such representation were entwined with the interests of empire.

The Act of Union led to the exodus of the art-purchasing class from Ireland, and Irish artists who had not already gone to London followed them. Here, many were quick to suppress their Irishness. Historically, violence or distress in art was softened for the sensibilities of the rich - distanced in time, and cloaked in mythology or allegory. Artists painted for an elite market, for aristocratic and merchant classes who simply would not acquire pictures of rotting potatoes, emaciated bodies, or diseased corpses to hang in their homes. Undoubtedly, the monetary nature of the engagement between artists and patrons softened the focus of artists when it came to addressing the interests of the purchasing classes. The careers of Irish artists, especially, would not have survived otherwise. Over and over, those who witnessed the horror and suffering lamented their inability to describe or delineate what they saw.

In December 1846 Nicholas Cummins, a Justice of the Peace in Cork, wrote:

the scenes that presented themselves were such as no tongue or pen can convey the slightest idea of ... six famished and ghastly skeletons, to all appearance dead, were huddled in a corner on some filthy straw, their sole covering what seemed a ragged horse-cloth and their wretched legs hanging about, naked above the knees ... in a few minutes I was surrounded by at least 200 of such phantoms, such frightful spectres ... Their demonic yells are still ringing in my ears, and their horrible images are fixed on my brain.

In an age that prided itself on morality, how could one depict the immoral? How could a desperate people, crazed with hunger and despair, living in filthy hovels among open sewers, fevered and fearful, be transformed into art? James Mahony lamented: "neither pen nor pencil ever could portray the misery and horror" (*ILN*, February 1847). Even George Frederic Watts's lack of specificity (as we shall see below) provoked one reviewer to rebuke him: "You come too close home Sir to

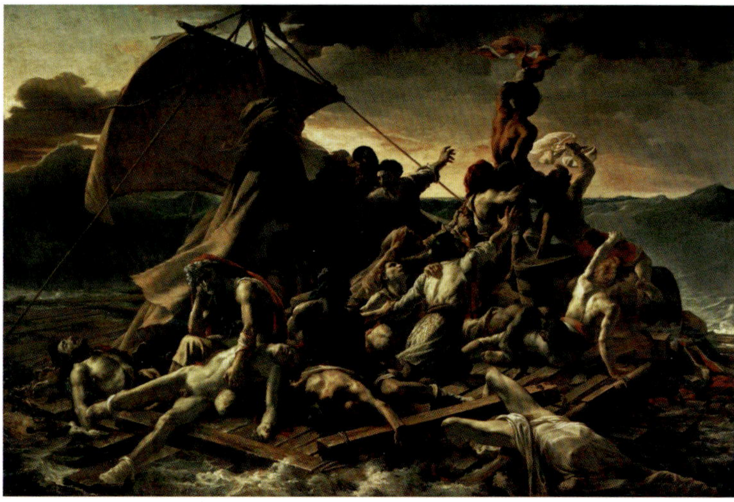

8 Gustave Courbet, *Burial at Ornans*
9 Francisco De Goya, *No hay quien los socorra*
10 Théodore Géricault, *Raft of the Medusa*

our consciences, to be agreeable" (*Spectator*, January 7, 1882).

The great humanitarian from Connecticut, Elihu Burritt, decided to see for himself: "I can find no language nor illustration sufficiently impressive to portray the spectacle." Yet he was eloquent in his inarticulation, describing stark-naked "breathing skeletons":

If they had been dead, they could not have been such frightful spectacles, but ... mirabile dictu, *they could stand upon their feet and even walk, but it was awful to see them do it. Had their bones been divested of the skin that held them together, and been covered with a veil of thin muslin, they would not have been more visible ... an appearance ... seldom paralleled this side of the grave.*

Burritt likened the scene to "that of the battle field when the hostile armies have retired, leaving one-third of their number bleeding upon the ground". He described the soup house "surrounded by a cloud of these famine spectres, half naked, and standing or sitting in the mud ... like famished beasts".[20] Accounts of the ravage of the bodies of children are particularly distressing: "Little boys and girls presented a hideous sight. In many instances, their heads had become bald and their faces wrinkled like old men and women of seventy or eighty-years-of-age."[21] In his study of "homicidal starvation", Alfred Swaine Taylor concluded that "life is commonly terminated by a fit of maniacal delirium".[22]

■ ■ ■

Irish artists went to Britain in pursuit of patronage, but British artists went to Ireland in pursuit of the primitive. The work of the Scottish artist David Wilkie predates the Famine, but had a major influence on subsequent artists. *The Peep-o'-Day Boys' Cabin in the West of Ireland* (1835–36, Tate Gallery) **[Figure 11]** and *The Irish Whiskey Still* (1840, National Galleries of Scotland) portray secret agrarian societies and illicit alcohol production – underground rural activities conjoined for their subversive potential. Wilkie's Irish

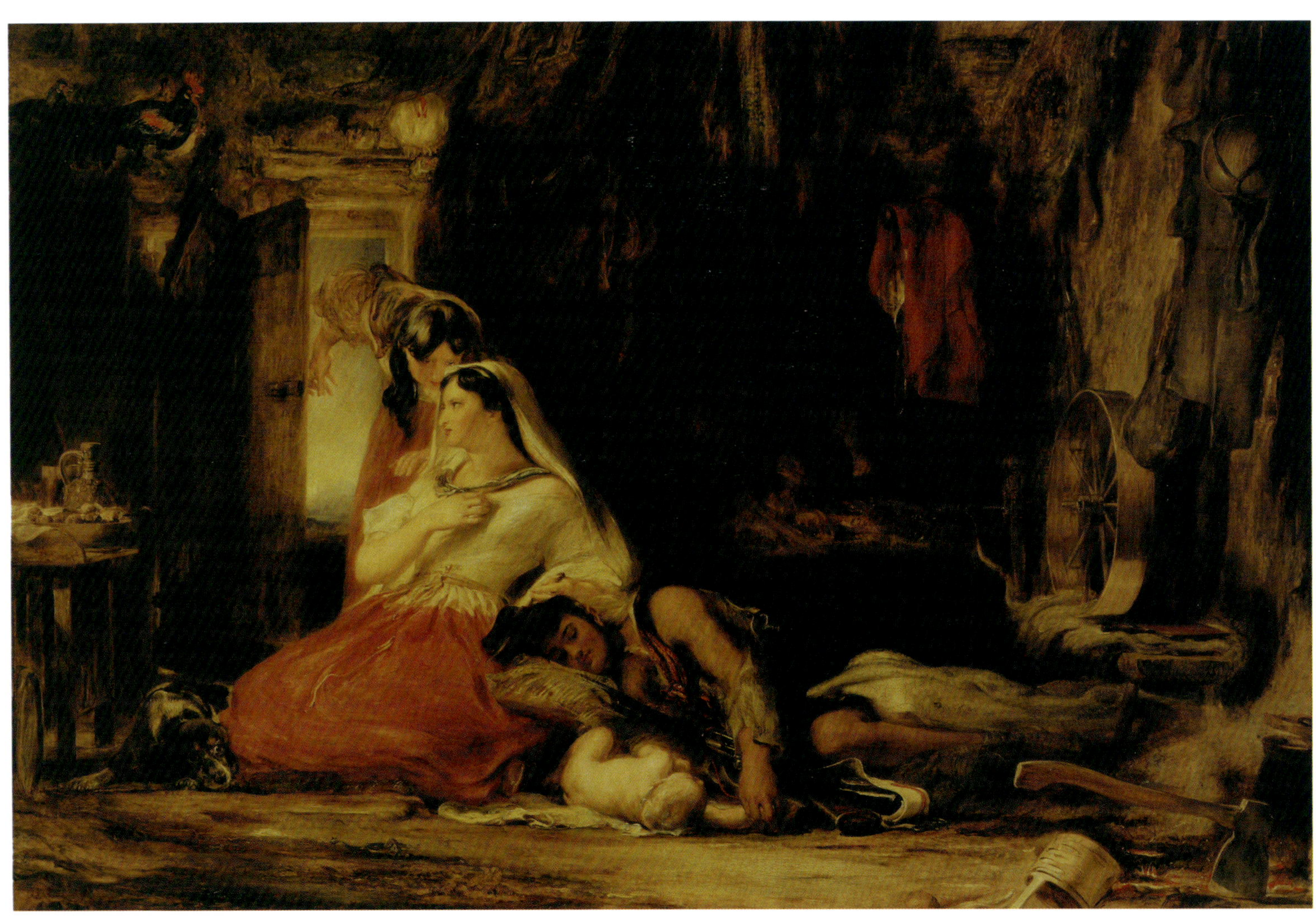

paintings were remarkable for their subject matter, scale, and execution, fueling what Fintan Cullen calls "centuries of generalized readings of Ireland: a peasant class who thrived on criminality".[23] But Wilkie found not only picturesque poverty but also a steadfast people, "whom no penalties could turn, whom no terror of military violence could overcome".[24] His rural scenes may have pandered to the expectations of the salon class in London, but they also underlined the resilience and ingenuity of the peasant. He saw such activities as representative of social problems, meriting "larger" treatment than mere genre scenes.

Wilkie saw himself practicing contemporary history painting, addressing important political and social issues. But in the work of another Scot, Erskine Nicol, Wilkie's high-mindedness degenerated into prejudice, as the Irish assume apelike visages in almost a hundred "humorous" paintings closer to caricature than characterizations of real life.[25] During a four-year stint in Ireland, from 1846–50, Nicol – with some notable exceptions – routinely portrayed the Irish as affronts to the work ethic and civility of their stolid British counterparts. The brown epidermis of his simianized characters reinforced the notion of the unwashed (or tanned-by-indolence) Irish as seen in *A Knotty Point* (1853, IGHM) **[Figure 12]**. But whether the artist was aware of it or not, Dr Daniel Donovan established that the "brownish filthy-looking coating, almost as indelible as varnish" was caused by a "secretion poured out from the exhalants on the surface of the [starving] body".[26]

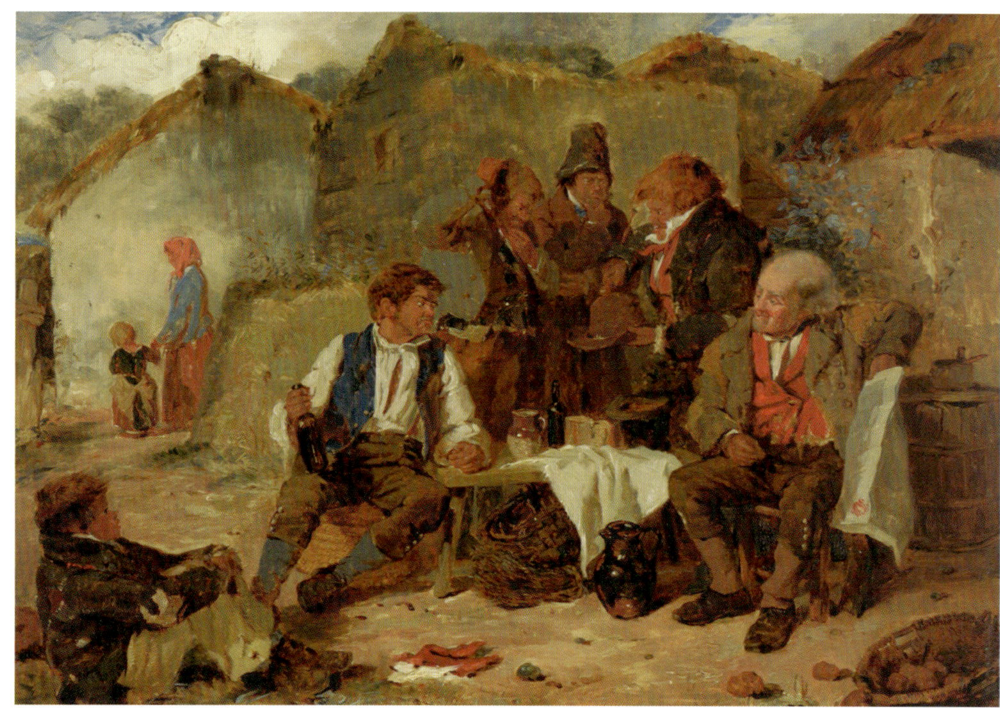

11 David Wilkie, *The Peep-o'-Day Boys' Cabin in the West of Ireland*
12 Erskine Nicol, *A Knotty Point*

Occasionally, however, Nicol put the expectations of patrons aside and produced some images sympathetic to the poor and critical of the regime. Of some complexity is a painting of a single figure, *The Tenant* (1880, Brian P. Burns Collection). Its title was derived from the novel by Maria Edgeworth, *Castle Rackrent* (1800); a subtle indictment of landlordism in the eighteenth century, it translates effectively into a nineteenth-century subject. The tenant sits in the hallway of a landlord whose demesne is depicted on a map, beneath which is a blunderbuss, showing that he regulates his affairs by what the prime minister Lord John Russell called "the lynch law of the landlords". The landlord is absent in the picture, as he so often was in life. As Kevin Whelan sees it:

The map represents a legal landscape, an abstract dehumanized world of numbers valued in property, power and money. The flesh-and-blood tenant disrupts this artifice, his head awkwardly breaking the map frame, embodying the moral and historical, rather than a legal relationship between land and people. He embodies a world of family, community and memory, in which invisible but powerful filaments of tradition kinship and occupation link him to a living not a legal landscape.[27]

Nicol's "humorous" images passed into painting from a new kind of popular illustration, exemplified by the comic magazine *Punch* **[Figure 14]**. As "a class which at best wallows in pigsties and hugs the most brutish degradation" (*The Times*, October 4, 1848), such characterisations were reinforced by Thomas Nast across the Atlantic **[Figure 13]**. But racial stereotyping also occurred in "serious" papers, where it was all the more damming for purporting to be realistic **[Figure 15]**. The racialization of poverty justified government policy on the Famine, leading the authorities to place blame for Ireland's problems on the Irish themselves **[Figure 16]**. As the

13 Thomas Nast, "St. Patrick's Day, 1867"

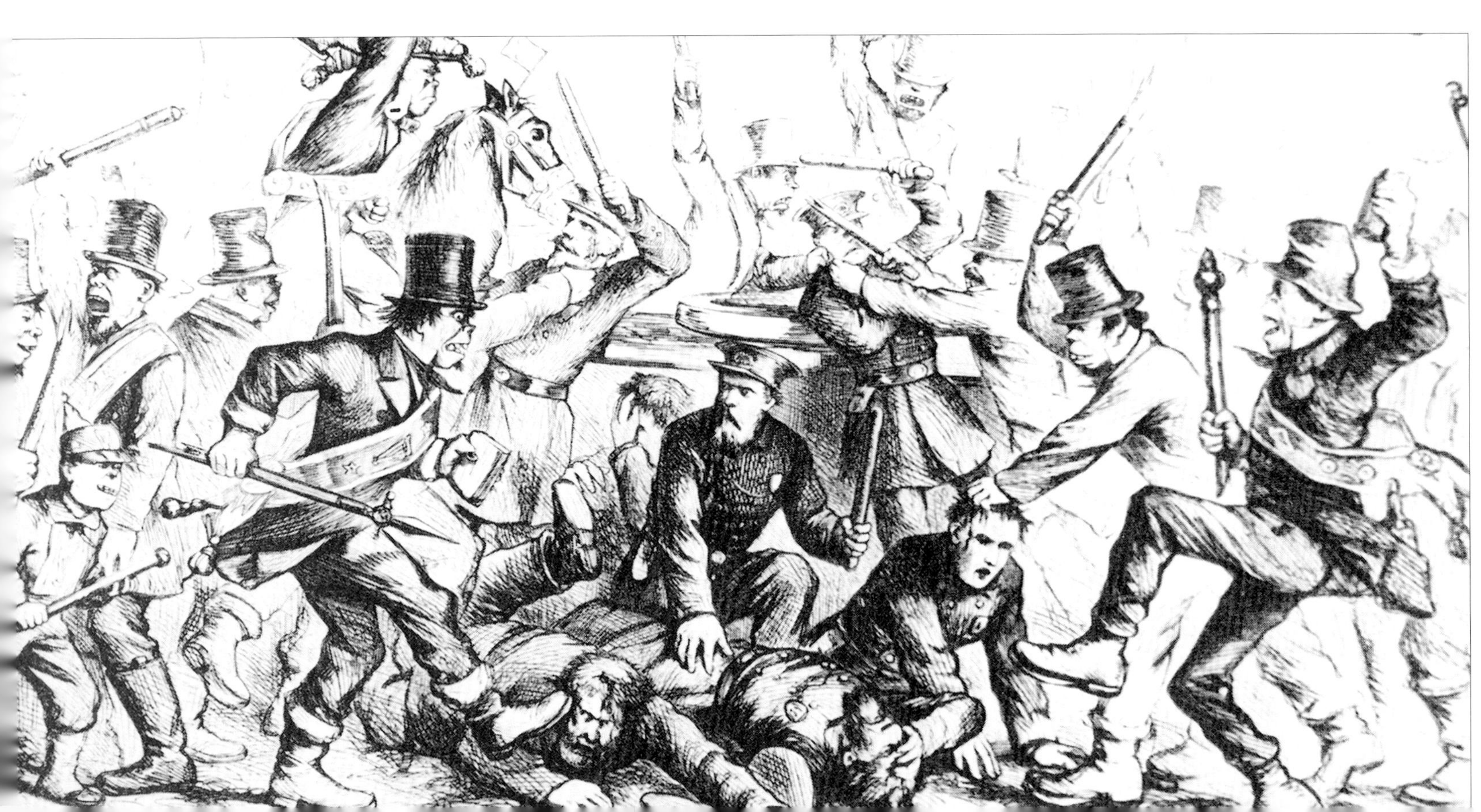

pseudoscience of phrenology gained credibility in tandem with evolutionary theory, the notion that man's moral and intellectual development could be read from his physiognomy culminated in an "Index of Nigrescence", in which the Irish were placed close to Cro-Magnon man and the "Africanoid" races. The prognathous jaw and low forehead, confirming low evolutionary status, supposedly explained Irish degeneracy and criminality.[28]

Not surprisingly, Irish painters recoiled from this, which makes the visual records of British artists all the more notable. In 1843 Francis Topham made his first visit to Ireland, returning in 1844 (and thereafter) with Frederick Goodall, Alfred Downing Fripp, and Henry Mark Anthony. These artists familiarized themselves with antiquarian debates, and would have known the artwork of George Petrie, George Victor du Noyer, William Wakeman, the illustrators for the Halls, and others. Anthony, Fripp, Goodall, and Topham's Connemara paintings are important visual records of the culture of the peasantry. And in their work the Victorian writer Mary Howitt perceived "the crushed and bleeding soul of the Irish people".[29] But as the Famine took hold, the empty skillet, the bare dresser, and the absence of a cooking pot over the fire alluded to the terrible conditions in which people struggled to survive, beyond which the ever-darkening story awaited visual realization.[30]

In Anthony's *Killarney* (1845, Royal Collection Trust) and *The Croppie's Grave* (1846, Walker Art Gallery), a more political vein is mined, as noted in a contemporary review that picked up

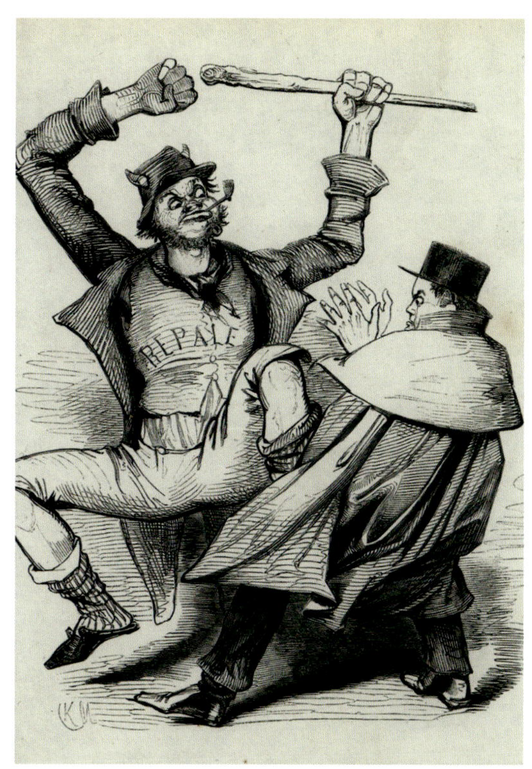

14 Kenny Meadows, "The Irish Frankenstein"
15 "Irish Physiognomy"
16 "Idiot and Mother"

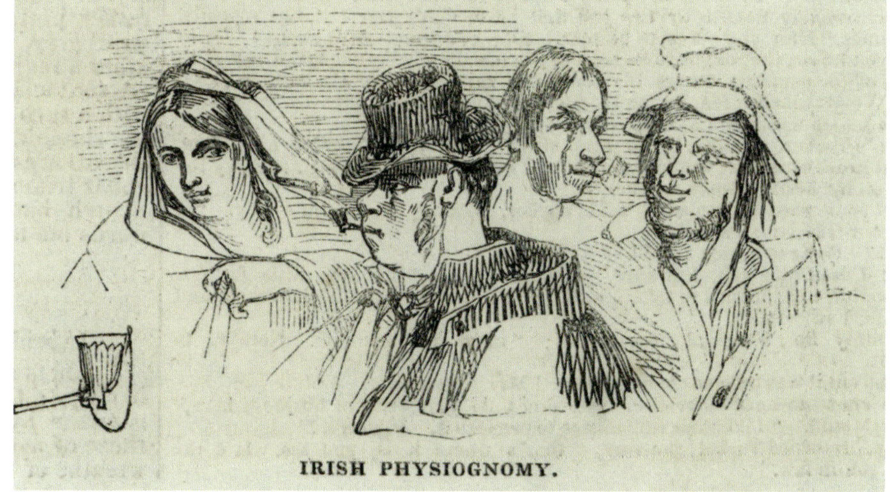

IRISH PHYSIOGNOMY.

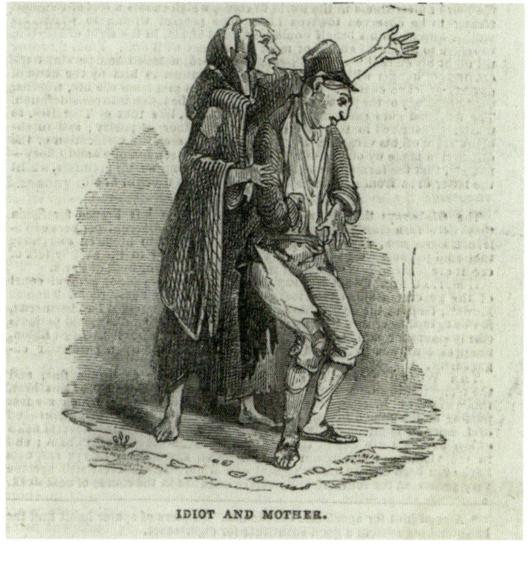

IDIOT AND MOTHER.

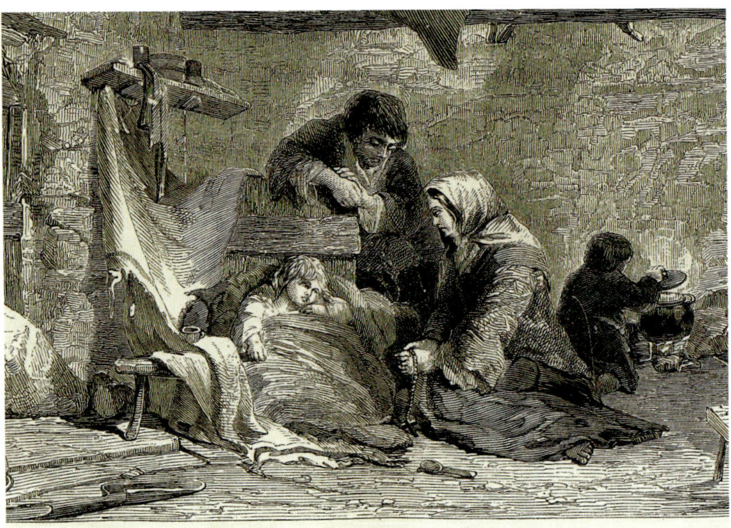

FAIRY STRUCK; OR, THE DYING CHILD.
By F. Goodall.

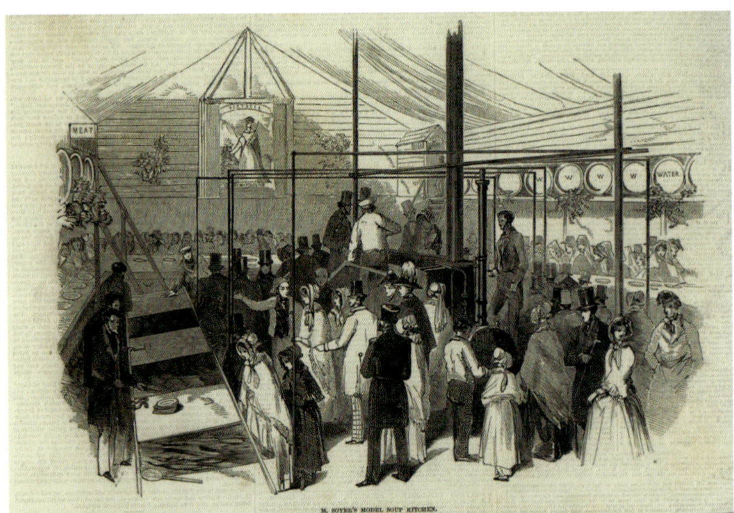

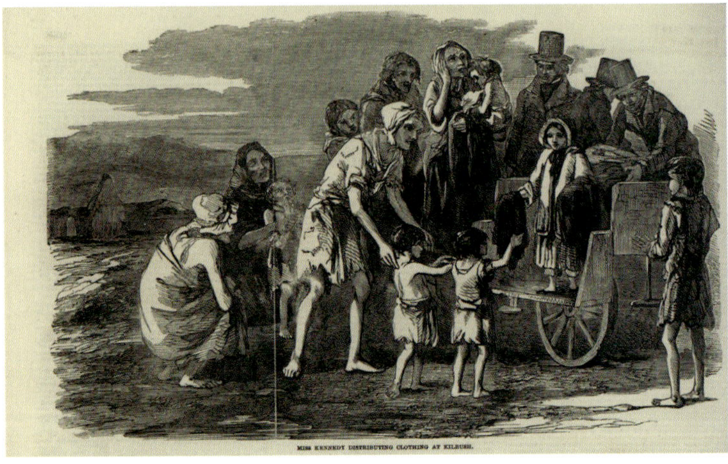

17 Frederick Goodall, "Fairy Struck, or, the Dying Child"
18 "M. Soyer's Model Soup Kitchen"
19 "Miss Kennedy Distributing Clothing at Kilrush"

on the "social and political cloud of ill that has hung over Ireland for so long" (*Manchester Courier,* September 14, 1850). From contemporary reviews we know that a number of lost paintings were richly informative of British takes on vernacular culture, while others were more overtly ideologically charged; the rediscovery of Goodall's "Fairy Struck, or, the Dying Child" (1847) **[Figure 17]** or Anthony's *Whiteboys' Retreat*, for example, would add to our understanding of the power of the image in both cultural-nationalist and colonial discourses.

■ ■ ■

David Lloyd notes that "The Famine, whatever else we wish to say about its contours and meaning, must be seen as a colonial catastrophe".[31] Lord John Russell, the prime minister from 1847, believed that relief measures were such as to encourage a culture of dependency rather than self-reliance. A new system of public works – hard labor, twelve hours a day, six days a week, for people already incapacitated by the previous year's shortages – brought people to their knees. The building of roads that led nowhere and walls that surrounded nothing were terminated in early 1847. The government next sent the *chef de cuisine* of the Reform Club in London to Ireland to provide soup for the starving, the *Cork Examiner* announcing that "there will soon be no more deaths from starvation in Ireland" (February 26, 1847) **[Figure 18]**. Philanthropy, charity, and local relief stepped in to compensate for the rigidity of central government. In a famous image we see Miss Kennedy, the seven-year-old daughter of the Poor Law inspector

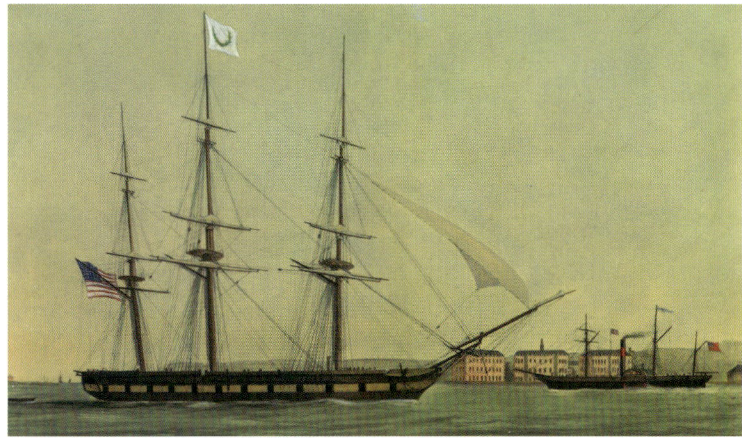

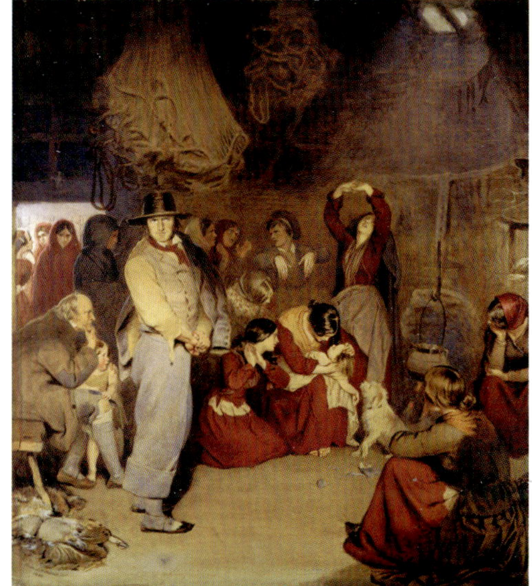

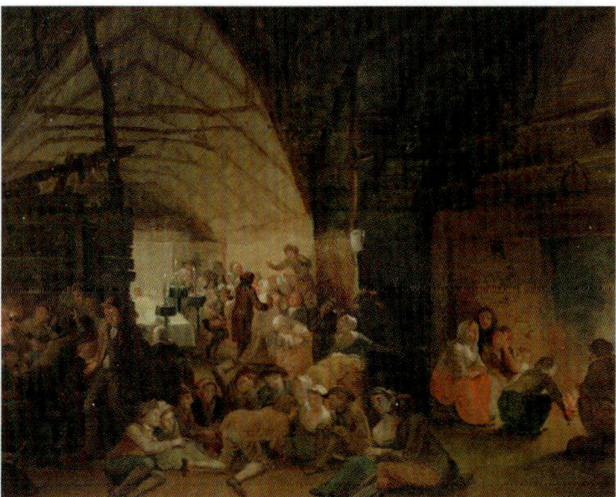

20 George M.W. Atkinson, *U.S. Sloop of War Jamestown*
21 Frederic William Burton, *Aran Fisherman's Drowned Child*
22 Nathaniel Gorgan, *The Wake*

of the Kilrush Union, daily distributing clothes "to the wretched children brought around her by their more wretched parents". A journalist saw a "woman crouching like a monkey, and drawing around her the only rag she had left to conceal her nudity. A big tear was rolling down her cheek, with gratitude for the gifts the innocent child was distributing" **[Figure 19]**.

When relief failed, there was the cold comfort of the workhouse, where conditions of appalling abuse and psychological cruelty obtained.[32] To gain admission the poor had to relinquish their small plots of land and endure segregation, causing indescribable familial distress: "the dormitories resembled pig-styes more than habitations of human beings, and the effluvia from them was overpowering to the highest degree" reported the *Economist* (January 2, 1847), while the pitch-dark punishment cells – four stone walls and a stone bed – attest to institutional callousness, even by Dickensian standards.

Without American relief, many more would have died. One of the most remarkable voyages of mercy was undertaken by Captain Robert Bennet Forbes, who published a record, *The Voyage of the Jamestown on Her Errand of Mercy* (1847). This featured the image *Departure of the "Jamestown", for Cork, Ireland, R.B. Forbes, Commander* (1847), which was commissioned of the great American luminist Fitz Henry (aka Fitz Hugh) Lane (Lane is also thought to have executed a painting of the ship, but this remains unlocated). When Fr Theobald Mathew escorted the captain around Cork, Forbes observed that the food in a soup kitchen he visited "would be refused by well-bred pigs in my own country". In reciprocation, he was presented with the framed lithograph *U.S. Sloop of War Jamestown* executed by George Mounsey Wheatley Atkinson **[Figure 20]**.

■ ■ ■

Before the Famine, the wake was the occasion of mourning, music, and dancing, amounting to both celebration and lamentation in the presence of the corpse, as we see in Nathaniel Grogan's *The Wake* (*c.* 1783, Fine Arts Museum, San Francisco) **[Figure 22]** and in a number of humorous sketches by Daniel Macdonald. Frederic William Burton's *Aran Fisherman's Drowned Child* (1841, NGI) **[Figure 21]**, however, is an image of raw grief, as family, neighbors, and friends gather around the fisherman and family to mourn the young child who lies lifeless across the lap of its distraught mother.[33] The accompanying rituals were important social and symbolic manifestations of community values and beliefs, attesting to vernacular cultures that lay outside Victorian ideologies of improvement and progress.[34] Keening – what Thomas

Crofton Croker call the "Irish funeral howl" – was an essential part of funeral practices, and in a rare linking of art to death, Croker tells us that the open hearse "used by poorer classes becomes perfectly grotesque, from the barbarous paintings of saints and angels with which it is bedizened".[35]

At the height of the Famine infant mortality soared, and part of the inconsolable grief was not only physical loss but the breakdown in respect for the dead. In one image, set in what appears to be a stable, a shaft of light illuminates the Widow Connor's child as she dies on the cold, earthen floor (*ILN*, January 5, 1850) **[Figure 24]**. Death occurred from dysentery, cholera, smallpox, and famine fever. Relapsing fever – transmitted through lice that fed on filthy, unfed people – led to hemorrhages, causing the foulest stench as it discharged while the poor person was still alive. The death toll was such that corpses were disposed of without shroud or coffin, wake or prayer: common civilities were also casualties, leading one correspondent to exclaim, "I fear we must bury the dead coffinless in future. My God! What a revolting idea! Without food when alive, without a coffin when dead" (*ILN*, January 16, 1847). In one of the most disturbing images of famine mortality, "Funeral at Skibbereen" (*ILN*, January 30, 1847) **[Figure 23]**, we see a man brandishing his whip to drive a half-dead horse across a barren landscape, with bodies slung across the cart, already eleven days' dead, heading for unceremonious disposal. Such was the impact of this image that it was republished in the *New York Herald* a few weeks later (February 28, 1847).

Poor housing and overcrowded workhouses, dirt and deficient diet, lack of clothing and hygiene were all factors in the spread of disease, and contagion was virulent, as in the illustration of a vicar keeping vigil with a dying man: "The Vicar sits while Mullins lies in the corner. Mullins died and 3 days later, so too did the Vicar."[36] Mullins's hut was less than ten-feet square, and in order to sketch the scene, "the artist had to stand up to his ankles in the filth upon the floor" (*ILN*, February 20, 1847) **[Figure 25]**. Mahony was appalled at the normalization of death: "so hardened are the men regularly employed in the removal of the dead from the workhouse, that I saw one of them, with four coffins in a car, driving to the churchyard, sitting upon one of the said coffins, and smoking with much apparent enjoyment" (*ILN,* February 13, 1847).

■ ■ ■

In Malthusian minds hunger was not only inevitable but necessary to keep the population in check; the blight culled the people and cleared the land, and was thus welcomed as an instrument of divine will. Charles Trevelyan, assistant secretary to the Treasury and chief administrator of famine relief, concluded: "Supreme Wisdom has educed permanent good out of transient evil."[37] As he saw it, "The judgment of God sent the calamity to teach the Irish a lesson, that calamity must not be too much mitigated ... The real evil with which we have to contend is not the physical evil of the Famine, but the moral evil of the selfish, perverse and turbulent character of the people."[38]

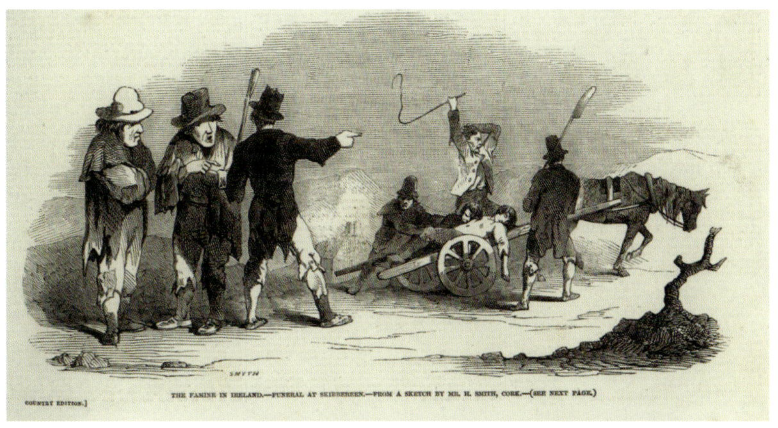

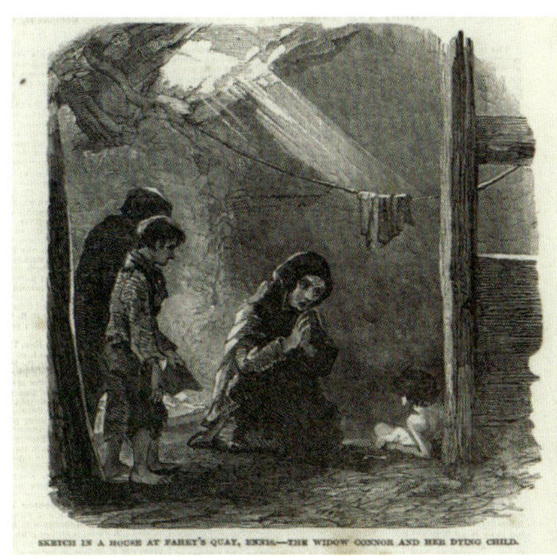

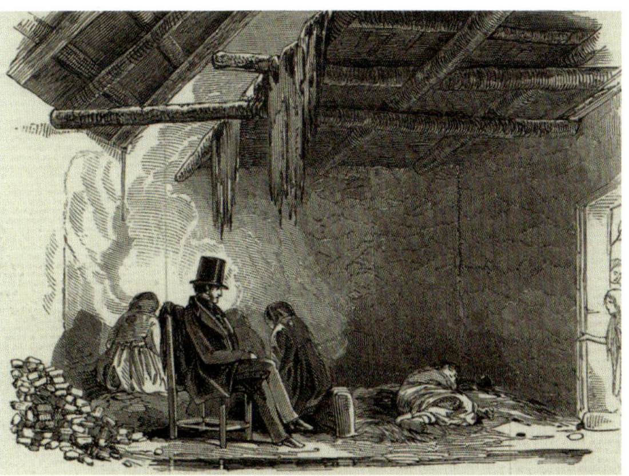

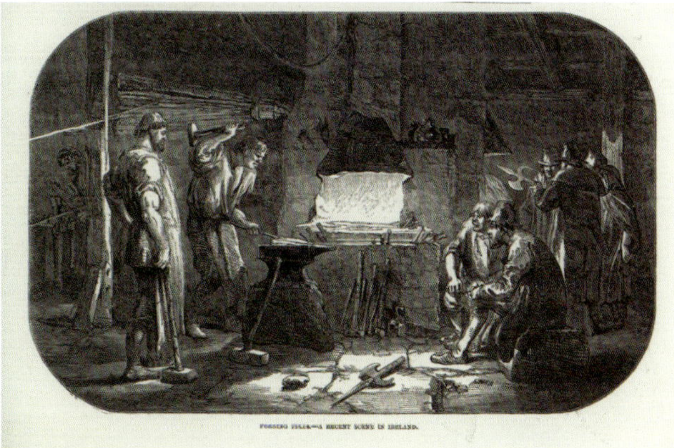

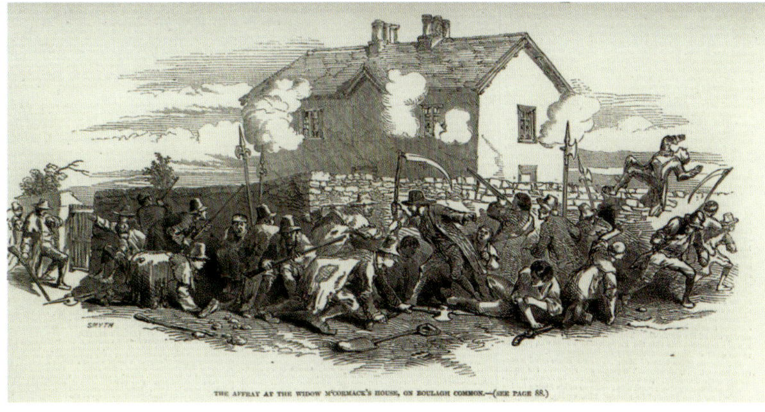

23 "Funeral in Skibbereen"
24 "Widow Connor"
25 "Mullins's Hut"
26 "Forging Pikes"
27 "The Affray"

In 1847 Lord Clarendon, Lord Lieutenant of Ireland, told the prime minister: "We shall equally be blamed for keeping them alive or letting them die, and we have only to select between the censure of the Economists or the Philanthropists. Which do you prefer?"[39] The logic of laissez-faire provoked John Mitchel's observation that Ireland "died of political economy".[40] Contemporary perceptions of ships laden with food "to feed the foreigner, leaving starvation and death the sure and certain fate of the toil and sweat that raised this food" ratcheted up the anguish and outrage (*Nation,* October 25, 1845). The consequences of paying the landlord regardless of the need to eat to survive were not hard to foresee: "Will not a starving population become justly indignant when whole fleets, laden with the produce of our soil, are unfurling their sails and steering from our harbour, while the cry of hunger is singing in their ears?" asked the *Waterford Freeman* (October 3, 1846). Mitchel protested that Ireland produced enough "to feed and clothe not nine but eighteen millions of people", yet "a government ship sailing into any harbour with Indian corn was sure to meet half a dozen sailing out with Irish wheat and cattle".[41] Although historians differ as to quantities and the mortality implications, large amounts of butter and corn, rabbits and seed, salmon and oysters, as well as porter and whiskey were exported.

Not surprisingly there are few images of food exportation, but there *are* some of British relief measures thwarted by Irish violence. In "Irish Armed Peasants Waiting for the Approach of a Meal Cart", brigands lie in wait to attack a cart bringing relief to the poor. The aggression of the Irish rather than the cold-blooded removal of food from the country is emphasized, as the text contrasts "a wise and humane Government" doing its utmost for "a destitute and famine-stricken population", and the "lawless ruffians ... who rather spill human blood to purchase a meal, than till the generous earth" (*PT,* October 30, 1847). Images of violence and resistance were more common in the realm of reportage. The illustrations "Forging Pikes" (*ILN*, August 5, 1848) **[Figure 26]** and the "Affray at the Widow McCormack's House, on Boulagh Common" (*ILN*, August 12, 1848) **[Figure 27]** suggest a country out of control when in fact the Young Ireland uprising of July 29, 1848 was but a scuffle. Although it was immediately obvious that no rebellion was afoot, the

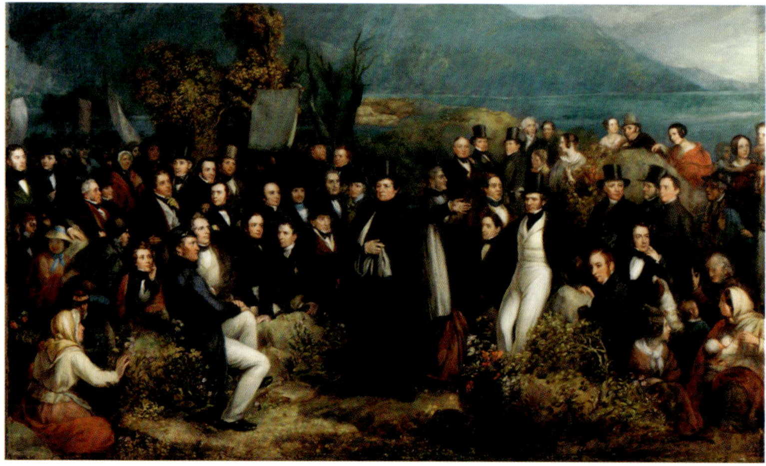

28 Joseph Haverty, *Monster Meeting at Clifden*
29 Daniel Macdonald, *The Irish Faction Leader* **[detail]** and *The Irish Faction Leader* **[detail]**

authorities made use of it to justify further coercion. In connecting hunger and violence, the press implicated the Irish in their own misery, leading the *ILN* to query whether too few had died in the Famine: "The aboriginal trait remains, and even cholera and famine have been lenient enough to spare a sufficient number of murderers to perpetuate the race, and to retard the improvement and the prosperity of the country" (October 30, 1852). Nassau Senior, economic adviser to the government, concurred, expressing his fear that the Famine "would not kill more than one million people, and that would scarcely be enough to do any good".[42]

There are few examples of Irish lawlessness, violence, and resistance in fine art, unless allegorized. In Maclise's *Marriage of Strongbow and Aoife* (1854, NGI), Strongbow's sword against the shattered high cross, the burning of Waterford city in the background, and the fallen heroes on the ground symbolize a surrender of Irish culture, spirituality, and power. The arranged marriage between Richard de Clare, Earl of Pembroke, and Aoife, daughter of the king of Leinster, signaled the invasion of Ireland by the Normans in 1169, but the connection to the more recent Act of Union did not need to be spelled out, any more than did other contemporary resonances: the corpses splayed across the foreground in an Irish painting of the 1850s could *only* speak of the Famine dead.

In the "Repeal Year" of 1843, the government banned the "monster meeting" to be held at Clontarf on October 7, asserting that Daniel O'Connell's ultimate aim was to

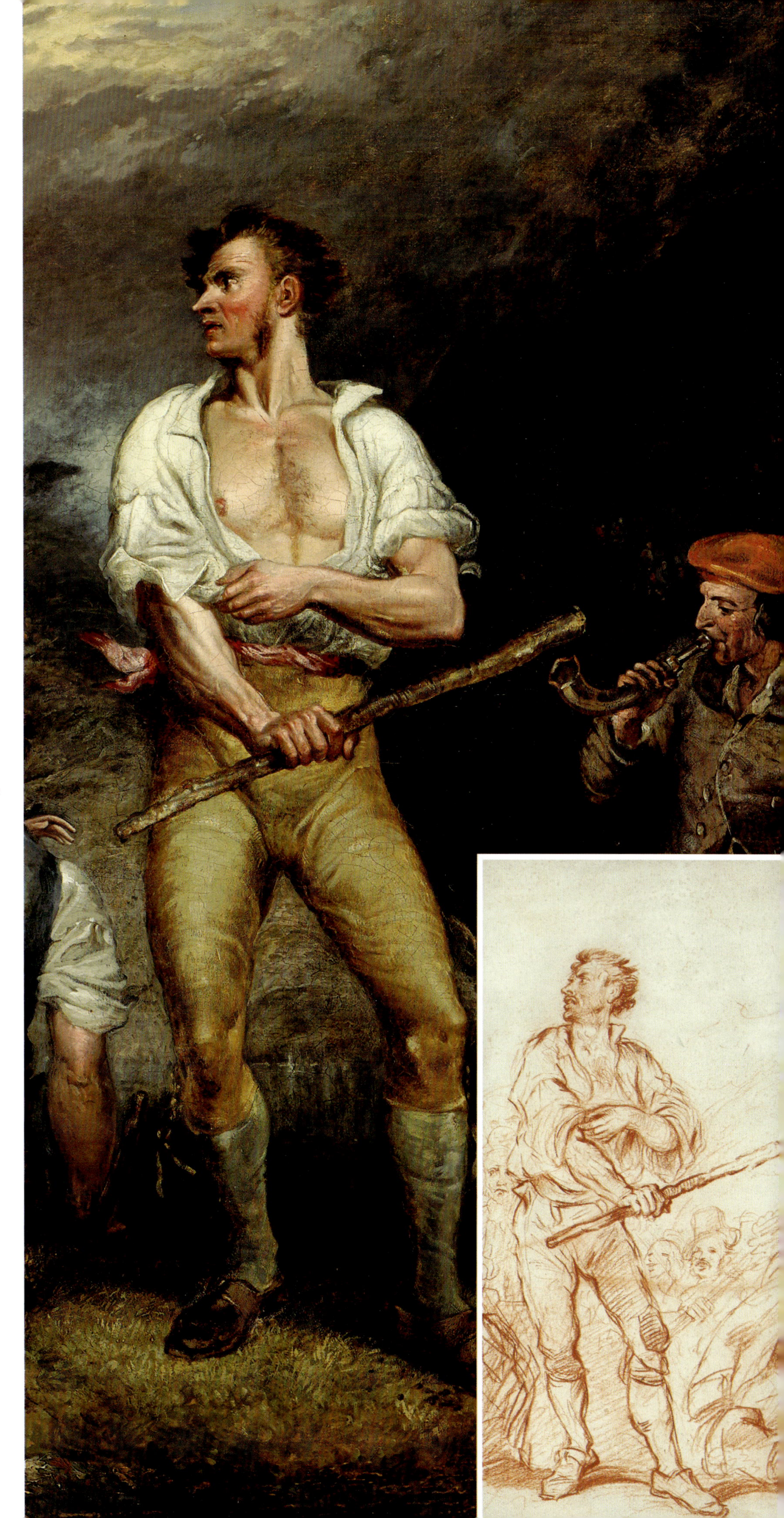

overthrow the government. Joseph Haverty's *Monster Meeting at Clifden* (*c.* 1844, NGI) **[Figure 28]** is a rare example of overt political imagery in fine art. More common were direct images in graphic form or indirect images in fine art.[43] Together with Maclise's *Installation of Captain Rock* (1834, private collection), these paintings are the antecedents of Macdonald's *Irish Faction Leader* (1844, private collection; preparatory sketch *The Irish Faction Leader* (1844, IGHM)) **[Figure 29]** executed on the eve of the Famine.[44] Faction fights - ferocious pitched battles - were expressions of empowerment by a downtrodden people, and kept sedition alive by enforcing the codes of a subaltern moral economy. Fights related to tenancy issues, land-grabbers, agents, or landlords resulted in guerrilla class warfare, family or neighborly disagreements, or Romeo and Juliet-type friction between feuding families. Agrarian insurgency had clear intent, but faction fights were also pre-planned, not simply "donnybrooks" or other spontaneous outbursts of uncontrolled violence. Outsiders saw such fighting as barbaric, but to insiders they were a form of social regulation, protecting the community against the state monopoly on violence. Rural disorder did not have to be subversive in intent to be subversive in effect, and to be treated accordingly.[45]

■ ■ ■

The Famine forced artists to rethink their capacity - conceptual and artistic - to depict the "truths too strong for fiction" noted by Maria Edgeworth. When the crop failed and people were unable to pay their rent,

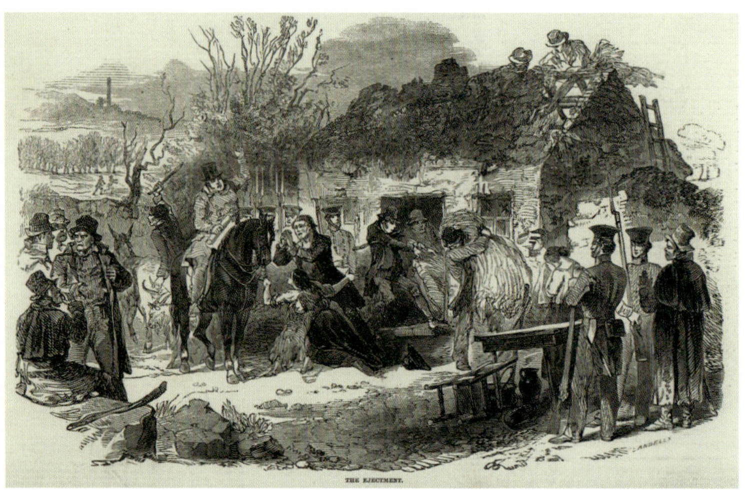

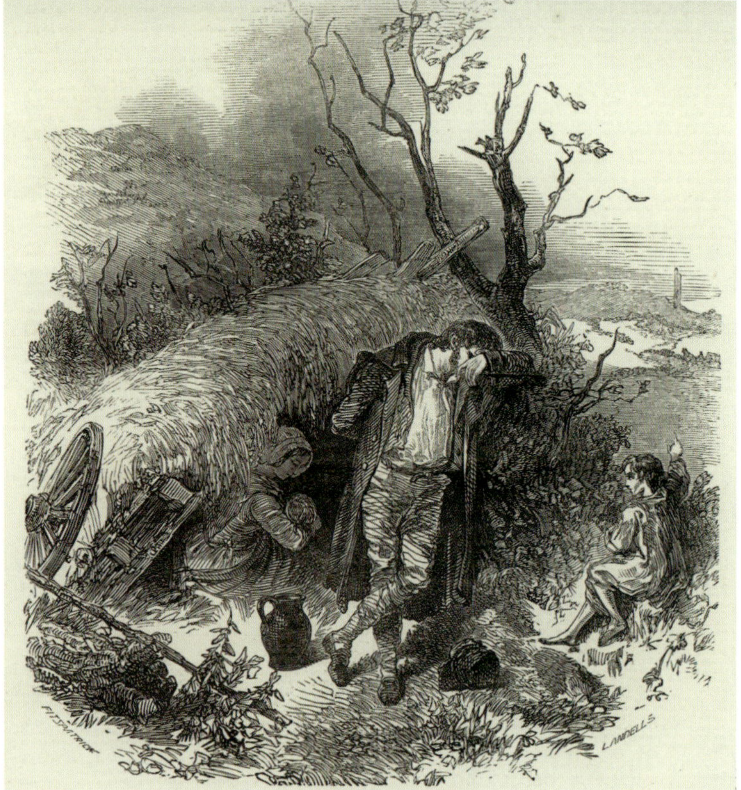

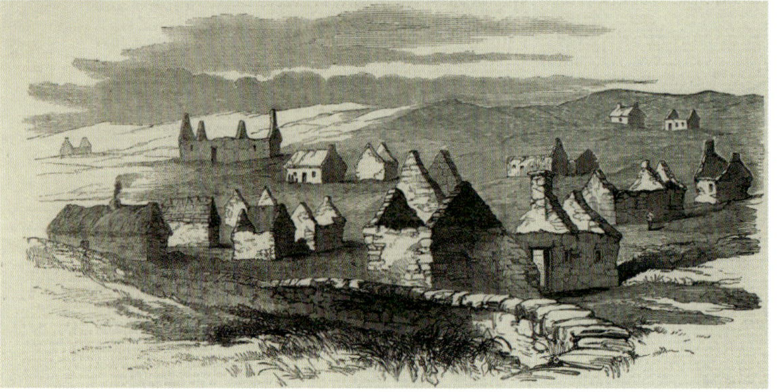

30 "Ejectment of Irish Tenantry"
31 "The Day After the Ejectment"
32 "Village of Moveen"

many landlords – realizing the profit in pasture – set about clearing their land of tenants. "Capricious" evictions required military and constabulary assistance, aided by hired "wreckers". In "Ejectment of Irish Tenantry" (*ILN*, December 16, 1848) **[Figure 30]**, a distraught family is dragged from their house. Later, in "The Day After the Ejectment" (*ILN*, December 16, 1848) **[Figure 31]**, we see them living in a ditch. Between 1846 and 1853 whole communities were evicted and over half a million people were made homeless.[46] To ensure that the evicted could not return to what remained of their cabins, landlords "tumbled" their roofs and had the foundations dug up. The deserted villages, according to the artist/illustrator James Mahony, "look like the tombs of a departed race, rather than the recent abodes of a yet living people". Mahony expressed relief at seeing "shrunken frames scarcely covered with flesh – crawling skeletons, who appear to have risen from their graves" as "evidence that I was not in the land of the dead" (*ILN,* "Village of Moveen", December 22, 1849) **[Figure 32]**.

Eviction in these conditions was a sentence of death. If unable to gain access to a workhouse, the destitute resorted to living in burrows two or three-feet deep (not unlike Eritrean, Afghani, and Ethiopian migrants living in the dunes of Calais today). But even from these "scalps" the poor were hunted, "unearthed, and left even without the shelter of what may be called a preparatory grave". Some were burnt out of these holes, including a child whose charred remains were brought out on a shovel (*ILN,* December 15, 1849). A number of paintings and post-Famine photographs of evictions are extant, but none depict such inhuman practices.[47] Emily Mark-Fitzgerald argues that "Images and accounts of eviction served as useful rhetorical tools utilized during the Famine and the 1880s land wars by nationalist sympathizers; few other experiences symbolized such an affront to moral decency and the sanctity of home and land."[48]

A number of such scenes were represented by both British and Irish artists, with some telling differences in approach and style. George Frederic Watts's *The Irish Famine* (originally called *An Irish Eviction*, *c.* 1848–50, Watts Gallery) shows an angry father, a terrified mother, a dying baby, and a grandparent abandoned to grief. Although the anatomical sturdiness shows just how little the artist knew of famine, Watts did go through a phase of acute social awareness, and was outraged by events in Ireland that he read about in the pictorial press. On the one hand, the mother's smooth face, the well-rounded bodies, and the decent dress would have confirmed the views of many: here go the Irish, nourished and healthy, looking for undeserved English charity. However, the fact that Watts did not exhibit the painting for over thirty years suggests that he may have known it would pander to the stereotype, when he wished to portray the Irish as stoical rather than abject in the face of suffering and injustice. Watts's eviction scene was loosely based on Aubrey de Vere's poem "The Year of Sorrow" (1849). In addressing a subject

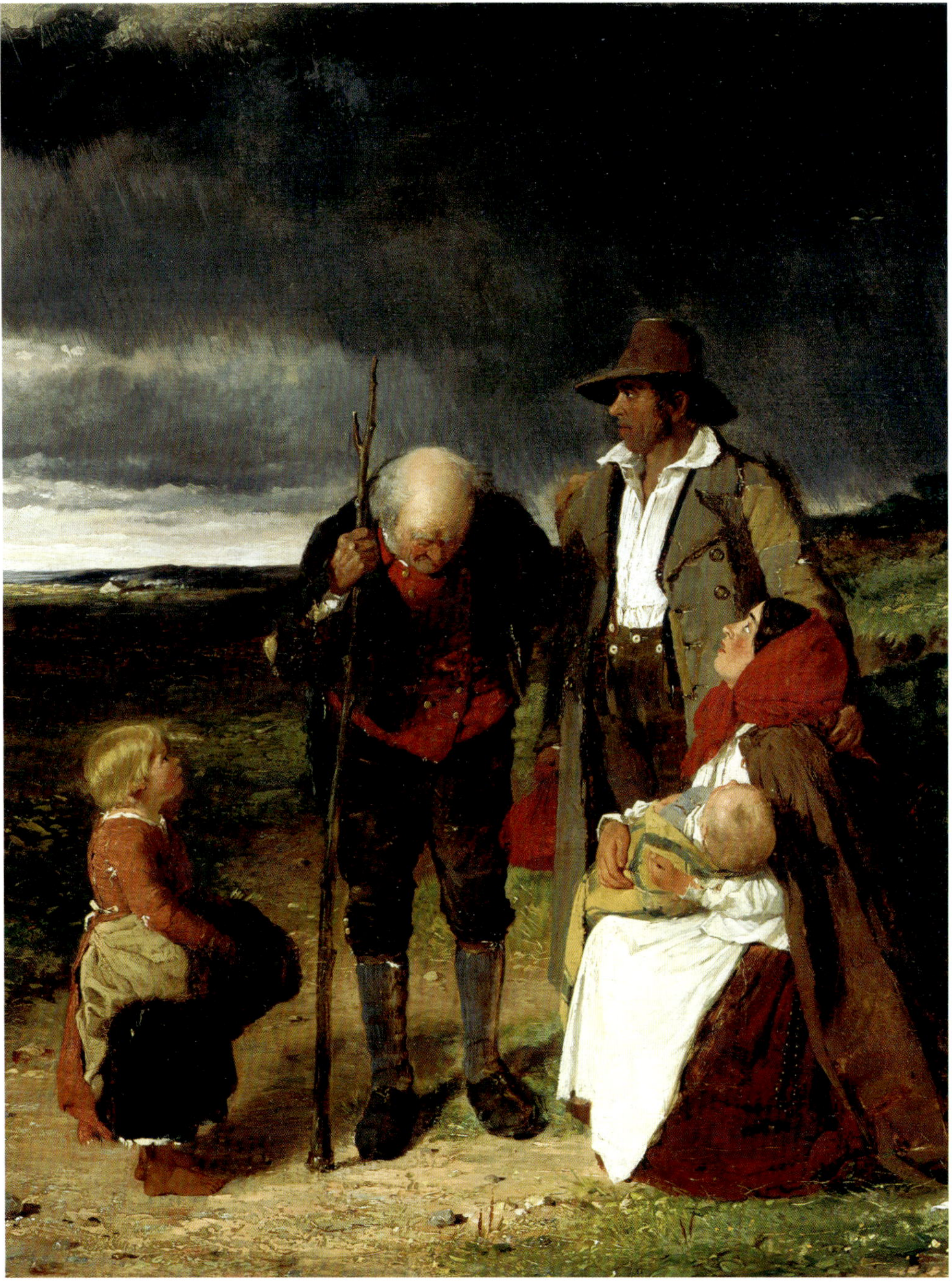

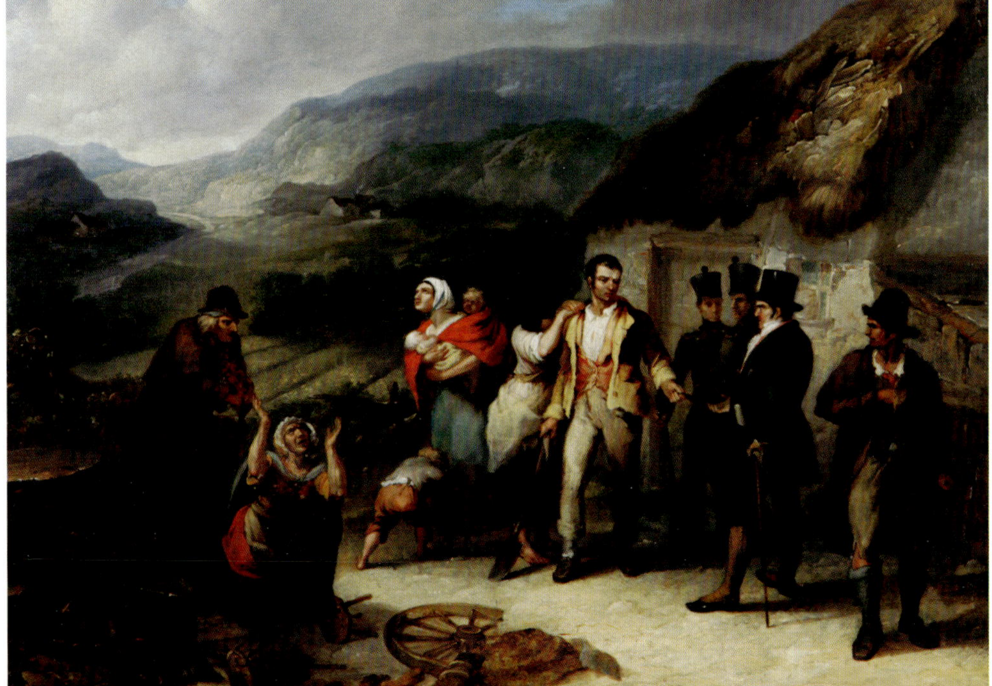

of contemporary topicality – one of profound and timeless relevance to humanity – he drew on the iconography of the Holy Family, thereby ensuring its history-painting status. It is worth asking what makes this such a commanding image. The large size (72 x 78 in/198 x 180.3 cm) signaled Watts's intention to produce a painting of high impact. Undoubtedly, his sense of morality, his understanding of the aesthetic purpose of art, his powerful universalizing skills, and his indignation are factors. The theme of expulsion had biblical and mythological resonances, which lent themselves to narratives of dispossession and suffering. But having never *seen* the suffering (in all its horrendous detail), Watts (who professed to painting ideas, not things) was able to elevate his image to one of transcendent empathy. Knowing that he had yet to visit the desolated country, de Vere credited him with "second sight", commending the truthfulness of his conception.[49] Watts's radical shift to contemporary social subjects – before his brother realists in France or his social-realist ones in England – was problematic for his conservative patrons, provoking the comment quoted earlier about the unwelcome disturbance to the consciences of his viewers.

Frederick Goodall's *Irish Eviction* (1850, Leicester Museum and Art Gallery) depicts the plight of a family shown the door of their home. The stone cottage may be a better class of dwelling than most, but the open door to the empty potato store tells of imminent

33 Erskine Nicol, *An Ejected Family* **[detail]**
34 Daniel Macdonald, *Eviction*

starvation. By the same token, such scenes of distress led Erskine Nicol to depart from his repertoire of stock images (as noted in relation to his *Tenant* painting). His *Ejected Family* (1853, NGI) **[Figure 33]** depicts a homeless family; the pathetic fallacy of black clouds, the grandfather stooping over in despair or stumbling with hunger, the mother and children looking to the young father/husband are more empathetic than we commonly get from Nicol.

In contrast to their British counterparts, Irish painters of the genre tended to layer detail upon detail, insisting, as it were, on their first-hand experience. In Daniel Macdonald's *Eviction* (*c.* 1850, Crawford Art Gallery) **[Figure 34]**, outrage is conveyed through respect – the dwelling is comparatively substantial, the family well dressed, their possessions relatively copious. The wreckers have already begun to tumble the roof and the door has been bricked up, indicating the landlord's intention of finding a higher rent for this dwelling. Taking over the holding of an evicted family was deemed unforgivable – another example of the persistence of a moral code at odds with "English political economy" (in John Mitchel's phrase). The vignette of the little boy trying to catch the dog, unaware of the enormity of what is happening, is countered by the man on the right putting his hand to his inner pocket where lies (it is implied) his pistol. This latter trope recurs elsewhere in Macdonald's work and in other illustrations of the period, signaling a

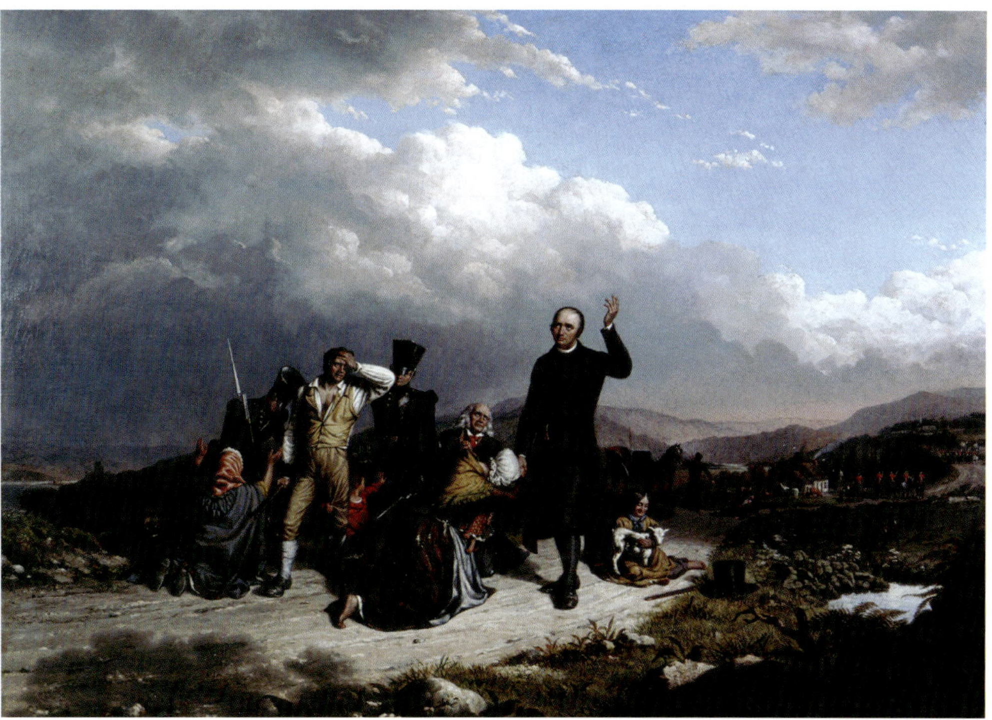

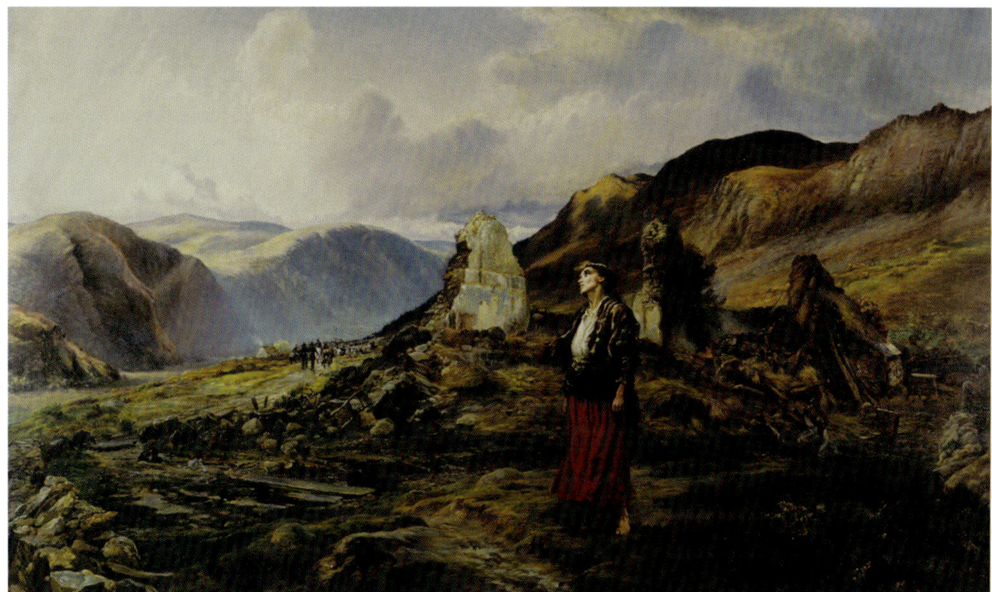

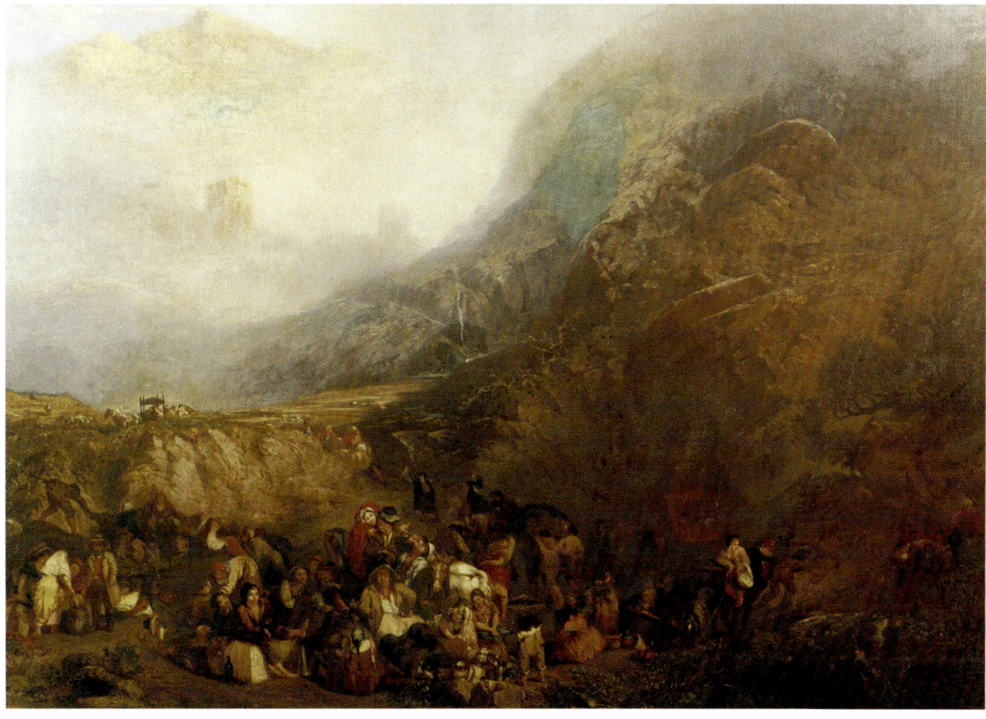

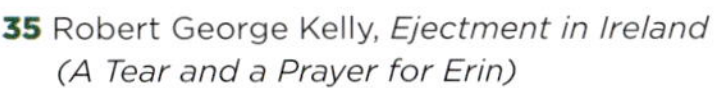

35 Robert George Kelly, *Ejectment in Ireland (A Tear and a Prayer for Erin)*
36 Lady Elizabeth Butler, *Evicted*
37 William Willes, *Mock Funeral*

temporal arc of a before (the small boy's innocence), during (the eviction), and after (resistance). In the middle ground, lazy beds (a rare example of tillage in fine-art form) once abundant with potatoes are putrified. This hard-working family is now unable to pay their rent. Failing charity, or emigration, eviction meant closing down the future, the despair of the workhouse, or a lingering death by a ditch.

In *Ejectment in Ireland (A Tear and a Prayer for Erin*) (1848–51, collection of Anthony J. Mourek) **[Figure 35]**, Robert George Kelly attempted a more complex narrative. The shock and shame of eviction was such that already debilitated victims remained passive. While Macdonald hinted at it, Kelly's is one of the rare depictions of violent response to ejectment. The tenant has murdered the bailiff. As his father is arrested, his son tries to repel the constable, while his wife and mother beg for mercy. The priest holds the hand of the wife, who cradles her baby. In the distance the sheriff's party marches down the road, on to the next assignment. Exhibited in the British Institution in 1853, the painting was considered "vulgar", and Strickland noted it was "much criticized as a political picture, which the artist never intended, and was discussed in the House of Commons" (although this is not recorded in Hansard).[50] It is hard to see how it could have been read as anything other than political, for as Catherine Marshall suggests, the problem "was not the depiction of poverty ... but rather the politicization of that poverty in a colonized country".[51] Later scenes of eviction, such as Lady Elizabeth Butler's *Evicted* (1890, NFC, UCD) **[Figure 36]**, Aloysius O'Kelly's "Eviction" (*ILN*, March 19, 1881), or Henry Jones Thaddeus's *Eviction Scene* (1889, private collection), attest to the upsurge in the ruthless efficiency of Irish landlords that led eventually to the outbreak of the Land War.

■ ■ ■

Front-line resistance involved staying at home, but it would be a mistake to view emigration only as flight: it was in overseas networks built up by exiles that the most determined opposition to British rule evolved. Ireland had long exported its poor; in the thirty years prior to the Famine, approximately one million emigrated to North America and half a million to Britain. From the early seventeenth century to the foundation of the Irish Free State, some seven million Irish emigrated to North America, creating a distinctive "culture of exile" in which, according to Kerby Miller, the Irish saw themselves as "driven out of Erin" by "English tyranny", like "the children of Israel". Although, in time, many did well, homesickness, alienation, bitterness, and nostalgia sustained "a distinctive Irish Catholic worldview rooted deeply in Irish history and culture".[52]

The notion of exodus along biblical lines informed the genre of quayside scenes, and allowed for narrative amplification: nostalgia for the past and/or a new lease of life in the future. Such subject matter encouraged fine artists to demonstrate their ability to handle crowd scenes à la Daniel Maclise, William Powell Frith, or Ford Madox Brown – the great modern history painters of Britain. Interestingly, when reimported into Ireland, history painting (including crowd scenes) was occasionally subverted for anti-establishment purposes, demonstrating its inherent versatility in presenting ideologically inflected versions of history; hence William Willes's *Mock Funeral* (1851, private collection) **[Figure 37]** - hailed, not quite accurately, for its originality of subject in art form[53] - brings a new ironic element to the wake. Set in the remote mountains of County Cork, the scene depicts peasants manufacturing "mountain dew" and transporting their "spirits" in a coffin to elude the detection of "gaugers" (customs men): "the busy and bustling crowd are stowing away the 'native' for its journey", as contemporary reviews noted (*Southern Reporter and Cork Commercial Courier*, June 26, 1852; *Cork Constitution*, June 26, 1852). Mock funerals, of the more somber kind, accompanied emigration, since for those left behind departure was a kind of death in life. "American wakes", marked by ritualized practices, permitted the ventilation of grief and bitterness, but also, perhaps, hope for a better life in the New World.

Some pre-Famine emigration scenes, such as *Emigrants at Cork* (attrib. George Mounsey Wheatley Atkinson, *c.* 1840, NFC, UCD), are light in tone (implying an element of choice), while later versions, such as Erskine Nicol's *An Irish Emigrant Landing in Liverpool* (1871, NGS) **[Figure 38]**, Margaret Allen's *The Last Hour in the Old Land* (*c.* 1877, Gorry Gallery), and Charles Henry Cook's *Awaiting the Emigrant Ship* (1867, Cork City Library), are suffused with nostalgia.[54] Others are attuned to the gravity and elemental nature of emigration: James Glen Wilson's *Emigrant Ship Leaving Belfast* (1852, Ulster Museum, Belfast) **[Figure 39]** and Edwin Hayes's *The Emigrant Ship, Dublin Bay, Sunset* (1853, NGI) are elegiac paintings capturing the mood, if not the circumstances, of leave-taking.

Although it is estimated that ninety per cent arrived at their destinations, some 100,000 died, and the state of survivors - diseased, starving, and penniless - was piteous. Of the actual voyages there are few images. It was not simply that artists had no personal experience of emigration, as a number of them were emigrants themselves: the painter and political activist John Mulvany is believed to have been a stowaway, and among other artist emigrants Thomas Hovenden's parents died during the Famine, and William Michael Harnett's family fled. The *ILN* wrote of the "splendid emigrant ships" transporting on average 250,000 people per annum. "The Tide of Emigration to the United States and to the British Colonies: Dancing Between Decks" communicates an unlikely bucolic picture of a leisurely cruise to America. Even the darker image "Searching for Stowaways" was a pale take on the grim experience of transatlantic refugees (*ILN,* July 6, 1850). Minimally converted cargo ships, gross overcrowding, inadequate food, and dirty and insufficient water suggest slave ships rather than ocean cruises. Below deck, disease spread rapidly, leading Captain Denham in his *Report to the Board of Trade* (May 21, 1849) to note that passengers on the *Virginius* sat upright for the entire journey: "The common offices of

38 Erskine Nicol, *An Irish Emigrant Landing in Liverpool*
39 James Glen Wilson, *Emigrant Ship Leaving Belfast*

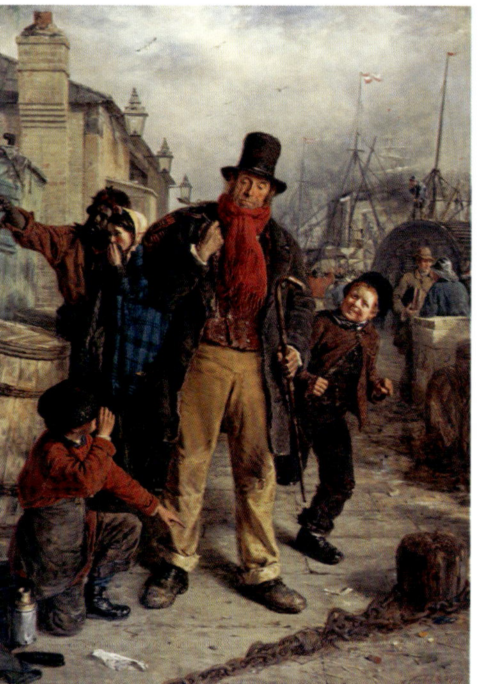

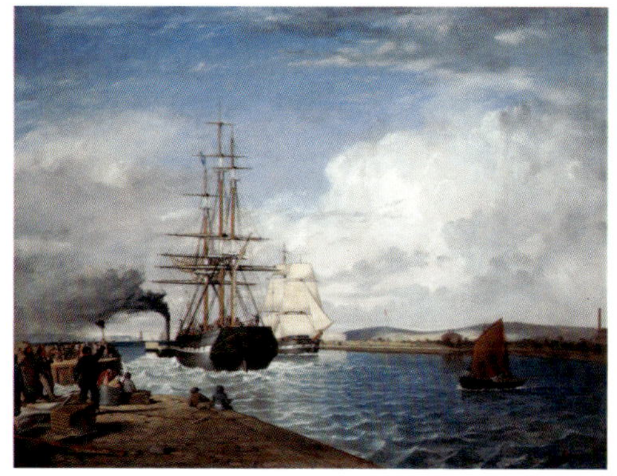

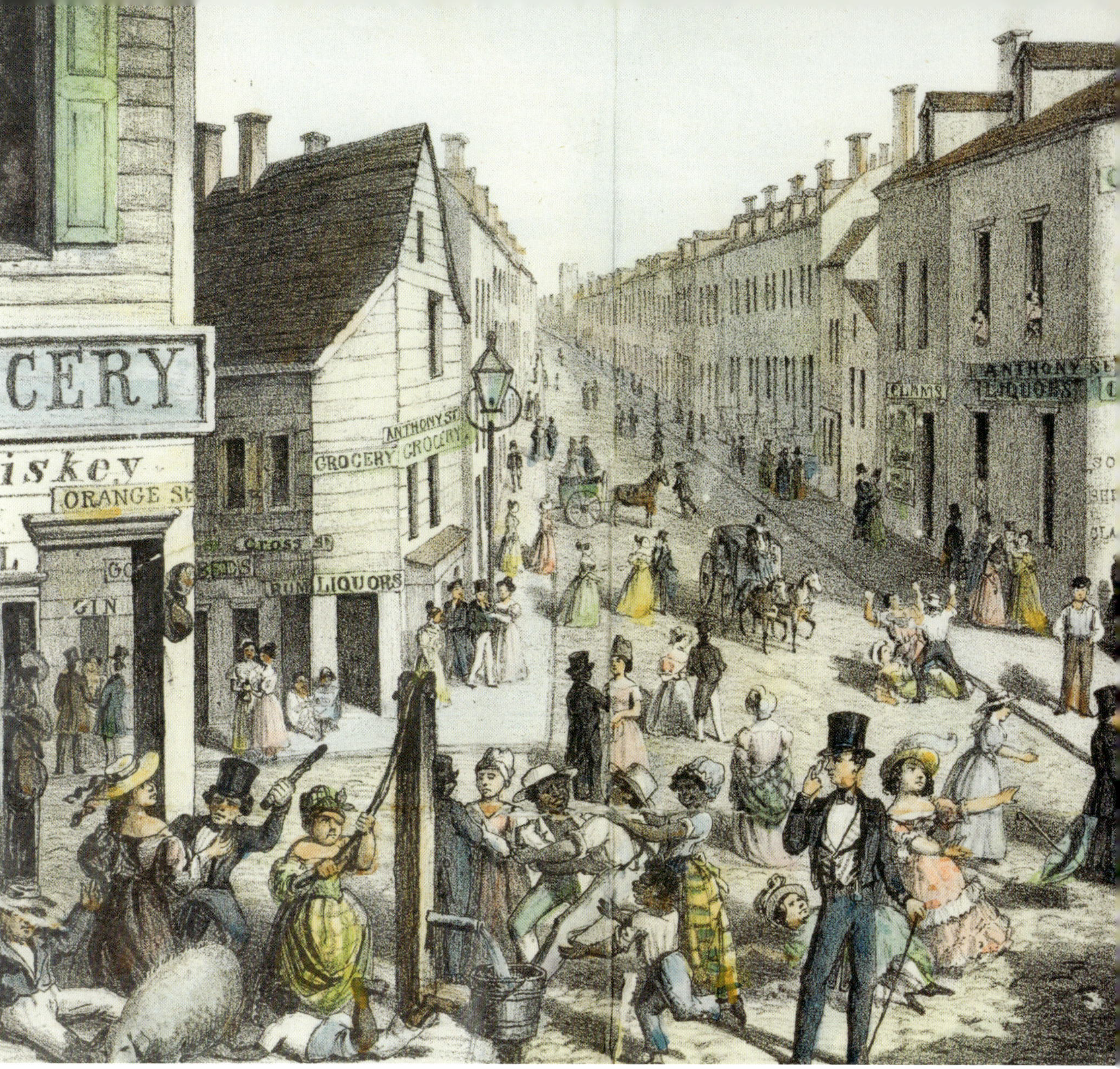

nature, including vomiting from sea-sickness, were consequently done on the spot ... The passengers and cattle were ... indiscriminately mixed together; the sea and urine pouring on their clothes from the animals, and they stood in the midst of filth and mire".

As most emigrants left with virtually nothing, the few museums devoted to the Famine have few artefacts. But Irish immigrants brought with them music and dance, storytelling, and song. The notion that they danced on deck may be risible, but there are a number of nostalgic and/or exuberant paintings from the period that attest to the importance of their native culture. In America Irish immigrants contributed hugely, as novelists, playwrights, poets, and journalists. Moreover, their contribution to Irish music, documented by musicologist Mick Moloney[55] and broadcaster and film-maker Philip King, among others, is significant. Indeed, the Irish contribution to American musical culture – from country and western to rock and roll – demonstrates a striking immigrant fusion.

■ ■ ■

The votive tribute marking the work of the selfless nuns at Grosse Île quarantine station in Théophile Hamel's *Le Typhus* (1849, Notre-Dame-De-Bonsecours Church,

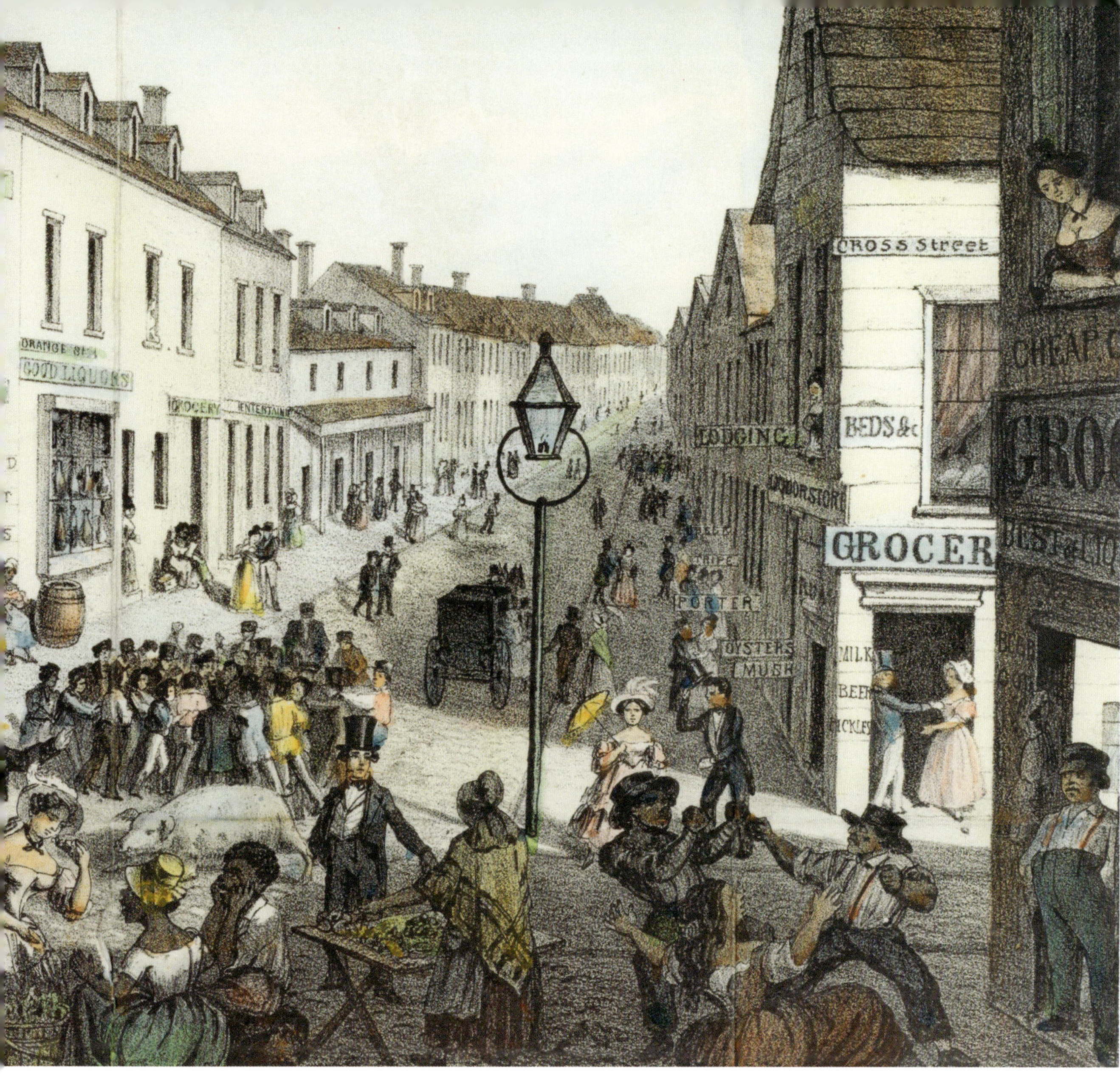

40 George Catlin,
Five Points, 1827

Montreal) gives some indication of the state in which immigrants disembarked.[56] But from the outset the unruly Irish caused outrage. George Catlin's pre-Famine *Five Points, 1827* (1827, private collection; lithographed in 1859) **[Figure 40]** is set in the center of Manhattan's sex-and-alcohol trade, where the Irish congregated. As immigration increased, Samuel Waugh's panorama *Immigrants Disembarking at the Battery, Castle Garden, 1847* (*c.* 1847, Museum of the City of New York) **[Figure 41]** shows the arrival of wealthy passengers among whom apelike Irish skulk, further reinforcing nativist hostility. In the Draft Riots of 1863, thousands of Irish immigrants provoked some of the deadliest street violence in American history; the frenzy of murder, arson, and looting was precipitated by class and racial conflict in the Five Points district.

One of the most striking images of Irish immigration is of recent arrivals in Britain: *Irish Immigrants* (*c.* 1847, Victoria Art Gallery, Bath) **[Figure 42]** by John Joseph Barker. The plight of the homeless family lent itself to Victorian moralism, for by 1847 throngs of Irish were arriving in the West Country, where they acquired a reputation for lawlessness and degeneracy. In Barker's painting, the off-the-shoulder and open-neck *demi déshabille* of the girls provided the opportunity for what Linda Nochlin described, in an "orientalist" setting, as "lip-licking and tongue-clicking".[57] The trope of the "dirty" picturesque is echoed in Walter Deverell's *Irish Vagrants*

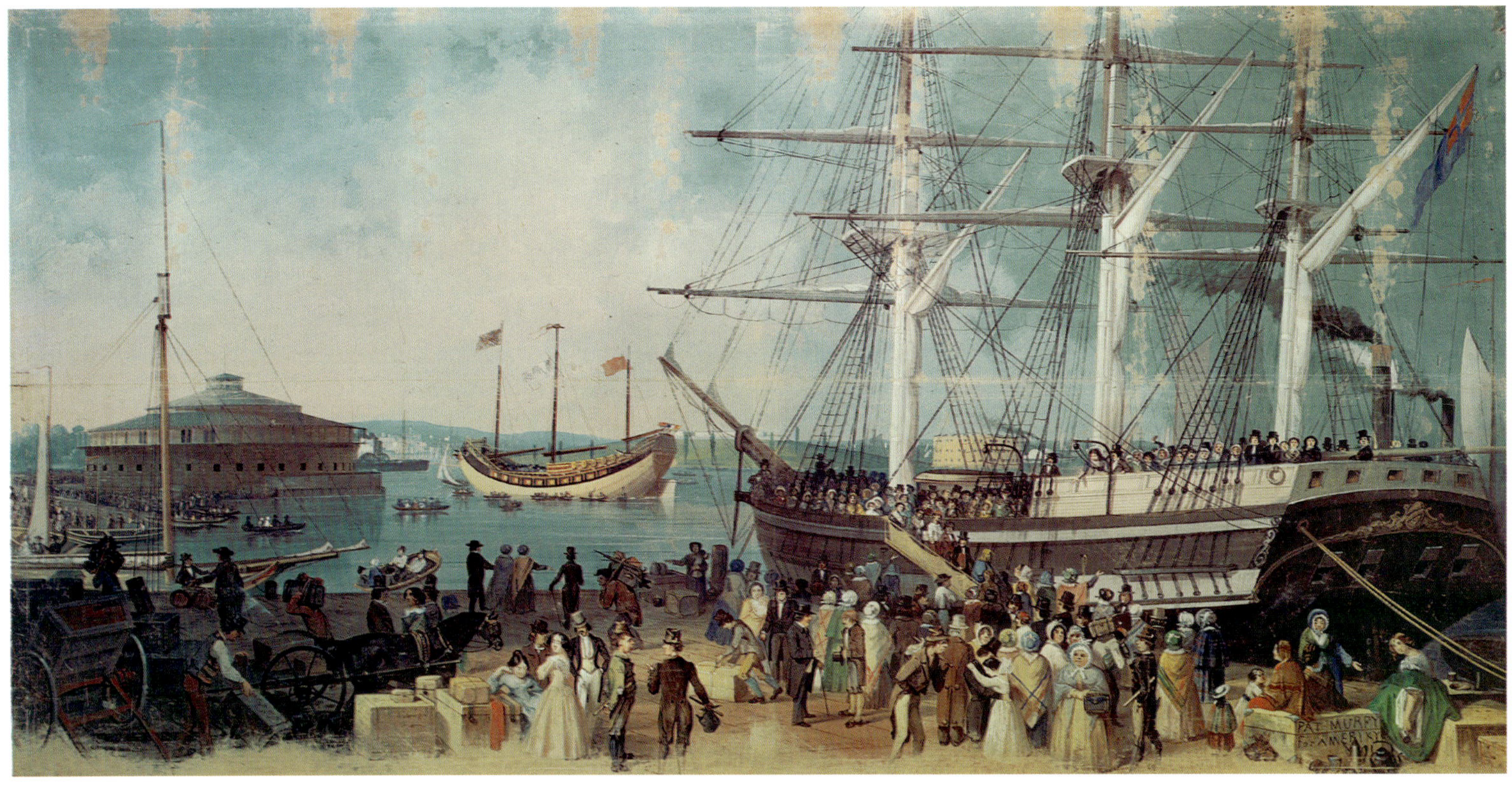

41 Samuel Waugh, *Immigrants Disembarking at the Battery, Castle Garden*

(*c.* 1853–54, Johannesburg Art Gallery), which shows Irish peasants following seasonal migration work across the water (but the haughty refusal of the mounted gentry to give alms augurs badly for their survival in England, too).

The Famine came to a gradual rather than an abrupt end, but, as Sir William Wilde ruefully observed, nothing would ever be the same again:

> *Even the ceremonial of religion has been neglected, and the very rites of sepulture, the most sacred and enduring of all the tributes of affection or respect, have been neglected or forgotten; the dead body has rotted where it fell, or formed a scanty meal for the famished dogs of the vicinity, or has been thrown, without prayer or mourning, into the adjoining ditch. The hum of the spinning-wheel has long since ceased to form an accompaniment to the colleen's song; and that song itself, so sweet and fresh in cabin, field, or byre, has scarcely left an echo in our glens, or among the hamlets of our land. The* Shannaghie *and the* Callegh *in the chimney corner, tell no more the tales and legends of other days. Unwaked,* unkeened, *the dead are buried, where Christian burial has at all been observed; and the ear no longer catches the mournful cadence of the wild Irish cry, wailing on the blast, rising up to us from the valleys, or floating along the winding river …*[58]

As "providential" accounts of the Famine took hold in evangelical circles in the late 1840s, Rev. Edward Nangle, presiding over his mission at Achill, County Mayo, remarked that "God is angry with this land. The potatoes would not have rotted unless He sent the rot into them … God never sends a scourge upon His creatures unless they deserve it" (*Achill Missionary Herald*, February 1847). God's anger was not easily appeased, for in the next generations famine did not recede into memory on the western seaboard but was an ever-present possibility. Alexander Williams's paintings show how fifty years after the Famine living conditions on Achill were as appalling as ever, and it was indeed the threat of another crisis that prompted James Connolly and Maud Gonne in 1897 to organize sustained relief efforts in counties Donegal, Mayo, and Kerry to prevent a recurrence of 1847. In their pamphlet *The Right of Life and the Rights of Property* they called for an end to fatalism and passive resistance: "The very highest authorities on the doctrine of the church agree that no human law can stand between starving people and their right to food, including the right to take that food whenever they find it, openly or secretly, with or without the owner's permission."[59] While the imposing ruins of antiquities or ancient monuments still provided the cultural iconography of a resurgent nationalism, it was in fact more recent ruins, those of evictions and roofless cottages, that featured in the magic-lantern slide shows projected onto public buildings by Maud Gonne during the visit of the "Famine Queen", Queen Victoria, to Ireland in 1897. Ruins were no longer relics of the distant past but the legacy of the harsh political realities of both the country and (as in the appalling slums) the city.

■ ■ ■

The visual impact of poverty and hunger, disease and death, and their treatment in memory and commemoration merits more extensive treatment than is possible within this essay, which builds on and complements the work of other scholars in visual culture who have worked specifically on the Famine, such as Catherine Marshall, Emily Mark-Fitzgerald, Niamh Ann Kelly, Justin Carville, Fintan Cullen, Tom Dunne, and Luke Gibbons.[60] Moreover, the wider field of Irish art history was greatly enriched by the publication of the magisterial five-volume *Art and Architecture of Ireland* by Yale University Press and the Royal Irish Academy in 2014, which has added considerably to our knowledge of individual artists in the IGHM Collection. Two years previously, the historiography of the Famine was given comprehensive treatment in the *Atlas of the Great Irish Famine*.[61] The terrain is now vast and includes significant work not only by historians and art historians but also by cultural theorists, geographers, philosophers, poets, musicologists, political economists, literary scholars, musicians, and novelists, who through their scholarship have expanded our knowledge and understanding of this subject. Many of these have contributed to the multi-award-winning series produced by Ireland's Great Hunger Museum, the *Famine Folios*, in which interdisciplinary collaboration has yielded new perspectives beyond the confines of history alone.

Although there are few paintings extant that represent the scale and depth of the losses caused by the Famine, it is left to the museum to pick up where lived memory leaves off, and to reimagine the archive for present and future generations. The point of the present exhibition is not just to represent the Great Hunger but also to contextualize and place it in its wider cultural and historical settings. James Mahony's *Consecration of the Roman Catholic Church of St. Mary's, Pope's Quay, Cork* (*c.* 1841, IGHM), for example, shows the determination of the Catholic Church to establish its authority within a disoriented culture. Jack B. Yeats's landscape of Derrynane is imbued with the memory of Daniel O'Connell, both as politician and landlord, in the immediate pre-Famine period. In Lilian Lucy Davidson's stark *Gorta* (1946, IGHM), narrative is eliminated in a Beckett-like fashion, as figures seem to look past one another into nothingness. The multiple narratives of popular memory are evident in Micheal Farrell's massive *Black '47* (1997–98, IGHM), in which a raking light shows Charles Trevelyan in the dock before a jury of the dead, arraigned for his mismanagement of the Famine - a fate he escaped in real life. As if extricating art from amnesia, a number of artists - such as William Crozier, Robert Ballagh, and Brian Maguire - informed by Irish history, engage with themes of injustice, cruelty, and abuse of power that characterized the Famine - themes that prevail in the growing gap between rich and poor in the world today.

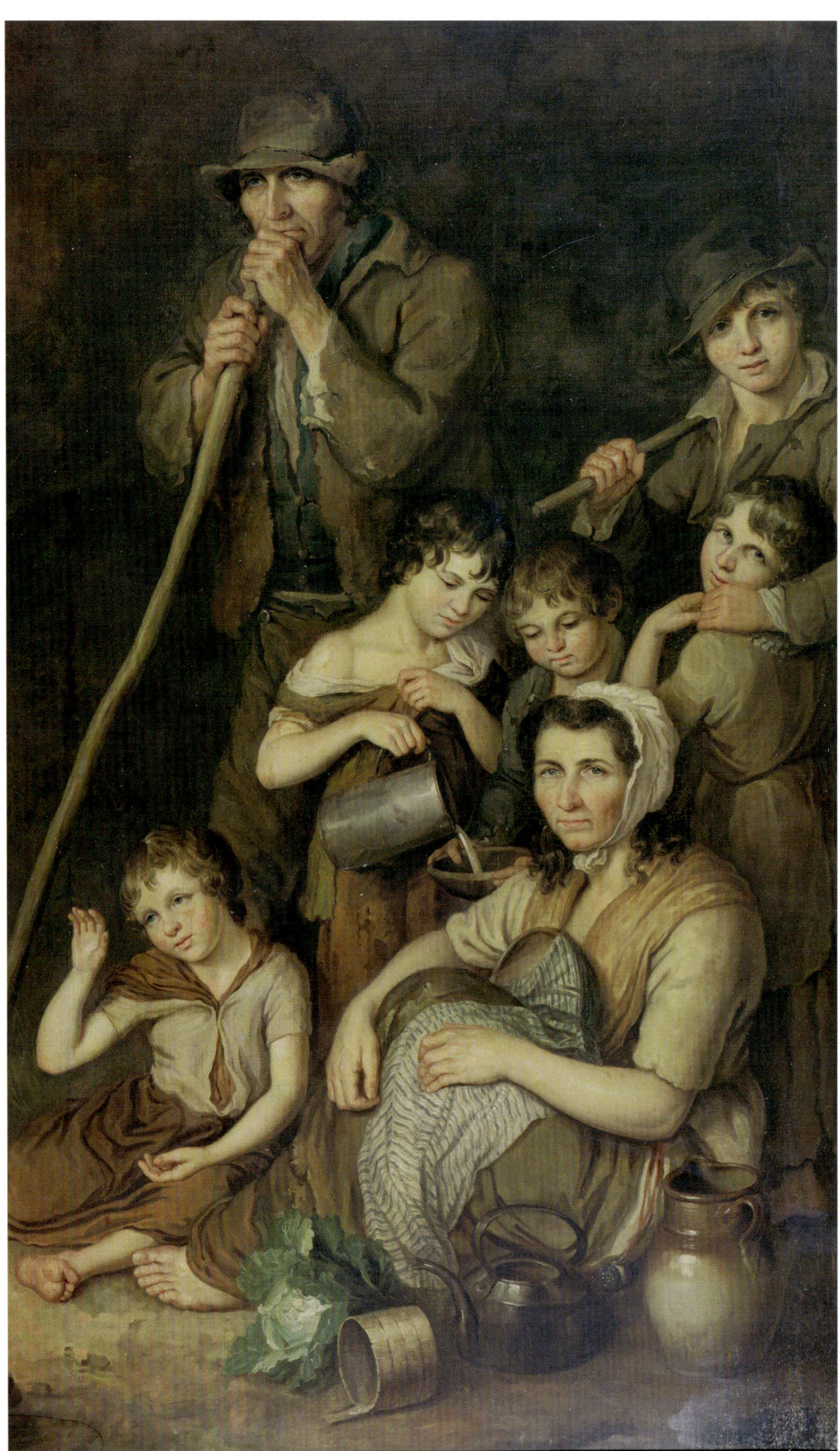

The art, spanning 170 years, is far from merely illustrative, and affords reflective expressions of who we once were, and how we became who we are today, each piece chosen for its quality as art as well as its capacity to bear witness. In consigning the past too readily to memory, we often forget that the past still throws its long shadow on the present. There is a sense in which a time interval is placed between a traumatic event and its representation, and to this extent it is not surprising that the Great Famine had 'a long gestation' (to appropriate W.B. Yeats's phrase) in Irish culture over successive generations. But even allowing for the passage of time, questions also arose, as we have seen, in relation to images themselves, and the capacity of mimetic realism or even figuration to capture inconceivable horrors. Modernism, and the catastrophe of the First World War, threw representation itself into crisis, looking to abstraction, expressionism, and other formal strategies to deal with the pressures of reality, and the late twentieth century ushered in new forms of artistic expression and production, ranging from time-based work, installations, video, and site-specific production to other innovative forms. Many of these experimental approaches lend themselves to negotiating aspects of the Famine that resist conventional genres, and the work of Hughie O'Donoghue, Alanna O'Kelly, and Dorothy Cross suggests that it is through "disfiguration, rather than the ordering illusions of mimetic art ... [that] disturbing areas of experience are rendered intelligible".[62]

In Hughie O'Donoghue's *On Our Knees* (1996–97, IGHM) (an expression borrowed from his mother), the landscape of the artist's Mayo family background, around Loch Carrowmore and Erris, is imbued with inner life, feelings of attachment, and yet alienation from the poverty and hardship that made living on the land so difficult. There are barely discernible boundaries between contour and ground, as if the environment seeps through the skin into impoverished bodies, becoming a state of mind. Reds, blacks, and browns are splayed over the canvas like body parts in Brian Maguire's more expressionist *The World Is Full of Murder* (1985, IGHM), conveying the impression that we are seeing bodies piled on each other, mass graves on the earth's suface without even the dignity of burial. Much of Dorothy Cross's work is site-specific in that it uses 'found objects' left on the surface on western landscapes, debris cast off by time. In *Basking Shark Currach* (2013, IGHM), the human and animal world are fused as if to compensate for the adversarial struggle between seemingly fragile currach boats and basking sharks once hunted on the Atlantic coast – a practice recreated for filmic purposes and perpetuated on the screen in Robert Flaherty's epic documentary *Man of Aran* (1934) long after it had ended in reality. This notion of time being extended in the image is central to Alanna O'Kelly's video installation *No Colouring Can Deepen the Darkness of Truth* (1992), in which sound – singing, chanting, sighing, breathing, keening – attempts to fill the void in images vacated by memory, as if the scarred landscape is itself lost for words. Time is reintroduced into the image, allowing for the gap between event and expression, but time in this case fails to find an adequate narrative form, as if memory is bent out of shape. Indirection and obliquity in these contemporary artworks enable us to go below the surface, revealing deeper truths. Through pushing the limits of visual form, new ways of thinking about the past allow us to imagine alternative presents.

The Famine Museum in Strokestown is an important precursor, but what is unique about Ireland's Great Hunger Museum is that it draws on art, both historic and contemporary, to confront, mourn, polemicize, and memorialize. Although much of the suffering took place beyond the visible, expressions of both the gaps and interconnections in Irish and diasporic history and memory contained in the collection lend themselves to exploration of issues of poverty, displacement, and violence as well as of class, gender, and identity in the contemporary world. For Paul Ricœur, "collective identity is rooted in founding events which are violent events. In a sense, collective memory is a kind of storage of such violent blows, wounds and scars", and it is these scars that are given form in Ireland's Great Hunger Museum.[63] In the end the best way to do justice to the past is to see that justice is done today.

42 John Joseph Barker, *Irish Immigrants*

Feasting in a Time of Famine:

DUBLIN CASTLE & THE GREAT HUNGER

CIARÁN REILLY

In the painting *The State Ballroom, St. Patrick's Hall, Dublin Castle* (*c*. 1850, Collection of Brian P. Burns) **[Figure 43]**, F.J. Davis captures one of the great social events of nineteenth-century Dublin. Here in the seat of British rule in Ireland, Davis's painting illuminates the pomp and ceremony surrounding the office of the Lord Lieutenant in Ireland. Dublin Castle receptions were grandiose affairs for which no expense was spared. In particular, the annual St Patrick's Day Ball, the highlight and culmination of the "Dublin Season", was much anticipated among the upper classes. As Denis McCarthy points out, the gentry and aspiring gentry eagerly awaited the Viceroy's gilt-edged invitation during these six festive weeks of balls and dinners.[1] It was, as Eilís O'Sullivan notes, "the pinnacle of Ascendancy social success" to be invited to a "ball, *levée*, dinner or masquerade".[2] The levee was the most popular event held regularly in Dublin Castle. Strictly for men only, these events were held at noon and included a formal introduction to the Lord Lieutenant or his representative.

With the onset of the Great Famine, the Dublin Castle levees and balls continued unabated, perhaps as a means of showing that "all was well with the ruling classes of Ireland".[3] During the Famine Dublin Castle was at the center of social life in the city and would play host to Queen Victoria during her visit in August 1849 as hunger, fever, and eviction prevailed across the country. In stark contrast, Dublin Castle was also home to the British government's Relief Commission, which oversaw the administration of Famine relief to over three million people, coordinating with over 2,000 local committees in the process. The presence and work of the Relief Commission was in obvious contradiction to the splendor and spending on entertainment in the castle throughout the Famine years.

From the 1780s Dublin Castle played host annually to a "Ball and Supper"; these austere events were very much the preserve of the "upper crust" of Irish society.[4] With the passing of the Act of Union in 1801, the St Patrick's Day Ball received a new impetus – something that was said to have greatly impressed the emerging Catholic gentry.[5] For the hordes of Dubliners who would never be admitted to such events, there was an element of mystique and wonder, and crowds thronged the streets leading to the castle in an attempt to catch a glimpse of the affluent, glamorous attendees. In keeping with the custom begun in the 1830s, on the eve of the Famine, Thomas Philip, the Lord Lieutenant, appeared from the castle balcony "swathed in shamrocks", although the gesture was largely ignored by the masses.[6] Whether this lack of interest reflected their objections to the extravagance of the occasion in the face of deprivation and poverty outside the castle remains unclear, but either way there was little public interest in the office of the Lord Lieutenant.

In March 1846, six months after the discovery of *Phytophthora infestans* (potato blight), Dublin Castle played host as usual to the elaborate celebration in honor of Ireland's patron saint. The route to be taken by carriages to the castle – which was publicized in advance in the national newspapers – was intended to avoid the throngs of destitute and hungry who sought sanctuary in the city.[7] Guests attending the castle ball were expected to adhere to a strict protocol, which included bringing "calling cards" that would be used to announce their arrival at the event.[8] Such was the excitement in anticipation of the "Dublin Season" that a Mr Burke provided "dancing and graceful exercises" for debutantes. Ladies were instructed to wear "feathers and lappets" and to appear in "Irish manufacture". When George William Frederick Villiers, 4th Earl of Clarendon, took the office of Lord Lieutenant in 1847, his wife Lady Katherine insisted solely on Irish dress for such occasions. Encouraging others to do likewise, in 1849 she ordered a dress "composed of the richest crimson Irish poplin, interwoven in colours of gold"; designed by a Mr Reynolds of Grafton Street, it was said to have been of the "most costly and gorgeous description".[9] As these events were attended by several hundred people, women were not allowed to wear trains on their dresses. Likewise, mourning clothes were forbidden, perhaps an indication that the organizers wished to forget what was happening all across the country.[10]

Those attending the St Patrick's Day Ball in 1846 could hardly have been oblivious to the reports of widespread hunger that were by now reaching Dublin Castle on a daily basis.[11] In addition, the first wave of Famine evictions had commenced, most notably at the Gerrard estate at Ballinlass, County Galway, which was something of a cause célèbre.[12] Regardless of the crisis developing across the country, the St Patrick's Day Ball in the castle's "splendid suite of apartments" was attended by more than 900 people, with the band of the 41st Regiment playing for the guests on their arrival. Commencing at nine o'clock in the evening, the ball opened with a "country dance" led by Augustus Frederick FitzGerald, 3rd Duke of Leinster; the crowd's favorite was undoubtedly the tune "St Patrick's Day in the Morning".[13] After dancing, refreshments were served in the Round Room, tea and coffee in the private Drawing Room, and supper in the Picutre Gallery (now called the Portrait Gallery).[14] Underlying the social importance of this event, the national and provincial newspapers printed the names of all 900 guests.[15] Throughout the spring of 1846 events continued at Dublin Castle under the patronage of the Lord Lieutenant, John William Ponsonby, 4th Earl of Bessborough. The castle events were quickly followed by balls at a number of the neighboring "Big Houses" as the festivities moved out into the country. In 1846, for example, Clontarf Castle played host to a *bal costumé* attended by more than 300 guests, and where the hosts, Mr and Mrs Vernon, dressed as an "Albanian chief and a Greek".[16] Newspapers teemed with advertisements congratulating the latest tenders to have won contracts to supply Dublin Castle with the finest delicacies and provisions.[17] It was little wonder that such excessive feasting in a season of distress was followed by calls for the office of the viceroyalty to be abolished;[18] for example, the editor of the *Kerry Evening Post* queried the exact role of the viceroy, who, it was argued, was absent more often than not from Dublin Castle.[19] In spite of such calls the social whirl continued, and as the *Illustrated London News* reported, no expense was spared for the 1848 ball, the highlight of which was the arrival of Prince George of Cambridge, a cousin of Queen Victoria.[20] That this occurred during a period of great alarm as revolution swept across Europe was somewhat surprising.[21] Clarendon, it appears, was reluctant to proclaim Dublin as agitation and conspiracy grew across the country.[22]

By 1849 numerous side events were held during the "Dublin Season", leading up to the annual St Patrick's Day Ball. Overseen by the castle chamberlain, Matthew Fortescue, and the gentleman's usher, Frederick Willis, a number of "drawing room" receptions were held in the weeks prior to that date.[23] The public were also invited to view the portrait of Lord Clarendon by the Irish artist M.A. Hayes on display in Mr Cranfield's premises on Westmoreland Street.[24] Not everyone was enamored of Clarendon's propensity for hosting levees; the *Dublin Evening Post* criticized the fact that the Lord Lieutenant and his wife had not allowed a week to pass without the hosting of parties, balls, and dinners.[25] Always lavish, at one event in early February 1849, over 1,600 people attended.[26] On that occasion the usual apartments were used: the Drawing Room, Dining Room, Picture Gallery, Billiard Room, Round Room and St Patrick's Hall. Statues modeled on those in the Parthenon lined the hallway, while flowers and shrubs were said to resemble an exhibition of the Horticultural Society. In another room an aquarium sixty-five feet by thirty-three feet, where "living fishes plied their fins, and several species of water-fowl glided along its surface", greatly impressed the guests.[27]

While these events were the highlight of the "Dublin Season", they were overshadowed by the arrival of Queen Victoria in August 1849. For weeks in advance of the visit the capital bristled with excitement, and as Cecil Woodham-Smith later wrote (quoting the *Freeman's Journal*), Dublin appeared to be a "city risen from the dead".[28] Although Clarendon initially had reservations about funding an elaborate visit, fearing that he would be expected to settle the bill, these concerns were quickly shelved.[29] In advance of the visit Dublin Castle was significantly overhauled, particularly the Drawing Room and St Patrick's Hall, which would play an important role in the proceedings, as depicted in the Davis painting. In addition, the ceiling of the Throne Room, which had been installed for the visit of George IV in 1821, was raised to reflect the architectural character of the day.

On August 8, 1849 Dublin Castle welcomed the royal party, and the queen hosted a levee where upwards of 2,000 gentlemen were presented to her. Somewhat pleased with the occasion, the queen later noted in her diary that

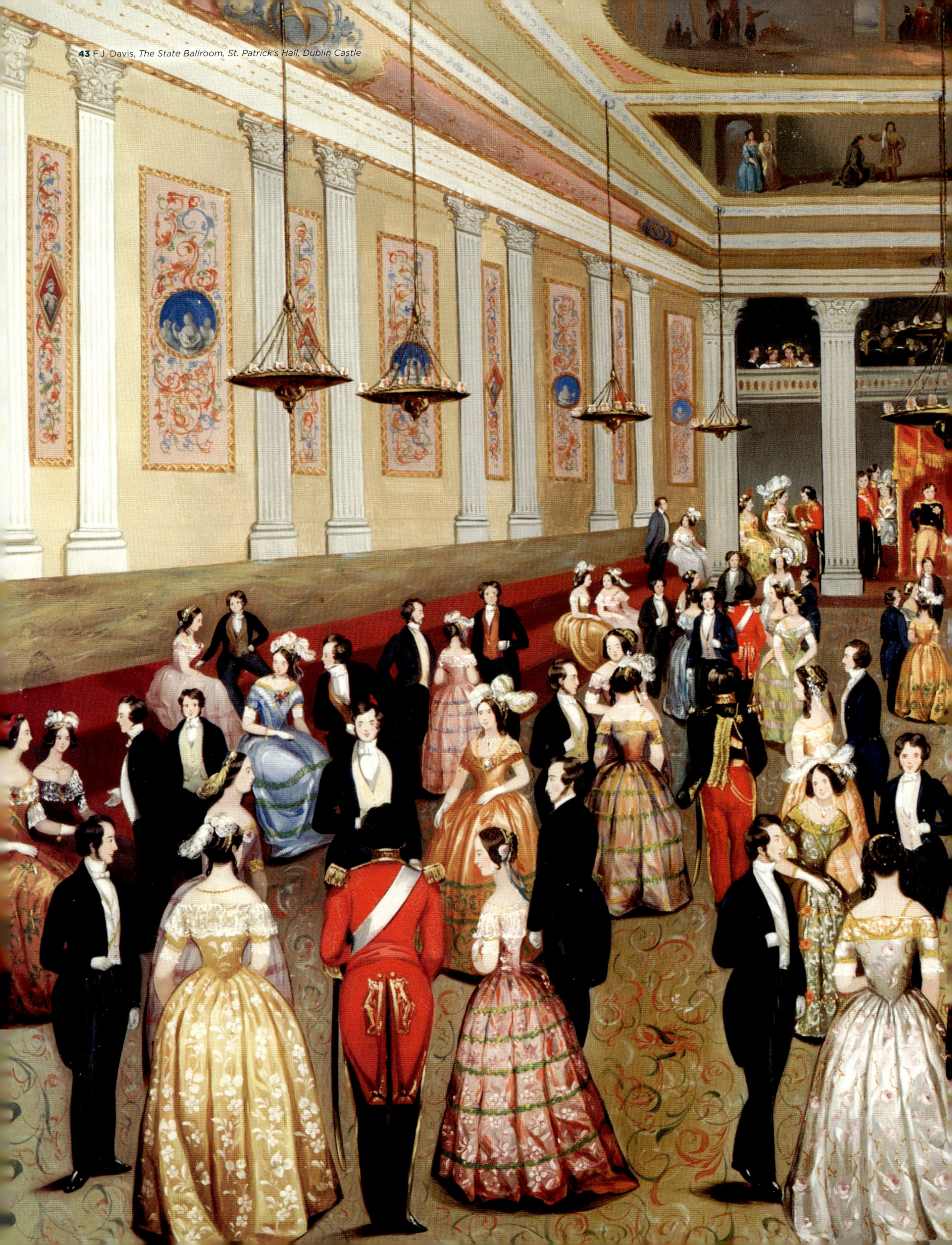
43 F.J. Davis, *The State Ballroom, St. Patrick's Hall, Dublin Castle*

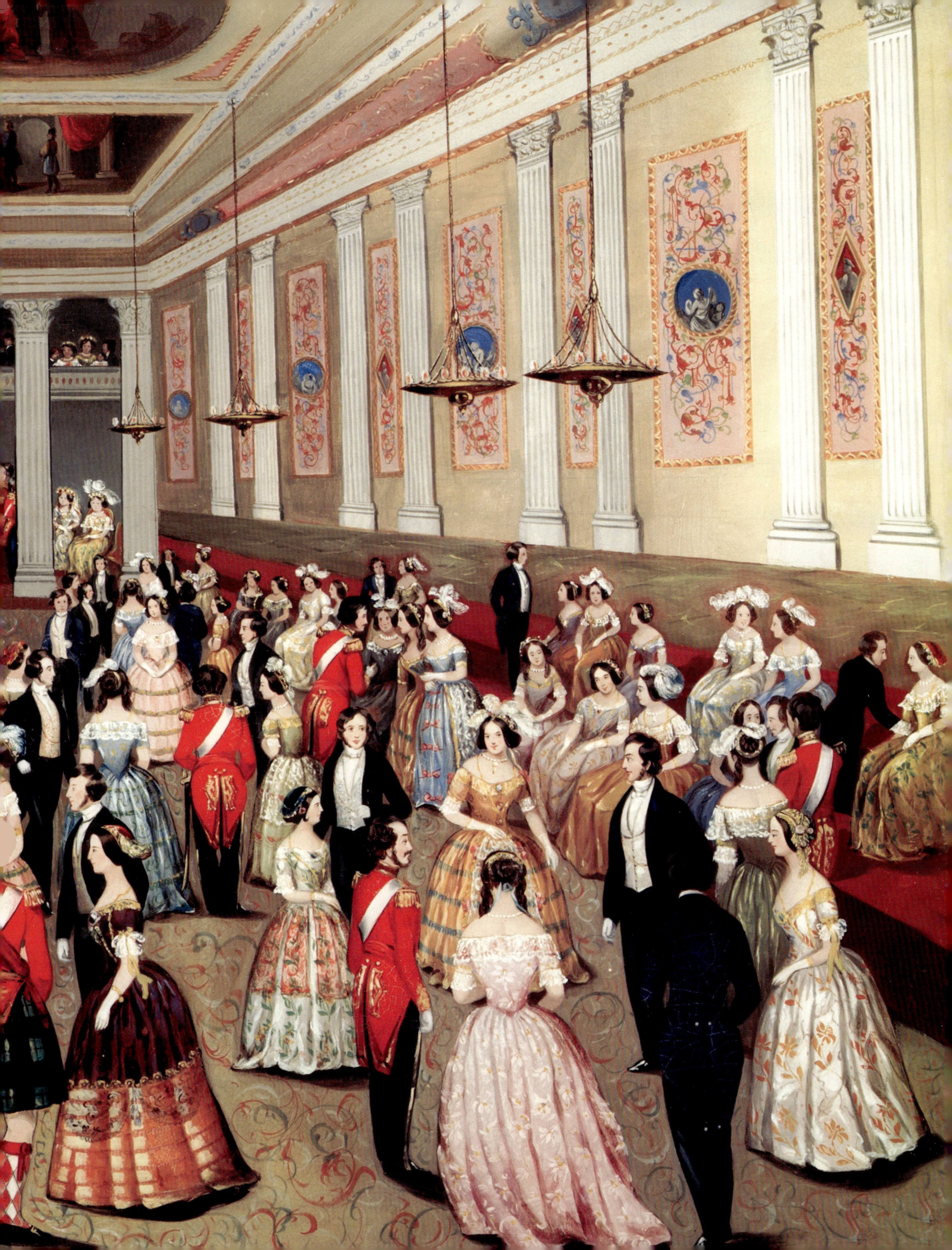

Everything was done in St James's style. The staircase and Throne Room are handsome and quite like a Palace. I sat myself on the throne, the seat of which was so high that I had great difficulty in sitting on it.[30]

However, she found that the levee was "hard work" and the "people are very awkward and some ridiculous". The following evening Queen Victoria returned to Dublin Castle for a "drawing room", where 1,600 ladies were presented to her.[31]

Unsurprisingly, given the condition of the country, there was widespread opposition to the royal visit. During the week of Queen Victoria's visit, a number of evictions were widely reported. As the *Roscommon Messenger* commented, the evicted had little interest in, or heart for, participating in the "joyous celebrations".[32] The *Freeman's Journal* went further, castigating the visit and pointing out that

one visit to a hut in Connaught, one view of a "cleared" estate in the south, a simple pencil etching by her Majesty of one unroofed cabin, with its miserable emaciated inmates cast out, and perishing on the dung heap beside it, would be a better result of this tour of the first magistrate of the empire than a week's festivities in Dublin Castle.[33]

■ ■ ■

Nowhere were the polarities between rich and poor in Famine Ireland more evident than in Dublin. As foodstuffs from all across the country were loaded for export, luxury goods continued to pour in. Indeed, the importation of such goods was largely unaffected during the Famine years, and there were ready markets for them. Most notably, Dublin auction houses fetched large prices selling a variety of potatoes, including Meyricks, Bangors, Peelers, Purple Kidneys and Cups, all unaffected by the potato blight, which raises the issue of culpability and the availability of potatoes in a time of severe shortage. Elsewhere, firms such as Scally's and Bewley's - among the largest importers of tea - appear to have been remarkably unaffected by the Famine; their imports included teas from Canton in southern China and Congo in central Africa. Dublin also boasted a number of "tasting shops" in which merchants were given an opportunity to try new brands, such as "Orange Pokoe" and Arabian coffee.[34] In one sale in March 1846 Bewley's had 800 casks of "middling and fine" tea.[35] Other merchants engaged in selling wines, spirits, and eau de cologne, ensuring that Dublin was well provisioned with the finest luxuries.[36]

In this world of apparent plenty, in the autumn of 1845 Dublin Castle officials were speedily deployed to meet the impending crisis resulting from the potato failure. Knowing that the failure of the potato crop would prove disastrous, a specialized Relief Commission was established. From here, under the careful watch of Sir Randolph Routh, head of the commissariat, and John Burgoyne, a senior engineer with the Office of Public Works, Famine relief was administered to almost half the population of Ireland. Chaired initially by the under-secretary, Edward Lucas, the Relief Commission was aided by a small team of civil servants and former military officers, including Colonel Duncan McGregor, John Pitt Kennedy, Dr Robert Kane, Sir James Dombrain, and Colonel Harry Jones. Much of the initial work fell to Lucas, who was quickly overwhelmed as thousands of letters poured into Dublin Castle on a daily basis to solicit help and support for the famished masses in every town and village in Ireland. Early on, the commissioners were also inundated with advice on how best to treat diseased potatoes and on providing alternative crops and foodstuffs to the poor.[37] While such advice was welcomed, a bigger challenge lay in ascertaining the extent of the blight and the likely consequences of the harvest failure. However, despite liaising with the constabulary and receiving input from a number of scientists and members of the gentry, the commission failed to anticipate the true scale of the calamity. It was not helped in this regard by landlords who appeared to be either misinformed about the situation or reluctant to adequately report it. For career civil servants, the sparse information offered little indication of the true extent of the failure of the potato. Even Ireland's premier peer, the 3rd Duke of Leinster, of Carton in County Kildare, was among those who greatly underestimated the extent of the potato rot.[38] Others were of the belief that "if but a fourth of them [potatoes] are saved all will be right".[39] The inability of Leinster and others to understand the crisis was probably due to the fact that since 1700 Ireland had experienced at least twenty-seven total or partial failures of the potato crop, which were usually followed by plentiful harvests.

The Relief Commission decided that small-scale intervention (primarily in the west of Ireland) through the provision of employment and imported Indian corn would stem the tide of Famine. However, by the spring of 1846 it was evident that a more concerted effort by the Relief Commission was needed, and that the solution lay with the establishment of local committees. As a means of providing relief for the more than three million people entirely dependent on the potato for their staple diet, the Relief Commission facilitated the establishment of more than 650 relief committees across the country (by mid-1847 the number of committees had increased threefold). The Relief Commission was not immune to criticism, and with the crisis deepening, newspapers such as the *Nation* sarcastically commented that the Relief Commission "is not an imaginary body", and assured readers that it did indeed meet in "the castle of Dublin".[40]

The local relief committees established in the spring of 1846 were tasked with distributing grain, facilitating loans, and establishing public-works schemes. Though the committees operated under the jurisdiction of the Relief Commission, the commissioners argued that responsibility ultimately lay with local relief committees. In particular, they was adamant that local committees should encourage the poor to continue to cultivate the land, frequently relaying the message that relief would not be a long-term measure. From the outset the establishment of local relief committees was often fraught with difficulty, and there was little the commissioners could do where local rivalries and petty squabbling prevented the establishment or effective operation of relief committees. Coupled with this it was widely argued that not enough of the "right people" (those who had experience in dealing with the lower orders) were appointed, which ultimately hindered the influence of these groups. Yet there were some who worked remarkably well and met with considerable success owing to the cordial relationship between Roman Catholic clergy and their Church of Ireland counterparts.[41] Although one of the later committees to be established, that at Rathkenny, County Cavan was among the most successful, and it received regular correspondence, support, and advice from the Relief Commission in Dublin Castle. Chaired by the local landlord Theophilus Lucas-Clements, the case of the Rathkenny committee demonstrates just how valuable such communication was, saving lives in the process as relief made its way to Cavan.

As elsewhere, during the late summer of 1846 Lucas-Clements and his fellow gentry realized that a second failure of the potato crop spelt disaster for the people of Cavan. While there had been intermittent demands on local farmers to contribute to ongoing famine relief, the local authorities now looked for other options to prevent mass mortality in the county.[42] Some, such as James Roberts, proposed that his local relief committee purchase Indian meal that could be sold to the laboring classes at cost price (charging only for the cost of carriage). A ton of Indian meal, Roberts estimated, would relieve fifty-five families from the grip of "extortion", but would not be accomplished "without a little trouble", perhaps suggesting that the members would themselves have to make financial contributions.[43] While commendable, these efforts were never enough given the sheer scale of the calamity, and the Cavan poor were soon in a "deplorable state ... dying of dysentery accompanied with slow fever, faster than they can be buried".[44]

The first meeting of the Rathkenny Relief Committee took place on March 29, 1847, with Lucas-Clements elected as chairman. Its initial business was made all the more challenging by the sheer scale of death, immediately made evident by the necessity to order extra coffins.[45] From its inception the Rathkenny Relief Committee was meticulous in its dealings, corresponding regularly with the commissioners in Dublin Castle. As relief included the daily provision of soup, on their advice a 130-gallon boiler was purchased from the Phoenix Iron Works in Dublin. These boilers (or "Famine pots") played a pivotal role in keeping people alive during the spring and summer of what came to be known as "Black '47". As per Dublin Castle's instructions, the committee was obliged to distribute rations to two groups: those under nine years of age and those over nine. Yet it was constantly striving to ascertain who the "deserving" poor were, and there were claims of personation and false applications – County Cavan no different from other parts of the country in this respect. In order to overcome these problems, the destitute were called in alphabetical order, and only the named person was given relief, not a member of the family. In the majority of cases the criteria were simple: applicants were to be "very poor" and possess "no means".

One of the problems the Relief Commission continuously faced was that the poor had little understanding of cooking Indian corn, or "yellow meal", as it was referred to. Circulars sent to relief committees instructed them to thoroughly cook the corn; this prevented people from reselling it at extortionate prices (being cooked, it would have to be quickly consumed). Despite the committees' initial successes in providing food for the poor, in most cases it was not enough to overcome the pangs of hunger. As a result, in late May the Rathkenny committee decided to increase the rations given to the poor by supplying eight ounces of bread with a quart of "stirabout" (soup). The committee was also actively engaged in the administration of public-works schemes in the parish. These were carefully monitored, with lists of those working on them sent to Dublin Castle on a weekly basis; however, deciding on who to include and recording their details took up much of the committee's time.[46] The committee was also required to send weekly reports to Dublin Castle for inspection. According to the regulations laid out for the relief committees, employment on the public-works schemes was only to be given to three groups: the destitute helpless; those destitute, able-bodied and not holding land; and holders of small portions of land. In addition, the waged were not meant to be given any relief, and those that did receive it were means-tested. As a result, the process of engaging workers on the public-works schemes was quite intensive, and decisions were not taken lightly. Where possible, members of the committee visited applicants to ascertain what possessions they had, and whether they were suitably "distressed".[47] This level of scrutiny, as advised by the Relief Commission, ensured that the system of relief was not grossly abused.

In spite of such a meticulous approach to the management of famine, Dublin Castle ideology and the work of the Relief Commission were ultimately shaped by events in London, and thus it was little wonder that when the British banking crisis commenced in 1847 the relief schemes were among the first casualties. Notwithstanding this, the banking crisis also coincided with the arrival of the aforementioned Earl of Clarendon as Lord Lieutenant. Widely ridiculed in the press and described as "My Lord Assassin" by some, Clarendon's appeals for help for Ireland were frustrated.[48] However, as with the "Dublin Season", there was no expense spared for his "swearing-in" ceremony, when Dublin Castle was said to have presented an "animated appearance".[49] After the elaborate ceremony, Clarendon hosted what would be the first of his many levees as Lord Lieutenant, entertaining the various Irish gentry and aristocrats. Despite such criticism, it was widely accepted that the work of the Relief Commission was of huge importance to the local committees across the country that strived to keep the poor alive. However, following the decision to phase out the public-works schemes in the summer of 1847, the Relief Commission became universally unpopular. By this time the government had decided that responsibility for relief should pass to the Irish Poor Law Commission, meaning the local boards of guardians.[50] In Rathkenny the relief committee realized that the relief schemes were insufficient to "answer the calls of destitution".[51] The following month, acting on the advice of the Relief

Commission, the Rathkenny relief account closed, although the need for providing for the poor had far from ceased.[52] Nonetheless, even in such a short space of time the committee had done a remarkable job. Meeting on only ten occasions between May and September, it had ensured that over £1,100 had been spent on local relief initiatives. In a practical way some 9,341 daily rations had been given to the poor, while hundreds were employed on a daily basis on the public works. While the success of the Rathkenny committee may have been atypical, it did prove that the assumptions that these were merely works that benefited the landlord or the aesthetics of uninhabited countryside were unfounded.[53] Certainly, mortality rates in Rathkenny would have been far greater were it not for the judicious management of the public-works schemes and the provision of over 9,000 food rations; the surviving committee records and correspondence with the Relief Commissioners in Dublin Castle testify to this.

■ ■ ■

In October 1847 the Relief Commission was instructed to prepare its final accounts and cease operations at once. In doing so the commissioners were confident in their belief "that it was thoroughly successful in its primary object", and that they had "diffused a degree of comparative content over the general mass of the community".[54] However, the commissioners conceded that the "discontinuance of this extensive system of relief ... must be attended with distress and difficulty", but hoped that local benevolence and charity would prevent further deprivation, championing the mantra that "Irish poverty must pay for Irish property".[55] In many respects theirs had been an unenviable task. With matters of finance strictly handled by the British government, at times there was little that the relief commissioners could do. Indeed, some - such as the under-secretary, Edward Lucas - regularly pressed government to increase spending on poor relief, warning that if they did not there would be "death from famine".[56] On other occasions castle officials inveighed against government policy, and were outraged that, despite their efforts, subscriptions remained low in certain parts of the country; they rebuked the landed gentry and others of means for their inaction.[57]

Unquestionably, the most important business in relation to Famine relief was carried out at Dublin Castle during the years 1845 to 1847. At its height, during the summer of 1847, the Relief Commission presided over the distribution of almost three million rations, which were provided through the network of soup kitchens made possible by the "Temporary Relief Act" of February 1847. Moreover, the exertions of some commissioners were remarkable: for example, John Pitt Kennedy, the secretary of the commission, was untiring in his duties, just as he had been over a number of years in connection with the Devon Commission that returned its findings on the eve of the Famine. However, even with these successes there were a number of flaws in the system: communication and distribution systems remained slow, which ultimately cost lives, while the quality of provisions was often considered below standard and highly objectionable. While the commissioners were conscientious and admirable, they sometimes fell short of what was needed and were not without blame. Indeed, even in November 1845, as the commissioners pored over the Scientific Commission's report on the extent of the blight, among their immediate concerns was the provision of a sanitary convenience in Dublin Castle.[58] In addition, their sometime self-congratulatory commentary to the effect that they had "improved the hitherto haggard appearance of the people" deflected from the true extent of the Famine crisis.

It is difficult to reconcile the contrast between the work of the Relief Commission and the lavish entertainment provided in Dublin Castle during the Famine years. Castle social life continued apparently unaffected by the Famine, and in many ways was the epicenter of Dublin social life, where the aristocracy and gentry could mingle when in the capital. Even if the horrors as relayed to the commissioners from local committees across the country seemed far removed, they did not have to look far for hunger, poverty, and the effects of Famine. Dublin of the late 1840s was described as being the "worst sewered, lighted, cleaned and watered city in the empire",[59] and, as Ó Gráda has argued and to use a modern parlance, it quickly resembled one huge refugee camp.[60] There was little empathy with the poor, particularly those who were overcrowded in substandard housing; indeed, the better-off inhabitants of Dublin, it was asserted, knew more of the "want, and misery, and suffering of the cottier population of Skibbereen, of Mayo, and of Clare" than of the "hundreds of human beings who huddled together in the lodging houses of Dublin".[61]

This study of Dublin Castle during the Famine illustrates how two starkly varying worlds existed there: on the one hand, the meticulous approach of the Relief Commission to the crisis, and, on the other, the pomp and ceremony of the "Dublin Season". In the decades that followed there was widespread hostility towards "the profaned salons",[62] and the apparent "sullen incapacity" of Dublin Castle during the Famine years came to represent the attitude of the British government in general.[63] As Ó Gráda notes, rarely were Dublin Castle officials cited in the folk memory of the Famine; this despite the fact that the fate of millions hinged on the decisions of a handful of men who composed the Relief Commission in Dublin Castle.

"Frightful and fearful is the havoc around me":[1]

THE GREAT FAMINE IN CORK CITY & COUNTY

LAURENCE GEARY

We stop the press, with very great regret, to announce that the potato murrain [blight] has unequivocally declared itself in Ireland … Where will Ireland be in the event of a universal potato rot? (Gardeners' Chronicle, *September 13, 1845)*

Two Cork artists, James Mahony and Daniel Macdonald, were responsible for some of the most significant visual records of the Great Famine. In a series of sketches in the *Illustrated London News* in 1847, Mahony depicted Famine realities in and around Skibbereen and Clonakilty in west Cork – a young mother begging in Clonakilty, an adolescent boy and girl potato gleaning in a harvested field at Caheragh.[2] Mahony's illustrations were journalistic and urgent, unfolding news captured in images at a time when photography was in its infancy. Macdonald's *An Irish Peasant Family Discovering the Blight of Their Store* **[Figure 44]**, executed in 1847 and thus contemporaneous with Mahony's work, offered a more measured, reflective, and stylised Famine narrative.

The scene is set in a rugged, mountainous landscape, beneath a turbulent, lowering sky. Against this background, itself ominous, Macdonald portrays a group of individuals, adults, and children – probably a multigenerational family – confronted with the loss of their pitted potatoes, the method of storing the harvested crop at the time. The spade has been cast to the ground, next to the halved and blackened potatoes. The bowed heads and forms of the women convey their anguish. The two men face in different directions. Their staring, unseeing eyes register the shock of the moment, the incomprehensible present, and the family's dimmed, blighted prospects. Potatoes were both the currency of the pre-Famine Irish peasantry and the key to their survival. They fed the people and their animals, and determined the rhythm, pattern, and tenor of their days, their present, and their future. The potato's loss presaged the demise of an entire class of people and their way of life.

In September 1845 potatoes in Ireland were struck by a new phenomenon, the fungal disease *Phytophthora infestans*, commonly called potato blight, which resulted in the loss of about one third of the country's second, or main, crop of potatoes. The impact was less severe in County Cork, where the deficit was slightly more than twenty per cent.[3] In the following year, blight returned and destroyed almost the entire potato harvest, a portentous occurrence that marked the commencement of the Great Famine in Cork city and county, no less than in the country generally.

The speed with which potato blight spread and the devastation it caused were vividly captured by Fr Theobald Mathew, the Cork Capuchin priest and respected temperance advocate, who, on a journey from Cork to Dublin on July 27, 1846, noted that the potato "bloomed in all the luxuriance of an abundant harvest". On the return journey a week later, he beheld "one wide waste of putrefying vegetation". In many places, according to Fr Mathew, "the wretched people were seated on the fences of their decaying gardens, wringing their hands and wailing bitterly [at] the destruction that had left them foodless",[4] a contrast to the muted, terror-stricken response of the family in Macdonald's painting.

PERCEPTIONS & REALITIES: CORK CITY

The winter and spring that followed witnessed the utmost distress in Cork and throughout the country. This was a period of extreme and debilitating food shortages, spiraling food prices, food stealing, and food riots, and a grossly inadequate public-works program. The resident population of Cork city was augmented by starving people from the county and further afield, who swarmed into the city in search of relief, "walking masses of filth, vermin and sickness", as one local newspaper described them.[5] These rural refugees scattered famine-related diseases in every direction and swamped the city's limited charitable and relief resources. Dr John Popham, one of the physicians attached to the North Infirmary, recorded:

The pressure from without upon the city began to be felt in October [1846], and in November and December the influx of paupers from all parts of this vast county was so overwhelming that, to prevent them from dying in the streets, the doors of the workhouse were thrown open, and in one week 500 persons were admitted, without any provision, either of space or clothing, to meet so fearful an emergency. All these were suffering from famine, and most of them from malignant dysentery or fever.[6]

Dr Callanan, one of the workhouse physicians, captured the situation in Cork during the fateful winter and spring of 1846–47 in imagery that was such a haunting feature of contemporary writing on the Great Famine:

From the commencement of 1847, however, Fate *opened her book in good earnest here, and the full tide of death flowed on everywhere around us. During the first six months of that dark period one-third of the daily population of our streets consisted of shadows and spectres, the impersonations of disease and famine, crowding in from the rural districts, and stalking along to the general doom – the grave – which appeared to await them at the distance of a few steps, or a few short hours.*[7]

On April 14, 1847 Captain Robert Bennet Forbes, commander of USS *Jamestown*, which had arrived in Cork Harbour from Boston a few days earlier with some 800 tons of relief provisions for distribution in Cork, visited the city in Fr Mathew's company and was shocked by the scenes he witnessed in Cork's side streets and back lanes. In a celebrated passage, which graphically captured the plight of the famine-stricken poor, he noted:

I went with Father Mathew, only a few steps out of one of the principal streets of Cork, into a lane; the valley of the shadow of death *was it? Alas, no, it was the valley of death and pestilence itself! I saw enough in five minutes to horrify me – hovels crowded with the sick and dying, without floors, without furniture, and with patches of dirty straw covered with still dirtier shreds and patches of humanity; some called for water to Father Mathew, and others for a dying blessing.*

Forbes recorded that hundreds of "spectres" stood about a police-patrolled public soup kitchen, begging for a portion of poor-quality soup. The city streets were thronged with beggars and with starving and sick children and adults, and, Forbes added, the situation was even worse in the countryside.[8]

The arrival of famine refugees from without the city provoked conflicting responses among city dwellers: anger, fear, hostility, and rejection among some; sympathy and concern among the more generous and charitably minded. Ratepayers resented the increased costs associated with the expansion of workhouse and hospital accommodation to meet the continuing crisis; business people were concerned with the impact of importunate beggars on trade and commerce; everyone feared the prevailing famine-related diseases, and blamed mendicants and vagrants for their diffusion. On April 23, 1847 a meeting of church wardens, health officials, and magistrates in the city called on the mayor to activate legislation that allowed for the expulsion of infected persons and paupers in order to prevent contagion, and requested the civic authorities "to organise a staff of able bodied and if possible well-disciplined men", and to station them at the key approaches to the city to prevent country paupers from entering.[9] The meeting and the mayor's acquiescence to its demands prompted Fr Mathew to complain to the government of this "heartless and cruel" response to the Famine, which, he said, was contrary to the word of God. According to Fr Mathew, strangers who were caught begging for food were confined without sustenance in an open market overnight, after which they were handed over to the constables, taken five or six miles from the city, and given a modest quantity of bread to sustain them.[10] The implications of such actions were obvious, their outcome inevitable.

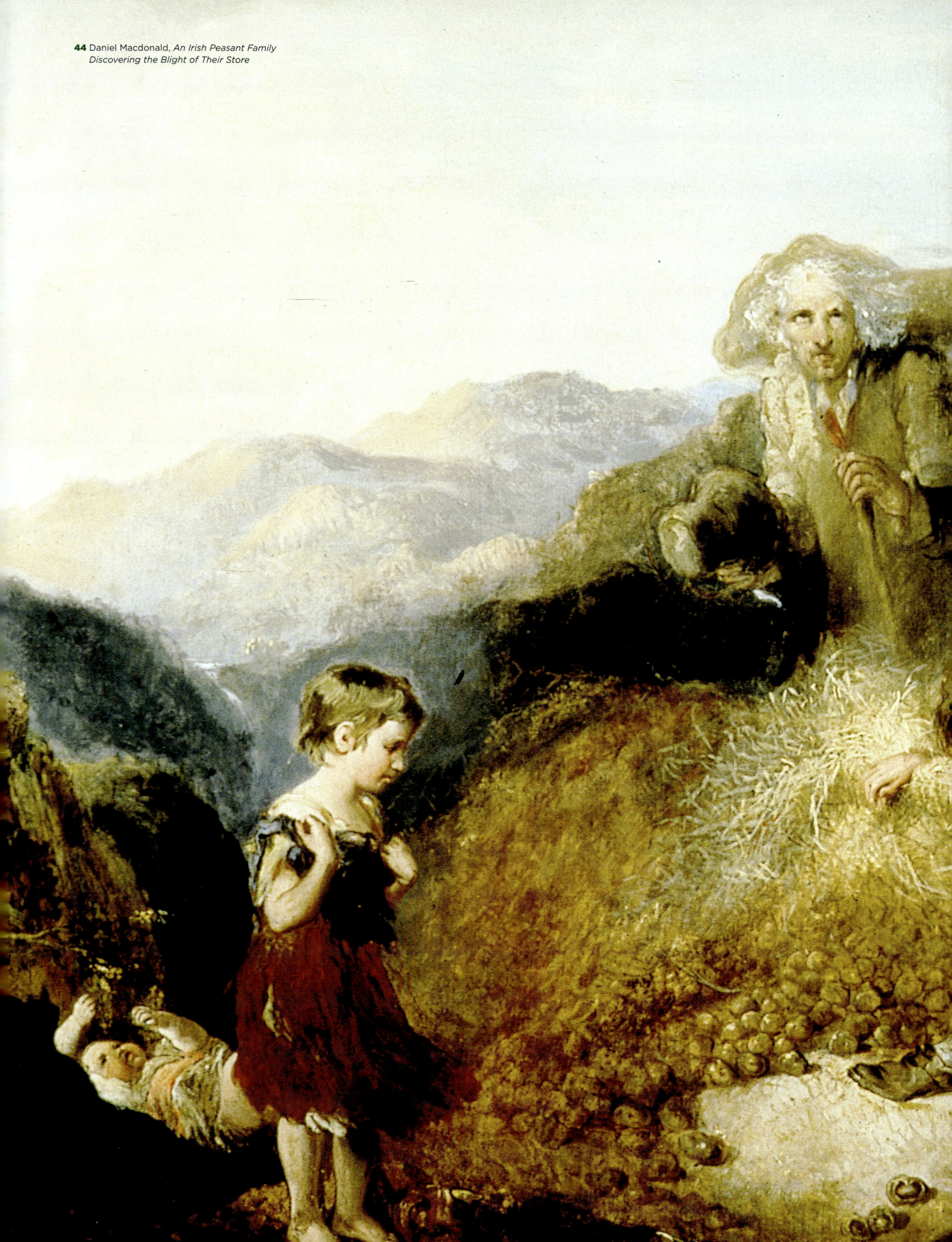

44 Daniel Macdonald, *An Irish Peasant Family Discovering the Blight of Their Store*

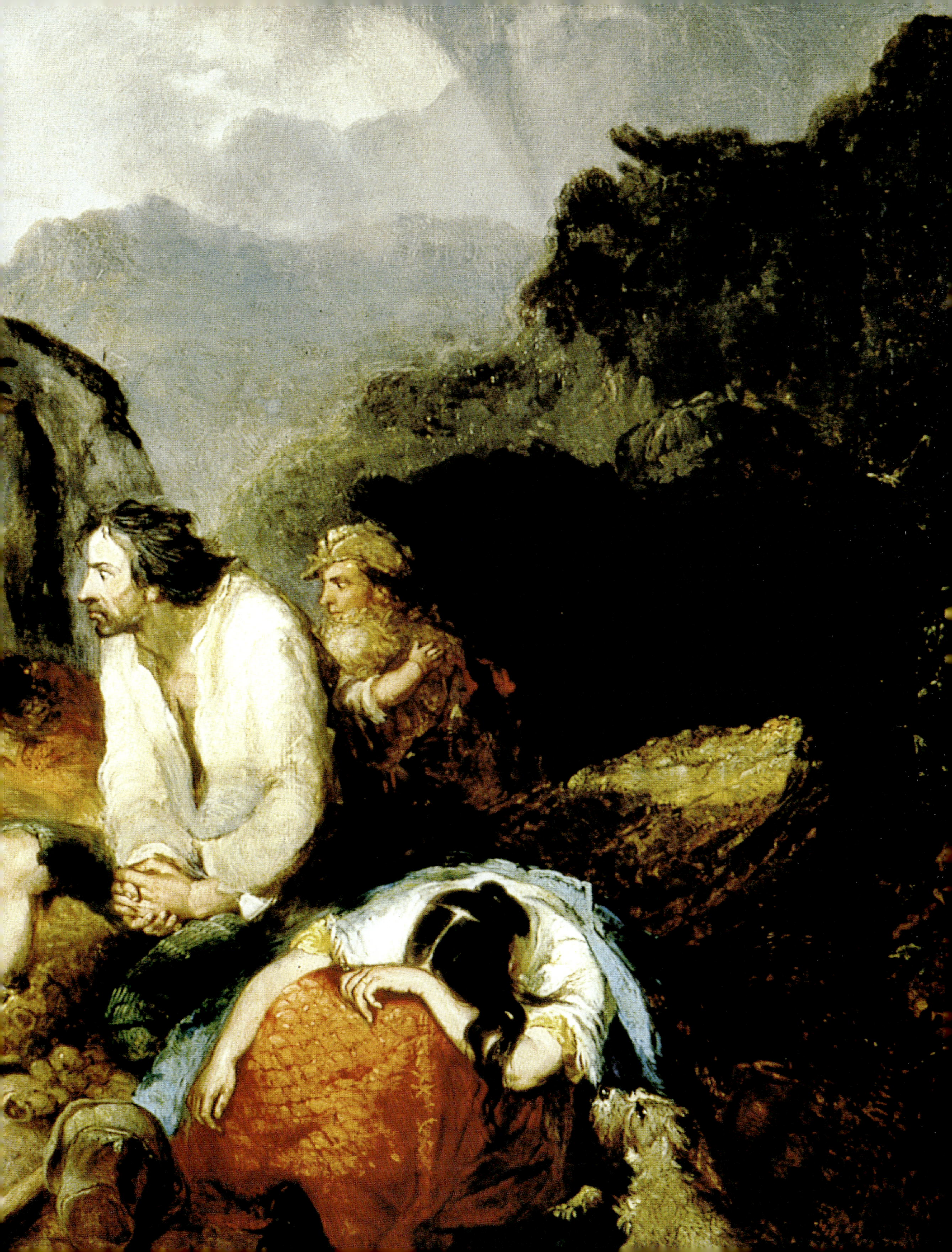

PERCEPTIONS & REALITIES: WEST CORK

The starving and diseased peasantry who abandoned the countryside did so because the land – and their government – had failed them, and the testimony of humane visitors to the worst affected parts of the county attested to their distress. On December 21, 1846 two members of the Society of Friends, William Harvey and Joshua Beale, left Cork city to investigate conditions in west Cork. They discovered that provisions were in short supply in Skibbereen Poor Law Union and in the surrounding districts, and that the food that was available was increasingly beyond the reach of the poor because of the disjunction between wages on the public works and the spiraling cost of food. The Quaker visitors concluded that direct government intervention was required to address what they described as the "complicated trials" of the peasantry.[11]

However, such intervention was unforthcoming. The prevailing ideological constraints of political economy, moralism, and providentialism left Lord John Russell's Whig government with a singular lack of appetite for addressing the consequences of potato failure, starvation, and disease among the affected population.[12] Six weeks after Harvey and Beale's visit, an Aughadown resident informed the Central Relief Committee of the Society of Friends that the locality was "one mass of famine, disease and death", with people succumbing to a complication of diseases. The correspondent added that the dead were wrapped in calico bags and conveyed to the churchyard in a reusable coffin, colloquially known as a "trap" or "sliding" coffin, which was fitted with a hinged bottom that swung open like a trapdoor when released.[13]

The synonymity of west Cork with famine was captured in the depiction of Schull and Skibbereen in one newspaper as "the two famine-slain sisters of the south".[14] The district's famine-stricken notoriety can be partially explained by the advocacy of some of its middle-class residents, notably Rev. Dr Robert Traill, rector of Schull, and Dr Daniel Donovan and Fr John Fitzpatrick, medical practitioner and parish priest respectively in Skibbereen.[15] Traill and other active residents publicized the plight of their respective localities in a series of graphic and harrowing letters to local and national newspapers, and their efforts may have been responsible for focusing disproportionate attention and aid on Schull and Skibbereen.[16] A medical practitioner, Joseph Kidd, who located temporarily to Bantry in the spring and early summer of 1847, suggested that the town and its neighborhood may have suffered even more severely than Schull and Skibbereen, but had not attracted as much attention or received the same amount of publicity, which he attributed to a lack of engagement by Bantry's resident gentry. Kidd described the homes of the Bantry poor as "hovels crowded with human beings in the most loathsome state of uncleanliness". He calculated that more than 400 individuals, almost ten per cent of Bantry's population, were suffering from fever or dysentery. Mortality was so great that trap coffins were used and the local relief committee engaged a team of men with horses to bury the dead as their families were generally unable to do so or even to accompany their loved ones to the grave.[17]

In February 1847 the British Relief Association dispatched ninety-six tons of food to Schull on the naval vessel *Scourge*. The ship's commander, J. Cruford Caffin, was shocked by what he saw on arrival. He claimed that three quarters of the people of Schull were reduced to skeletons, and he was particularly struck by the physical decline and beggar status of adult males. Caffin had read reports of the Famine in the district and thought they were highly colored to attract sympathy, but realized there had been no exaggeration when he saw for himself the reality. In Dr Traill's company he visited several poor Protestant families. The first had possessed a cow, a few sheep, and potato ground, but their animals had been stolen, and Caffin concluded that their situation was hopeless. In another cabin a woman who longed for death had blocked up the door with dung so that she might not be disturbed. She had some money but her frailty and the distance she lived from the village prevented her from purchasing food for herself. Caffin and Traill found a female corpse on the floor of the next cabin they visited, "cramped up as she had died, with her rags and her cloak about her, by the side of a few embers of peat". The dead woman's son-in-law had absconded, leaving his wife with three moribund young children, and the abandoned woman had neither the means nor the strength to dispose of her mother's corpse.[18]

The publication of Commander Caffin's distressing account of his experiences prompted Rev. F.F. Trench, curate of Cloghjordan, County Tipperary, to visit west Cork. Trench encountered abnormality – whole communities in disarray. He noted the absence of children's games, the abandonment of funerary customs, the defilement and dismemberment of unburied bodies by vermin and dogs, the ubiquity of coffins, and mass graves. Trench experienced the sight, smell, and sound of death and decay – in effect social disintegration.[19] Trench's depiction of communal implosion was corroborated by his cousin Richard Chenevix Trench, who was drawn to the area in early April 1847 after reading Rev. Trench's account in a Dublin newspaper. The stark reality of the situation was brought home to Richard Trench in Ballydehob, where he witnessed a "mass of wild fierce hunger", which he described as "almost unmanageable".[20] Like many other observers, he was struck by the abandonment of customary funeral rites throughout west Cork, by the debasement of the living and the dead.[21]

On February 18, 1847, a few days after Caffin recorded his shocked impressions of conditions in Schull, the American pacifist, philanthropist, social activist, and evangelical Christian Elihu Burritt journeyed westwards from Cork city, and found the road to Bandon "lined with apparitions of human misery" – poor, starving people who offered a stark and startling contrast to the surrounding green and fertile fields. In Bandon he found individuals crouching in the dark corners of their mud-walled cabins, looking like "famished beasts" while trying to hide their misery in darkness. In a parting comment, before he left Bandon for Skibbereen, Burritt observed that "if suffering could purchase salvation", the Irish poor would already have "earned the best provided mansions of heaven". In Skibbereen he witnessed wan children who appeared as if "they had just been thawed out of the ice in which they had been imbedded until their blood had turned to water". On a wet and cold afternoon he inspected an impoverished area of the town, where, in windowless, straw-roofed cabins, he encountered the dying and the dead lying on the same "pestiferous straw upon which their predecessors to the grave had been consumed by the wasting fever of famine". Burritt encapsulated his three-day stay in Skibbereen in the comment, "A quiet, listless despair broods over the population, and death reaps a full harvest." Further west the conditions and prospects of the people were just as grim, and Burritt's experiences in west Cork were to haunt his dreams for years to come.[22]

WEST CORK: A MEDICAL LABORATORY

The Famine precipitated rolling waves of infection, particularly fever and dysentery, and the impact of these diseases was exacerbated by the presence of others, especially tuberculosis, smallpox, diarrhea, influenza, pneumonia, and measles, and by the reappearance of the dreaded Asiatic cholera in 1848–49. Medical practitioners testified to the ubiquity and virulence of disease throughout west Cork. Dr Daniel Donovan, who practiced in Skibbereen and was familiar with the local people and their illnesses, described 1847 as a "disastrous year". He claimed that "famine and pestilence broke out at an earlier period, raged more severely, and committed greater ravages" in the neighborhood of Skibbereen than in any other part of Ireland. According to Donovan, the fever epidemic in Skibbereen followed inexorably in the wake of escalating food prices and widespread starvation, and he predicted the transmission of the disease from the lower to the higher social classes and its diffusion beyond the shores of Ireland. His analysis of starvation and disease in Skibbereen in 1846 and 1847 was as stark and explicit as its implications were obvious: medical practitioners' training and skills and the medicines they employed were no match for the prevailing fever and dysentery, which, he claimed, originated in Ireland in "squalor, misery, and starvation". Donovan concluded that the politician had a bigger role to play in curbing disease than the physician, that economic and infrastructural investment would have a greater impact on public health than "placing hospitals in every townland and doctors in every hamlet".[23]

Daniel Donovan in Skibbereen, Joseph Kidd in Bantry, and their medical colleagues throughout the country were severely challenged by the starvation and diseases that surrounded them, and so, too, were the hospitals, dispensaries, and workhouses these doctors attended. When the Famine began, Cork city and county were served by sixty-eight dispensaries, thirteen fever hospitals, and three infirmaries – the North Infirmary and South Infirmary in the city and the County Infirmary at Mallow.[24] After the second failure of the potato crop in 1846, pressure mounted on these and on the country's medical and relief facilities generally. As a result, overcrowding became the norm; so, too, did inadequate and insecure funding, indebtedness, and ubiquitous fever, dysentery, and other infections. Sickness and occasional absenteeism among medical personnel, not to mention increasing levels of mortality, were other features of these institutions.

Excessive numbers of institutional inmates, which resulted from the indiscriminate admission of the hungry, the sick, and the moribund, created logistical problems and gave rise to serious public-health concerns. On November 18, 1846 ninety starving individuals applied for admission to the Skibbereen workhouse. The Poor Law guardians who administered the institution were aware of the possibility of importing infection, but the lamentations of the applicants and their resolve to lie down and die around the walls of the workhouse rather than be driven out into the heavy rain overcame the guardians' misgivings. Skibbereen workhouse, which had been built to accommodate 800 individuals, contained 1,169 by the first week of January 1847.[25] In mid-March, according to a local solicitor, the number of inmates had swollen to 1,450, and the institution was in a "most alarming condition". Fever and dysentery were rampant, and 104 deaths were recorded in the first ten days of March. In a period of just over four months, November 1, 1846 to March 10, 1847, 728 individuals died in the workhouse, "nearly the number it was built to accommodate".[26]

In the opening months of 1847, many Cork relief and medical facilities faced similar pressures. In the second week of February 1847, forty-nine inmates died in Fermoy workhouse, where dysentery was "raging violently".[27] At about the same time there were 5,300 paupers in the Cork Union workhouse, a thousand more than the recommended number, and mortality was increasing alarmingly. There were ninety-one deaths in the last week of January, 127 in the following week, and 164 in the second week of February, one every hour; disposing of the dead had become a major problem. The Central Board of Health, at the instigation of the Poor Law Commission, dispatched Dr Richard Stephens in mid-February to conduct a medical inspection of the workhouse. The two administrative bodies feared that overcrowding would result in disease outbreaks that could not be contained within institutional walls. Invariably, fever and other contagious diseases began among the poor and spread to the higher social classes, among whom disease generally proved more lethal, possibly because of a lack of acquired immunity. Stephens reported that Cork workhouse was in a grossly overcrowded and chaotic state, and he attributed the institution's escalating morbidity and mortality rates to the debilitated or moribund condition of the poor on admission, and to the overwhelming pressure on the building's rudimentary sanitary arrangements as a result of overcrowding.[28] The situation continued to deteriorate, and on March 29, 1847, after the deaths of 757 inmates during the month, the guardians halted admissions pending assurances from the medical staff that the institution was in "a wholesome and healthy state".[29]

Immediately after completing his inquiry into the Cork Union workhouse, Stephens conducted a similar investigation in Bantry workhouse, where fifty-six deaths had occurred in the week ending February 6, 1847. Stephens found the workhouse clean and orderly when he visited on February 19, but he was shocked by the state of the fever hospital. He had never experienced "such an appalling, awful, and heart-sickening condition as it presented", nor did he think it possible that such a situation could exist in "a civilised or Christian community". He witnessed naked patients lying on straw beds in their own excrement, and the living sharing bed space with the dead from the previous night. Some of the patients begged for water, others for food, stating that they were hungry and weak rather than sick, a claim that was subsequently borne out by the removal of thirty of their number from the fever hospital to the workhouse proper. There was a dreadful stench throughout the hospital, generated possibly by the prevalence of dysentery among the patients. There was no doctor in attendance, and nursing was provided by one of the paupers, who was untrained and unfit for the duties.[30]

The experiences of the Cork and Bantry workhouses and their hospitals in the opening months of 1847 reflected the extreme pressures that the Famine imposed on the country's relief and medical institutions. Mortality levels varied over the course of the Famine, and were obviously higher during periods of particularly acute distress – in the winter and spring of 1846–47, for instance, and in the second and third quarters of 1849. Disproportionately high mortality rates during the latter period may have been due, in part at least, to the Asiatic cholera epidemic that commenced in December 1848 and to increased evictions resulting from the Poor Law Amendment Act, 1847. These factors contributed to the Famine's overall demographic impact of at least one million deaths from starvation and disease.

FEARFUL REALITIES: DEATH & ITS TRAPPINGS

The many references to social implosion and abnormality in Irish, English, and American visitors' perceptions of west Cork, noted above, were corroborated and substantiated in newspaper reportage and commentary. In mid-December 1846 a special correspondent of the *Cork Examiner* reported that the most extraordinary feature of the prevailing distress in the Skibbereen district was "the total apathy and singular indifference" with which death was regarded. He claimed that the better feelings and sympathies that formerly characterized the Irish people had disappeared, and their familiarity with death had rendered them indifferent to its ravages. An editorial comment added substance and texture to the reporter's palpable sense of shock:

A terrible apathy, like that which oppresses a plague-driven people, seems to hang over the poor of Skibbereen ... One scanty funeral is fast followed by another and that by another. The dead are enclosed in rude boards, having neither the appearance nor shape of a coffin and are committed to their silent resting place in the night time, when no eye can rest curiously on the rude contrivance, or observe the absence of friends and mourners, and the want of all that ceremony so grateful to the pride and consolatory to the feelings of the Irish peasant.[31]

The reporter encountered "the same unaccountable and extraordinary apathy" in Bantry a few days later. The general feeling among the people was that they were "doomed", that they would be found dead in the fields or on the mountains without either the consolation of religion or the comfort of friends.[32] A similar miasma of fatalism hung over other parts of west Cork. A report from Castletown Berehaven in mid-February 1847 noted the "anguish of mind" and "wretched depression" that afflicted the peasantry. The observer added that these feelings arose from a sense of inevitability, from a conviction among the people that they were "doomed to die".[33]

The abandonment of traditional funerary rites and customs, and the disrespect (almost desecration) shown to the dead were stark features of the Famine.[34] Early in 1847 Rev. John Fitzpatrick of Skibbereen reported that the respect that the Irish were so fond of paying to their deceased friends, and their accompanying of the remains to their last resting place, were no longer a feature of the district. He noted: "there is now no concourse of people following the corpse, no weeping or wailing is heard, no manifestation of grief". The people were oblivious to everything other than obtaining "a morsel" to rescue them from starvation.[35] A similar response to famine deaths was detected in the Cork Union workhouse. The medical officer there noted that "there was no sorrowing, no tears, no wailing even of mothers for their children". The latter "went out of life like bubbles bursting on the stream".[36]

The dead were interred at night or early in the morning, from shame, it was suggested, because they could not be given a decent burial.[37] In mid-January 1847, when the number of deaths in the parish of Schull was about twenty-five per day, the local famine-relief committee informed the Lord Lieutenant of Ireland that "the most careful mode of interment now practised is to scrape by night a hurried grave in the shallow soil and use a few loose stones as covering".[38] Increasingly, corpses were buried without coffins. In late February 1847 the secretary of the Skibbereen famine-relief committee reported that the dead were being "thrown" coffinless into graves.[39] The dead were interred wherever they fell, in ditches, in corners of fields, behind their cabins.[40] Many were in such an advanced state of decomposition that their houses were pulled down around them and burned.[41] As mortality increased, bodies were left unburied and were eaten by vermin and dismembered by pigs and scavenging dogs.[42]

THE RECKONING

The population loss that County Cork experienced could not have been anticipated when potato blight first appeared in the early autumn of 1845. The county and the country generally emerged relatively unscathed from the initial season of potato failure, but the winter and spring of 1846–47, following the almost complete destruction of the 1846 crop, was a period of terrible distress, perhaps the worst of the entire Famine. During these months, fever and dysentery raged epidemically, their malignity intensified by the effects of starvation, and these diseases cut a swathe through the immunocompromised population of west Cork and other badly affected areas. The government's response to the failure of the staple food of the poor was determined by the prevailing ideology of political economy, and was grossly inadequate.

The overwhelming burden of attempting to feed the hungry, care for the sick, and bury the dead fell to local, rather than central, initiative, and devolved primarily on the middle class, or at least on responsible representatives of that class. These were the individuals who wrote letters to newspapers, canvassed public opinion and more concrete support, served on committees, and joined delegations to Dublin Castle and Westminster. The engagement of middle-class local residents and their articulation of the plight of the helpless and the voiceless of west Cork and elsewhere was of crucial importance. Their distressing, often harrowing accounts of starvation and suffering and their emotional appeals for assistance were published in the national and international press. In the winter of 1846 and in the following spring and early summer, a succession of visitors prompted by the publication of local accounts of the Famine arrived in Skibbereen and Schull, and the response of these individuals generated further attention, publicity, and practical assistance. There may have been a degree of anthropological inquiry or even ghoulishness in their interest, but the vast majority of those who involved themselves in famine-relief initiatives, whether they were visitors or locals, are likely to have been motivated by charitable and humanitarian impulses, by an overriding sympathy for, and sense of duty to, their fellow man. However, the often heroic work of responsible and committed citizens – medical practitioners such as Daniel Donovan of Skibbereen and clergymen like Robert Traill of Schull – was dwarfed by the sheer scale of the event, and the Famine's toll on the population of west Cork and of the country generally was horrific.

In the late 1840s and early 1850s the Irish people were confronted with a catastrophe of unprecedented dimensions and with morbidity and mortality rates on a scale never before experienced. The poorest and most vulnerable were stripped of entitlement and choice. For the more advantaged, there was the option of flight, and some two million emigrated from Ireland in the decade 1845–55. Nationally, the numbers who died during the Famine years were on a par with those who emigrated. Death and emigration reduced the population of County Cork from 854,118 to 649,903, or by almost twenty-four per cent, between the census of 1841 and that of 1851, although the city's population increased from 80,720 to 85,745 as a result of the influx of rural migrants.[43] The demographic impact was the most dramatic and enduring of the Famine's seismic shocks, but there were others – political, social, and economic – that were to rumble on for the remainder of the nineteenth century and into the twentieth.

Entering the Gray Zone:

HUGH DORIAN & "THE YEARS OF FAMINE"

BREANDÁN MAC SUIBHNE

On April 25, 1914 Hugh Dorian died aged about eighty at 55 Nelson Street in Derry's Bogside; the cause of death was "senile decay" - that is, old age. For the previous eleven years the widower had shared that two-up, two-down house with his daughter Ellen, her husband James Kyle, a docker-cum-laborer, and their family, now numbering three children. Another daughter, Maria, a "factory girl", had lived with them until the previous year, when, at forty-four, she married Thomas Curry, a widowed laborer employed in the Cow Market. A few years earlier, a widow, Annie McLaughlin, and her children - Daniel, a laborer, and Maggie, who took in laundry with her mother - had been renting one of no. 55's four rooms, and they may still have been there in April 1914. Known to have been present at Dorian's death was his youngest son, James (b. 1877), who lived nearby on the Lecky Road. A printer, he alone of three brothers who survived into their twenties acquired a trade. The other two, Hugh and John, became laborers; indeed, the old man, while usually employed as a bookkeeper or writing clerk, had occasionally resorted to manual labor.[1]

Dorian's death passed unnoticed in Derry's three main newspapers, and no memorial today marks his grave in the City Cemetery; it likely never had any marker other than a simple wooden cross. Yet he himself crafted an extraordinary memorial to the poor who perished in the Great Famine and, controversially, those who prevailed and prospered: a narrative written over nearly 400 pages of a copybook in 1889–90 **[Figure 45]**, which comprises the most extensive account of the Famine committed to paper by anybody rooted in the underclass decimated by it. And it is one that defies easy categorization. For sure, it is a nationalist narrative. Dorian blames Britain, in the long term and the short, for the disaster that befell Ireland. For instance, he identifies public-work schemes as the point where

government advisers dealt out the successful blow - and it would appear premeditated - the great blow for slowly taking away human life, getting rid of the population and nothing else, by forcing the hungry and the half-clad men to stand out in the cold and in the sleet and rain from morn till night for the paltry reward of nine pennies per day.[2]

Still, in an assessment of the Famine's consequences he expresses cold satisfaction at the fate of "many" of his neighbors:

Arising from death, emigration, and dispersion to all parts, the population soon dwindled away. And indeed I hope it will not be any way uncharitable to say it, but with the multitude also disappeared many turbulent and indifferent characters who were only a disgrace to the good, the honest and the well-doing, and if there was poverty, there was peace too.[3]

Given Dorian's politics and, indeed, the vividness of his descriptions of the physical and mental toll of hunger, these remarks strike a strange and discordant note. They become decidedly disturbing when one realizes that Dorian himself was on occasion a "disgrace to the good, the honest and the well-doing": he drank and brawled, feuded with neighbors, and fell foul of his priest and the law. And so his narrative, in which there is great emphasis on divisions between the poor, serves as a reminder that there is more to the Famine than an event in Anglo-Irish relations or a problem of public administration, and, most especially, that men, women, and children are not simply receptacles of food or members of a social class – they belong to households and kin groups, and have cultural and political bonds, and such filiations and affiliations can, in a time of dearth, make the difference between life and death. Given how the narrative illuminates how some people "who were comparatively poor, who really had nothing to spare in the good times, those who might be called the lower class" managed to "creep up in the world" during the Famine,[4] it helps to check what Cormac Ó Gráda has described as a tendency, in popular discourse, "towards a version of famine history in which the descendants of those who survived all become vicarious victims".[5] Dorian brings the land-grabber[6] and the meal-monger into view.[7] And, above all, he directs attention, intentionally and otherwise, to a moral space where judgement is, at best, not easy – a space between victim and persecutor that is itself integral to many humanitarian crises. Primo Levi gave that space a name – the gray zone. In *The Drowned and the Saved* (1986) he recalled the "brusque revelation" on entering Auschwitz that "hope of solidarity from one's companions in misfortune" was a grand delusion: the interior of the camp, he insisted, could not be divided into blocs of victims and persecutors, for some prisoners took advantage of others, or, for a variety of reasons, collaborated and received rewards and favors from their captors.[8] Dorian, by explaining why, in the years of the Famine, the poor lived in dread of each other,[9] disturbs accounts that simply oppose victims and persecutors, and brings readers into the gray zone of the Great Famine.

■ ■ ■

Many artworks in Ireland's Great Hunger Museum bring passages in Dorian's narrative to mind. Most obviously, this remarkable collection includes fine representations of the social life of the Irish poor in the mid-nineteenth century and after, as well as works that help the viewer to apprehend how, when the blight came, there was, in Dorian's words, "nothing but stillness, a mournful silence, in the villages; in the cottages, grim poverty and emaciated faces showing all the signs of hardships".[10] And it also features many works that represent the condition of post-Famine Ireland, when, as Dorian described it, people who gathered at night to chat found "their subjects were lacking words, more silent, and of a more mournful nature" than their conversations in former years.[11]

Less conspicuous in the collection than in the narrative is the *reduction* of people, how famine pushes people below the waterline of what they had previously considered civilized behavior; moreover, many works seem intended less to provoke a reflection on the moral dilemmas that the poor faced or, indeed, issues of complicity than to stir pity.[12] But such concerns are there, most strikingly in modern pieces such as Alanna O'Kelly's *A Kind of Quietism* (1990, IGHM) and her *No Colouring Can Deepen the Darkness of Truth* (1992, IGHM), and, more obliquely, Charlotte Kelly's *Abandonment* (2011, IGHM). And some critics have discerned them in contemporary works, too: one interpretation of Daniel Macdonald's *Irish Peasant Children* (1846, IGHM) sees the absence of parents and the disturbed expression of a child as hinting at a disintegrating family.[13] Still, after Dorian, and his insistence that sometimes "a man's very neighbour is very often just as pitiless a tyrant as any man",[14] one cannot look on the most sentimentalized depictions of Irish rural families – for example, the work of Topham (*Feeding Chickens,* 1848 IGHM), Goodall, and Fripp (*An Irish Peasant and Her Child*, n.d., IGHM) – and not recall that it was families just like them that observed with an unpitying eye the fate of those deemed a disgrace to the good, the honest, and the well-doing. And changed, too, after Dorian, are those ruined houses that have become emblematic of the Famine: harm, his narrative insinuates, did not always come from without.

TURBULENT & INDIFFERENT CHARACTERS?

Hugh Dorian was not a native of Derry; neither was his wife Catherine (née Gallagher) nor six of their nine children (b. 1859–77). Rather they were the remnants of what the *Derry Journal* once called the city's "fugitive population" – that is, people who had "flocked into the city from rural districts after the Famine".[15] There had been work then in Derry for women, but little for men. Yet here those fugitive families had remained, the males chronically underemployed. And others followed: the city's population swelled from 15,196 in 1841 to 20,187 in 1851, and it was just shy of 40,000 in 1901. Derry's working-class streets and laneways, like those of other Irish towns, were home to the "depressed urbanized surplus of the countryside".[16] The condition of those people was that of "static vagrants ... unemployed attendants", as John Berger described the inhabitants of twentieth-century shantytowns – "attendants in the sense that they wait ... cut off from the past, excluded from the benefits of progress, abandoned by tradition, serving nothing".[17]

243 ~ Years of Famine ~

appear, but to work were not able, nor yet much inclined. While on the g
and apparently working, a man in every gang, or as they were called "gan
kept a lookout for the approach of the "gaffer" whilst the rest of the gang
or stood idle, and when under the eyes of the gaffer itself, their efforts
such that the slowest manoeuvres of a now Corporation brigade man
swift motion in comparison. Here is where the government advis
dealt out the successful blow, and it would appear premeditated, t
great blow for, slowly taking away human life, getting rid of the popula
and nothing else, by forcing the hungry and the half dead men to stan
in the cold, and in the sleet and rain from morn till night, for the paltry su
of Nine pennies per day. Had the poor pitiful creatures got this allow
small as it was, at their homes it would be relief, it would be charity, it wo
convey the impression that their benefactors meant to save life, but in the wa
thus given, on compulsory conditions, meant next to slow murder.

With every hardships and so small a recompense, still the man who g
work at the lucky Nine pennies per day considered it a great favour, an
thought himself happy at earning even so small a sum, while at the sam
time the Yellow Indian Meal was bought at two pence per pound.

Oh! the thought then of the Nine copper coins, worth of Indian meal,
means for providing a supply for the twenty four hours, and keep life in
family of perhaps five or six, and in this calculation of not omitting, or
forgetting the Sunday.

There were private laws made by the "Committee" men, and those who had
distribution of the relief and amongst their law acts were such that any m
possessing a four footed animal - not a dog or cat - but one which could be
at fair or market, as long as he had such was in consequence

45 Hugh Dorian manuscript

Donegal 60 Years ago. 244.

...rred from government aid. The absurdity of this enactment is manifest ...or the result was that very soon a great many were brought to the same ... in poverty, and then the want and suffering became general with few ...tions. Every conceivable means were resorted to, for getting something ...nything to support life, by soliciting on trust, by borrowing even in the ...llest quantities, from those who had a little to spare from day to day, and if ...ccessful in entreating at one house, would try another and another, ...at last some neighbour would be found to share for the time, as a loan ...ugh pity and during the while, the hungry family were praying for ...successful return of the messenger that they might get something in the ...e of a repast for the day. Things and substances never heard of ...as being used to support human life were of necessity resorted to, in ...any substance which the palate did not completely rebel against, was ...to alleviate the pangs of hunger.

Many affectionate parents reduced themselves to mere skeletons from the too repeated acts of withholding from themselves the necessaries they were so ...h in need of and giving it to the silent helpless children, therby feeling ...at comfort in the act, but unawares feebleness would steal upon them, ...d so overcome would they be from weakness caused by want of food ...actually apparently strong ablebodied men, who on managing to get into ...neighbour's house, without any business whatever but purposely to while ...time and be relieved in being out of sight of the distress if only for a ...minutes, and from exhaustion would after sitting on a chair or other ...t, soon fall asleep and on attempting to get home again, would have to ...hands to a wall or fence to keep from staggering, and as the saying is ...multiplicity of stars before their eyes.

Dorian had been born *c.* 1834 in Fánaid, north Donegal, and that rugged peninsula, although never named, is the focus of his narrative. He belonged to a family poor in land; his father, of all smallholders in the townland of Cashel, had least "cow's grass". Still, his family's precocious literacy had allowed Hugh to clutch at advancement. Neil Dorian, a close connection, had kept a hedge school in the 1820s – he may be an itinerant teacher who looms large in the narrative – and in 1851, when Fánaid's population had declined by about twenty-five per cent in the space of five years, Fr Daniel O'Donnell appointed the seventeen-year-old Hugh as master of Fanavolty National School.[18]

It was a step away from the spade, and first in Fanavolty and then in nearby Tullyconnell School, to which he moved in 1854, Dorian thrived, consistently impressing inspectors. But between politics and public houses, he lost his footing in the lower middle class. First, in 1864, Dorian opted to move to a new school at Ballyhoorisky managed by an unpopular landlord, William Clements, 3rd Earl of Leitrim, setting himself on a collision course with the Catholic clergy. Then, in January 1866, his priest "read him from the altar", declaring there was "none more wicked in the place" and ordering him from the chapel. Dorian, he claimed, had penned a letter that "went to show" that a "number of people" had met at the chapel to plot a murder and that, if they followed through with their plan, it would be the cause of people being evicted. Frustratingly, available sources (including some letters from Dorian to Leitrim) do not clarify whether the priest was condemning him for promoting the Ribbon Society or the Fenians, both of which had a presence in Fánaid, or for informing on such a group. But it seems to have been the former.[19]

Thereafter, the once diligent teacher lost interest in his "scholars": in May 1866 he was admonished for the low proficiency of his pupils and his school's "want of cleanliness", and a year later, in May 1867, an inspector formally threatened to close Ballyhoorisky if things did not improve. And things did not improve. In May 1868 the Commissioners of National Education reprimanded him "very severely" for involvement in a row in a public house, and warned him that if he were again "guilty of brawling or associating with drunken people" he would be dismissed. The number of children attending the school was now falling, and he was playing truant, being reprimanded in 1870 for late attendance. In 1871 he was convicted of being drunk and disorderly, and in summer 1872, aged only thirty-eight, he resigned his position and left for Derry with his wife Catherine (they had married in 1856) and six children.

Dorian found work as a clerk, and by 1874 the family was living at Alexandra Place, near the docks.[20] It was there, in 1877, that Dorian's ninth and last child, James, was born. Three of those nine children died young, all from diseases that still relentlessly stalked the poor: ten-year-old Ellen of smallpox in 1874 (a daughter born the following year was given her name); three-and-a-half-year-old Annie of whooping cough in 1876; and in 1885 nineteen-year-old Thomas of "the decline", a euphemism for wasting diseases, especially pulmonary tuberculosis; he had suffered with it for three years. Alcohol brought other troubles. Catherine's body was taken from the Foyle on December 27, 1899. She had been last seen two days before Christmas, when, at 6.45 p.m., she had been arrested for public drunkenness in a gateway on Waterloo Place. Taken to the Strand Road barracks, where a policeman thought the "old woman" (she was fifty-four) to be "weak and famished", she had been released at 10.00 p.m. to get somebody to fetch a daughter who had also been arrested for drunkenness. A doctor who examined the body noted a flesh wound on the right side of the forehead and a slight contusion on the lip, both of which had been caused before her death.

At a coroner's inquest, convened in a public house on Sackville Street and chaired by one of the managers of Watt's Distillery, a constable deposed that there had been no wound on her face when she had been discharged from the barracks, suggesting she had either fallen or been assaulted before entering the water. Hugh, described in the press as "a respectable, hard-working man", told of searching the streets of Derry for her:

He stated that he last saw his wife alive between two and three o'clock on Saturday. At that time he was home for dinner. He gave her some money to make necessary purchases for the household. He returned home again from work after six o'clock, but his wife was then absent and did not come back. He waited for her to return up to eleven o'clock. After that hour his daughter came in and inquired about her mother. Witness then left the house and walked around the city, searching everywhere for the deceased, but in vain. He walked through almost every street in the city, and also along the quay, but found no trace of her or of any person who had seen her.

The jury returned a verdict of "death by drowning, accidental, instantaneous".[21]

There were other drink-related incidents. Notably, in 1901, James Dorian, then aged twenty-two, appeared in court charged with having thrown a crockery bowl at a neighbor, Sarah Quigley, who had been visiting a sick person in their house. Quigley, a laborer's wife then in her fifties, testified that she did not believe the bowl was thrown with any ill intent, but the court fined him anyway.[22] Then, a few weeks later, James was prosecuted a second time for being drunk "at his own residence", suggesting the constabulary had been called to calm him down.[23] And there were other sources of trouble. For instance, in 1897 Hugh Dorian Jr. was fined for beating a railway laborer opposed to a strike called by the Amalgamated Society of Railway Servants; he himself was not a railway employee.[24] Finally, failure to locate some family members in census returns (searchable online for the country) raises the possibility that they may have been imprisoned: in 1901 Hugh Jr.'s wife, Margaret, was not at home on census night, but she was still living (he was "married" not "widowed"), and she cannot be found in any other household. Likewise, in 1911 Ellen's husband, James Kyle, cannot be found in the census. Prisons, like poorhouses and asylums, only entered their inmates' initials on census returns.

And so there is a certain irony in Hugh Dorian's satisfaction at the "disappearance" of "turbulent and indifferent characters" during the Famine, for the respectable (and the constabulary) sometimes placed himself and his family in that category. But there were many in the same category: in 1899, the year that Catherine drowned, there were 2,097 arrests for drunkenness in Derry (pop. 1901: 39,892), giving it a rate of such arrests more than three times that of the country as a whole and twice the average of all major urban districts; only in Waterford city were arrests for drunkenness more common.[25]

The Dorians, then, were typical of Derry's laboring poor. And for that reason, in his last years Hugh may have been a disappointed man, ruminating on the condition of his children and their spouses, who, despite receiving an elementary education better than most people of his generation, remained underemployed manual workers mired in poverty, waiting for a change. There had once been hope that change was imminent. Indeed, in 1889, when Dorian began his narrative, Charles Stewart Parnell was in his prime and nationalists believed home rule was on the cards, which may have contributed to Dorian's optimistic tone in his "Concluding Remarks".[26] Yet, in December 1890, after he had finished it, the O'Shea divorce case had split nationalists, and soon home rule seemed as far away as ever. Parliamentary change had blown the flame of hope in the early 1910s. But, on the night before Dorian died, unionists landed massive consignments of arms and ammunition at Larne, Bangor, and Donaghadee for distribution to the Ulster Volunteer Force; the police and military stood by, stalling a process of democratization that had progressed, however fitfully, through his lifetime. Hope would spring again, in 1916–21, before it, too, was extinguished by partition and civil war. Some of Dorian's grandchildren likely lived to avail of the United Kingdom's welfare programs rolled out after the Second World War, and, if he had great-grandchildren, they may have been beneficiaries of the 1947 Education Act that introduced free secondary education. But down to the late 1960s, sectarian discrimination blighted the prospects of most of those born beneath the walls of Derry; over half a century after Dorian's death, the people of the Bogside were still "static vagrants", "unemployed attendants", still waiting.

A REASON TO WRITE

Politics gave Hugh Dorian a reason to write of the Famine. In February 1889, in Gweedore, west Donegal, District Inspector William Martin of the Royal Irish Constabulary attempted to arrest a priest, James MacFadden, wanted for promoting resistance to landlords. Martin did so as MacFadden was leaving Derrybeg chapel after having said Mass. Grabbing hold of him, he drew his sword, causing the dispersing Mass-goers to surge forward and beat him to death with paling posts and stones. The state responded in a heavy-handed manner, flooding the district with police and soldiers, who detained forty-eight men and three women and conveyed them to Derry Gaol. Ten people, including the priest, were charged with murder, and thirteen others with conspiracy; they were brought to trial in October. Fearful that a glaringly packed jury would find at least one prisoner guilty of murder, the defense counsel reached an agreement with the attorney general: the priest pleaded guilty to obstruction and was immediately released. Nine others also received short sentences for obstruction, while seven were convicted of manslaughter.[27]

The entire episode, from killing to court case, became part of the contemporary debate about home rule. For unionists and conservatives, the "barbarous murder" by Mass-goers was evidence of the "savagery" of Irish Catholics, and established that they were incapable of self-government. In a variation on an old theme, Rev. R.R. Kane, a prominent Orangeman, told a massive "indignation meeting" in Belfast that the people of Gweedore were "as innocent and credulous as the painted children of the prairie" but manipulated by their priest for his own sinister ends.[28] The message was clear: home rule would be Rome rule and destructive of life and liberty. Nationalists and liberals, on the other hand, presented the people of west Donegal as a monolithic group of simple peasants persecuted by avaricious landlords and an alien state; the excessive state reaction became the "Gweedore Terror", and it was held up as evidence of the need for further land reform and home rule.

Indignation at the smallholders' treatment, in print as much as in prison, forms the starting point of the narrative. Dorian alludes to "recent events" and "sufferings" having drawn international attention to Donegal, and, in a note, describes the Gweedore prisoners arriving, under massive military escort, at Derry Gaol:

Anyone who had seen or witnessed the procession from Pennyburn to Bishop Street Queen's Hotel, can never forget it. England's strength, cavalry, infantry with swords drawn, guarding barefooted girls with a piece of shawl about their shoulders. Pity they had not a few field pieces to make the victory more complete. It could not be compared to Roman victory or procession in days of paganism. It was more like Hell opened until the iron gates closed upon their prey, a few defenceless young men and young women handed over to the cruelty of unmerciful gaol keepers.[29]

And the Gweedore case also provides the narrative with its central purpose: to debunk the notion that the Irish rural poor were inherently savage (and thus incapable of self-government) by relating their alienation and violence not to distant history but to their lived experience of social injustice and sectarian discrimination and, especially, starvation and disease in the late 1840s. The Famine accounts for about twenty per cent of the narrative, including two substantial chapters ("The Years of the Famine" and "The Landlord Extermination"); the remainder is largely concerned with illuminating the society obliterated by the Famine and that made by it.

ENTERING THE GRAY ZONE

Four decades after the blight came on the potatoes, Hugh Dorian could recall its color and its smell: "in one night, smitten with the blight and changed from the natural green to that of polished black, the real resemblance of death; today the crop green and in blossom, tomorrow dark, withered, and an unpleasant and offensive smell, which could be felt at distance away".[30] And he could remember, too, the face of hunger: "the cheekbones became thin and high, the cheeks blue, the bones sharp, and the eyes sunk". He could recall how people's legs and feet used to swell and get red, and how the skin would crack, and the "weakness in the frame" that would come over the hungry - how they used to suddenly nod off to sleep and then tottered when they tried to walk:

Many affectionate parents reduced themselves to mere skeletons from the too oft repeated act of withholding from themselves the necessaries they were so much in need of and giving them to their silent helpless children, thereby feeling great comfort in the act, but unawares that feebleness would steal upon them. So overcome would they be from a weakness caused by want of food that apparently strong able-bodied men, on managing to get into a neighbour's house without any business whatever but to while away the time and be relieved, to be out of sight of the distress, if only for a few minutes, would sit on a seat and soon fall asleep from exhaustion, and on attempting to get home again would have to lay hands on a wall or a fence to keep from staggering - with, as the saying is, a multiplicity of stars before their eyes.[31]

Hunger's mental toll was not forgotten. Dorian remembered how some people, after several seasons living "between hope and despair", effectively gave up: "Men lost all energy, all activity merely creeping about like so many bundles of clothing".[32] Likewise, people became

negligent and drifted from bad to worse, selling everything they could dispose of for the merest trifle to anyone who could buy or exchange them - until the Workhouse, the last game of all, or (through the well wish of some friends abroad) the emigrant ship, shut them out of view of their native country for ever more.[33]

He remembered, too, anguish, sadness, and misery. Above all, Dorian remembered fear:

It came to this that even the few who had some worldly substance about them were afraid to own it and were afraid to use it except under pressing necessity, and not only that but the persons who had sufficient nourishment in food showed signs as if it did them no good. This in a sense was not to be wondered at, as it could not be otherwise for a man of feeling, knowing that his neighbour, his friend or near relative, perhaps his grandchild, was without food and hungry ... there was an uneasiness, a dread of the future preying upon their minds so that what they partook of served not what nature allowed, and along with this, the sleep was restless thereby disturbing the body, leaving it pale and sickly looking though nourishment was sufficient at the time.[34]

This general "dread of the future" included fear of the landlord and his bailiffs, and fear of those charged with the distribution of relief. But crucially, as want and suffering became general, there was fear of the neighbors, and that fear persisted into the years that followed:

self-preservation was the predominant thought of all men. Friendship was forgotten, men lived as if they dreaded each other, every one trying to do the best for himself alone, and a man would rather deny the goods he possessed than make it known that he had such or that he was improving in the world.[35]

Central in Dorian's account are land-grabbers. And his narrative, doubtless inflected by his own family having lost land, apparently to a cousin, brooks nothing but disdain for them:

The greedy man thinks deeply, his eyes see far, and it takes a length of time to fathom or bring to view his designs. The landlords are often accused, and justly, of their oppression, cruelty and tyranny, but unfortunately very often a man's very neighbour is just as pitiless a tyrant as any man. He first covets his fellow neighbour's property, strengthened in his thoughts from some certain signs arising of the latter coming to poverty or unable to meet his demands. The avaricious neighbour sees him going back in the world, he feels glad at this, but the declining man lingers longer in the way then at first supposed, and the man progressing in the world's goods has no claim at him, has not the law nor the power to grasp at him as he would wish, but to hasten his downfall he knows the way to do it. He buys up the bailiff, a thing not too hard to do, as food and drink will do that, next the agent, and lastly through them the landlord.

The poor man who is unable to meet his demands is at last turned out and this seemingly industrious man grasps – with apparent reluctance ... though he had for years previously used every means he could devise to fall wrongfully into possession. He pretends that he feels for the "outgoers", and there is a sort of a half promise just to keep matters cool for the present, that some recompense will be paid, or if in a few years the outgoing man is able to do the impossible, that is redeem, that he will be reinstated: "I do not want your land, I have as much as I can handle of my own, but you see I can't help it, unless I draw the anger of the landlord against myself and you see one does not like to do that."[36]

Certainly, Dorian remembered the courage of the poor in collecting together to plunder food stores guarded by "tyrannous, sneaking, place and promotion-seekers" (constables) or to prevent the coastguard removing meal from ships wrecked on their coast.[37] And he remembered the poor clutching to the vestiges of humanity by small acts of charity or by arduous journeys, undertaken when weakened with hunger, to bury their dead.[38] Importantly, too, he was conscious of class differences. The poor, he wrote, "were treated and despised as if they were beings of quite a different creation": the proverb *Ní thuigeann an sách an seang* he perfectly translates as "the satiated never understand the emaciated".[39] And he makes much of corruption in his local relief committee, with funds intended for alleviating distress "smuggled and converted into other uses".[40] But it is his preoccupation with the readiness of some among the poor to take advantage of people in distress and, most especially, his own indifference to the loss of many of his neighbors that give edge to his extraordinary narrative.

coming home:

ART & THE GREAT HUNGER EXHIBITION CATALOGUE

NIAMH O'SULLIVAN

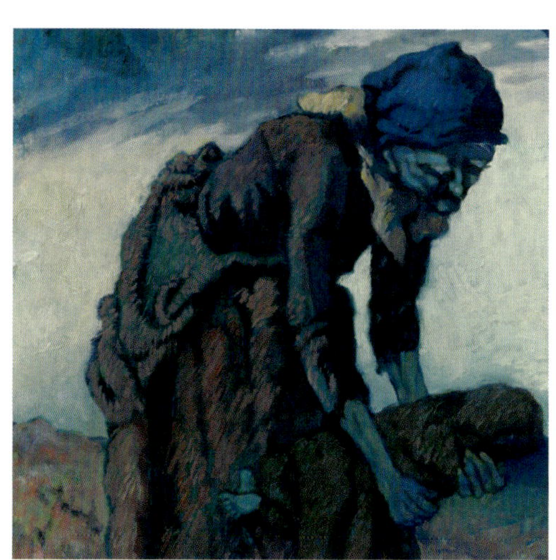
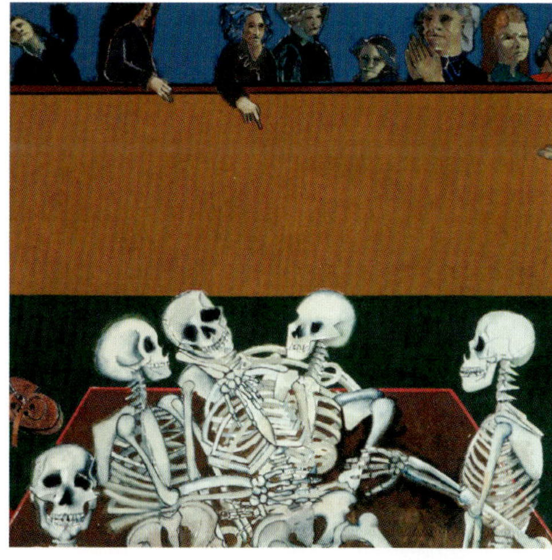
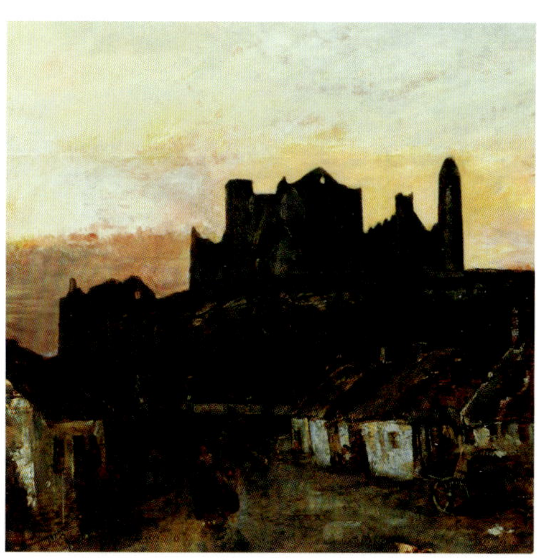
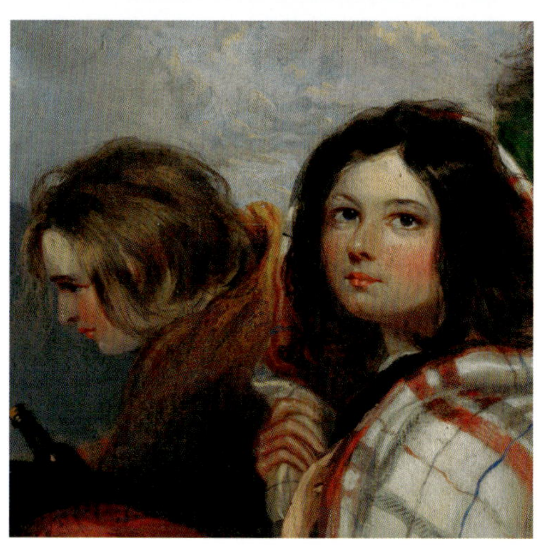
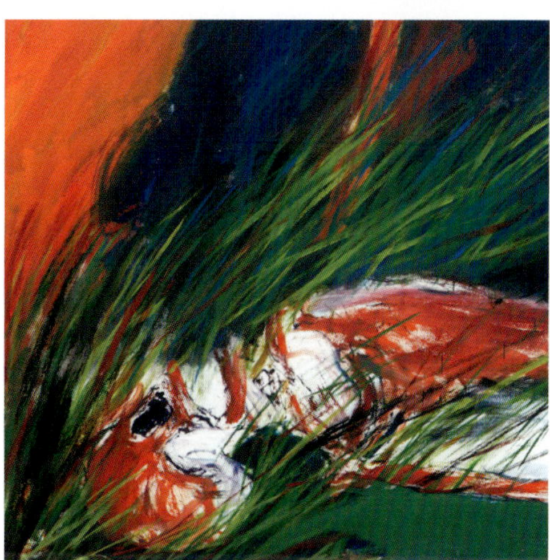
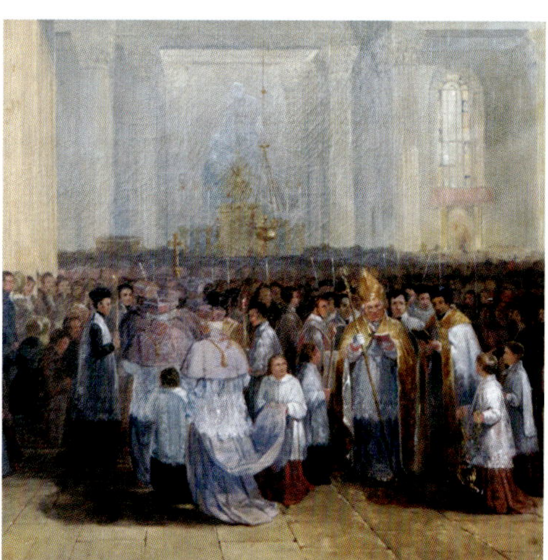

Allan, Henry

RHA (1865–1912)

The Rag Pickers, 1900
Oil on canvas, 26.5 x 40 in (66 x 101.5 cm)

This painting is one of two versions of the same subject. This *Rag Pickers* was exhibited at the RHA in 1900, and was owned by the artist Joseph Malachy Kavanagh. Allan studied in Belfast, Dublin and the Académie Royale, Antwerp in the *antiek* class with Vincent Van Gogh (Allan passed, Van Gogh failed!), followed by the life class with the renowned Charles Verlat.[1] Walter Osborne, Richard Thomas Moynan, and Roderic O'Conor were also there at the time. Allan returned to Ireland about 1888, when he began exhibiting small interiors à la Jozef Israëls. Allan's *The Little Match Seller* was awarded the Albert Prize at the RHA in 1893. Other works include *Old Beggar Woman, Carting Sea-weed in the Ards,* and *Martial Law: An Episode of an Irish Rebellion in 1798.*

In *The Rag Pickers*, described by Julian Campbell as "a remarkable piece of Social Realism", Allan enlarged his scope and lightened his palette.[2] The topography is consistent with the dunes of Ringsend, Dublin seen from South Lotts in 1900. Ragpickers eked a living by collecting scraps (as well as dead cats and dogs that could be skinned to make clothes). In the painting, women are collecting for the paper mills at Rathfarnham, Kilmainham, or Clondalkin. Ragpickers turned over what they salvaged to a master, who would sell it. Although it was the reserved occupation of the poorest, anything of value was confiscated. Here, two crones point at a group of other pickers, suggesting some disagreement.

Ragpickers lived on the margins of society. Realist artists and writers turned the ragpicker into a type of street philosopher who – unburdened by material things – understands human nature. In Victor Hugo's *Les Misérables* (1862), la Vargouleme rag picks, and in *The Rag Picker* (*c.* 1865–70), Édouard Manet sites him within his beggar-philosopher series, depicting his picker as a social type representative of the age. *Chiffonniers* (as they were called) were forced out of existence by the Haussmannization of Paris in the 1860s. And when Eugène Poubelle devised the garbage can in France in 1884, he was denounced for interfering with ragpickers' livelihoods. Even today, rag-and-bone men play a role in the waste management of cities, especially in Third World countries, where it continues to be a source of income for the urban poor.

The lot of immigrants was a matter of substituting one life of misery for another. Throughout the nineteenth century, almost three million destitute Irish streamed into America. By 1855 the population of New York was thirty-seven per cent foreign-born Irish. The Irish concentrated in slum roosts, such as Five Points in Manhattan's Sixth Ward, said to average a murder a day. Immortalized in Herbert Asbury's *Gangs of New York* (1928) and in Martin Scorsese's film of the same title (2003), the Irish were synonymous with crime and violence (in 1859 fifty-five per cent of people arrested in the city were Irish).

In Mulberry Street, horrendous conditions pertained. And here the ragpickers lived. In September 1873 *Harper's Weekly* carried the illustration "A Tenement House in Mulberry Street", observing that "Not in Rome, nor Paris, nor London can be found worse abodes of foulness and misery than the lower class of tenement-houses in New York." A single tenement contained twenty families, over forty adults and as many children, "the lowest class, steeped in ignorance and degradation":

The house is never cleaned, and the floors and walls are saturated with offensive effluvia ... and the atmosphere within is rank poison. Decaying garbage and filth of every description cover the

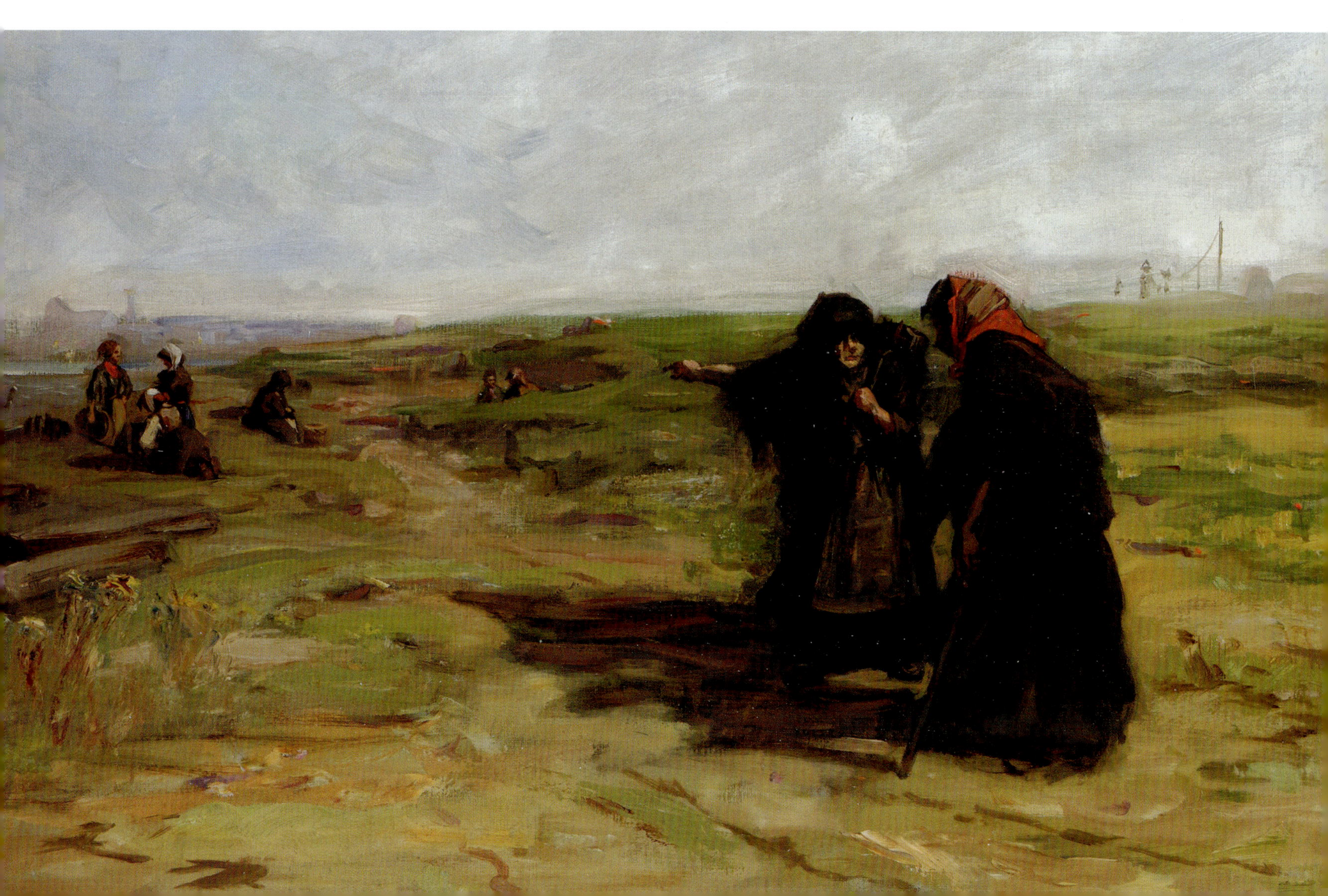

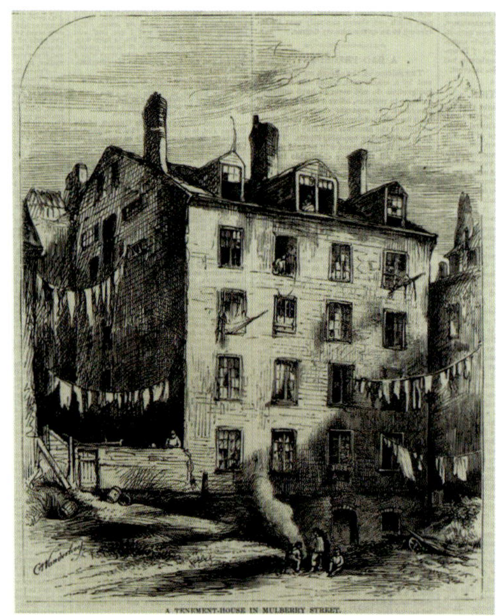

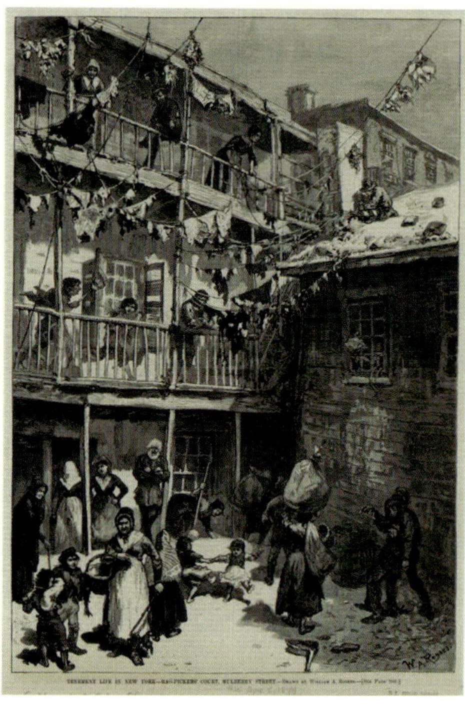

Charles A. Vanderhoof (1853–1918),
"A Tenement House in Mulberry Street"
Harper's Weekly, September 13, 1873
17 x 11 in (43.18 x 27.94 cm)

William A. Rogers (1854–1931),
"Tenement Life in New York –
Rag-Pickers Court, Mulberry Street"
Harper's Weekly, April 5, 1879
17 x 11 in (43.18 x 27.94 cm)

passage-ways and court, and sickening odors and gases rise from the choked sewers, and penetrate every part of the building.

Here resided the Irish: "At night nearly all the adults were generally drunk, and their dismal orgies were a great annoyance and terror to the neighborhood."[3]

In the new spirit of investigative journalism, when William A. Rogers returned to Mulberry Street for *Harper's*, things were even worse; the squalor he described constituted a biting social document of the age (April 5, 1879).

By the turn of the century, immigrants comprised some seventy-five per cent of the city's population, prompting nativists to post "No Irish Need Apply" signs around the city. As immigrant groups competed for jobs, racial tensions rose. The Draft Riots of 1863 turned into ugly race riots, with white, chiefly Irish rioters, attacking blacks (an estimated 100 black people were killed). Gradually, the status of the Irish changed. Tammany Hall helped immigrants find lodgings and jobs in exchange for votes, and the Irish came to dominate the political machine, but prejudice lingered long. Jacob Riis, the "muckraking" photojournalist, argued that at the bottom of the tenement ladder resided the "low Irish"; that, indeed, the "tenement possessed an affinity for the Celt",

to whose best and strongest instincts it does violence and soonest and most thoroughly corrupts him ... the Irishman does not naturally take kindly to tenement life, though with characteristic versatility he adapts himself ...[4]

The response to Riis's *How the Other Half Lives* induced the police to close down the lodging houses that featured therein, including Mulberry Street.

Allen, Margaret

HRHA (1832-1914)

A gentleman farmer and his wife are portrayed in their comfortable kitchen. They are the essence of decency. But a newspaper story causes the woman to sink to the floor, sobbing into her green handkerchief. Her needles splay as she drops her knitting (the ball of green wool already undone by the kitten). The man, clutching his newspaper, stares fixedly ahead. They have just read of the arrest of their son in connection with the dynamiting campaign in London.[5] The newspaper story, the subject of the painting, concerned a barrage of "outrages" perpetrated on January 24, 1885, when Westminster Hall, the House of Commons, and the Tower of London were subjected to dynamite attacks, courtesy of Irish and Irish-American conspirators. The Fenian/Clan na Gael dynamiting campaign in Britain coincides with the time the painting was conceived and executed.

The chromolithograph in the background - hooded by the gridiron above - shows the alluring Erin about to be ravaged by a vulture, confirming the political message of the painting. The iconographic origins of this image are Titian's *Rape of Europa* (1562) and a then recent illustration from *Punch* (October 24, 1885). Historically, "heroic rapes" or mythological rapes were commissioned by princes of the Church and state as metaphors for patriarchal power.

In 1882 the National League was established in Dublin, provoking a series of trenchant cartoons. The *Punch* image, by British cartoonist Sir John Tenniel, shows Charles Stewart Parnell, personifying the National League, transformed into a vampire bat about to prey on beautiful Erin, personifying Ireland. In the face of the evil from within - as Tenniel perceived the National League - attempts to liberate Ireland from her English protector are portrayed as monstrous. In the painting the message is reversed - the bat is replaced by a vulture, a carrion-eating raptor, more dangerous and deadly than the bat - and now Britain is clearly identified as predator.

According to the *Freeman's Journal* (March 11, 1886), Allen's painting *Bad News in Troubled Times* illustrated the announcement that an "important arrest has been made". The reviewer went on to say that the elderly couple are

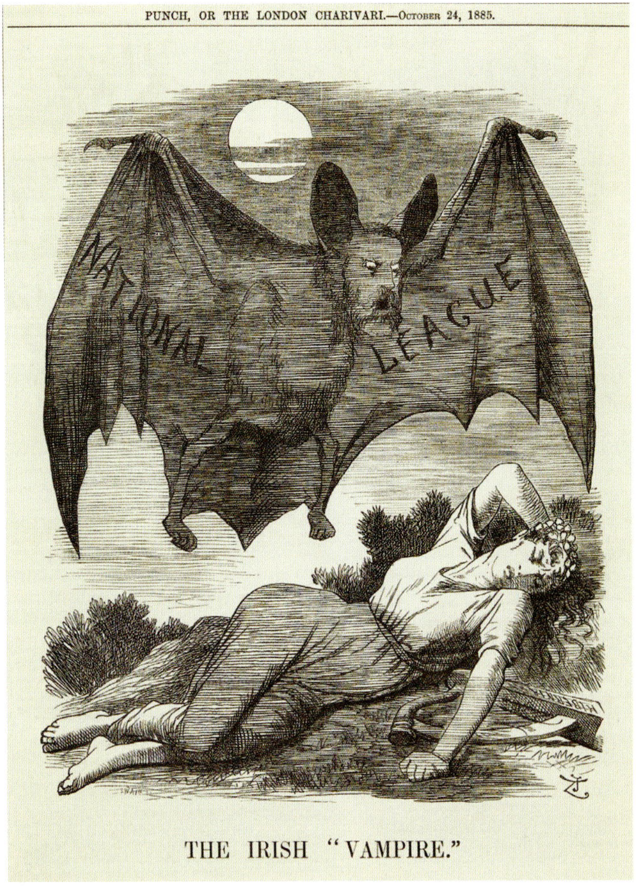

John Tenniel (1820–1914),
"The Irish 'Vampire'"
Punch, October 24, 1885
Wood engraving,
10 x 7.5 in (25.4 x 19.05 cm)

"represented as stricken with horror at the announcement, which it is to be supposed relates to their son."

When the painting was exhibited in 1886, the RHA catalogue referred to the story as reported in the *Freeman's Journal*, but when it was exhibited in 1888, the source was given as the *Irish Times*. On January 31, 1885 the *Irish Times* reported that the arrest related to a lithographic printer, Goodman, an American with Irish relations in New Cross (the mention of Goodman's trade is interesting given the chromolithograph in the background). On February 2 the *Irish Times* mentioned that a brother in Croydon "was first informed of the arrest on reading the morning newspaper". On February 4 another "important arrest", that of twenty-two-year-old James Gilbert Cunningham, alias Dalton, alias Gilbert, from Gortnamorra, County Cork, also for dynamiting activity, was effected. And on August 20, 1885 the *Irish Times* reported the "important arrest" of yet another dynamiter.

But there would appear to be a number of threads to this painting. A further arrest in November 1884 – the story continued to run in the press into 1885 – was of an Allen namesake, one Fred Allan, a leading Fenian and senior member of staff of the *Freeman's Journal*, indicating perhaps a direct connection with the artist Margaret Allen. Moreover, William Philip Allen, one of the three Manchester Martyrs executed after the escape of two Fenians and the death of a police officer in 1867, may indicate an additional connection: Allen was from Tipperary, near Balleen, where Margaret Allen was eventually buried.

According to the *Freeman's Journal* (March 1, 1886), the RHA exhibition that year showed 596 pictures, and was "one of the best that the academy has had for years". In its review, the *Freeman's Journal* (March 11, 1886) declared *Bad News in Troubled Times* "decidedly clever, though not of a high order of merit". Two years later, in 1888, it was exhibited in the Irish Exhibition at Olympia, with the intention of not only demonstrating "the worth and significance of Irish art" but also "to help to moderate the prejudices ... at the very root of misunderstanding between people and people"; the catalogue described the exhibition as "part of a movement entirely outside the arena of politics; freed from all sectarian or class influence".[6] Notwithstanding such protestations of neutrality, *Bad News in Troubled Times* was here exhibited alongside other works with definite political inflections: Catterson Smith's *Portrait of Daniel O'Connell*, *Notice to Quit* by James Brenan, and Aloysius O'Kelly's *Mass in a Connemara Cabin*.

The role of Irish America in the dynamiting campaign in the early 1880s was fueled by bitter memories of Anglo-Irish landlordism and British misgovernment, rekindled by fresh reports of hunger and evictions in the late 1870s. A series of poor harvests – the worst on record since the Famine – and increasing numbers of evictions – not witnessed on such a scale since the 1840s – precipitated a new wave of immigration, which reinvigorated Irish-American hostility, thereby consolidating an inclination to violent retribution among Irish-Americans. Irish-Americans believed that landlordism "was the last link which keeps Ireland bound to England", which, once removed, would destroy British power in Ireland; this view underpinned the campaign of explosions in British cities in 1881–85.[7] Now, for the first time, the Irish question was a matter of daily concern to private British citizens, who feared for their own lives. As one journalist put it, what Irish nationalists desired was

> *not merely the repeal of the Union, but the establishment of a perfectly independent Irish Republic [and] the only method of obtaining their ends is by frightening England and the English people … until at last [England] shall be only too glad to let Ireland go her own way.*[8]

Although she was the first woman elected an honorary member of the RHA, little is known about Margaret Allen. She showed fifty-three works there, including the powerful eviction scene *The Last Hour in the Old Country* (1876), but felt obliged to soften her subject matter in response to negative criticisms of her more political paintings.

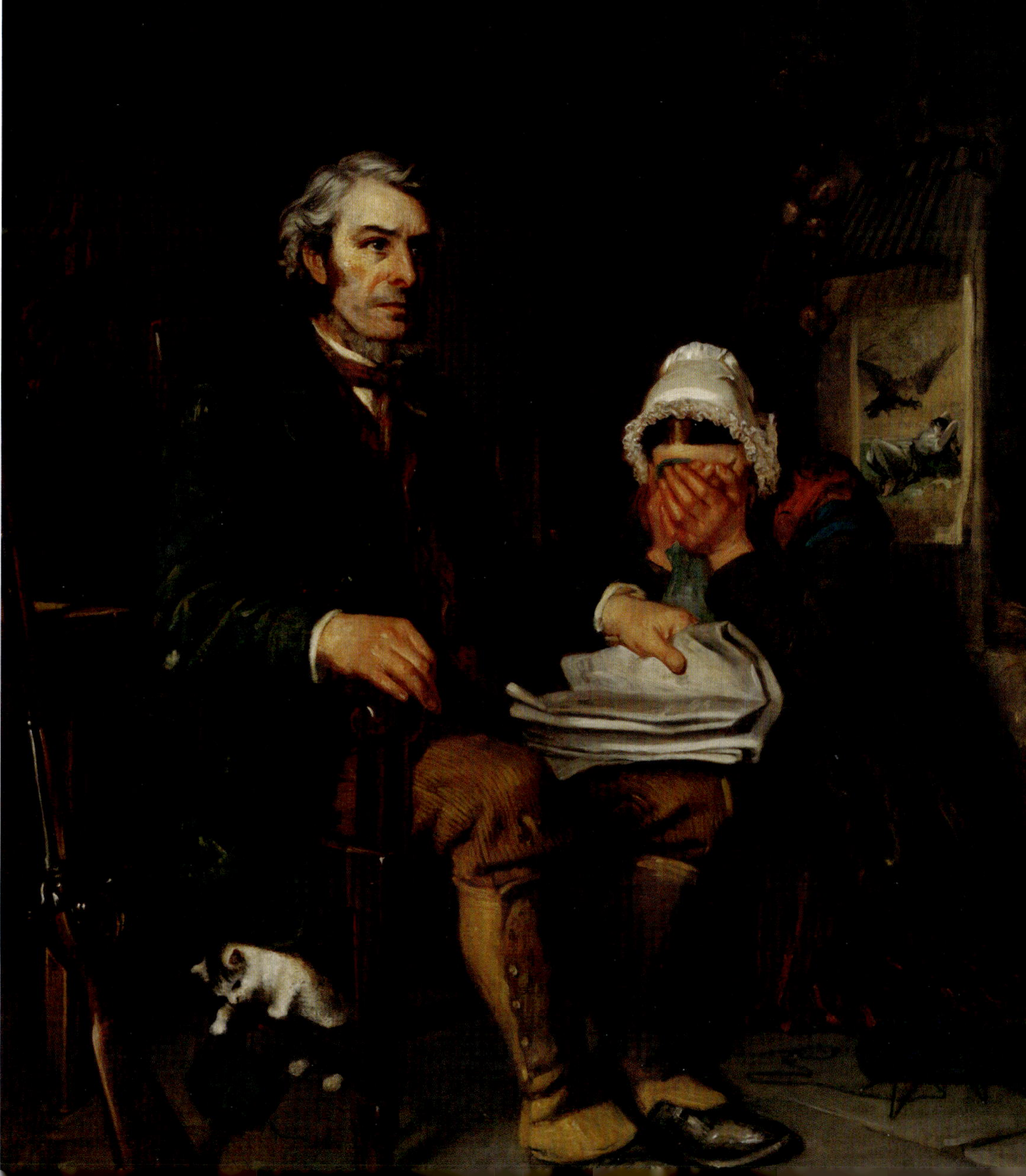

Bad News in Troubled Times: "An important arrest has been made, that of a young man named –." – Freeman's Journal, 1886
Oil on canvas, 38 x 32 in (96.5 x 81 cm)

Anthony, (Henry) Mark

(1817–86)

One of the most original British landscape artists of his generation, (Henry) Mark Anthony acquired a reputation for powerful, daring work, albeit at a time when originality was an all-but-suspect quality. Anthony was admired by Ford Madox Brown, Dante Gabriel Rossetti, William Michael Rossetti, and John Millais. William Holman Hunt rated him one of "the men of sterling merit" (alongside Maclise, Dyce, and Mulready).[9] The lawyer/dealer Sergeant Ralph Thomas paid Anthony sixpence a minute for his pictures, and his work was collected by the major collectors of the day, including James Leathart, John Miller, and Dominic Colnaghi. Anthony exhibited to considerable acclaim in the salons of London and the major provincial centers, as well as the 1857–58 American Exhibition of British Art in New York and Boston.

In 1854 Anthony was awarded Liverpool Academy's annual prize, and his reputation soared. Of his work in the London Pantheon, Ford Madox Brown declared "every one of them well-nigh look gorgeous, colour like Constable, only better by far".[10] A leading light in the Society of British Artists, Anthony resigned in 1852 in the expectation of election to the Royal Academy, but unedifying details of his private life led to a fall from grace. Not only had he seduced the maid but also assaulted his wife, and, to excuse himself, accused her of stealing and drinking.[11] When he failed to secure a place in the Royal Academy, he lost status, resulting in his important Irish work, dating to Famine times, slipping into obscurity.

The critic Frederic George Stephens insisted that "no English painter surpassed him in profound sympathy with the grave, melancholy, and dignified subjects he affected."[12] Described as "the founder of a new school of art" (*Fine Arts Journal*, April 3, 1847), his detractors noted "a morbid taste for novelty" (*Evening Mail*, April 12, 1852) and a tendency to allow style degenerate into mannerism. Epithets such as "theatrical", "execrable", "perfect", "truthful", and "preposterous" divided critics, collectors, and audiences, who praised and damned his work in equal measure.

Divergence of opinion centered on the crux of "finish". Academic standards demanded a smooth, licked look. Anthony employed the broken brushwork and bold contrasts of the avant-garde, long before most of his compatriots. With its emphasis on individuality and the imagination, Romanticism paved the way for the Barbizon School in France, in which Anthony played a part. He was the first British artist at Fontainebleau, where he became friendly with Corot and Dupré. The Barbizons were interested in the effect of light on landscape allowing the artists' temperament to show through, thereby heightening the "sketch-finish" conflict. It was believed that only by reworking the initial impression into a refined work could an artist show his mastery. Anthony's "originality" frustrated those critics who desperately wanted him to "finish" his work.

One critic noted that the "thickness of colour" would suggest that he painted with a palette knife and mahlstick rather than a brush – "a grievous blunder" (*Aris's Birmingham Gazette*, October 16, 1848). The *Illustrated London News* equivocated: "Mr. H.M. Anthony is the Mr. J.M.W. Turner of Suffolk Street", and not one of his paintings "is without its characteristic absurdities, or without its undoubted evidence of genius" (March 30, 1850). Of *Ruined Church and Tower of Aghadoe with View of Lake* (probably *Killarney, A View of the Lower Lake*, purchased by Prince Albert), one critic thought it "worthy of imitation" (*Critic*, April 15, 1845), but another noticed how "the paint is so rough in places as to impose impediments to the progress of the finger along the canvas" (*Globe*, March 26, 1845). And of *Ancient Round Tower and Stone Cross at Monasterboice, Louth, Ireland*, *Bell's Weekly Messenger* complained that "he will never enjoy an eminence ... whilst he yields to the extravagancies of a fervid imagination, and sets all rules of colour and drawing at defiance" (April 21, 1849).

The Pre-Raphaelites acknowledged Anthony as a major influence on their development, but he himself never reconciled the freedom of *plein-air* painting with the detailed observation of Pre-Raphaelitism. Nevertheless, William Michael Rossetti argued he was "by far the greatest of our living landscape-painters"; "Massive Force, instant grasp and realization of his subject are his great characteristics". According to Rossetti, he "realised some of the principles of the sect before Pre-Raphaelitism was a word known to man".[13] In particular, his "powerful paintings" between 1847 and 1857 "were certainly very remarkable, and stood out saliently".[14] Those dates include his Cashel painting.

The symbolic markers embedded in the ruins of the Rock of Cashel are steeped in legend and history, and, in Anthony's tondo, are juxtaposed with the raw facts of life in the 1840s, revealing the abject poverty of the people. Cashel is a spectacular complex, built on a limestone outcrop. Stone walls enclose a ninety-foot-high round tower, the finest twelfth-century Romanesque chapel in Ireland, Cormac's Chapel (containing some of Ireland's oldest frescoes), and a 210-foot-long thirteenth-century Gothic cathedral. According to the *Globe*, "it is in his twilight scenes that this artist comes nearest the truth of nature. His motionless masses, and cutting outlines against clear skies ... produces astonishing effects with his remorseless and unmitigated contrasts of light and shade" (March 30, 1852).

Cashel was extremely important ecclesiastically and politically. Before the Rock became a religious site, it was chosen in the fourth century by the Eóghanachta, who went on to become kings of Munster. St Patrick is believed to have baptized Aengus, king of Munster, here in AD 448. Brian Boru, later high king of Ireland, was inaugurated king of Munster here in 978. In 1101 King Muircheartach O'Brien presented the Rock to the Church in order to curry favor with the bishops and to end secular rivalry with the Eóghanachta (then known as MacCarthys). Shortly after, in 1127, Bishop Cormac MacCarthy began Cormac's Chapel, which was consecrated in 1134. In 1169 Domhnall Mór O'Brien founded a cathedral, which was replaced in the thirteenth century by the present structure, whose vicissitudes, especially from the Reformation onwards, resulted in total ruin by the eighteenth century. The Rock became a site of massacre in 1647 during the Confederate War with Britain: an estimated 1,000 were killed here, with bodies in the churchyard described as being five or six deep.

By the late eighteenth century the cult of ruins had set in. A ruin, Kieran Flanagan suggests, can function "as picturesque, as salutary, as an object of guilt but also of instruction ... as an archaeological resource, as an enigmatic remain, whose longevity demands scrutiny ... a deposit for contemporary culture to grapple with".[15] Visits to an abbey would often take place at night, the solitary figure dwarfed by the surroundings.[16] Anthony's *Tintern Abbey* fits this genre. The tripling of Tintern, Turner, and Wordsworth is one of those high moments of Romanticism, but Wordsworth's "Lines" contain no reference to the abbey itself because neglect had desacralized contemplation.[17] The ruin is absent, arguably because Wordsworth could not handle the contamination of the site, whereas beggars, decay, and neglect are conditions Anthony confidently confronted in Cashel.

Richard Lalor Shiel saw the Rock "as an emblem as well as a memorial of Ireland ... on which it is impossible to look without feeling the heart at once elevated and touched by the noblest as well as the most solemn recollections".[18] Mr and Mrs S.C. Hall concurred: "All the ecclesiastical ruins ... sink into insignificance compared with those that crown the far-famed Rock of Cashel", which they described as a city – "for the rank belongs to it" – although it consists of little more than a thousand houses, most of which were "mean and wretched".[19]

By the 1840s the impoverished minor gentry were evicting tenants in their hordes to convert their land to profitable pasture, making Tipperary the second worst county in Ireland for ejections. Those who could, emigrated, those left behind lived in appalling penury. As a result, intense class feuding made Tipperary one of the most violent districts in Ireland. Indeed, a number of Anthony's Irish pictures were political. His *Croppie's Grave* (1846, Walker Art Gallery, Liverpool) and *The Whiteboys' Retreat* (1846) indicate a neglected vein of Irish political pictures from this period.

During the 1840s Anthony visited Ireland with Frederick Goodall, Alfred Downing Fripp, and Francis Topham, returning himself in 1855 to paint the landscape and historic ruins. He familiarized himself with antiquarian debates. George Petrie's description of Cashel as "that sacred and magnificent acropolis" led to a reawakening of interest in Ireland's ruined past. In his *Essay on the Round Towers of Ireland*, Petrie wrote of "the piety, art and learning of remote times", and suggested that at such sites "we are among the dead ... forced, as it were, to converse with men of other days", a melancholic reflection that seems to have found its echo in Anthony's work.[20]

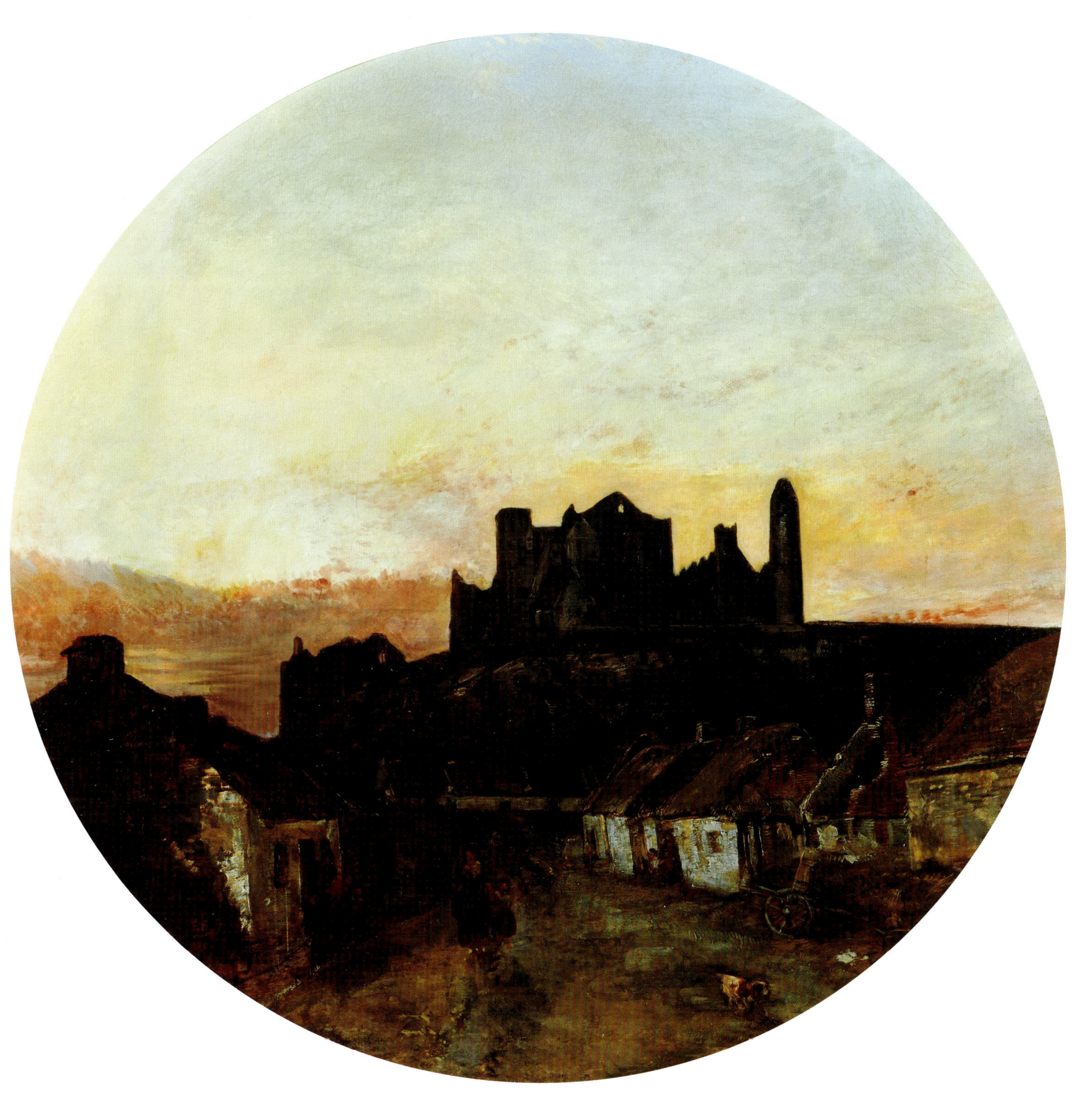

Sunset (also known as *Rock of Cashel*), c. 1847
Oil on canvas, 45 x 45 in (114 x 114 cm)

Ballagh, Robert
(b. 1943)

Roimh After, 2017
Oil on canvas, 19.6 x 15.7 in (50 x 40 cm)

Ballagh studied architecture, which he abandoned to play in a showband, The Chessmen. In turn, he defected from architecture to become Ireland's number-one pop artist (as he sees it, the *only* Irish pop artist). While the academism of Seán Keating coexisted with the modernism of Cecil King, the decidedly urbanist Ballagh, to compensate for his lack of academic training, and emboldened by the first Rosc exhibition in 1967, adapted the simplicity and irony of international pop art to Ireland.

In 1972 John Berger, the controversial art critic for the *New Statesman*, wrote and presented *Ways of Seeing* for the BBC. This salvo – a riposte to Kenneth Clark's highbrow *Civilization* three years previously – was the foundation stone of the new discipline of visual culture, with its emphasis on art and society. In its wake Ballagh set out to demystify the role of the artist and make art accessible. He also sought to reconnect with the past, at least aesthetically, depicting himself in conversation with Vermeer, Holbein, and Velázquez, Laurence Sterne, James Joyce, and Joseph Sheridan Le Fanu.

Ballagh has executed many portraits, observational, allegorical, and even medieval altarpiece-style, with their "attributes" or, in contemporary parlance, their signifiers: Dr Noël Browne – doctor and politician who did so much to eradicate the scourge of TB in Ireland, and came up against the Church with his Mother and Child scheme – is depicted cruciform, while Bernadette Greevy, the acclaimed singer, is portrayed through her professional publicity persona. In others, he resurrects the dead: Charles Stewart Parnell, leader of Irish nationalism in the late nineteenth century, or friend and mentor, the artist Micheal Farrell. These portraits are palimpsests, layered with irony and humor, allusion and quotation. The *trompe l'oeil* effects demonstrate Ballagh's consummate skill. In his portrait of Charles Haughey, the former Taoiseach is dwarfed by his own political image, showing Haughey to be his own myth-maker – "I've always enjoyed ... the concept of a play within a play", Ballagh told Brian McAvera.[21]

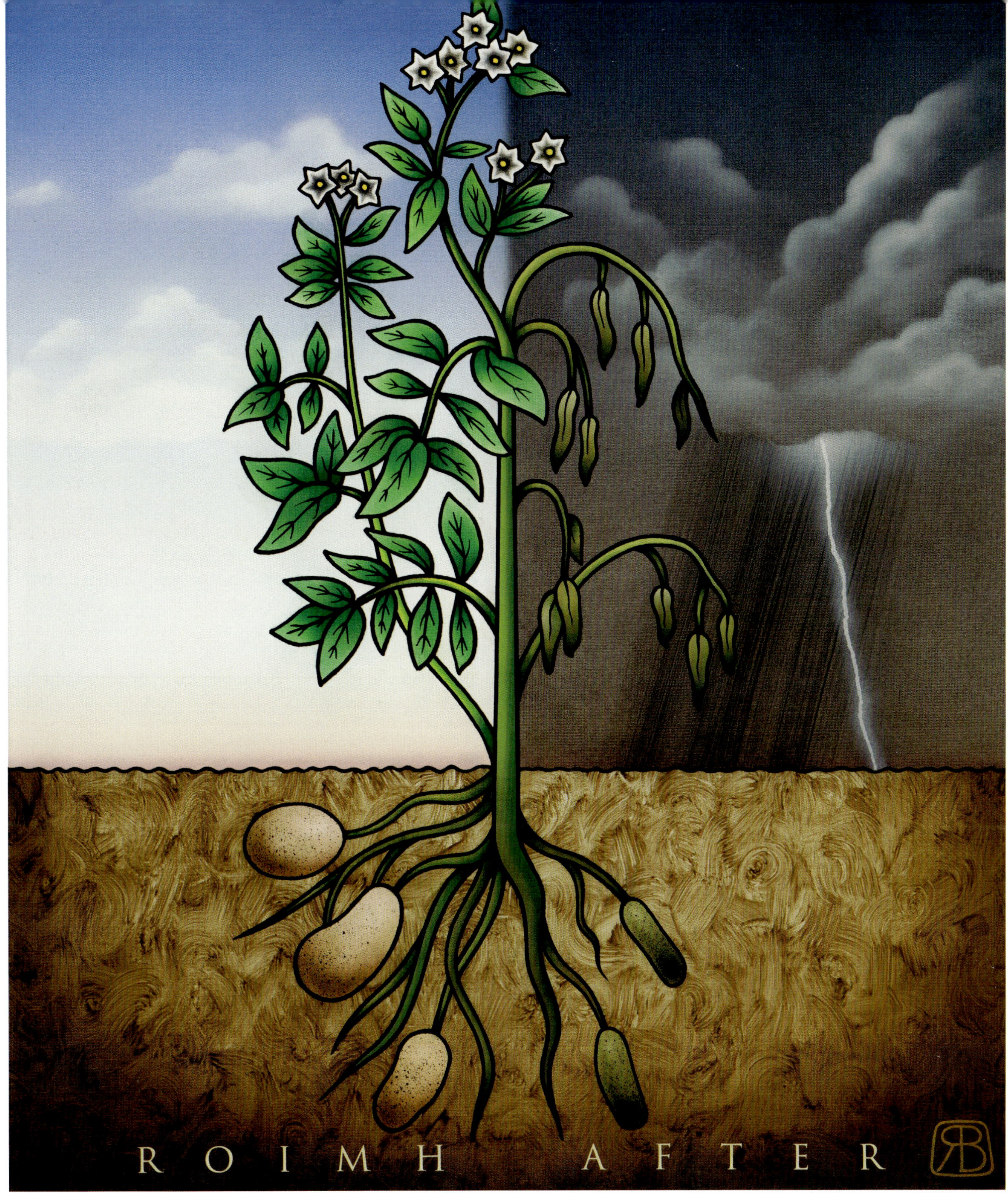

Ballagh is also a respected designer. He has designed stage sets for Beckett's *Endgame* and Steven Berkoff's version of Oscar Wilde's *Salomé*, while corporate commissions include designs for *Riverdance*. He has designed almost seventy stamps and the last Irish banknotes before the euro, providing him with opportunities to combine national themes with new technologies, projecting a progressive image of Ireland. He also designed the opening ceremony for the Special Olympics World Games in 2003. At the heart of his art is a commitment to activism. Patrick Murphy says that Ballagh occupies the position equivalent to state artist while simultaneously being the state's biggest critic.[22]

An Gorta Mór, 2012
Stained glass, 58.5 x 58.5 in
(148.59 x 148.59 cm)

Following the outbreak of the "Troubles" in Northern Ireland in 1969, Ballagh's work took on a political hue. He drew on historical imagery, such as Goya's *Third of May*, to comment on the presence of British troops in Northern Ireland, and to expose the killing of fourteen unarmed marchers gunned down by British paratroopers on Bloody Sunday in Derry in 1972. Ballagh remains deeply immersed in Irish history. Ever the polemicist, he continues to lay bare injustice and oppression around the world, the continuity of themes extending to the freeing of political prisoners and victims of a politicised miscarriage of justice, among them Nelson Mandela and the Birmingham Six.

The artist and critic Brian O'Doherty notes that Ballagh "is seen as a nationalist by some, an international socialist by others, a retro anti-progressive and a critic of emblematic sentimentalism, an uncomfortable retriever of old nationalist injuries and an idealistic European progressive".[23] While some of the references of this figurative artist are literal, others are erudite, and all address serious questions about the nature of modern art and its audiences. Throughout his career Ballagh has campaigned for artists; he was a founder member of the Artist's Association of Ireland, and a member of the International Artists' Association and of Aosdána. Notwithstanding official patronage, in 2006 he challenged the Irish government in the courts for its failure to implement an EU directive about artists' resale rights.

An Gorta Mór prompts the question what do pop artists Roy Lichtenstein, Andy Warhol, or Robert Ballagh have in common with medieval stained-glass artists? The urge to communicate without privileged knowledge, perhaps. John Berger points out that seeing and understanding come before words - a crucial factor in "reading" medieval art.[24] If the written word was indecipherable by most, images proffered another route to knowledge. And at the core of narrative sequencing in medieval art was a Church instructing its adherents. Stained glass provided the opportunity for wandering minds to be cathechized, and enabled preachers to instruct through reference to the illustrative windows in their sermons. The ability to grasp highly compressed narratives in sequence, and interpret the dogma as intended, demanded active engagement. The transept window at Canterbury may have been known as the *Biblia Pauperum*, but it required a visual vocabulary to understand the theological links. And, of course, stained glass also gave pleasure. Given spectacular expression in Chartres or Reims cathedrals, for example, Gothic windows were the graphic books of the medieval period.[25]

Born to a Southern Catholic mother and an Ulster Presbyterian father, Ballagh understands the interstices of theology and politics in Ireland. As Catherine Marshall says, he straddles "several of the many faultlines to which Irish 20th century culture falls prey".[26] Marshall sees Ballagh's model for himself as "the journeyman artist of the medieval craft system who serves his community".[27] His adaption of stained glass to tell the story of the Famine is thus both homiletic and aesthetic. Like his medieval antecedents, Ballagh expects his viewers to be versed in the doctrine of the Famine (and not that according to Trevelyan). The synergy of his ideology and iconography emphasizes the Famine as unfinished business:

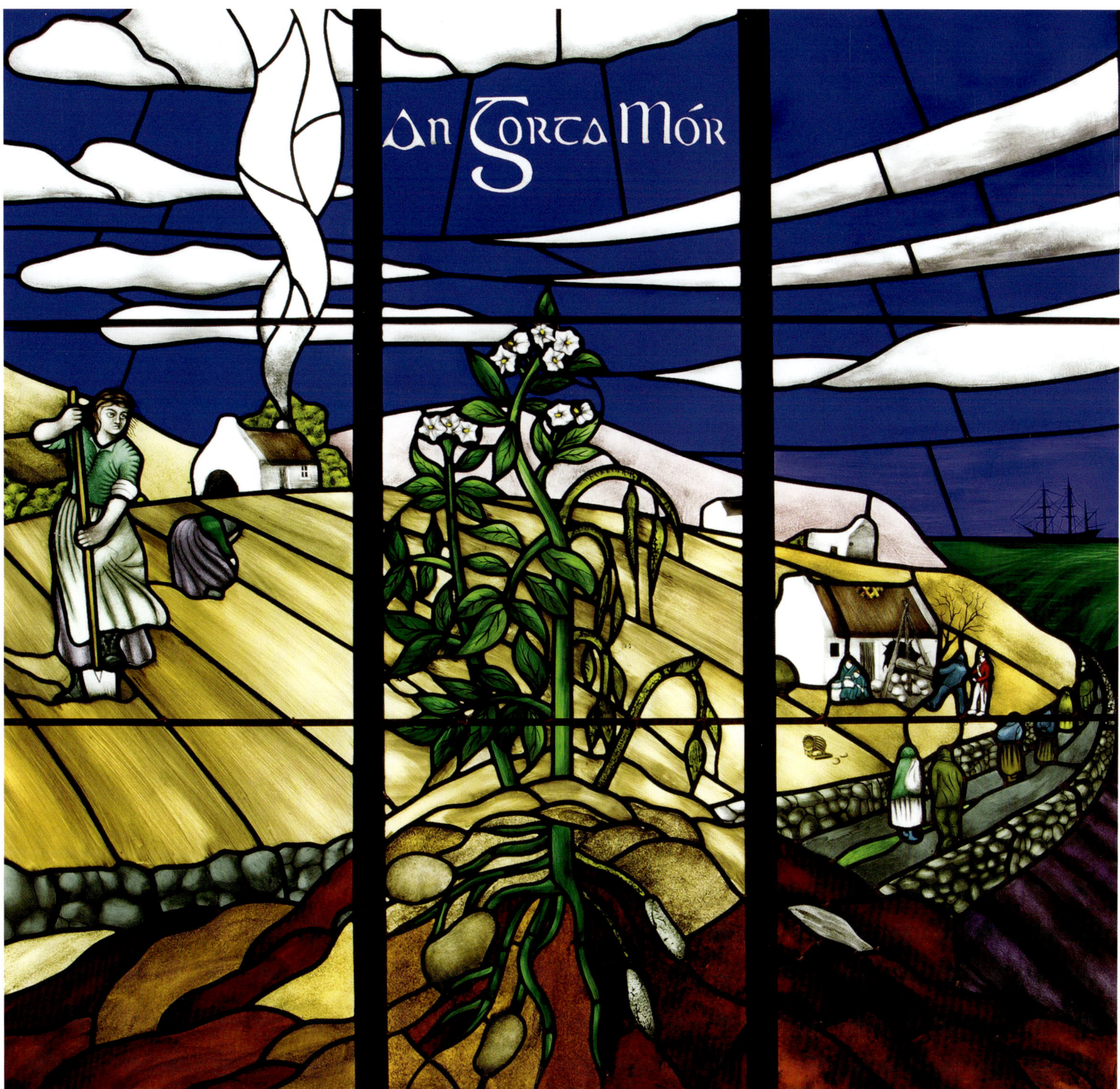

I elected to underscore the piece with a clear and simple narrative. On the left side of the triptych the potato plant is flourishing while on the right side it has been afflicted by blight. The potato barely sustained a peasant population in Ireland, living in frugal conditions – this is represented on the left-hand panel – however, when the potato crop failed, catastrophe followed. The population was halved by starvation, disease and emigration. The right-hand panel represents an eviction scene, where starving tenants, unable to pay their rents, have been evicted, their homes pulled down and thus "encouraged" to emigrate. A soldier is included in this sorry scene to underline the failure of the authorities to adequately respond to the needs of the people. Finally, a ship "lies waiting in the bay", to take the fleeing emigrants to foreign shores where the Irish story continues ...[28]

In *Roimh After* Ballagh reiterates elements of *An Gorta Mór*. The leading of the stained glass is echoed in the tripartite division of the oil. The left of the painting shows potatoes growing abundantly under a serene sky; after, on the right, shows the food of the peasantry, symbolically struck by lightning and shrivelling on the stalk. The bilinguality of the title alludes to the cultural ruptures that changed Ireland for ever.

Behan, John

RHA (b. 1938)

An inner-city child from Sheriff Street, Dublin, John Behan spent hours in his local library; his work thus tends towards the classical, literary, and legendary. He watched drovers herding cattle from "Cowtown" to the port of Dublin for export, and spent his childhood summers on his grandfather's farm. Birds and animals, mythic and real, recur throughout his work, as do boats from the quaysides of the Liffey and the Corrib. And he has an abiding interest in music. From these disparate elements, Aidan Dunne credits Behan with "constructing an indigenous school of figurative sculpture".[29]

Aged fifteen, he began a seven-year apprenticeship with a metalworking company, during which time he studied with Paddy McIlroy in North Strand, and as a night student at the National College of Art and Design under Seán Keating, Maurice MacGonigal, and John Kelly. He went on to study at Ealing College of Art, London and at the Royal Academy School, Oslo. Behan was a founder member of the New Artists group, the Independent Artists and Group 65. He was a founder member of the Project Arts Centre, and is a member of the Arts Council, Aosdána, and the RHA. He founded the Dublin Art Foundry in 1970 with Peter O'Brien; previously, Irish sculptors had to have their work cast in England. The foundry now casts the work of world-renowned artists.

When he first exhibited in the Irish Exhibition of Living Art (IELA) in 1960, the IELA had lost its edge, representing the "epigones of whatever fashionable movement of the time penetrated into Dublin – usually at second hand, and several years too late".[30] The urge to internationalize among young Irish artists seeking to escape the taint of provincialism was great, but the result was an importation of an Anglo-American internationalism, exemplified in Britain by Anthony Caro – the academic style of the day. This, Brian Fallon argued, was the residue of colonialism, as it disavowed anything that was in and of itself Irish.[31] Behan, however, had his own ideas, some of which were international but within a vernacular idiom. He cultivated a ruggedness that suggests European rather than American influences – expressive rather than formal, emotional rather than abstract. Seamus Heaney said that in Behan "you are encountering what the 'Upanishads' call the ancient self, something previous to and underlying individual character, some kind of psychic bedrock".[32]

Behan says of his art,

My art is related to ancient culture as well as to modern technique. I feel that every artist, be they poet or writer or sculptor or painter, must have roots, roots that will tap into the ground. It's not to say that you don't live in the modern world – I use all the technology that I possibly can to express myself – but in terms of Irish art, we have had a gap between the Middle Ages and the 20th Century – so I had to go back: the future was in the past, if you like.[33]

From his first bull sculpture, shown in 1960, Behan has drawn on mythology, especially the Táin legend. He started making bulls from scrap metal, before modeling and then casting them, increasing their solidity and mass. Contrastingly, his bird series is characterized by more open volumes. Both show sophisticated patination and rich textural effects that enrich the narrative, conveying at once a contemporary and traditional feel.

From the Children of Lir to the bulls of Cooley or the bittern of Cathal Buí, Behan tends to work thematically. Hilary Pyle argued that "his dabbling with mythology has gone on too long, and to little purpose", but the Famine offered him a new theme, and, from the one-hundred-and-fiftieth anniversary in the mid-1990s, he has intensely exploited it on a range of scales within an output of some fifty sculptures a year.[34]

Adrian Frazier says that

when John Behan took on the Famine in all its psychological and historical dimensions, he went beyond being a lyric poet who happened to work in bronze; he assumed a bardic role in relation to his people. With full seriousness, he meant to do justice to their past by means of his art.[35]

Behan's *Potatoes: Famine* (2001) starts at the beginning: in 1845 blight struck, the spores of *Phytophthora infestans*

Famine Mother and Children, 2000
Bronze, 23 in (58.42 cm)

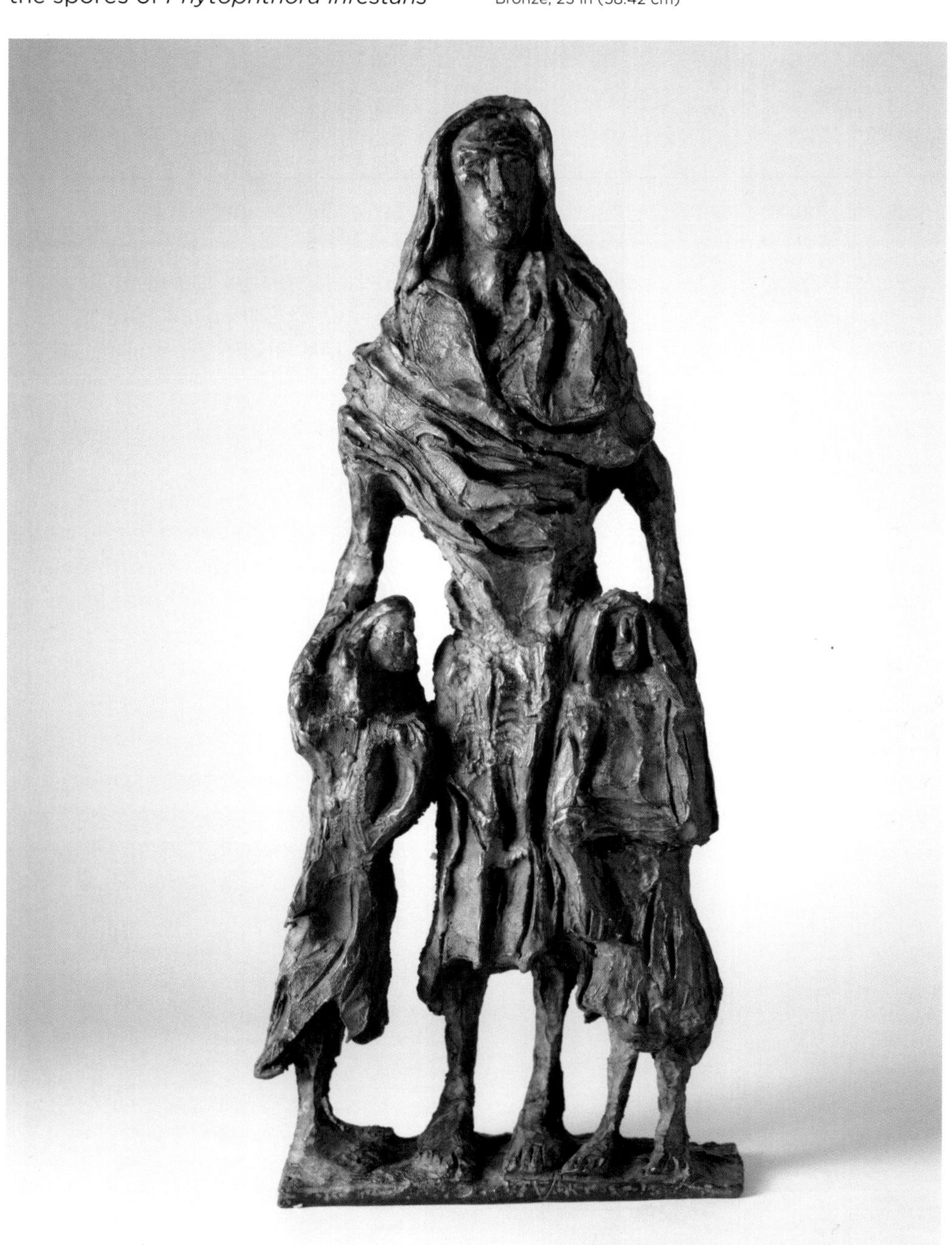

being carried by wind, rain, and insects, spreading from Mexico to the Americas, and on to Europe. The blight's effects in Ireland exceeded anywhere else due to the reliance of Irish peasants on the potato. The Irish male ate ten to fourteen pounds of potatoes a day, women and children somewhat less. A family could subsist for almost a year on the yield of a one-acre plot. The blight cut the population and cleared the land speedily, ruthlessly, and efficiently. Episodes of famine were common in Ireland, but tended to occur in single years.

When the Great Hunger entered its second year, Fr Theobald Mathew wrote to Assistant Secretary to the Treasury Charles Trevelyan: "A blast ... has passed over the land, and the hopes of the poor potato cultivators are totally blighted, and the food of a whole nation has perished" (August 7, 1846). In both *Evicted* (2001) and *Immigrant* (2001), Behan addresses the anger and shame that forms part of our post-Famine psyche. This is a man at his most elemental, lost, and dispossessed. His *Famine Cart* shows how those dead "fortunate" enough to have anyone left to see to their burial, however perfunctory, were carted to the grave. This famished and exhausted beast will soon go the way of the poor people he carries. Contrastingly, *Famine Grave* (2001), notwithstanding the suffocating subject matter – skeletal bodies stacked as if in a grave – is light and ethereal.

The emotional register is heightened in *Famine Mother and Children*, based on the story and illustration "Bridget O'Donnel and Children":

I had fever, and was within two months of my down-lying [confinement]; they commenced knocking down the house ... I had the creature born dead ... and one boy thirteen years old died with wants and with hunger while we were lying sick. Dan Sheedey and Blake took the corn into Kilrush and sold it ... I had not a bit for my children to eat when they took it from me. (ILN, *December 15, 1849)*

Famine Ship (2000) is an iteration of the National Famine Memorial (1997, Murrisk, County Mayo) sited at the foot of Croagh Patrick, a place of annual pilgrimage. The largest bronze sculpture in Ireland, it was commissioned to commemorate the loss of life in Ireland, while also reminding us that famines continue around the world. The ship is a powerful reminder of the millions who emigrated during and after the Famine, especially those who did not survive the "coffin ships". The three masts rise above the ship like the crosses on Calvary. The ribs of the ship evoke potato ridges, and the rigging is entwined with the flattened bodies of those who died on board, fused into a powerful semi-abstract but expressive piece of art, producing an intricate horizontal pattern of considerable impact. Fourteen nations were represented at the foot of the "sacred" mountain for the dedication ceremony, but, it was then noted, no British representative attended.

Behan's monuments, Frazier argues,

are produced by somebody who knows the trade of metal work, who ... knows the behaviour of bronze, as it was known in the workshops of Rodin and Michelangelo. And yet in spite of the down-to-earthness and this-worldness ... there is also present in them and behind them a sense that they are vessels of the spirit, symbols of human knowledge ...[36]

Frazier suggests that they "amount to a communal effort by people in the postcolonial Republic to rectify the historical erasure of the experience of many Irish people".[37]

So many left from Westport, County Mayo in despair but arrived in New York in hope. *The Arrival – The New Dawn* (2000) was commissioned by the Irish government and presented to the United Nations. It is sited on the Sculptural Plaza in New York, alongside works by Henry Moore and Barbara Hepworth. In place of the skeletal rigging at Murrisk, here survivors disembark to start a new life. Analogously, *Immigrants: Mother and Daughters* (2000) is a work of great tenderness and compassion, showing a mother and two daughters landed in America – conjoined, they brace themselves to face the future together.

Famine Ship, 2000
Bronze, 26 in (66.04 cm)

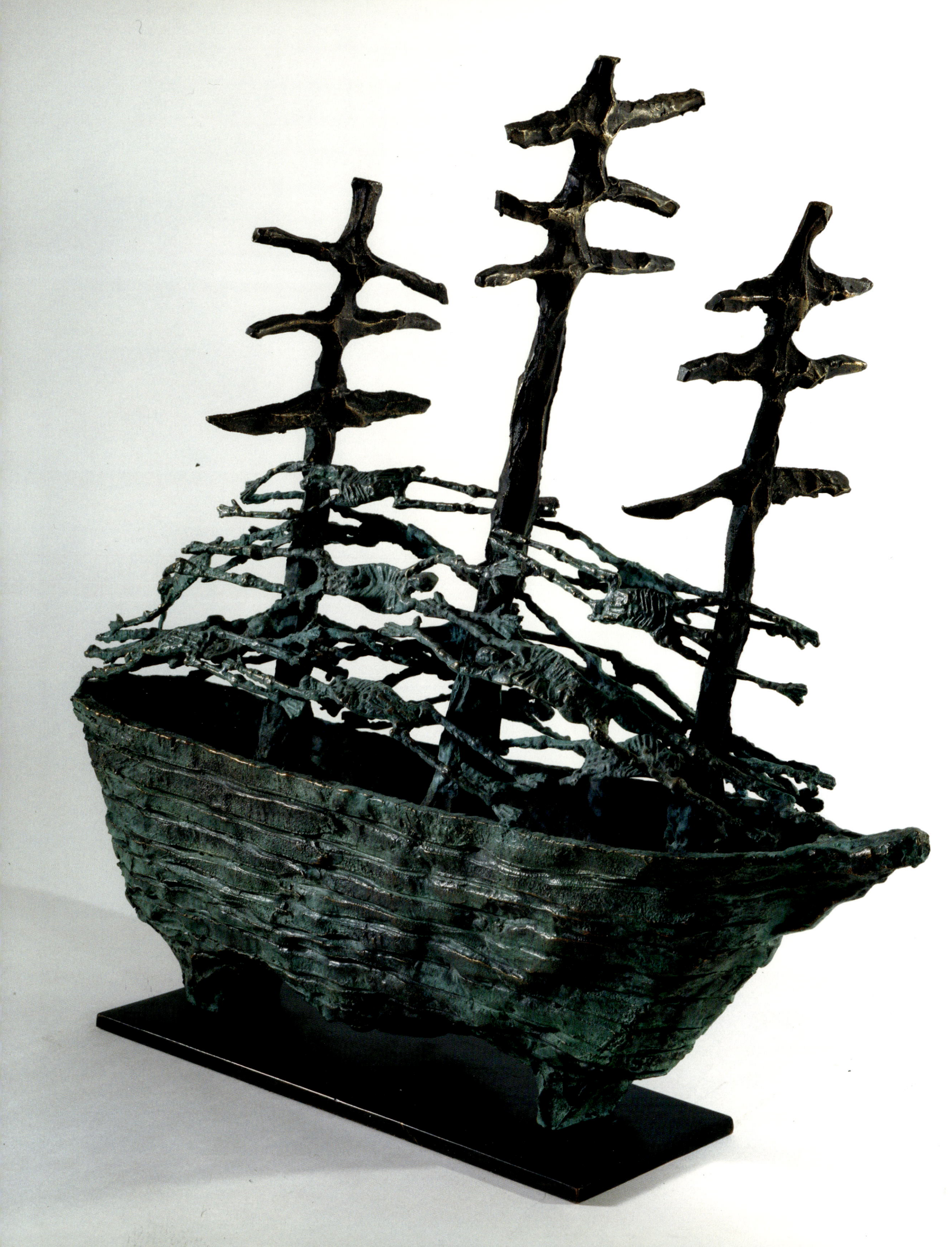

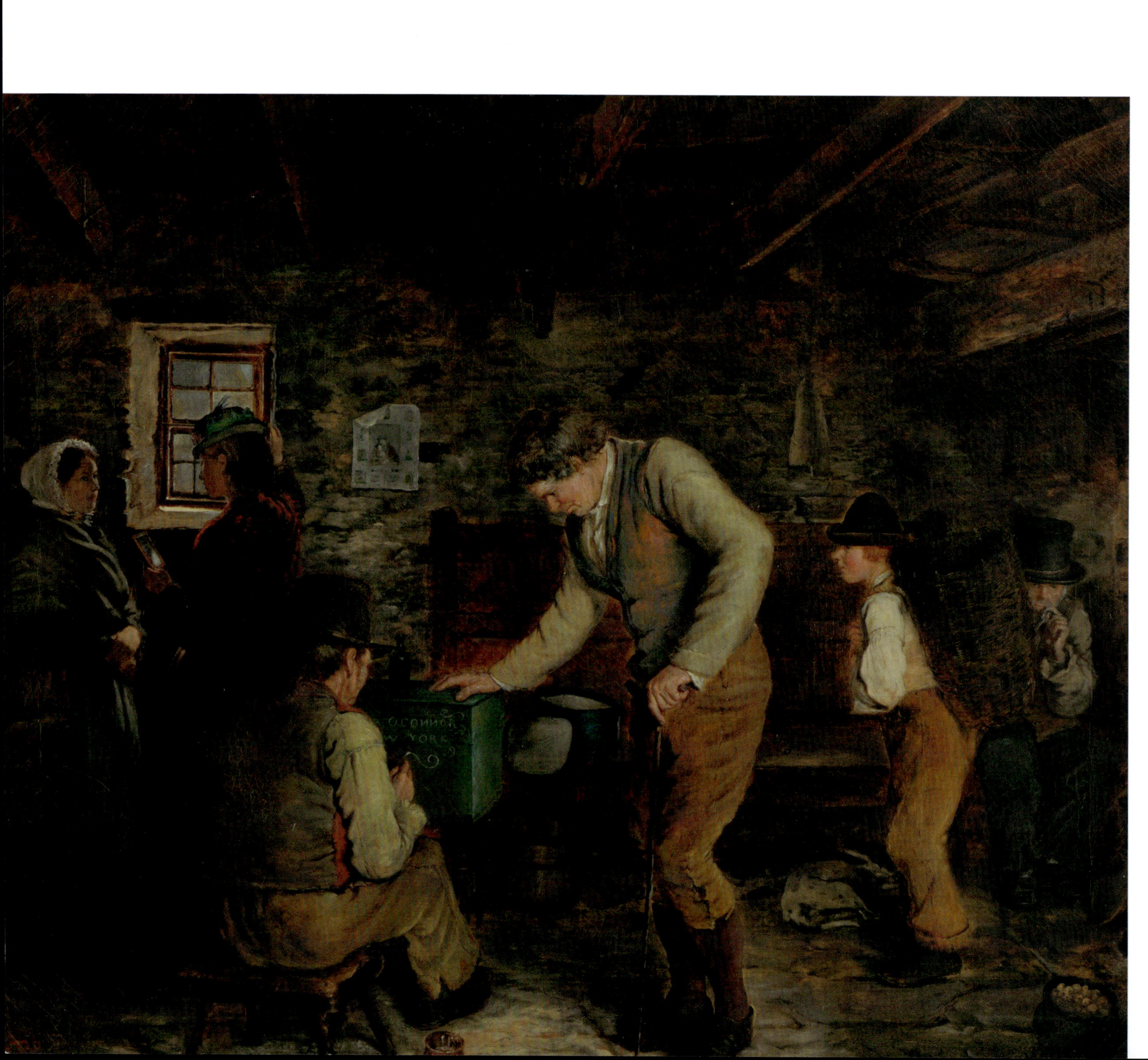
O.CONNOR
W YORK

Brenan, James

RHA (1837–1907)

The Finishing Touch, 1876
Oil on canvas, 25 x 30 in (64 x 76 cm)

Traditionally, emigration paintings were set on quaysides: for example, Margaret Allen's *The Last Hour in the Old Country*, G.M.W. Atkinson's *Emigrants at Cork* (*c.* 1840), and C.H. Cook's *Awaiting the Emigrant Ship* (1867). Brenan's emigration scene, *The Finishing Touch*, is all the more poignant for its homely setting. The Irish cottage negatively connoted poverty and primitivism, but also, positively, traditional family and community values, albeit dented by decades of famine, eviction, and emigration.

Brenan attended the Dublin Society Schools and Royal Hibernian Academy in Dublin, and the Government School of Design, London. He studied with Owen Jones and Sir Matthew Digby Wyatt, the secretary of the Great Exhibition in 1851 and architect of the Pompeian Court in the Crystal Palace (1854), on which Brenan collaborated. Having taught in Liverpool, Birmingham, Great Yarmouth, Taunton, and London, Brenan was appointed headmaster of the Cork School of Art at the age of twenty-three, a post that culminated in 1885 with the opening of the Cork School of Art and Gallery. In 1889 he became headmaster of the Metropolitan School of Art in Dublin, where "his work influenced the whole art-industrial life of Ireland" (*Irish Times*, August 7, 1907). This position ensured the exhibition and positive reception of his work in the exhibition venues of Dublin, Liverpool, and London. Although he was prolific, it was in a manner less to the taste of our times than his. William Laffan describes him as "somewhat pedestrian", more focused on social detail than style or originality; Brenan portrayed dignified, decent people, but marred, Laffan argues, by "a patronizing sentimentality" that ultimately serves to "reinforce, rather than question, the status quo".[38] But in his own time, "the grace and accurate sense of art values seen in his work enlisted the keenest admiration" (*Irish Times*, August 7, 1907).

His underlying concern with social issues, such as eviction and emigration, shows him to have been one of the relatively few artists of his generation, however didactically, to address such fraught subject matter. Aesthetically, Brenan was influenced by David Wilkie and William Mulready (and antecedently Dutch seventeenth-century painting). Certainly, the impressionism of the 1870s and 1880s passed him by. But most Irish artists, even in the mid-to-late nineteenth century, continued to look to London. At its best his work was more aligned with the social realism of the Newlyn School in England – progressive in content if not style – rather than deficient in vision, as some contemporary critics intimate.

While there are few paintings of the Famine contemporaneous with the Famine, Brenan's paintings are highly informative of post-Famine conditions, and illustrative of the ongoing struggles of a country that continued to be ravaged by poverty and emigration. In the late 1870s, once again people were hungry and on the verge of famine, and problems in the fishing and mining industries resulted in a flow of emigration to Britain, Australia, Canada, and America. With memories of the Great Hunger still vivid, *Letter from America* (1875, Crawford Art Gallery) and *The Finishing Touch* (1876) reflect the everyday realities of a time when fear of the Forties remained live.

Brenan exuded empathy for country people. The links he forged between art and industry as preludes to industrial development in Ireland were forward-looking. He was a much-loved teacher and pioneer of the lace industry (lace making and classes in drawing and design were taught in many Munster convents, notably Killarney, Kinsale, and Kenmare), supervised by Brenan, as his painting *A Committee of Inspection* (1877, Crawford Art Gallery) attests. Brenan's admittance to family intimacies confirms the trust he earned by his support of their domestic endeavors.

This painting shows a young woman preparing to emigrate to America. The local signwriter, sitting on the "creepie" stool, is inscribing her name and destination, "O'Connor, New York", on her modest traveling box. Although emigration was not the hazardous journey it was in the "coffin ships" of the 1840s and 1850s, it continued to signal the break-up of families. Many elderly parents would never see their children again. In the post-Famine period, Irish men married late, hence the elderly, infirm father, who, with heavy heart, places his hand on his daughter's box. And he knows that his young son, carrying the turf into the kitchen in a creel on his back, will be next. Only the old and infirm remain behind. The girl is trying on her new hat from the open box on the settle, while her already grieving mother looks on. On the cabin wall is an unframed wood engraving of the Madonna and Child, the mother's only future comfort. The grandfather sits morosely by the fire.

The story of emigration continued unabated throughout the nineteenth century, and was the cause of a number of Irish artists working in America, such as Thomas Hovenden, whose *Breaking Home Ties* shows another mother's farewell to her son but in an American setting. Hovenden had been a student of Brenan at the Cork School of Art prior to his emigration to New York in 1863.

Chamberlain, Margaret Lyster

(b. 1954)

New England artist Meg Chamberlain is interested in issues surrounding loss and compassion. She draws on the work of Auguste Rodin and Käthe Kollwitz – artists of passionate expression – in the creation of *The Leave-taking*.

Born in St Johnsbury, VT and raised in Reading, MA, Chamberlain learnt to spin, weave, and embroider from her mother, Patricia Lyster, a textile artist. She studied fine art and now works in a variety of media, including sculpture. This sixteen-figure bronze was commissioned by Quinnipiac University to interpret the Famine experience from the perspective of Famine refugees.

Rich in narrative detail, her work "explores aspects of human life which we share, but find difficult to express, things that lie beneath the form – life, love, youth, old age, death, rebirth, sorrow, prayer, joy, moment of despair, moment of enlightenment". She claims

a strong link to the Jewish Holocaust [and] used photographs of those victims to study the effect of starvation and despair on the human body. I went within myself to integrate this experience into each figure's persona: I have been a baby, a girl, a sister, a wife and a mother. How would each of these have endured such suffering, privation, humiliation and loss? I created a narrative based on these imagined experiences ...[39]

This sculpture recreates the journey from despair to hope in the New World. To remain was most certainly to die, to emigrate an attempt to grasp for life and start anew, to leave a desperate present and dare an uncertain future.

In their hundreds of thousands, the homeless and hungry boarded what were in many cases "coffin ships". Some estimates suggest that up to thirty per cent died en route or on arrival; those who made it did so in severely diminished condition. The tenants of Lord Palmerston (foreign secretary in Lord John Russell's government) were reported as traveling almost naked, having been lured by false promises of clothing and money on arrival in Canada. Emigration was a dreadful experience. Shipping regulations were lax: many of the vessels were minimally converted cargo ships owned by rapacious profiteers; "brokers" sold tickets at inflated prices; and emigrants were given dirty or too little water and inadequate food (one pound of food for each adult per day).

Stephen de Vere, a landlord from County Limerick, made the three-month passage to Grosse Île in 1847. He reported:

Before the emigrant has been a week at sea he is an altered man ... How can it be otherwise? Hundreds of poor people, men, women and children, of all ages from the driveling idiot of 90 to the babe just born, huddled together, without light, without air, wallowing in filth ... sick in body, dispirited in heart ... lying between the sound in sleeping places so narrow as almost to deny them ... a change of position ... by their agonised raving disturbing those around them ... living without food or medicine ... dying without spiritual consolation and buried in the deep without the rites of the church.[40]

They voyaged below deck in the dark. There were dreadful scenes of drunkenness as the crew sold alcohol to starving and dehydrated passengers. They died in Ireland, they died while the ships lay at anchor, and they died in quarantine. In this piece the shrunken and starved board the ship with their meager possessions. The figure at the top stands as witness, relinquishing the past and kindling hope for the future. Chamberlain's great-grandmother, Mary Regan of Millstreet, Cork, had escaped the Famine as a teenager, and came to America, where she worked as a house servant. She inspired one of the pivotal figures at the base of the ramp.

In its shadow three women huddle together, waiting for the blessing of death. Behind them squats an old man sifting the noxious soil through his fingers. At the base a man holds back a young woman who has just said goodbye to her young brother. She has been his only comfort since their mother and other brothers and sisters died, but her father only has fare for two, and that only by promising his daughter in service to the gentry. At least she would eat. The distraught father disengages the boy from this last embrace. Weak with the hunger, he can barely hold his son, as the terrified boy reaches for one last loving touch. They will likely never meet again.

A young couple has gathered all that remains of their household into a *cliabh* (used for carrying potatoes or seaweed). The young mother whispers comfort to her infant son, restless with fever. A grown son helps his aging mother along the difficult slope, fulfilling his father's dying wish. At the top of the ramp a father steps forward, encouraging his son, who turns in a moment of wistful hesitation. Glancing back to the hills, he fixes them in his memory with his mother's dying words: "Never forget from where ye came."

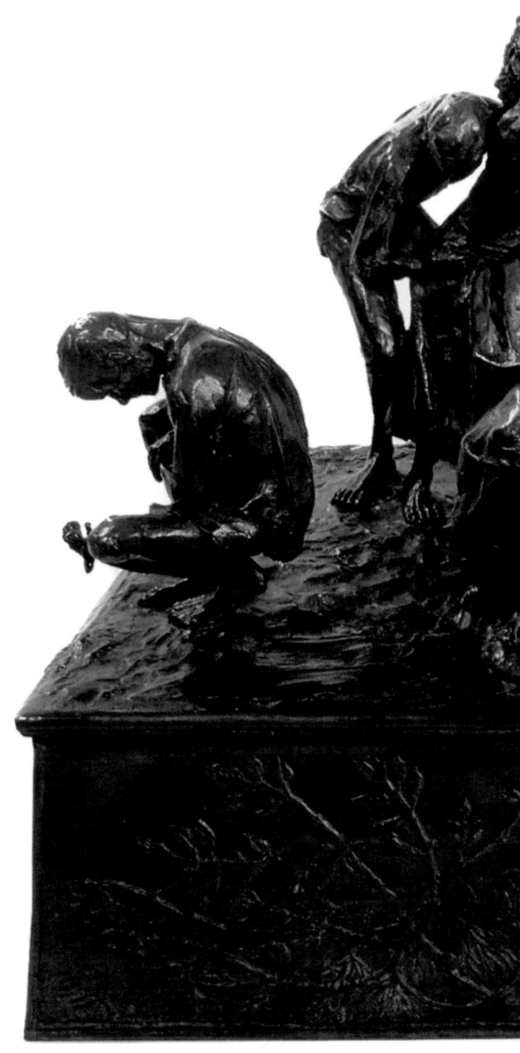

The Leave-taking, 2000
Cast bronze, 25 in (63.5 cm)

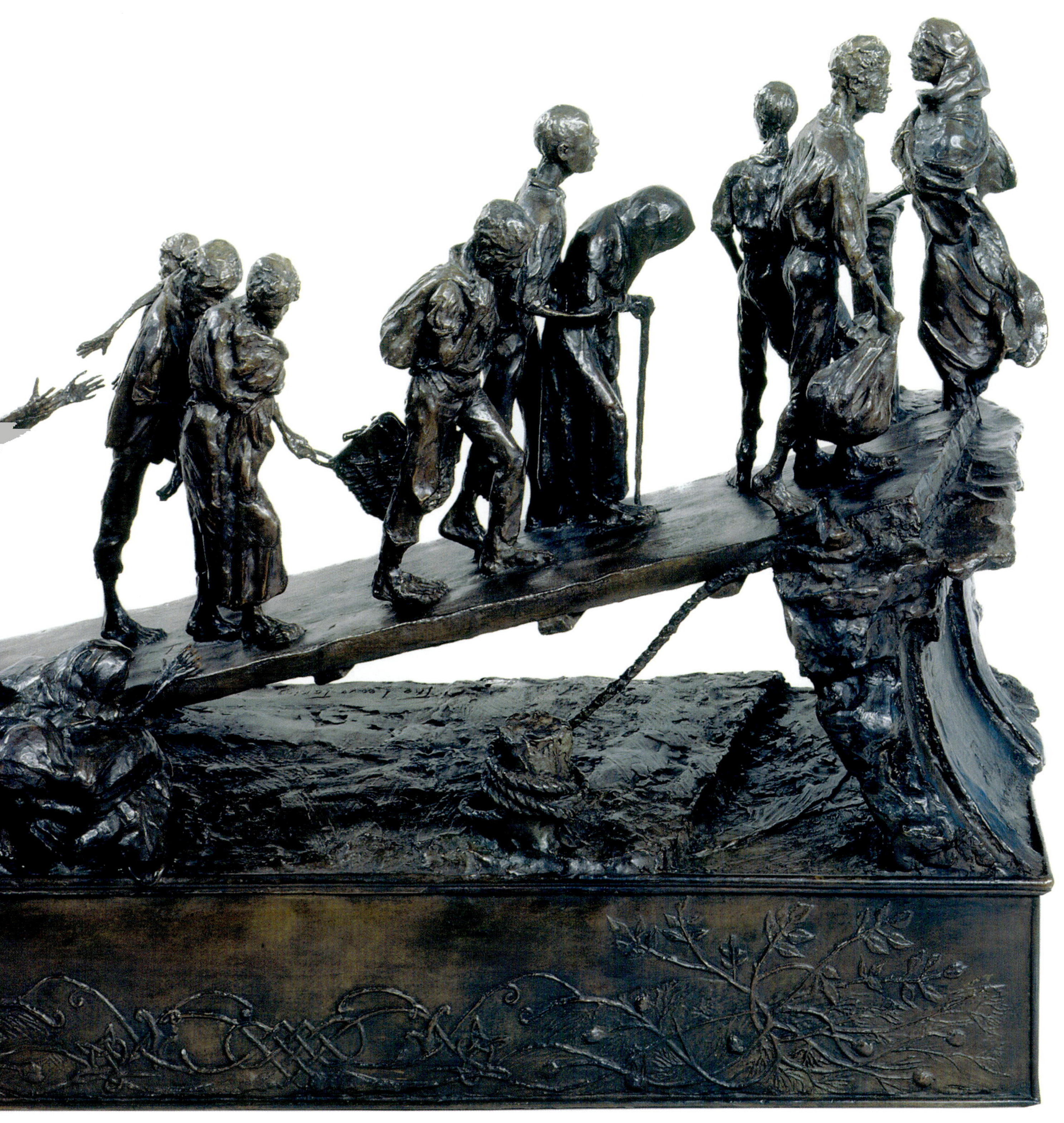

Coll, John

(b. 1956)

Famine Funeral
Welded bronze and brass, 11 in (27.94 cm)

Coll participated in *Famine* (1995), an exhibition organized by the George Moore Society in Claremorris, County Mayo to commemorate the one-hundred-and-fiftieth anniversary of the Great Hunger, and which traveled to Northern Ireland, the United States and Canada. The Burns Library in Boston College acquired *Famine Burial* from the society. In this related work, *Famine Funeral*, Coll depicts four standing figures, "living, wailing ghosts", hollowed out, and run through by a corpse wrapped in binding cloths. The procession is making its way to the grave, although we know that, by then, the Hunger had dealt a savage blow to long-cherished funeral practices demonstrative of the civility of the Irish and of their respect for the dead.

Viewed from the side, this work projects a cruciform outline, invoking the Christian message of afterlife. That one is dead and the others alive is but an illusion. The one stands for the all. The host figures are less than skin and bone, their extirpation imminent. It was this haunting that traumatized the American evangelist Asenath Nicholson:

In all my former walks over this island, by day or night, no shrinking or fear of danger ever retarded in the least my progress, but now the horror of meeting living, wailing ghosts, or stumbling upon the dead in my path at night inclined me to keep within when necessity did not call.[41]

In Christian iconography, the death of Jesus, impaled on the cross, is confirmed by the lance, the Spear of Destiny, piercing his side, confirming him as both God and man – the blood symbolizing his humanity, the water his divinity. As the dead figure "inhabits" his pallbearers, he excretes and merges with them, adumbrating their deaths. The gouged figures, carrying the dead within – powerful images of death by starvation – are monstrous in their metamorphoses, yet far from untender in their ministrations.

Coll is interested in the fact that post-war children often show psychological symptoms of deprivation even though they never suffered the trauma themselves.

In such cases, epigenetic marks – fragments of DNA that attach to the parents' genes as part of their survival mechanism – pass to the offspring, and become a genetic memory of that original trauma.

In this piece, at the tipping point of life and death, the corpse is subsumed by the hollowed-out skeletal figures. David Lloyd writes of "a specter that continues to haunt because we are not yet free, collectively, of the shadow of processes of dehumanization".[42] The dead body is tightly bound and gagged – representing fear of contamination by loved ones, and fear of reprisals by authorities, who chose not to alleviate the suffering of those they saw as recalcitrant.

Following an initial career as a marine biologist, John Coll became a sculptor, and has executed many works of national interest, including the Dublin canal monuments to the poet Patrick Kavanagh and the writer Brendan Behan, and to the patriot Countess Constance Markievicz in Rathcormac, County Sligo. Coll worked in stainless steel for a time, but as he felt the need for more texture and color, shifted to copper, brass, and bronze. And from zoomorphic forms he now embraces the human. He exhibits at home and abroad, and holds regular exhibitions at Kenny's Gallery, Galway.

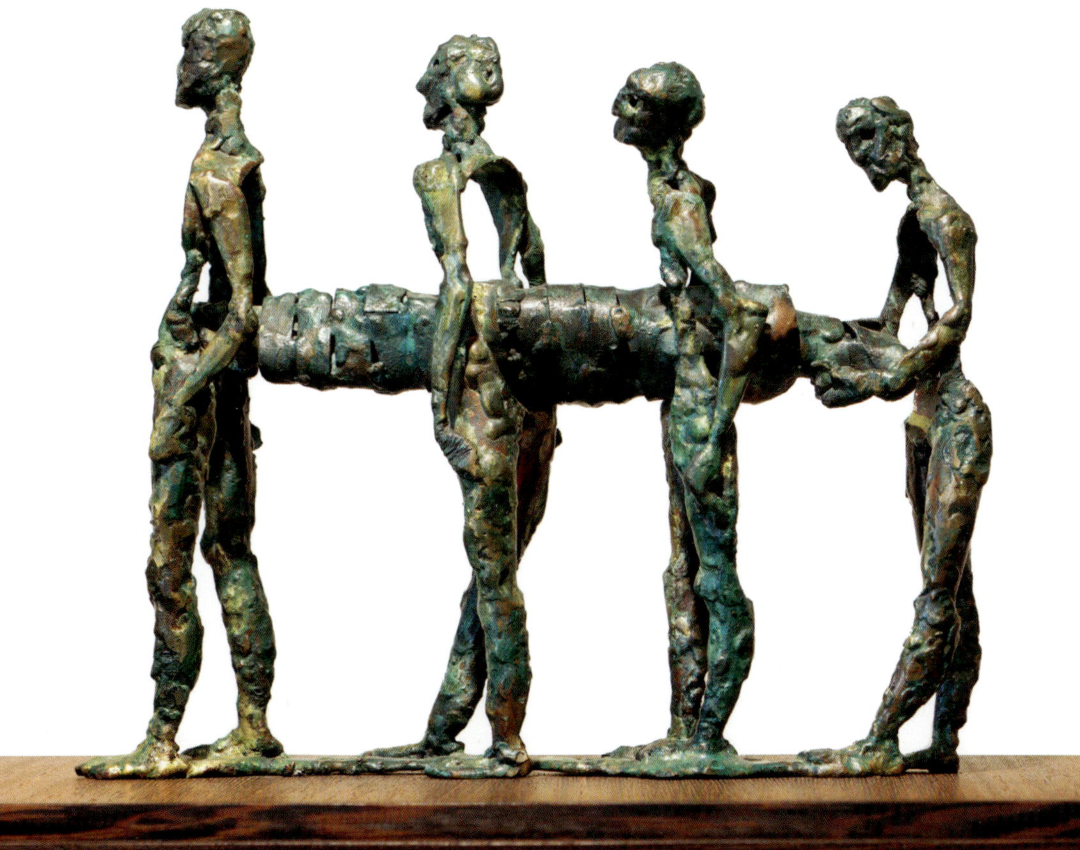

Cross, Dorothy

(b. 1956)

Since representing Ireland at the Venice Biennale in 1993, the scale and conceptual sophistication of Cross's work is formidable. She exhibits in a variety of media: sculpture, photography, and video. She is known for her public site-specific projects, notably the award-winning *Ghost Ship*, the ethereal lightship that haunted Dublin Bay in 1999. According to Robin Lydenberg, Cross "produces works that honor the materiality of objects and bodies marked by lived experience and time's gradual effects – rust, wear, wounds. The beauty she achieves in her art reflects an aesthetic of growth and decay that is as much tactile as it is visual."[43] Much of Cross's recent work is about Connemara, where she now lives.

Basking Shark Currach was exhibited in *Connemara* (2014, Turner Contemporary; RHA Gallery, Dublin) and shown in *Legacies: JMW Turner and Contemporary Art Practice* (2017, New Art Gallery Walsall). Unlike other artists, Cross did not go to Connemara for the scenery or the romantic associations that the west represents in Irish culture, but to dive. She bought a field that stretches down to the sea, on which she built a shed. She purchased a house at the mouth of Killary Harbour, and there built her studio, looking across the sea.

Cross's work features ocean and fjord, cave and boat, pearl and fossil, shark and whale. If Cross embodies any one element, it is water. She swam competitively, and the photograph of her floating in that geological wonder the Worm Hole on Inis Mór, at the bottom of the cliffs of Dún Aonghasa, is an image of someone at one with water.

The sea is both a source of life and death. Cross is also drawn to found objects. Since Picasso, Duchamp, and Beuys, artists have used *objets trouvés* both to make art and to subvert it. In Cross's hands they alchemize – recognizable, but transformed. Her combinations are challenging, disturbing, witty. Innocent objects take a sinister turn, dangerous ones become humorous. In one, a cow skin shrouds a wedding dress draped over a dressmaker's dummy seen from behind, with the teats of the udder providing the circlet of the virgin's headdress, signifying bridal sacrifice. Her unexpected juxtapositions encompass both the ancient and modern, the exquisite and the repulsive, the natural and the manufactured.

Before completing her MFA in San Francisco, Cross took a course in Jungian psychoanalysis, which she found helpful in opening up ideas within her work. When preparing a memoir dedicated to her mother, she was aware of many of the connections between her childhood and her work, but also discovered that things she hadn't remembered resonated with art she had made - for example, "A photograph of my mother standing next to an upturned currach".[44]

Currachs - handmade wooden boats over which animal skins are stretched - were used by fishermen in the west of Ireland for centuries. Both currachs and sharks recur in Cross's work, not just as motifs but as allusive devices. "I am very interested in what is repulsive and what is beautiful, because in our own bodies we are so confused about that, in terms of sexuality and our own mortality. The shark epitomises that, too, in terms of fear and desire and misunderstanding." The shark is thus a metaphor for terror, repulsion, and vulnerability, but also for survival, longevity, and power. Hal Foster's description of avant-garde practices concerning "ruination, recovery, resistance" is relevant here; Cross interweaves the past and the present, the natural world and the human body, creation and destruction.[45]

So why did people die during the Famine when Ireland is surrounded by ocean? When the potato failed, those fortunate enough to own a currach had to pawn or sell their equipment to buy meal. A contemporary visitor to Ireland noted, "So rude is their tackle and so fragile and liable to be upset are their primitive boats ... that they can only venture to sea in fine weather and thus, with food almost in sight, the people starved."[46] And as access to deep-sea fish was beyond reach, the winkles and mussels closer to shore were soon depleted by starving people.

During the 1990s Cross cured cowhide and stuffed snakes, drawing on their symbolic associations across cultures, before moving on to sharks. The surreal *Shark Heart Submarine* shows a paint-spattered easel displaying a model submarine, gilded in white gold, encasing a shark heart in a specimen jar - its tiny heart pumping the engine of this man-made machine, as it were. In Cross's work, "place is sedimented with unconscious as well as ideological and historical elements".[47] *Teacup* (1997) - her storm in a teacup - marked her shift to time-based art. Here, she inserted a clip into a photograph of a porcelain cup and saucer from Robert Flaherty's *Man of Aran* (1934), the controversial documentary film featuring a shark hunt in a currach. In *Basking Shark Currach*, a one-man currach is stretched with the skin of a basking shark (rather than the usual cowhide). In addition to its skin, fins, and meat, the basking shark was once fished for the oil produced from its liver (Dublin was lit by shark oil in the eighteenth century). The coast from Slyne Head to Achill was known as the Sunfish Bank, so plentiful were sharks. Sharks inspire terror, yet the basking shark is a peaceful creature. The fact that a large shark and a currach are about the same size, however, meant danger to fishermen. But in *Basking Shark Currach*, "the combination of a mysterious animal, generally feared, and the ribs of a small boat have formed a lifesaving relationship. The dorsal fin of the shark reads like the keel of the boat which is the structure that balances the vessel as it moves through the water", says Cross.

While working on a set for Vaughan Williams's opera based on Synge's *Riders to the Sea*, Cross found Meitheal Mara in 2008, an organization that teaches traditional boatbuilding to young unemployed people. She persuaded the group to sell her a currach, which sat in her studio for a number of years until she came upon the remains of the basking shark washed up on the shore. Working against the incoming tide, she got help in skinning the carcass, and pickled it herself. When she realized it was a fit with the currach, she grafted the skin onto the skeleton of the boat. The partial coverage allows for an ambiguous outcome when it comes to reading the elements of the piece and their combination. Cross tends to avoid narrative closure in favor of dissolves, convergences, and ruptures, and in this instance the timber work is not fully covered, signaling the possibilities, but also the dangers, involved in fishing by currach. Cross's historical interests are more about destabilizing fixed ideas about the past, affirming uncertainty in the search for meaning.

Virgin Shroud (1993), *Teacup*, and even the early shark works were as much about gender as other issues. From her Jungian studies, the anthropomorphic archetypes of the unconscious mind - the animus and the anima - are tropes in Cross's artwork. *Teacup*, for example, contains the world of macho adventure within a fine porcelain cup. Equally, the hide on *Basking Shark Currach* alludes to the male contained and protected by the more fragile female. The social behavior of basking sharks in summer months has been studied and is thought to represent courtship. Some have pregnancies that last for more than three years, and there is evidence that some store sperm, resulting in "perpetual" pregnancy, while others have two uteruses, so they are not only always pregnant but doubly so. Indeed, female sharks of several species can reproduce without any help from a male - a phenomenon known as parthenogenesis - fertile Cross territory.

In *Everest Shark*, on the bronze cast of a blue shark, in place of its fin sits a scale model of Mount Everest - Cross's take on how humans perceive time. Sharks have existed for over 400 million years, and Everest rose from the bottom of the sea sixty million years ago, she explains. Sharks evolved to their present state 100 million years ago, "perfectly suited to their environment and have not changed. Everest, the highest point of our world, the pinnacle of aspiration, is only 60 million years old" - the enormity of time.[48]

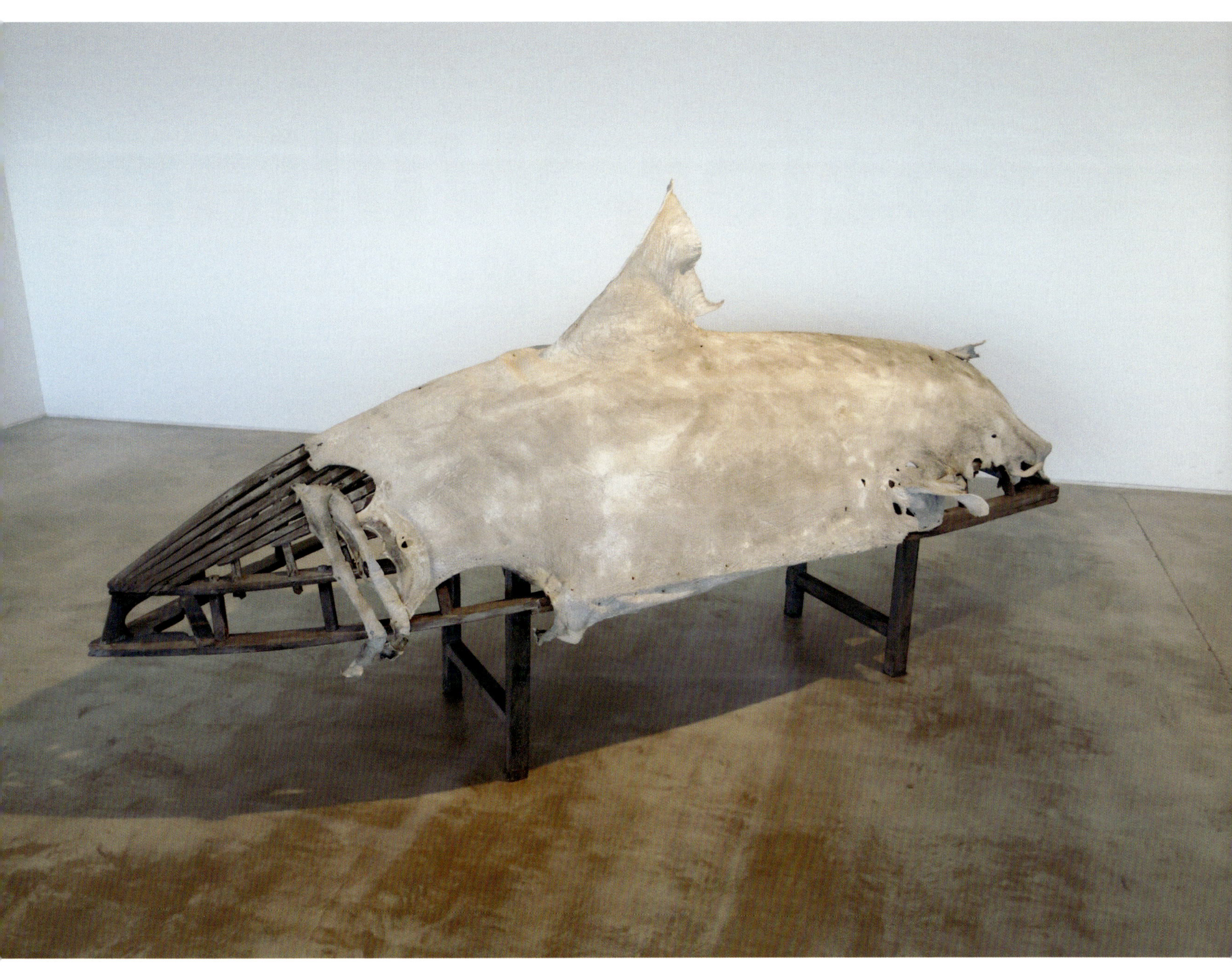

Basking Shark Currach, 2013
Basking-shark skin, wooden-currach frame, 36.22 in (92 cm)

Crozier, William

(1930–2011)

Rainbow's End, 1970
Oil on canvas, 71.7 x 47.8 in (182 x 121.5 cm)

In *Rainbow's End* a human cadaver decomposes. It could be anywhere, and yet nowhere more typical than west Cork, where in summer gorse fires rage, and where Crozier later lived and worked for some thirty years. The febrile reds, yellows, and oranges together with blacks, greens, and blues reverberate in the apocalyptic blaze. The powerful movement of the towering tree and the counter arc of the rainbow suggest a charnel ground.

Crozier has been compared to Francis Bacon, an artist with whom he shared an intensity of emotional pitch (rather than subject matter or style). He believed Bacon "was the only major painter in Europe ... the only artist dealing with the central theme which is how one depicts man".[49] *Rainbow's End* features a landscape at once fertile and inhospitable. The putrefying body speaks of inhumanity across the ages, and resonates with the paradoxes of the Famine that occurred in a country that produced abundant food while people died in their hundreds and thousands. In the face of mass death, as in the Great Hunger, the death of one, seen here, represents the death of many.

William Crozier was born in Glasgow in 1930 and grew up in a home as Irish as it was Scottish. On graduating from the Glasgow School of Art in 1953, he went to England, and then Paris, where he immersed himself in philosophy, art, and politics. Many years later he reflected: "my art, my concept of freedom and responsibility have their roots in the Boulevard St Germain".[50] This racination nourished his *oeuvre*, yet Crozier's passionate involvement in Ireland and Irish history subsequently became for many the most distinctive feature of his work. He was the subject of a major retrospective in 2017 at Uillinn: West Cork Arts Centre and at the Irish Museum of Modern Art.[51]

One of the foremost European artists of the post-war period, Crozier was artistically and philosophically influenced by the existentialist movement. If Paris was his intellectual home, Ireland was his spiritual one. In the mid-1950s he lived in Dublin, and moved in literary circles, with Anthony Cronin and Patrick Kavanagh (the latter had a profound effect on Crozier, not least his "Great

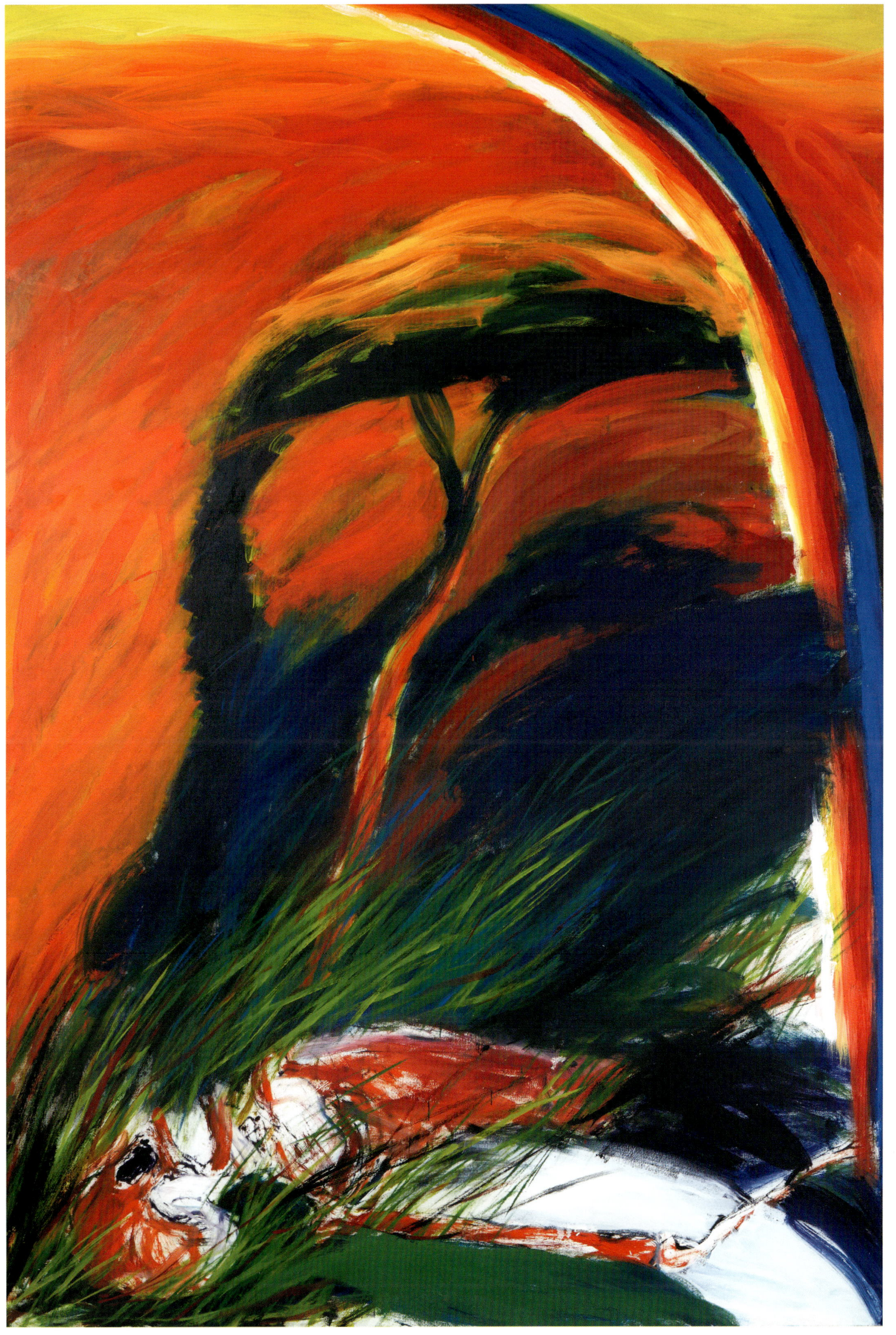

Hunger").[52] But it was in London that he established his reputation in the vanguard of contemporary landscape painting, creating what Katharine Crouan calls "powerful images that drew their inspiration from a visionary experience of place reinvented as an abstract, expressionist image" that, in Crozier's own words, "convey a sense of austerity and isolation, of emotional unease and perhaps a sense of tragedy".[53]

In the 1960s and early 1970s, human figures appeared in his landscapes, at first as self-portraits or portraits of friends, but they soon took on universal meanings. In relation to figures in a state of stress, he said it was his intention "to extend the state of mind of the person into a depiction of the landscape". He drew on photographs of the First World War and the concentration camps of the Second World War for paintings such as *Bourlon Wood* (1962, Imperial War Museum), perceiving "the landscape and the person to be one in nature ... in the factual sense that someone who is in a state of stress or is in a state of isolation sees the world as a projection of themselves".[54]

Crozier always painted quickly – emphasizing the materiality of the pigment – but not without prior reflection. His skeleton paintings, begun in 1969, predate the New Expressionist German painters of the 1980s, and were shaped by Crozier's visits to the death camps of Auschwitz and Bergen-Belsen. He described the 1945 newsreels of the liberation of the concentration camps as the rationale for the series, notably *Rainbow's End*. Some months before painting it, in 1969, he visited Bergen-Belsen, and afterwards wrote:

I saw the landscape as where a holocaust had taken place, where some enormous tragedy had been acted out ... The very thought of Belsen had haunted my imagination all my life and I froze with terror when I turned a corner and saw a sign marked Bergen-Belsen. The enormity of that horror I have not fully dealt with.[55]

If he gave utterance to his emotions regarding the traumas of Irish history, the two world wars, and especially the Holocaust through his skeleton series, in 1969, when British troops entered Northern Ireland, notwithstanding his commitment to pacifism, Crozier relinquished his British passport and became an Irish citizen. Despite his outrage at the atrocities carried out by all sides, and despite a lifelong commitment to pacifism, photographs of his studio in London in 1970 show "Troops Out" posters, indicating his position. *Rainbow's End* may be a reworking of an earlier canvas, or, more likely, a revisiting of the theme he explored in *Fallen Man* (1962, Glasgow Museums). Crouan suggests that the concept of "fallen", implying a loss of innocence or moral evil, may well have been prompted by his experience of the world in 1970, especially of the "Troubles".[56]

In London, in the late Fifties and the Sixties, Crozier was considered one of the most innovative landscape artists of the post-war years. He had exhibited with David Hockney, Peter Blake, and Terry Frost, as well as Francis Bacon. His interest, however, was in the sublime, not the picturesque, in the sense that his work evinces existentialist concerns and a preoccupation with universal issues. In *Rainbow's End*, the black sky, the blood-drenched landscape, the palpable horror are, to borrow the critic Philip Vann's word, "hallucinogenic" in intensity.[57]

Crozier chose his titles to expand the meaning of his subjects. Notwithstanding the inclusion of a rainbow in several paintings of the series – symbol of hope in European art – Crouan says that he found working on paintings such as *Rainbow's End* such a harrowing experience that he thought he might never paint again. But he did, exploring themes of evil, trauma, and alienation that allowed him to universalize. His links with Ireland, especially west Cork – the scene of some of the most needless Famine-related suffering and death – makes this painting particularly apt for Ireland's Great Hunger Museum. In the abstract, this skeleton represents all those who died and remained unburied and unremembered. Like millions of Irish scattered around the world, Crozier saw exile as his life; this is what his work is about: "I have always felt in a permanent state of exile ... It's about a sense of loss, a problem of identity."[58] Landscape, he believed, "is not the subject; it is the vehicle through which I can express intangible things. Things which have no narrative. Loss, memory – all can be done through the language of landscape."[59]

Davidson, Lilian Lucy

ARHA (1879–1954)

In Davidson's *Gorta*, one age of anxiety meets another. There is nothing like it in Irish visual culture. Its echoes are of the European tradition – artists who engaged with the dark side of the landscape in the years leading up to and between the two world wars. And, perhaps, antecedently Edmund Burke:

Whatever is fitted in any sorts to excite the ideas of pain and danger, that is to say, whatever is in any sort terrible, or is conversant with terrible objects, or operates in a manner analogous to terror, is a source of the sublime; that is, it is productive of the strongest emotions which the mind is capable of feeling.[60]

The restricted palette intensifies the emotion. Blue has a long tradition in Christian symbolic iconography, and is also associated with mourning. Its dominance here heightens the sense of loss. This family has lost its child to starvation. Davidson provides a glimpse of terrifying grief. Notwithstanding the grandfather's rosary beads, it is without religious hope or heroic overtones. It may have been painted a hundred years after the Famine, but, Davidson reminds us, hope did not grow out of loss. All narrative is eliminated, and yet, as an invocation of Famine, its subject is indisputable. These people have come from nothing; now traumatized, they look past one another into nothingness.

The bareness of the setting would suggest a *cillín*, where those prohibited from interment in consecrated ground by the Catholic Church were buried.[61] Unbaptized children, stillborn children, illegitimate children, convicted murderers, the mentally disturbed, the shipwrecked, those who took their own lives, and those whose religion was unknown were buried there. And, in the 1840s, many victims of the Famine.

Archaeologists, anthropologists, and sociologists relate the characteristics of *cillíní* to the concept of Limbo. Since unbaptized infants were not Christian, they were excluded from Heaven, prompting the Church to create the in-between space of Limbo. The unbaptized dead were believed to be capable of malevolence – even as infants – giving rise to rituals of burial that could be distressingly inhumane. Such interments took place at night (especially for illegitimate or stillborn children), usually by the father or a male relative. Oral accounts suggest that, while the denial of burial in consecrated ground was devoid of compassion, the marginality of the burial ground would ensure that such babies would rest undisturbed. The creation of a *cillín* within bogland or woodland is consistent with notions of liminality. Davidson excelled at twilight scenes, and twilight is quintessentially liminal. Here, the presence of both parents and, it would seem, a grandfather intimates the death of a slightly older child, but a more desolate, hopeless place would be hard to imagine. Ironically, Lilian Lucy Davidson, one of nine children brought up as "poor as church mice", was herself buried in an unmarked grave.[62]

Gorta was exhibited in the *Thomas Davis and the Young Ireland Movement Centenary Exhibition of Pictures of Irish Historical Interest* (1946), the government's response to the hundredth anniversary of the Great Hunger: the exhibition was illustrative of Irish history from the founding of the *Nation* newspaper in 1842, through the Fenian movement and the War of Independence and up to the year of the anniversary. A number of works directly relating to the Famine were exhibited: *Famine* by George Campbell; *An Ghorta* by Muiris Mac Conghail; *Connemara Cottages Abandoned During the Famine* by Louis Le Brocquy; *Bliadhain na Gorta* by Pádraic Woods; *Famine* by Muriel Brandt; *Ocras, 1850* by Cathal Mac Lúain; *The Emigrant* by Louis Le Brocquy; *Evocation of 1846–47 Famine* (decorative design) by Michael O'Farrell; and Lilian Davidson's *Gorta*. Forty-seven works were selected, and thirty-nine others acquired on loan from the National Gallery (now Dublin City Gallery, The Hugh Lane), the National Museum, and Áras an Uachtaráin, residence of the president of Ireland. In addition to the works directly depicting the Famine, a number of others can be considered Famine-related, addressing emigration and eviction – for example, works by Fr Jack Hanlon and George F. Campbell.

In its review the *Irish Times* deplored the "mournful and depressed" art in the exhibition, citing Muriel Brandt's *Famine* as "too realistic". Surprisingly in this regard it did not mention Davidson's *Gorta*, although – given its description of Nano Reid's eviction scene, *Feudalism, 19th Century*, as "witty and light-hearted" – the omission might be to Davidson's credit (July 23, 1946).

Davidson earned a reputation for empathetic, naturalistic work. In her early years she was influenced by Stanhope Forbes, whose heightened palette, square-brush technique, and strong impasto highlights became characteristics of her style. Traces of Paul Henry can be seen in *The Flax Pullers*, but, most importantly, the influence of Jack B. Yeats is evident in her choices of subject and her fascination with the vibrancy of Irish rural life, as seen in *Fair Day in Miss O'Dowd's*. In her fair and market scenes she was drawn to the social aspects as much as to the opportunity to experiment technically.

Katherine Cahill describes Davidson as "a journeyman artist" and "not in the vanguard with Mainie Jellett, Evie Hone or Mary Swanzy in bringing experimental art to Ireland". Her perception of Davidson as "rooted in the somewhat narrow, Victorian focus of the South Kensington system", however, is harsh: *Cottages – Keel, Achill* (1938), one of several night scenes depicted with a restricted palette of mauves and earthy browns, is decidedly modernist. Of her 1926 exhibition, the *Irish Times* noted "a strong individuality in her painting" (November 3, 1926); reviewing her 1934 exhibition, it declared that "She has vision, and crude and rude, as some of her subjects may be, out of very human sympathy with the humblest she composes scenes of life and interest" (February 6, 1934); and of her 1940 exhibition, it observed that "Human sympathy is an elemental urge in her outlook" (November 4, 1940).

Davidson was prolific and proficient across a range of media: painting, book illustration, poster design, and set design for theatre. And she was both a critic and writer in her own right; she wrote under the pseudonym Ulick Burke. "Her Only Son", published in the *Bell* (October 1942),[63] concerns a poor mother of a mentally ill son – who would assuredly be buried in a *cillín* – who tried to kill her.

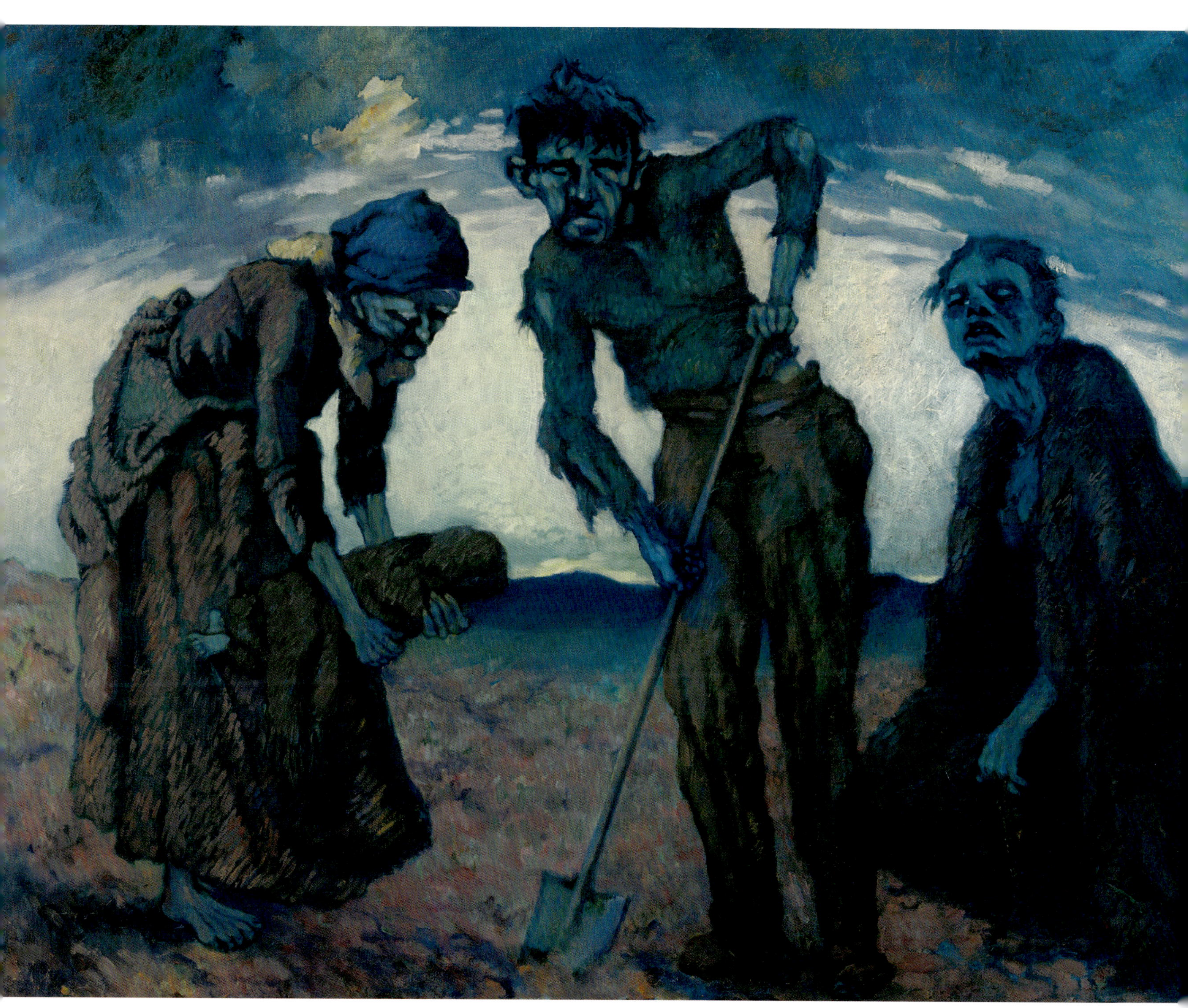

Gorta (previously known as *Burying the Child*), 1946
Oil on canvas, 27.5 x 35.5 in (69.85 x 90.17 cm)

Farrell, Micheal

(1940-2000)

Seen as charming, flamboyant, and outrageous, fellow artist Brian Bourke described Farrell's life as "a narrative of woeful behaviour, domestic chaos and bad luck ... If it were not for the reproduction of the work it would be a miserable saga".[64]

Farrell attended St Martin's School of Art, London. In 1961 he showed with the Young Contemporaries, and, aged twenty-three, was awarded the Prix de Rome. Although pop art was the rage and Farrell was immersed in the work of Hockney, Stella, and Kitaj, his early work, such as the *Cairn* series, conveyed "an authentically Celtic language of visual expression" combining motifs from early Irish art with the techniques of geometric hard-edge abstraction through the new medium of acrylic, exploring how "art, religion, colonialism, national identity and violence are as enmeshed as the intricate traceries of linear motifs in the Book of Kells".[65] Farrell insisted his language was pictorial, not political, but it wasn't long before one became the other.[66] "I had arrived at a totally aesthetic art with no literary connotations. I wanted to make statements, using sarcasm, or puns, or wit, and all of these I could not do before because of the limited means of expression I had adopted", he said.[67]

In 1966 a teaching position at the Pratt Institute, New York ended with his outspoken opposition to the Vietnam War. There - described by Noel Sheridan as "a full-blown extravagant enigma" and by Brian O'Doherty as "a walking opera" - he met Mark Rothko, Roy Lichtenstein, and Larry Rivers, and was seen as an up-and-coming international star. In 1967 the Musée d'Art Moderne, Paris purchased a painting, and also that year he was awarded the Carroll Prize at the Irish Exhibition of Living Art. But, controversially, he was rejected by Rosc '67.

Outraged by British policy in Northern Ireland, he announced that he would not exhibit there "until that state has achieved the basic fundamentals of a decent society".[68] As he saw it, "Ireland is getting fucked by the opposition, getting screwed up by Britain, by the Protestants".[69] Irish identity and politics, violence and sex, religion and death were now interwoven with autobiographical elements. After the Bloody Sunday massacre in Northern Ireland in 1972, he politicized his *Pressé* series, while the Dublin and Monaghan bombings of 1974 led to even more visceral pictorialization.

In 1971 he moved to the artists' colony La Ruche, Paris. In 1976 he spent six months in Florence, where, based on François Boucher's 1752 portrait of the Irish child courtesan Marie-Louise O'Murphy, he discoursed on the body politic. Farrell's *Madonna Irlanda: The Very First Real Irish Political Picture* (1977) allegorizes Ireland as both whore and victim. But if Farrell's political and sexual allegories objectified women, he also laid bare his male ego.[70] The Hugh Lane Gallery purchased *Madonna Irlanda* in 1977 (but did not exhibit it for ten years). His sardonic anti-establishment polemics continued in his depiction of a bishop and a nude woman in flagrante delicto in his *Lune de Miel de l'Évêque* series, following the Bishop Eamonn Casey scandal in 1992.

Farrell's work was sometimes romanticizing, sometimes lacerating, but, given his penchant for absolutism, rarely nuanced. He subscribed to a secular European cultural agenda, but also harbored deep nationalist sympathies, though from the often-skewed vantage of exile. Aidan Dunne describes his Famine and Bloody Sunday works as a "potent reflex": "What links these themes, however, apart from their role in national history, is the issues of justice that they raise - justice, but not - and this may be true of all Farrell's work - reasoned historical analysis."[71]

Incensed by Bloody Sunday - the killing of fourteen unarmed civil rights marchers by British paratroopers in Derry in 1972 - he also saw Ireland as mistress of her own miseries. His views on the Great Hunger, however, were unequivocal. By focusing on the failure of the British government to address the Famine, Farrell vested in the assistant secretary to the British Treasury in London (with responsibility for relief) all the spleen he could muster: to his *Portrait of Charles Trevelyan* he appended the dedication, "For crimes against humanity, never brought to justice - MF". Trevelyan saw the Famine as a "mechanism for reducing surplus population" and defended the export of food from the starving country on the grounds that the government should not interfere with free trade: "The real evil with which we have to contend is not the physical evil of the Famine, but the moral evil of the selfish, perverse, and turbulent character of the people", he argued.[72]

For *Black '47*, Farrell studied horrifying Holocaust photographs taken at Auschwitz. Projected as though from outside the picture, a raking light - as if a searchlight - bisects the painting, falling full force on Trevelyan, breaking the boundaries between pictorial and gallery space. Trevelyan holds forth, justifying the withholding of food, and pointing to the potato as the root cause of the Famine.

Skeletons are relegated to a hole in the floor. Although a consequence of societal collapse during the Famine was the breakdown of communal ties, here two skeletons are wrapped around one another - the dead have come together to

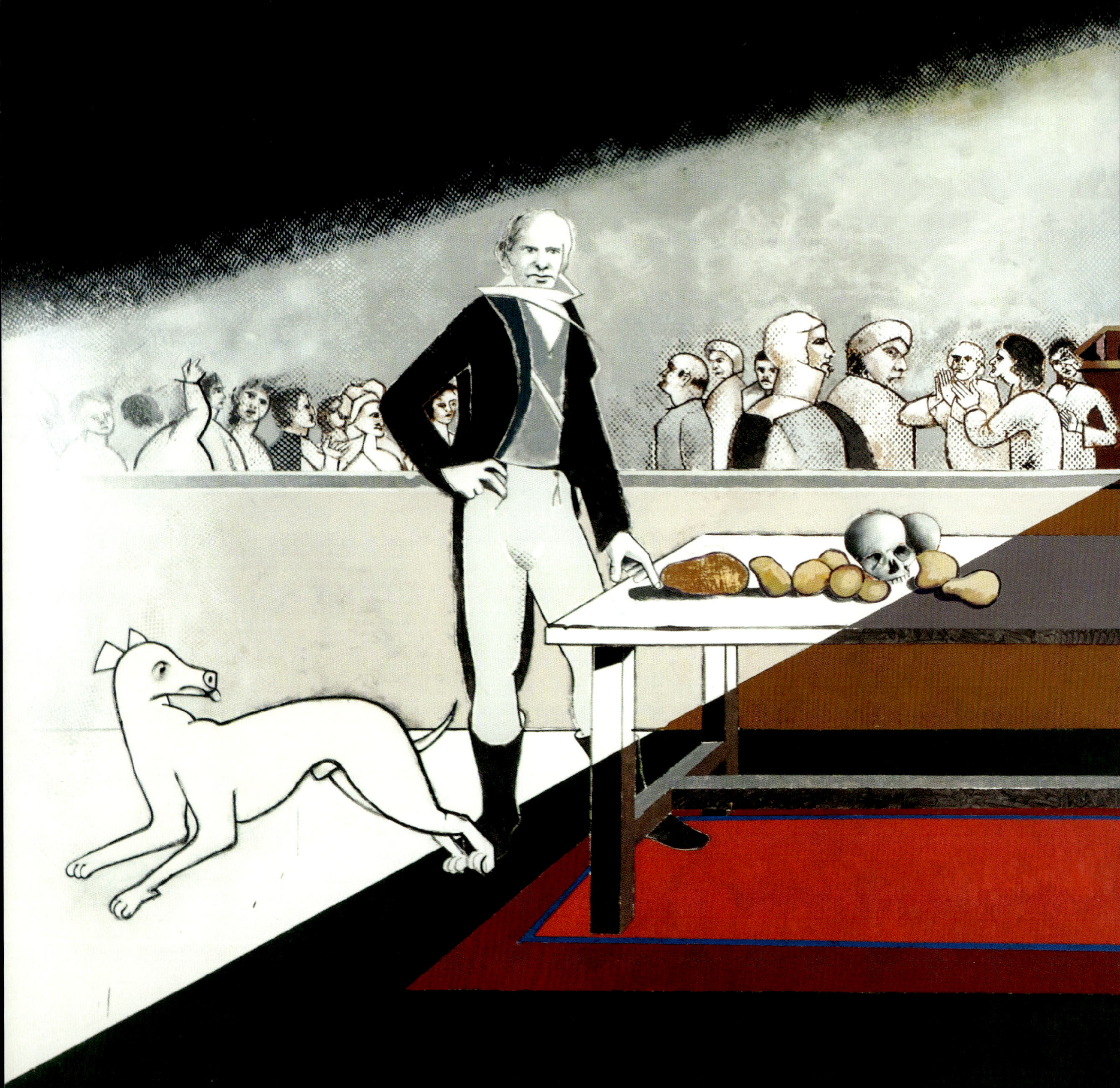

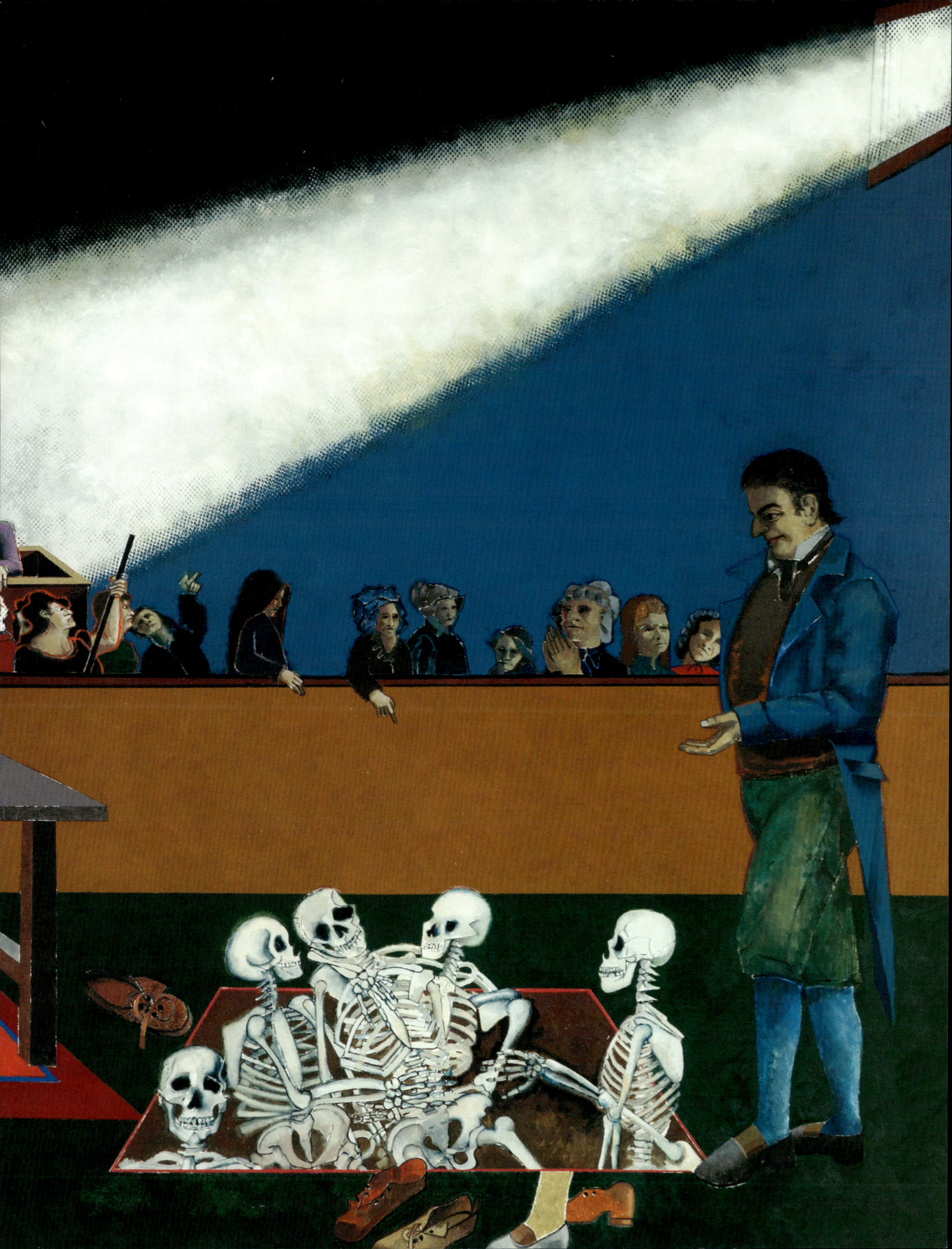

support each other. Beneath are shoes – all that remain of once-living people – although one foot remains standing, Farrell himself perhaps, with one foot in the grave. The feet beneath the exhumed skeletons recall the discarded shoes found at Nazi death camps. A smug landlord smiles down on the human remains – with so many deaths and departures, his mission is accomplished. A wolfhound flees from the scene of the crime. A symbol of Ireland in nationalist iconography, the Irish wolfhound was identified as the dog of Irish kings and warriors of old. The wolfhound migrated to America, where it was incorporated into memorials such as the Irish Brigade Monument at Gettysburg.

The bodies in the grave sprout up as witnesses for the defense. The crowd in the darkened gallery point to the victims, while the British turn their backs on proceedings. And there is a group of Turks. In 1847 Sultan Abdülmedjid sent aid to Ireland, encouraged probably by his Irish physician, Justin Washington McCarthy from Cork (the sultan employed many physicians). Initially, he pledged £10,000, but, allegedly, to avoid embarrassing Queen Victoria reduced it to £1,000 (and, according to some uncorroborated accounts, secretly sent three ships of grain).[73]

One of Farrell's visual sources was Gustave Courbet's *Burial at Ornans* (1849–50), executed coincidentally during the Famine. Courbet saw his burial of an unremarkable man as a "statement of principle". With its frieze-like composition, gaping grave, and stark contrasts of color, its radicality appealed to Farrell, who, 150 years later, drew on it to comment on the inhumanity condoned in Ireland during the Great Hunger.

At the opening of his last major exhibition, featuring his Famine and the Bloody Sunday series, he announced that "[t]he potato was only an excuse to get rid of us and get the land", and quoted George Bernard Shaw: "It was not a famine – it was organized starvation." In the related lithographs (one being one of the biggest stone lithographs in the world), Trevelyan and the Golden Wonders star. In *The Wounded Wonder*, skulls and potatoes commingle, as if exchangeable commodities; from them blood splashes into the open grave beneath – the blood of Famine victims, as well as Farrell's own blood, an intimation of his mortality. While Brian King's assertion that "Micheal took on all the political cows, and slaughtered them one by one" may be true, so, too, did Farrell see the Famine series as a premonition of his own impending death.[74]

The Wounded Wonder, 1997–98
Hillier's medium and acrylic on canvas,
55 x 62 in (139.7 x 157.48 cm)

Portrait of Charles Trevelyan, 1997–98
Hillier's medium and acrylic on canvas,
19.7 x 15.7 in (50 x 39.9 cm)

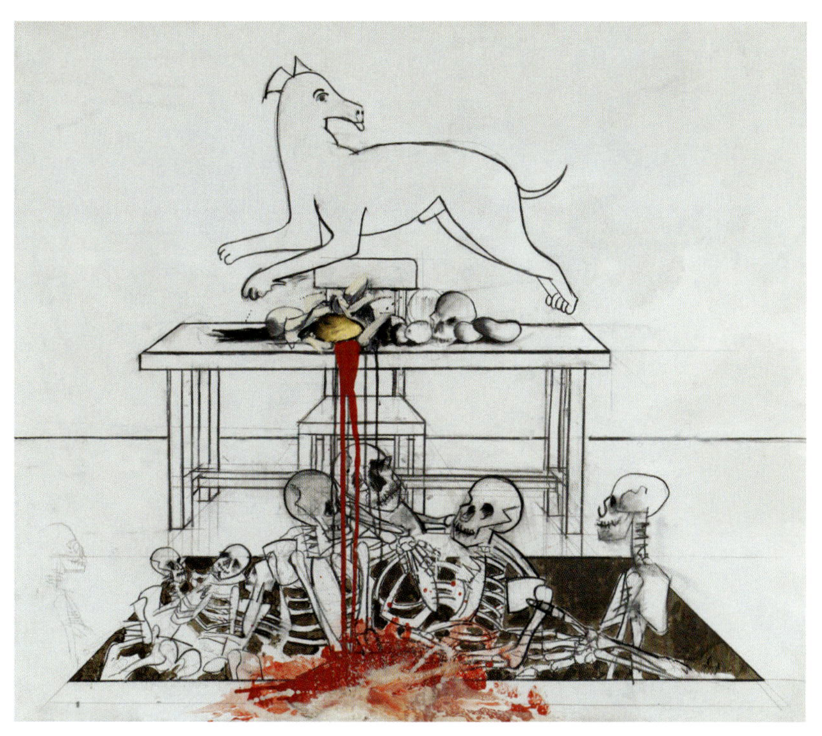

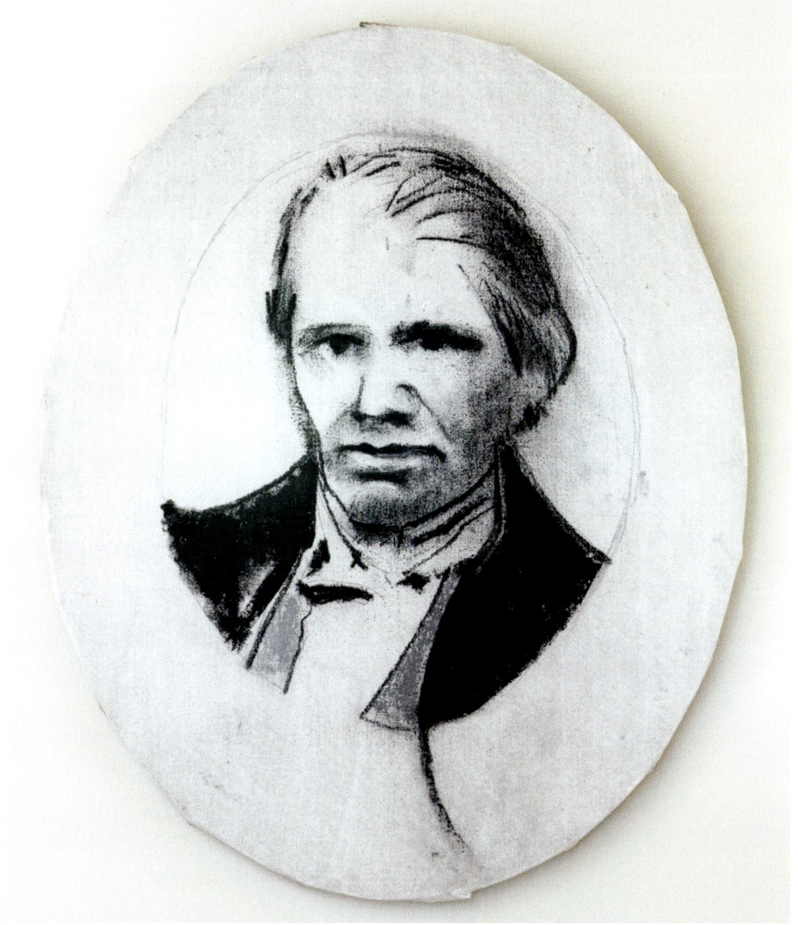

Fripp, Alfred Downing

RWS (1822–95)

An Irish Peasant and Her Child, n.d.
Oil on canvas, 12.5 x 9.75 in (31.75 x 24.77 cm)

In 1843 Fripp made his first trip to Ireland; in 1844 and thereafter he returned with Frederick Goodall, Francis Topham, and (Henry) Mark Anthony. While Anthony plowed a different furrow, the others painted homely scenes of domesticity set in dreadfully poor hovels. While many of their works now seem sentimental, they are what remain visually of the conditions endured by Irish people in the lead-up to, and during, the Famine. But all were also capable of producing commanding pictures – in Fripp's case *The Poachers Alarmed* (1844, Whitworth Museum, Manchester), garnering him a not insignificant reputation among important critics, such as John Ruskin and F.G. Stephens. Stephens described Fripp as

an indefatigable leader of the highest influence and importance ... a subtle chiaroscurist, a good colourist, a poet in painting with a rare and delicate sense of what is peaceful and idyllic in Nature and expressible by art, and potent in treating simple themes with a due regard for style, massiveness and breadth.
*(*Magazine of Art*, 1895)*[75]

These British artists caused consternation in Connemara when a rumor that they had come to convert the people from Catholicism resulted in them being staked out for three days until the curate, Fr Rooney, rebuked the locals in "a short harangue in Irish", thereby curing the natives of "the ridiculous fear they had cherished, that when they were actually being sketched, their names were being put down in a book for purposes of enlistment", wrote Goodall. Ironically, it was Fr Rooney who underwent transformation! On leaving Connemara the artists left him paints and brushes. When Fripp and Topham returned the next year, they found Fr Rooney in his "studio"; he had become an artist, and was exhibiting at the RHA.[76]

A rare painting from the Famine period, *Sympathy*, signed and dated "Seaan O Ruanadh Sagart 1847" (John Rooney, priest) (*c.* 1809–50) (NFC, UCD) attests to his skill. The priest suffered from a heart condition, and had shattered his arm in a shooting accident in 1839. In 1844 he asked the historian James Hardiman to write to the antiquary George Petrie on his behalf, *as there is no provision in this dioces [*sic*] for disabled journeymen, I have taken to the canvas and brush for my support, I have just ready to send to the Dublin exhibition of this year, a picture* The Denial of Peter *... I will not publish my own name, for the Art Union Committee I'm told are of a certain class, and if they discovered the artist to be a priest perhaps he would have very little to boast of at their hands. The name I assume is "John Clarke quasi Joannes Clericus" – and this is the name I wish to have introduced to Mr. Petrie.*[77]

Fr Rooney's own parish of Oranmore lost forty per cent of its population during the Famine years; his *Sympathy* depicts a woman seated at a spinning wheel and a girl holding a dead bird – a metaphor for the sorrow of a child confronted by death, symbolic of the Famine. The rise of the curate as artist has the hitherto unknown backstory involving Fripp and friends, who provided the means towards his new profession.

The Victorian writer Mary Howitt described Fripp's paintings as "mournful poems" in which she perceived "the crushed and bleeding soul of the Irish people ... a brave and noble nature, suffering hopelessly and undeservedly with all the strength of a martyr".[78] Although they appear ruddy and well fed, the melancholy mother, the moody landscape, the darkening skin of mother and child, and the withered stalk in the background suggest otherwise. In 1848 a painting entitled *The Irish Mother* was exhibited in the British Institution with identical dimensions, which may identify it as this painting. Fripp additionally executed a watercolor version (1846, IGHM). In Fripp's 1848 contributions to the RA, the *Illustrated London News* observed the "dirt and idleness", and lamented that they were "scarcely pleasing enough to be picturesque" (February 26, 1848).

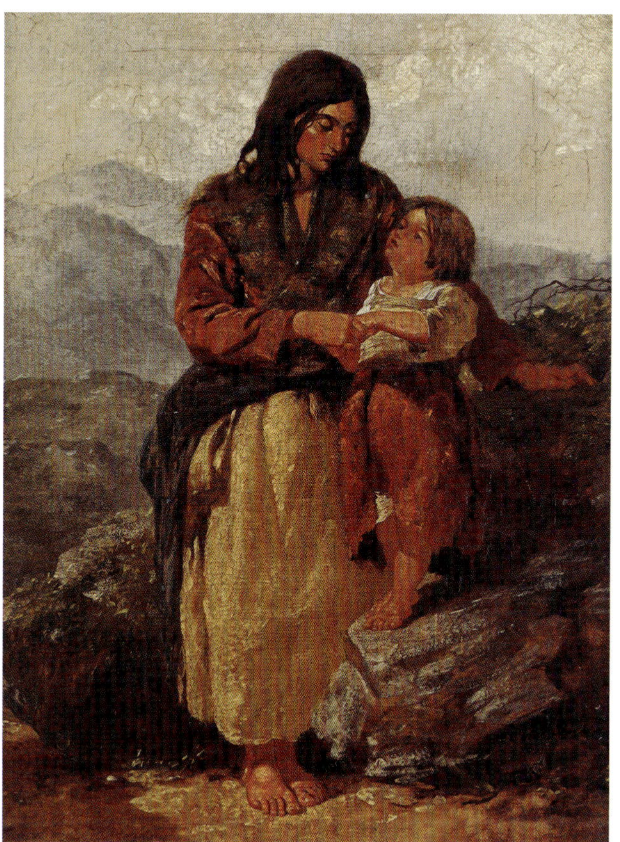

Gillespie, Rowan

(b. 1953)

The Victim, 1997
Bronze, 9.5 in (24.13 cm)

The Victim represents each of the millions who died from starvation and disease or who emigrated. The scale of the figure contrasts with the scale of the horror. He has suffered pain, loss, and humiliation, he sees nothing, hears nothing, utters nothing, yet, as Gillespie says, this piece "is about the miracle of human life in a galaxy of indifference".[79]

The Victim is part of a series of works commemorating the one-hundred-and-fiftieth anniversary of the Great Hunger that culminated in Gillespie's memorial, *Famine* (1997, Custom House Quay, Dublin), in which seven people (and a dog) stagger toward the docks to board the *Perseverance* that sailed on St Patrick's Day 1846, landing in New York two months later. Inspired by Joseph O'Connor's *Star of the Sea* (2004) is a sister group, *Migrants* (2006, Toronto, Canada). At a time when the population of Toronto was only 20,000, 38,560 famine refugees arrived, as if by deluge, in 1847. Gillespie's figurative style is a natural for Famine commemoration. The roughened surfaces, the etiolated figures, the lengthening and stretching of forms all add to the emotional charge of the work. *Footsteps Towards Freedom* (2017), in Tasmania, completes the trilogy.

Gillespie's Quaker background and historical interests led him to a remarkable story. In 1957 a parking lot was built over what had been a mass grave on Staten Island, just across the water from where the World Trade Center once stood. In 2007 the Friends of Abandoned Cemeteries halted the construction of a new courthouse. A row of human remains, cut off at the knees when a bulldozer rolled over them, was found. A quarantine station had operated there.

During the Famine period, Irish refugees streamed into New York Harbor. All ships underwent medical inspection. The sick were consigned to the Marine Hospital, and the remaining passengers quarantined for thirty days (in the case of yellow fever, six months). The unquarantined wandered Staten Island, penniless and disoriented, preyed upon by unscrupulous profiteers, as they waited for the interned to die or be discharged.[80] In an effort to contain the spread of lethal diseases, as they died they were carried from bed to grave without death

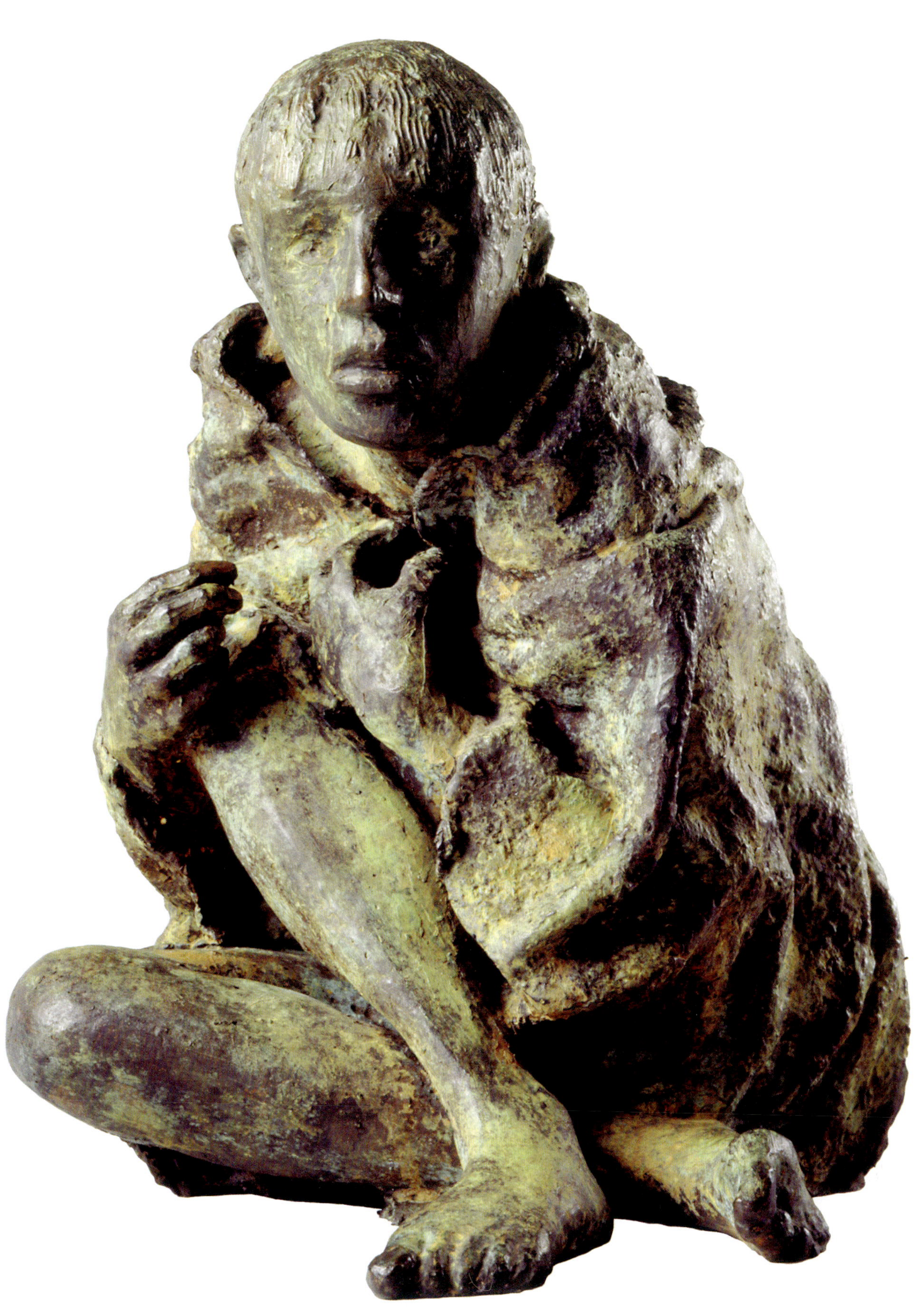

certificates or burial records. On September 1, 1858 a mob of Staten Islanders and older Irish immigrants, fearing contagion, evacuated the facility and set fire to the buildings.

There are two cemeteries. One – where tens of thousands of bodies were buried in trenches – is today a golf course. But when New York State initiated plans to build the new Supreme Court on the other parking lot, having been made aware of the sensitivity of the site the state paused to allow research. Over a period of two years archaeological fieldwork defined the boundaries of the cemetery, and the human remains were forensically examined. Jennifer Hyatt-Morgan identified 650 people, now immortalized by Gillespie. His litany in bronze provides the name, age, disease (typhus, phthisis, cholera, bilious fever, dysentery, hepatitis, albuminaria, pneumonia), and date of death of each one:

Having spent some time at the site and with those involved, I felt the need to offer some small dignity to those forgotten dead by cutting their names into bronze. It was my way of taking time to contemplate the horror behind these statistics. I would need to make 5,000 tables like these to record the known deaths resulting from the Famine in Ireland.[81]

Gillespie studied at York School of Art (where Sally Arnup introduced him to the lost-wax casting process); Kingston College of Art (where he was tutored by woodcarver John Robson, and through whom he was mentored by Henry Moore); and the Kunst og Håndverke Skole in Oslo. For three years he lectured at the Munch Museum, and became enthralled by the work of Edvard Munch, a discernible influence on his work. A master craftsman, Gillespie displays impressive technical proficiency. He uses phosphor bronze for its durability, and employs the complex and labor-intensive lost-wax technique. Unusually for a monumental bronze worker, he works alone – from conception, through casting, to completion – in his purpose-built bronze-casting foundry in Dublin:

... to be one man alone in a workshop with nothing more than the notion of an idea, then to start bending and welding, covering in clay and wax, changing, forming, deforming, reforming, discovering something, loving it and hating it, days and weeks of journeying, Then the moulding, baking, melting, lifting and shovelling, sweating, exhaustion and exhilaration until almost abruptly, one day, there is something ...[82]

At a time when one in four New Yorkers were foreign-born, nativists assigned blame to the stigmatized Irish immigrants for the social ills of the day. Underlying the 1858 arson was an intricate web. On the one hand, the largely Irish contingent of the "Quarantine mob" operated at a time of virulent prejudice on the part of a predominantly Protestant public towards the Irish. The Irish perpetrators, however, were part of an older immigrant demographic that preceded the Famine immigrants of the 1840s, and were relatively established members of the populace. The arsonists were thus an alliance of older Irish and eminent American families who had lived on Staten Island for generations. The existence of the Quarantine, as it was called, gave rise to a widespread fear of disease among both groups, but also, paradoxically, to a fear among WASPs of social contagion, and among the already settled Irish resentment towards the new arrivals.

The new immigration of the 1840s swamped the slums of New York. Cholera (known as the "Irish disease"), smallpox, and typhus accompanied poverty, poor sanitation, and overcrowding, and were blamed on the Irish, fueling nativist resentment and inspiring new "Irish-centric animosity".[83]

In turn, the Irish rounded on southern and Eastern European immigrants, as well as African-Americans, practicing their own exclusionary tactics and generating their own stereotypes in order to advance their own integration. The arsonists conflated the medical risk posed by newly immigrated Eastern European stevedores who staffed the Quarantine with the moral degeneracy implied by their ethnic inferiority. The *New York Times* condemned the mob as diabolical, and suggested rebuilding the hospital on the same site so as "to spite the arbiters of its destruction", and named Irishmen John Carroll, Patrick O'Hare, and Michael O'Brien as perpetrators.[84] The threat the Quarantine posed was very real, but combining the forces of nativism, racism, and xenophobia to legitimate epidemiological fears was opportunistic.

In contrast to other groups who endured short-term or sporadic stigmatization, antebellum Irish immigrants were subjected to sustained loathing from Americans intent on blaming them for the deadliest diseases spread amongst them, discounting slum subsistence and dirty water as the real causes. The Irish withstood the most appalling working and living conditions, thereby confirming the stereotypes. Such conditions prevented them from upward social mobility, which in turn fostered greater racism, as people perceived Irish inferiority in terms of what were seen as their genetic characteristics: laziness, degeneracy, and immorality.

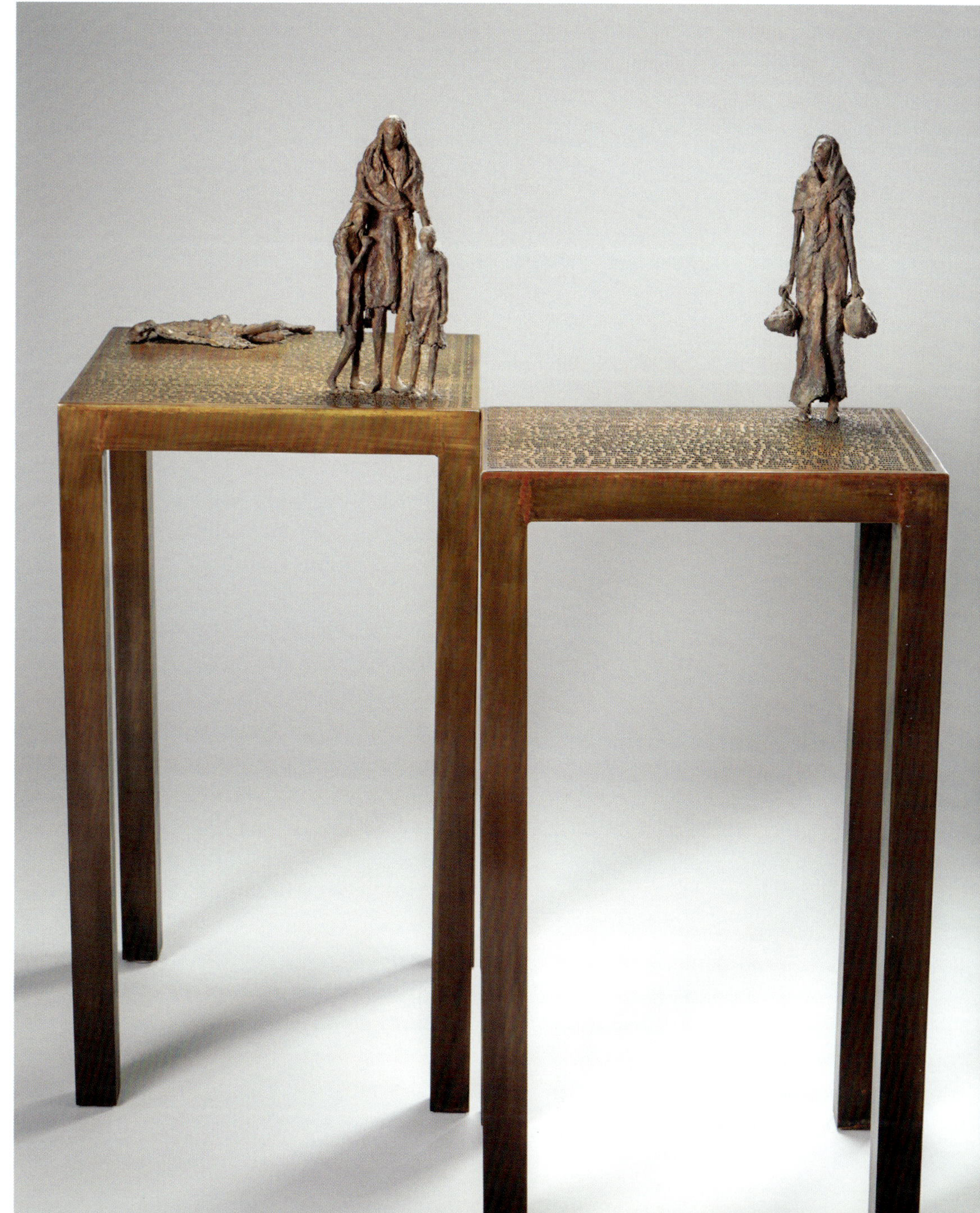

Statistic I & *Statistic II*, 2010
Bronze, Statistic I: 49 in (124.46 cm),
Statistic II: 49 in (124.46 cm)

Goodacre, Glenna

(b. 1939)

Anguish, 2002
Bronze, 17 in (43.18 cm)

Goodacre studied at Colorado College and, in 1967, at the Art Students League of New York (with Bill Draper, whom she considers one of the finest portrait painters). Her work was so figurative she considered medical illustration as a career, eventually settling on sculpture. She is renowned for her *Vietnam Women's Memorial* (1993, National Mall, Washington DC) that acknowledges the contribution of the 11,000 women who served in the United States military during the war. Goodacre's work is highly narrative - sculptures that speak to the heart. She has executed more than 500 works, and is represented in more that forty countries.

To commemorate the one-hundred-and-fiftieth anniversary of the Great Hunger, a $3 million *Irish Famine Memorial* (2003, Philadelphia) was commissioned. An international competition - which drew over a hundred submissions - was won by Goodacre. It took seven years to raise the money, and she was given fourteen months to execute the work, and fourteen months to have over 450 pieces cast. In 2003 the thirty-five life-sized figures were installed in the park that overlooks the Delaware River, at Penn's Landing, by the shore where so many Irish disembarked.

The work is designed in the form of an arc, with a strong diagonal axis. Approximately twelve feet high, thirty feet long, and twelve feet wide, it rests on a two-foot-high concrete plinth. It depicts the Famine in Ireland, the destitute embarking for America, and immigrants stepping onto American shores. The east end suggests a landscape decimated by hunger, the higher end a ship, facing west, with many disembarking sick and others rushing forward in hope. Described as Rodinesque, the figures are modeled loosely and impressionistically.

Goodacre's work is forcefully literal, but she says she is no slave to detail.

I work the clay surface in a looser manner, with what you might call almost "soft edges". It has enabled me to simply suggest rather than overwhelm with detail. It really emphasizes movement. In the Irish Famine Memorial, *the committee liked the idea of maintaining the broad, loose treatment of my maquette. I was so glad that they realized the richness it would bring to the form. If I ever hear someone say when they are walking through my studio, "My goodness, that shoelace looks so real, so detailed", as soon as they leave, I'll reach down and rework it. I'm looking for the broader impact rather than a collection of details.*[85]

In a national competition for a new dollar coin, the winning design was Goodacre's *Sacagawea* (2000), a member of the Shoshone who interpreted for explorers Lewis and Clark on their westward journey nearly two centuries before. Unveiled at the White House by Hillary Clinton, it features a three-quarter profile, the first such on any United States coin; it is also the first coin to feature a woman and child, and the first designed by a woman.

Goodacre tends to sketch in clay. From tiny bas-relief, such as *Sacagawea*, to the imposing *Irish Famine Memorial*, to the twice-life-sized *General "Hap" Arnold* (1993, Air Force Academy), she demonstrates massive control of scale. For the *Famine Memorial* she did several maquettes – six-inch-tall figures. "When you realize that these have to be enlarged 15 to 16 times and you end up, much to your surprise, with 35 to 40 figures, you wonder, what have I gotten myself into", she said.[86]

In 2003 Goodacre held an exhibition, *Inspirations from the Irish Memorial*, at Cavalier Galleries, Greenwich, CT, comprising editions of single and double heads that extended the highly narrativized memorial. By naming the pieces – for example, "Mr O'Toole", "Rose", and "Bernadette" – she sought to heighten the sense of authenticity (although, anachronistically, some, such as "Erin" and "Shannon", were not names of immigrants but names given later, nostalgically, to the children of immigrants). As in all Goodacre's work, the patina and the facial and gestural expressions are roughened to intensify the emotion.

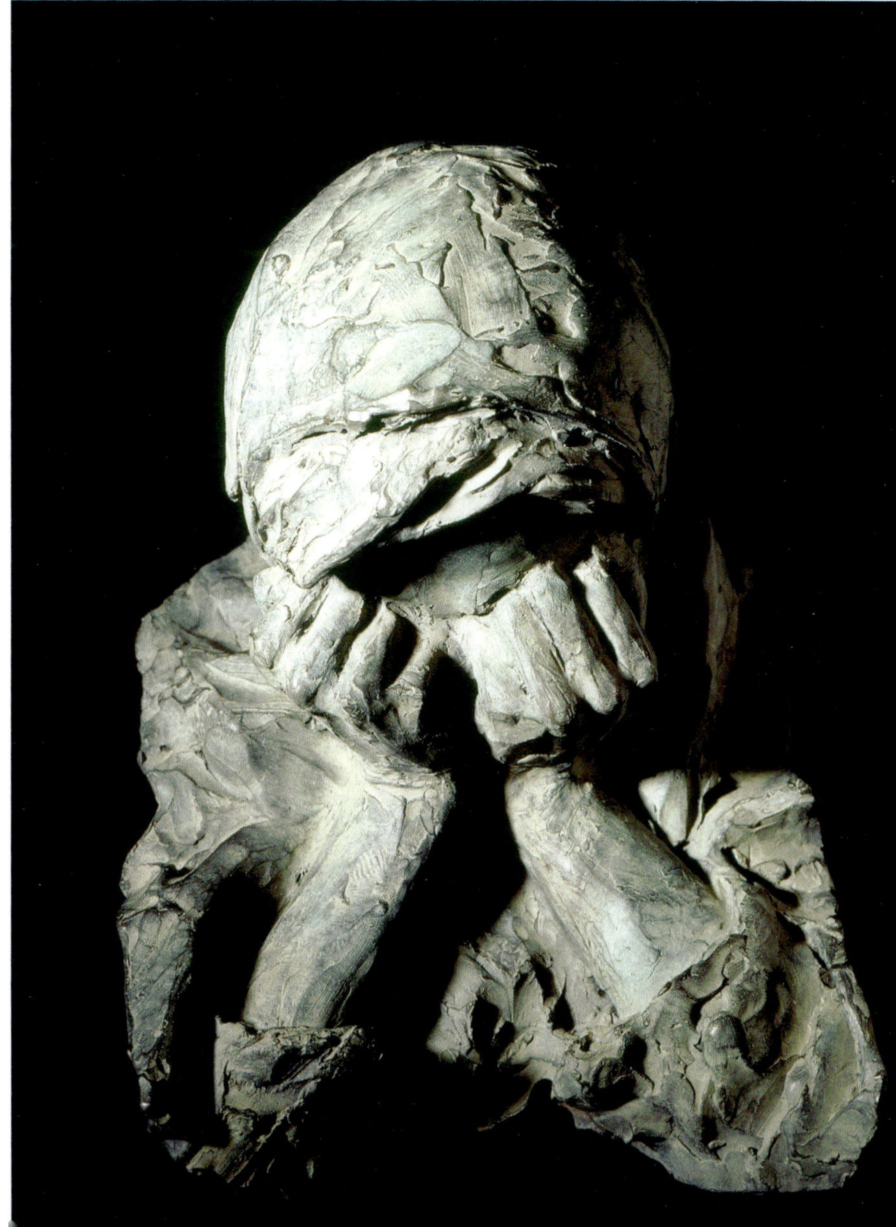

Helmick, Howard

(1840-1907)

Mending Nets, 1886
Oil on canvas, 21 x 30 in (52 x 74.29 cm)

Howard Helmick loved Ireland. Born in Zanesville, Ohio, he studied at home before enrolling in the studio of Alexandre Cabanel at the École des Beaux-Arts, Paris in 1866, where he was friendly with Americans Robert Wylie, Thomas Eakins, Mary Cassatt, and Frederick Bridgman. His artistic formation also evolved in the colony of Écouen, north of Paris. In October 1870 he left Paris - then under Prussian siege - for London, where he stayed until 1887. During this time he made frequent visits to Kinsale, Kenmare, and Connemara, where he studied rural character and life.

"The Irish are full of weaknesses", he told his American writer friend Julian Hawthorne, "but I like them. Their chief merit is that they are superior to the English."[87] In Ireland, according to the American critic Clarence Cook, Helmick found "in that land of changing lights and shadows in human life ... so many picturesque subjects, [all he needed] to supply the demand for his pictures. It was a field till then almost undiscovered ... and [he] was left in almost undisturbed possession of the quarry he had opened."[88]

"For foreigners, the truth of grinding poverty, frequent famine and substandard housing was veiled by ... manipulated images of the 'dear little cabin'", at which Helmick excelled, argues Claudia Kinmonth.[89] The scene here is a traditional cottage. The grandmother sits by the fire, the heart(h) of the family. There is a lively sense of suspense as the grandfather rests his pipe to emphasize a moment in his story. Two young, barefooted girls listen to their grandfather tell tales of old, one disentangling the net as the other hangs it on a rope from the rafters to dry.

The subjects of fish and famine recur. Of course, there were fishing communities, but they lived precarious lives. The cliffs, rocks, and currents rendered long stretches of the Irish coast treacherous. According to contemporary sources, big fish were many miles out at sea; currachs were too small to weather the wild Atlantic waves, while larger boats had trouble with rocky seabeds (and timber was in short supply). Distance from markets, poor transport, and irregular supply prevented an industry from developing. Moreover, much of the coast was

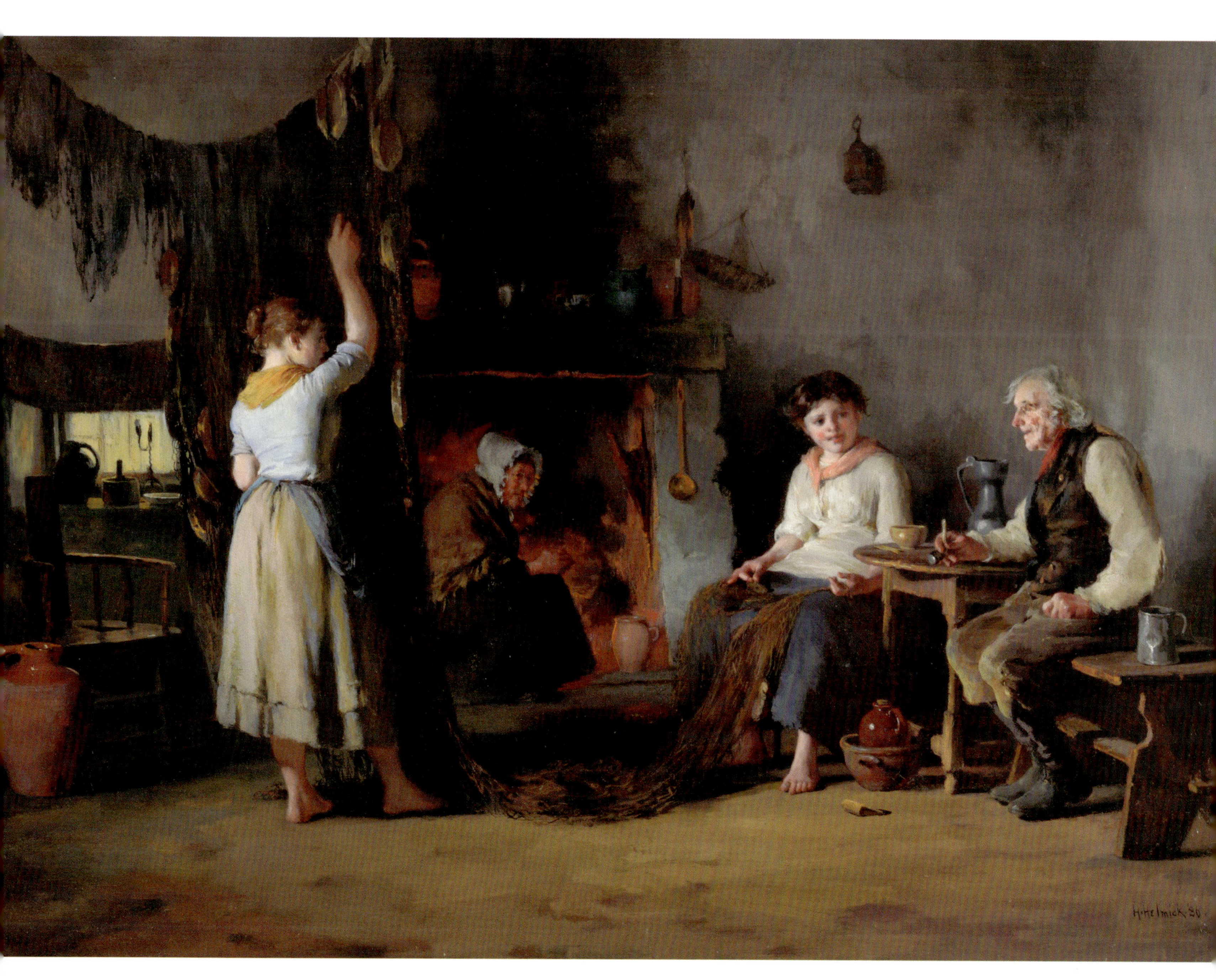
H. Helmick 80

"owned" by landlords, whose tables groaned with salmon, sole, and turbot, while the poor, in their desperation – and in the hope that the following year would yield a successful crop of potatoes – pawned their boats and nets to buy meal. Once pawned, they were difficult to redeem. Even after a successful catch, they were often too poor to buy salt to preserve the fish for their future consumption. At Claddagh in January 1847 (an exceptionally severe winter) "all the boats were drawn up to the quay wall, stripped to the bare poles, not a sign of tackle or sail remaining ... not a fish was to be had in the town, not a boat was at sea".[90] Between the Great Famine and the 1870s, the fishing population of Galway alone was reduced by a third. But when times were better, peasants augmented their diet with herrings found near the shore.

Several British artists who visited Ireland during the Famine featured net making or mending. Nets were valuable assets. As we see, making and mending was women's work. Helmick thus displays not only his technical skill but also knowledge of daily family life. His later images of African-Americans were not dissimilar in approach to his paintings of the country people of Ireland. Barbara Weinberg describes as significant Helmick's move "from history with a pronounced genre component to historical and contemporary 'exotic' genre – peasants, craftsmen, and free blacks".[91]

The American romanticization of Irish poverty was countered in Katherine Tynan's "Irish types & traits", paradoxically illustrated with Helmick's romanticized paintings. Tynan, the nationalist writer, noted as late as 1888 that "one of the most pitiful signs of a workhouse child's degradation [is] that it does not know how to play", going on to observe that it was only "within the last two or three years that the old games of football and hurling were revived ... since the heart of the country received almost its death-blow in the famine of '48 and the resulting exodus". She prayed that "the dances at the cross-roads in summer-time, which were such an innocent and happy feature of the good old times in Ireland, be revived".[92]

Helmick was attuned to such aspirations, setting his paintings in large farmhouse kitchens, like the one in this painting:

The walls and rafters are blackened with the peat smoke, and the whole atmosphere saturated with its most penetrating and clinging smell ... in the wide chimney there are, if the people are well-to-do, hanks of onions and a flitch of bacon; the turf lies on the earthen hearth without any intervention of a grate, and on either side of it are generous seats of banked and cemented clay, where the urchins bask in winter evenings listening to the tales of their elders, till their mottled shins show, as the peasants say, the map of Ireland printed upon them. The furniture is of the simplest: a dresser with gorgeous crockery – there used to be jugs of a certain coppery hue and sheen, which one does not see nowadays ... the whole, lacking the ordered neatness of an English peasant's cottage, but picturesque to a degree, with dancing flame and Rembrandtesque masses of shadow, and highlights on occasional spots of colour.[93]

Helmick did not return home until the early 1890s – "one of the army of the expatriated-charmed – and who shall blame him! – by the ease and comfort of life-abroad, and finding there all the success he needed", as Cook saw it.[94] Back in the United States, "freighted with well-won honors", he became professor of painting and design, and history and philosophy of art, at Georgetown University, Washington DC, and taught at the Washington Art Students' League.

His 1892 exhibition of Irish peasant life at the Reichard Gallery on Fifth Avenue featured "[d]elicious examples of a cheery and refinedly humorous genre" in which "[t]he ghosts of Wilkie and Mulready" were discernible.[95] Throughout Helmick's work "runs a vein of that gayety with which the Irish poor, even in their uttermost misery and destitution, relieve the melancholy of their laborious lives. They are character studies of the truest kind, as well as artistic productions of the first order."[96] Cook thought that it was in Helmick's larger pictures of family groups that he was at his most original, finding there an "[a]rtless nature, free and happy with the happiness that only poverty can know".[97]

Henry, (Emily) Grace Mitchell

(1868–1953)

Not for Grace Henry the romanticized cottages of husband Paul. Crowded and dilapidated, hers are more closely observed. She is the superior colorist, and her broad brushstrokes, heavy outlines, and bold use of impasto show her to be more radical than her more famous husband. They exhibited together and their work was reviewed together, yet Grace was overshadowed and cut out by Paul to the extent that after twenty-six years of marriage he didn't even mention her in either of his (later) biographies. Her modest output (numerically), the absence of letters and papers, and no one to fan the flames of her reputation meant that his prolific output of over 1,350 works (documented by S.B. Kennedy) and the dissemination of his work through posters, prints, and photographs ensured not only a place for him in the canon of Irish art but, to many, the status of national artist, while Grace's often more avant-garde work is overlooked. Even before Mary Swanzy, Evie Hone, and Mainie Jellett, she experimented with abstraction, although never relinquished representationalism. Notwithstanding their differences, personal and aesthetic, the reputations of husband and wife remain entwined, culminating in their joint posthumous exhibition in 1991.[98]

Daughter of a manse, Grace came from a well-off family of ten children. She was brought up in the Scottish Highlands – a landscape that did not excite her artistically – moving to Aberdeen in 1894. She was taught at home, followed probably by finishing school in London, but became estranged from her family. In 1899 she went to Holland and Belgium, and she attended the *académies* Delecluse and Julian in Paris. There, alone and penniless, both of northern Protestant clerical families, Grace met Paul Henry in 1900. In 1901 they moved to London, and married in 1903. Eight years older than her husband, she was Emily to family, Grace or Mrs Paul to others. They lived in Surrey for several years, and from there moved to Achill Island in 1910. In the early years on Achill, partly to experiment with night light à la Whistler, she painted around the old bridge at Dooagh using orange lamps to simulate daylight. She also painted nocturnal landscapes, such as *The Long Grey Road of Destiny*.[99]

Both Paul and Grace were influenced by the French realists, such as Millet; post-impressionists, such as Van Gogh; Whistler, with his simplified forms, sense of pattern and narrow tonal range; and, closer to home, by Synge. Paul's *Potato Diggers* (1910–11) and Grace's *Top of the Hill* (Limerick City Gallery of Art), in their simplicity and breadth of execution, reflect these influences.

Notwithstanding their traditional subject matter, each was cognizant of modernist trends. Wearing her plaid shawl, the heavily outlined woman in this painting, à la Rouault (with whom Grace later exhibited), dominates her environment, dwarfing the cabins, with their tiny windows and doors, stacked one on top of the other. The application of lilacs, grays, and purples, accentuated by Prussian blue and black impasto, are typical of this late Achill period, *c.* 1915–19, during which time she painted the people in a progressively more expressionist manner.[100] The superimposition of the melancholic woman against the diminutive dwellings signals the role of women in surviving harsh island life at the time. In fact the *Freeman's Journal* noted in her work "the wistful loneliness of the West" (April 9, 1919). That Grace executed two versions suggests that the lone figure resonated with her personally.[101]

In 1913 the Henrys were offered Corrymore House, former home of the infamous Captain Boycott, but were unable to buy it; it was subsequently purchased by the American Robert Henri, but, strangely, there appears to have been little contact between the three artists. Described as a vivacious, passionate, outgoing woman, Achill was purgatory for Grace, and their marriage became strained. In 1919 they moved to Dublin. The Dublin art scene was controlled by the conservative Royal Hibernian Academy, leading them to found the Dublin Painters' Society in 1920, which included among its membership Jack B. Yeats, Mary Swanzy, Harry Clarke, Mainie Jellett, and Charles Lamb. Shortly after, in 1924, Grace – then aged fifty-six – briefly studied with French artist André Lhote, but remained more Fauvist than cubist.

Grace and Paul continued to exhibit together, but with mixed success. In 1931 they separated. She sued him for the restitution of conjugal rights, and was awarded £3 a week alimony, following which she had a romantic association with Stephen Gwynn, with whom she traveled in Europe (later trips were probably financed by Mrs Creed Meredith). Her later work, characterized by bold colors and daring brushwork, was executed in France, Spain, and Italy. She attained levels of artistic creativity akin to that of the Scottish Colourists, who were her contemporaries.

In 1939, at the Calmann Gallery, London, she showed thirty-four paintings to considerable acclaim. Reviewing it, the poet (and later director of the National Gallery) Thomas MacGreevy praised her pictorial quality:

As surely as Verlaine wanted his poetry to be all music, she wants her painting to be all poetry. And she seldom fails to attain it. It may be the obvious, but beautifully realized, poetry of an Irish village street in moonlight, the less obvious but more powerful human poetry of the Rouault-ish Potato Diggers, *it may be the cool serenity of a northern landscape like* Strangford Lough, *or the Mediterranean vivacity of* White Pigeons, *whatever her theme the artist strives to give it the appeal of poetry. Her drawing is sensitive, her colour is invariably harmonious and she has the rare gift of being able to make portraiture as poetic as any other branch of art.*[102]

Subsequently, MacGreevy reviewed her "enchanting" exhibition at the Victor Waddington Gallery, describing her as "the most feminine of painters" and doubting that "we have another artist whose work is marked to such a degree as hers by the sense of the sheer loveliness of paint as a medium of expression":

This is the sort of work that triumphantly and beautifully justifies an artist's existence; for Grace Henry manages to convey the impression that it comes as easy to her to evoke a lovely picture out of a blank canvas as it comes to some women to arrange flowers beautifully in a vase. As a matter of cold fact, however, her technique is a highly-developed instrument of expression. It had to be perfected over years to this pitch of mastery in order to convey the more nearly ultimate, and, therefore, less easily attainable, realities to which, cutting through mere everyday accidentals, the artist's vision penetrated ... where everything is as delicately in harmony with everything else as the strands of sound in a quartet by Debussy or Borodin.[103]

For all her *joie de vivre* and painterly exuberance, she ended life a sad and lonely figure.

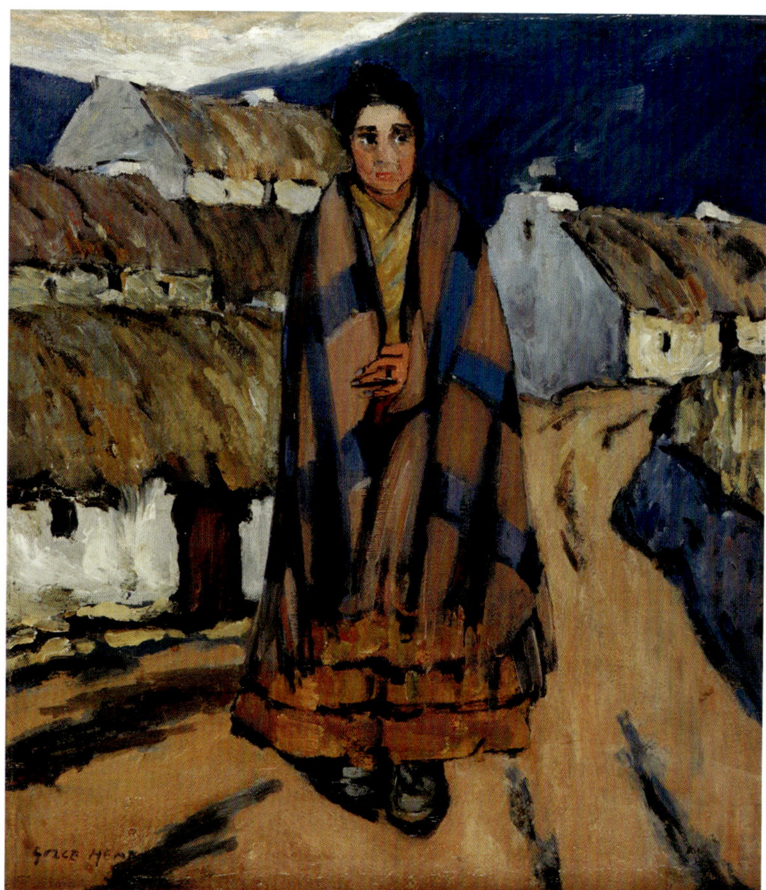

Lady of the West (previously known as *In the West of Ireland* and *Woman of Connemara*), c. 1912–19
Oil on canvas, 18 x 14 in (42 x 36 cm)

Henry, Paul

(1876–1958)

"Time ... has taught me that I can never be really happy if away for very long from, at least the sight of, the mountains, and the proper setting for the vast declivities and the purple shadows is the light on the cottage wall at evening, when the sun is in the west, and the rooks are trailing lazily home", Henry reminisced in his autobiography.[104] Given such desideratum, most of Henry's work was set in the west of Ireland.[105]

Henry's father was a Baptist minister in Belfast who converted to the Plymouth Brethren, ensuring a strict childhood for his sons. His grandfather, Rev. Barry, preached in Achill as part of Edward Nangle's mission there in the 1830s. Henry's northern evangelical Protestant background – against which he rebelled – would have resonated with the Protestant mission that offered food for conversion to Catholics during the Famine, and which continued its mission for many years after.

In 1898 Henry went to Paris, home of the avant-garde, where he studied with Jean-Paul Laurens at the Académie Julian and at Whistler's Académie Carmen with Alphonse Mucha. He was influenced by Millet and the impressionists, and especially Cézanne and Van Gogh, who "took visible nature, and by alchemy distilled by themselves, turned it into something entirely different".[106]

In Paris he sported "a mass of brown curly hair which I wore very long, a black velvet jacket of unusual cut, a green velvet waistcoat, also of unusual cut, very baggy peg-top trousers and an enormous black bow tie".[107] And here he met Grace, his artist wife, whom he married in London, where they became part of the Fitzroy Street Group that included William and Albert Rothstein and Walter Sickert. While working as an illustrator there, he knew the then dealer and collector Hugh Lane, who encouraged him to return to Ireland.

In 1910 the Henrys went to Achill on the recommendation of Paul's friend Robert Lynd; they remained there for nine years. Early work, such as *The Potato Diggers* – painted under the influence of Millet and Van Gogh – showed concern for the social conditions of the poor, but gave way to people-less landscapes from the 1920s, suggesting a resistance to change and a covering up of the ongoing "hungry bareness of things", as Lynd described it. Despite idyllic appearances in Henry's paintings, life in the west of Ireland, fourscore years after the Famine, remained shockingly harsh. Henry noted that for the inhabitants it "would be simply impossible were it not for the money coming in from [relatives in] America".[108] Yet the rye-thatched, whitewashed cottages Henry painted, over and over, with two or three windows and two chimneys, were four star, and, in reality, few and far between.

Notwithstanding the terrible poverty, Henry felt at home there, claiming a "deep buried ancestral feeling".[109] Yet for all his romanticization, his description of the living conditions of his friend Michael Mangan shows that he was well aware of the truth:

There was just one miserable room and the cabin ... was falling to pieces from age and neglect. On one side, where it threatened to fall over into the garden, it was shored up with baulks of timber, driftwood picked up on the strand. The one window was about two feet square and was built in and could not be opened, and the only ventilation came through the door which was always open as it helped to lighten the gloom of the interior. The chimney had partly fallen in and the room was always full of smoke. The roof had not been freshly thatched for years ... and the whole thing leaked abominably.

To the left of the ruined hearth stood Michael's bed, just a few planks covered with straw, sheets of brown paper, sacks and old rags and raised a foot or so from the earth floor which often held pools of water from the dilapidated roof.[110]

As Seán Ó Faoláin put it, "No man can look on the lovely face of Connemara without feeling the tragedy of mortal impermanence, the harshness, indeed the unfairness, of the struggle between man and nature which wears him out and outlasts him." "Lost" was the word he used: "lost islands, lost land, lost consciousness, lost time".[111] But the sense of timelessness that emanates from Henry's paintings is aesthetic rather than ideological, historical, or political – surprisingly so, given the upheavals of his time.

Whether it be the hush before dawn or the murmur of sunset, in Henry's work the dominant sky, the mountains in the distance, the bog stretching far and wide, the hand-won turf stacked against the gable walls sought to redress the defects Rosa Mulholland observed. To his critics his work is formulaic and repetitive; Ó Faoláin, however, perceived him as "an Impressionist *au font*", noting his "sure observation of nature", and, insofar as his work is about "light caught in a flux", argued that "he never repeats himself".[112] Although his landscapes portray a sense of fidelity, Henry was not interested in accuracy, which he described as "a very minor virtue"; he said "it was not the thing seen ... but how you saw it" that mattered.[113] The novelist Mulholland concurred:

Whether it be due to the scantiness of our sunshine, and the coldness of our atmosphere ... too many brushes seem to have learned a trick of moderating the hues of the prism with an infusion of soot. In a land of rain, cloud and mist, we crave for the sun; yet these artists grudge us a little warmth, as though the sunlight were a sin. After all, our sun does sometimes shine and when it shines our artists ought to paint. When it does not shine, they ought to have recourse to the stores which they limned in a happier season.[114]

Henry professed himself "crazy" about Whistler. His use of aerial perspective and strong patterning, verging on the abstract – turf stacks echoing mountains – are Whistlerian. Typically, Henry structured a two-part division of the picture plane, with a prominent cloudy sky characterized by a narrow tonal range, with a heavy application of luscious pigment. He was red-green color-blind – he rarely painted sunrise or sunset – and by 1945 had lost his sight.

Synge's *Riders to the Sea* resonated with Henry. The veracity and sincerity of their respective work was striking. Synge "touched some chord which resounded as no other music ever had done", said Henry.[115] Correspondingly, Henry's autobiographical account of life long after the Famine described houses

of one room or at the most two; in this all the family lived; and one could sometimes see a cow and a couple of calves and a donkey, not partitioned off but just living in the same room as the family. The hens found their resting places on the rafters; I need not say that the atmosphere was foul, and the manure from the cattle was forked out every day and thrown to one side.[116]

And yet the dignity, good taste and sturdiness of character of its inmates shone through for Henry. "Lift the latch in any promising house, and share the hearth with these people ... for nowhere are such warm, hearty, hospitable folk as beyond the Shannon", wrote Ó Faoláin.[117] The *Freeman's Journal* said that Henry "redeemed from sordidness [the] unkempt cabins", so that they become "not merely dignified but epical, a symbol of the spirit of the West".[118]

One third of the native Irish population was either killed or shunted to Connacht by Cromwell's forces between 1641 and 1652. In time Irish nationalists and literary revivalists came to see the west as the repository of Ireland's ancient language, culture, and spiritual values. In *Twelve Irish Artists*, Thomas Bodkin identified landscape painting as the litmus test by which the progress of any national school could be rated; he ranked Paul and Grace Henry among the greats.[119] The identification of Henry's paintings with the spirit of the west was reinforced in 1925 when the London, Midland and Scottish Railway Company published a poster of his *In Connemara*; distributed across Europe and the United States, it sold almost a thousand copies, and two more posters were commissioned. Contemporary debates gave rise to the notion of a distinct school of Irish painting, many focusing on Paul and Grace Henry as "reformers who have established a new intellectual and artistic tradition in Ireland".[120]

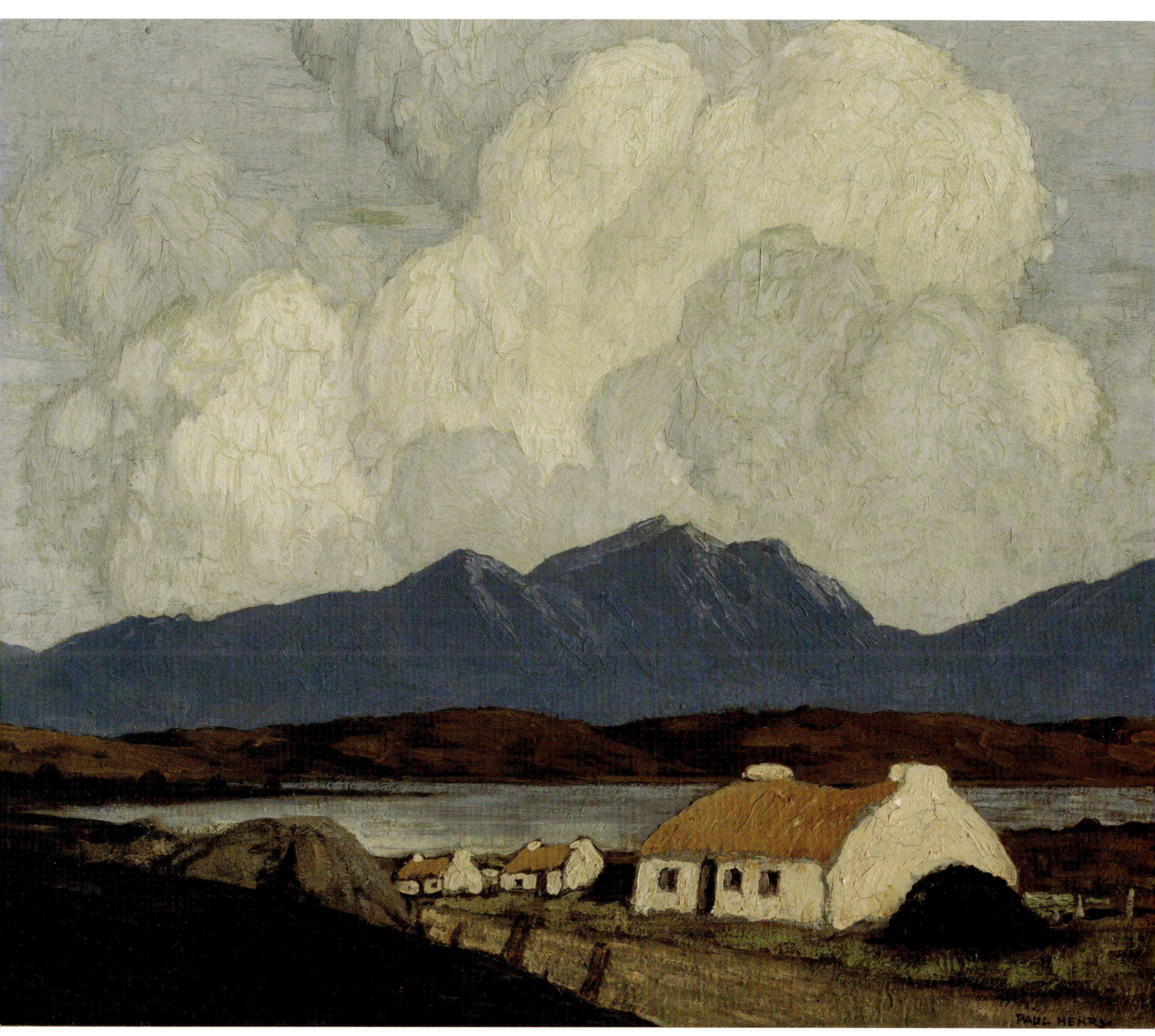

Cottages, West of Ireland, c. 1928–30
Oil on canvas, 22 x 26 in (56 x 66 cm)

Irish School

The Connemara Spinner, c. 1840
Oil on canvas, 25 x 29.9 in (63.5 x 76 cm)

Contrary to the negative portrayal of the Irish at the time, this painting is a paean to industriousness, decency, and respectability, probably of the Protestant rather than Catholic variety.

As Claudia Kinmonth's research shows, this interior is rich in the material culture of a well-off, "strong" Connemara farmer and his family in the immediate pre-Famine period.[121] At the end of a busy day, the farmer lights his pipe with a turf ember taken from the fire on the floor. His top hat sits on a ladder leading up to a capacious half loft. Above his head hangs a horseshoe, for good luck. The women wear madder-dyed petticoats typical of the west of Ireland. The mother, balancing on a 'creepie stool', reaches into the cast-iron cooking pot. The number of domestic vessels signals a substantial household that boasts of implements in every possible material: a cooper-made metal-hooped tub (used as both washtub and soup or stew pot); a rolled-top tin can (used to carry water from the well); blue-and-white willow-patterned ceramic meat platters, cups, and teapots; a broom and baskets (some shop bought, others home-made); wooden-hooped coopered vessels; a large noggin for eating or drinking; a piggin for carrying; a huge jug; and large, black-glazed earthenware vessels (probably "Buckley ware" imported from England).

The studious boy is charming. As ink, quill, and book attest, this family is educated. The operation since 1831 of a National school system meant that, by 1841, literacy, at twenty-eight per cent, was comparatively high. At stake now was denominational control. The evangelism of the Church of Ireland, manifested in the despised corruption of "souperism" (luring Catholics to convert for food during the Famine), versus the muscle-flexing of newly liberated crusaders following Catholic Emancipation in 1829 resulted in stark sectarian lines. The Church of Ireland, though the minority Church, operated in close association with the gentry, and dominated civil administration. It was dedicated to English interests in Ireland, and was maintained by tithes paid by penurious Catholics (unpaid contributions resulted in confiscation of livestock), giving rise to much ill will. *Odium theologicum* was such that, as James Johnson observed in 1844, "the tea of a Protestant grocer would stick in the gorge of a Catholic consumer, and *vice versa*".[122]

Evidence of outside labor is seen in the creel, for carrying turf, and the slane, for digging it from the bog. The presence of the "Connaught pig" - the "long-faced gentleman" - in the interior acknowledges the importance of the pig in the Irish rural economy. The young, bare-headed (therefore unmarried) woman sitting at the "latest" treadle wheel (introduced by government to improve the spinning of flax into thread for linen) is testament to home industry. Kinmonth describes it as "[s]ophisticated compared to the walking wheel usually used for wool". This "low Irish" or Dutch wheel was powered by a treadle; "This freed both the spinner's hands to feed a really fine, even thread onto the moving spindle ... Raised aloft the distaff holds the laboriously prepared flax cleanly within reach, so she can tease out each thread, to spin it."[123]

The fat cat eating his fish, the full pots, and the circular skib (knocked over by the pig) - through which the cascading potatoes would be strained, and from which they were eaten (flavored with salt, buttermilk, and salt herring (seen hanging on the wall)) - suggest abundance. From the head of the house to the baby tucked into the cradle, the scene suggests constancy and continuity in a world that would soon be utterly destroyed by the Great Famine. By 1851 three out of four spinners of cotton, wool, and linen were gone (dead or emigrated), and households of such affluence were decimated in comfort and number.

Aesthetically, this artist is more concerned with displaying his mastery of detail than the overall coherence of the scene, but interior paintings such as this are very rare, and constitute valuable records of Irish social life and mores.

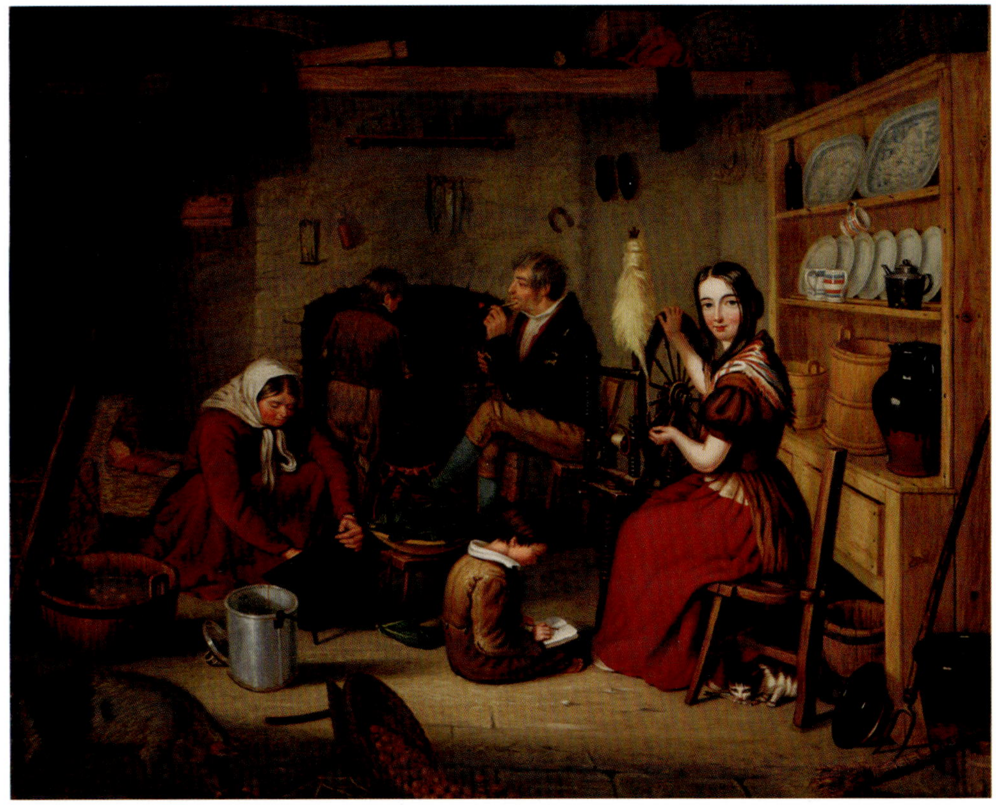

Irish School

Lest We Forget, c. 1880
Oil on canvas, 25 x 34 in (63.5 x 86.36 cm)

The setting is a traditional Irish cottage, where the hearth was the center of the home. Painted in the late nineteenth century, *Lest We Forget* depicts a rural world in the shadow of the Famine but on the verge of change. The painting shows three generations. The elderly man warming his gnarled hands by the fire has had a hard life; he sits apart, engrossed in the past – his thoughts are dark as he tries to keep bad memories at bay. The young woman and the musician, possibly her husband, are living very much in the present. The children and dog are enchanted by the fiddler, who attests to the vitality of Irish culture. The elderly man represents the past; the young woman, arms akimbo, ready perhaps to dance, is modern in demeanor, and the children represent the future.

The painting is about memories of the past and cultural renewal in the post-Famine period. In Överkalix in Sweden, research into the 1831–36 famine there reveals how environmental conditions created chemical markers that attached to genes and passed down the generations. That genes develop "memory" is a new concept. The original study of epigenetics, as this nascent science is called, found evidence that ancestral trauma can be passed down to subsequent generations. The transgenerational connections in *Lest We Forget* are thus perhaps as much physiological and psychological as social and cultural. Cultural memory allows individuals and groups to orient themselves in time and space, and to process transformative historical experiences. Society ensures cultural continuity by preserving its collective knowledge and forms of expression, and passing them from one generation to the next.

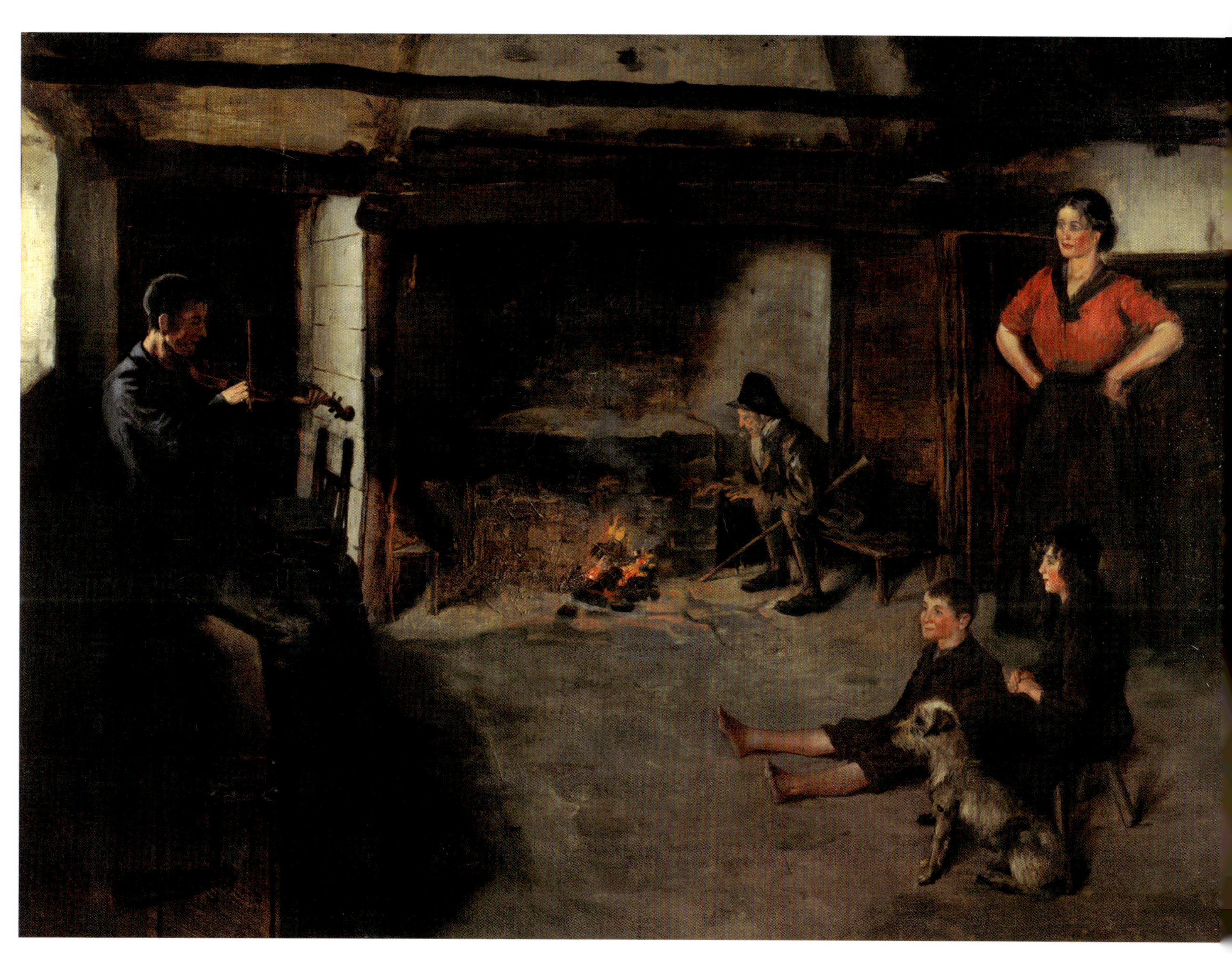

Jones, Sir Thomas Alfred

PRHA (1823-93)

Connemara Girls, 1880
Oil on canvas, 56 x 44 in (142.3 x 112 cm)

From the 1860s Thomas Alfred Jones executed a number of paintings featuring Irish colleens. In its monumentality, *Connemara Girls* is the best of the genre, surpassing perhaps *Molly Macree* (NGI).[124] The word 'colleen' is derived from *cailín*, the "ín" "denoting the diminutive and connoting both affection and junior status, not just in age terms, but, more crucially ... in social standing".[125]

Strickland, unfairly, dismissed Jones's portraits as "commonplace ... poorly painted, mechanical in execution, and without artistic merit", for Jones was an adept.[126] These enchanting colleens, with their lustrous black and red hair, are at once traditional and modern. The symbolic embodiment of Ireland as female has its origins in Celtic mythology. Representations of alluring, young women - the female colonial subject - in pretty peasant attire and posed in beautiful landscapes, took on an allegorical and, at times, political hue, and are indicative of the role of gender in the construction of national identity in nineteenth-century Ireland.

The wind-whipped skirts revealing the bare legs of the girls are more suggestive than most in this genre. The home-spun yarns enlivened by the madder dye connote both rural authenticity and sexual awareness. Shawls tantalizingly offered opportunities for both concealing and revealing the body; the shrouding of the girls on the right suggests modesty, while the bare head and trailing shawl of the girl on the left emphasizes her bodily contours. The impressive scale (and price of £105) of *Connemara Girls* drew admiring attention. The *Freeman's Journal* noted the "lovely ideal picture of three-arch-looking colleens on a country road" in its review of the RHA that year (February 2, 1880).

Unlike images of Mother Ireland or the Maid of Erin, wherein the female figure personifies Ireland, the colleen represents the national feminine ideal, but supposedly in a "real" way. Alluring but chaste, colleens were perceived as civilizing influences on an emerging nation scarred by famine, riven by colonial oppression, and depleted by emigration.

The depiction of three beauties, bathed in summer twilight and set against a

Connemara mountain pass, suggests good times. The girl on the left carries a basket with bread and turf, and all look well fed and happy. But memories of the Great Hunger were very live, as the west of Ireland was once more on the verge of famine in the late 1870s and early 1880s. Significant increases in evictions, rising prices, and severe shortages led to the Land Wars and the formation of the Land League in 1879.

The contrast between youthful, healthy beauty and the emaciation of victims of the Famine that had stalked these same hills not so long before resonates. Indeed, notwithstanding their carefree appearances, the lot of young women was far from easy. For example, in the 1860s more than half those in the Cork Union workhouse were female. Dowries were not to be had; after the Famine, records show a dramatic increase in female destitution and prostitution. And in the absence of dowries, there was an almost seventy-per-cent increase in the number of women entering convents; the alternative was emigration.

Set against the great tapestry of Connemara, the intense pre-Raphaelite type coloring and attention to detail are not unlike Augustus Burke's *A Connemara Girl* (NGI, 1865) and Aloysius O'Kelly's *Girl in a Meadow*, paintings that tie in with a European naturalism, as exemplified by Jules Breton and Jules Bastien-Lepage, showing Jones's knowledge of European trends in art.

Abandoned as a baby, Jones was thought to have been named by his adoptive parents after Henry Fielding's foundling character *Tom Jones.* He attended the Royal Dublin Society Schools. Following a number of years in Europe, during the Famine period, he returned and built a substantial portrait practice. Almost everyone of note sat for him. Urbane, popular, and prolific, he became president of the Royal Hibernian Academy in 1869. He was knighted by the Duke of Marlborough in 1880 – the first Irish artist to be so honored by the British Crown.

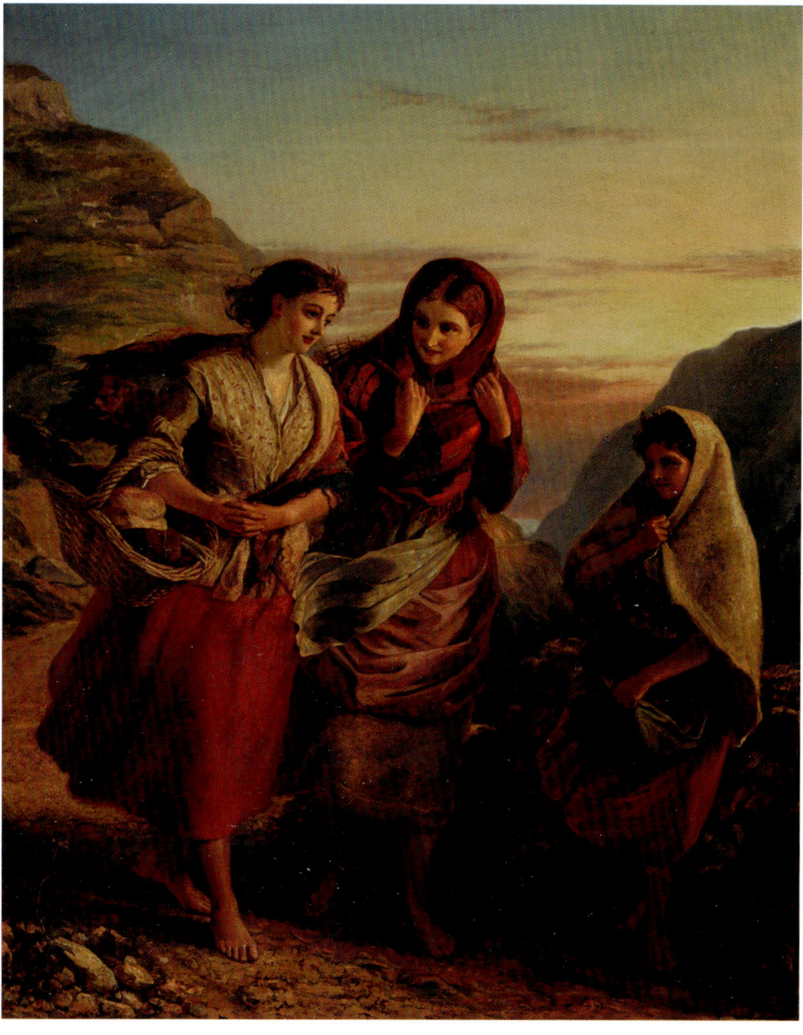

Macdonald, Daniel

(1820–53)

Executed at the height of the Famine, *Irish Peasant Children* does not represent the Famine per se but speaks of it. What might seem like an innocent blend of landscape and genre painting lends itself to interpretations beyond appearances. Aesthetically, the figures are not integrated into the landscape (as convention dictated) but dominate it, suggesting an awareness of the avant-garde art of a Daumier or Millet, who elevated the peasant from walk-on to lead part, with attendant political as well as aesthetic ramifications.

There are many ways of representing hardship other than head on. It was not just that the ravage of famine challenged the skills of artists, but the conceptual frames of reference of the time led artists to adopt shorthand features – tattered rags, spiky hair, and dirt – to imply rather than delineate hunger. The children on the rocky outcrop could be said to represent three faces of Ireland: beautiful, mischievous, and potentially dangerous. The alluring girl in the red skirt and plaid shawl has that Spanish look found in the west of Ireland; the boy behind the rock is quick and wily, and probably a handful; the girl on the left has seen terrible things, and has a desperate air (the bottle in her hand is cocked like a gun). Alone outdoors, all does not bode well for them, and there are no guardians to care for them.

Macdonald was pre-eminently a painter of national character. His figures play music and dance, make *poitín* and get drunk, court and marry, fight and die. His study of rural superstition, *Sídhe Gaoithe/The Fairy Blast* (1842, NFC, UCD), for example, shows how his work was thoroughly anchored in scholarly knowledge of rural Irish life. It is one of the rare paintings to engage with the rites, legends, and superstitions of the Irish – what Sir William Wilde called "the poetry of the people, the bond that knit the peasants to the soil". In its lived form, "folks' lore" allowed people to speak obliquely of events, conditions, or states of mind that may have been difficult to articulate by other means.[127] The painting is thrumming with anxiety and foreboding, an adumbration of catastrophe to come.

Macdonald was also steeped in the knowledge of rural unrest in Ireland. Stories of insurgents and outlaws were part of his boyhood. He knew the rebel ballads of old, not only those adapted for drawing-room entertainment but also the less refined originals, many of which were discovered by his father, James McDaniel. Macdonald's father was an erudite folklorist, painter, caricaturist, inventor, and musician. He was part of a remarkable group of Cork intellectuals that included Thomas Crofton Croker, Samuel Carter Hall, William Maginn, Daniel Maclise, Fr Francis Sylvester Mahony, John Hogan, Jeremiah Joseph Callanan, and others. Through his father and his father's friends, Daniel became aware of both the learned and political debates that animated the time.

But far from the Irish artisan stock they were long assumed to be, the Macdonalds were Scottish bluebloods. When James McDaniel discovered that he was in fact a Macdonald, he reverted to the name, as did his children. As well as being the 8th Macdonald of Castleton, James had a claim to the important Annandale and Hartfell peerage, dormant since 1792. Given complications of legitimacy (and lunacy), he remained a claimant and never an heir; nevertheless, the contention bore fruit when the family relocated to London in the mid-1840s.

Daniel was well informed about the parlous state of rural Ireland in the 1830s and 1840s. The 1798 Rebellion, the post-Napoleonic Wars economic crash, and the not insignificant 1817 and 1822 famines led to mounting unrest, so that the Irish were perceived as inherently rebellious. In addition to bitter sectarianism, rural grievances included tithes extracted from poor Catholics to pay Protestant clergy, conacre (letting small strips of poor land for growing potatoes on disadvantageous terms), high food prices, and low wages. The vast majority were employed on the land owned by a tiny minority. Secret societies retaliated, carrying out savage nocturnal maiming, raping, burning, and murdering that inspired terror in landlords.

In the Lion's Den: Daniel Macdonald, Ireland and Empire, the first retrospective of this artist, took place in the IGHM in 2016, and showed Macdonald to be an audacious artist who evolved a spirited form of realism that countered British stereotypes of Irish people - an acute observer of everyday life and national character.[128] Following the 1800 Act of Union, novelists began to focus on the "national tale", exploring a romantic unity of language, culture, and ethnicity. Macdonald was one of the few artists to visualize these coalescing sensibilities. Wry or deadpan, droll or satirical, he painted the rural story with incisional empathy and humor. But when the Great Hunger took hold, his work assumed more ominous tones. The Famine culminated in the depletion of the population of Ireland by over one half by the end of the nineteenth century. While eviction and emigration were painted (albeit infrequently), the Famine itself was not. Macdonald's *Irish Peasant Family Discovering the Blight of Their Store* (1847, NFC, UCD) was exhibited in London in 1847, and drew unequaled attention to the most cataclysmic event of the epoch. Macdonald returned to Ireland that year and traveled around the south and south-west, where he encountered scenes of unrepresentable distress, accounting no doubt for the somewhat hyperbolic tone of the painting. In 1966 the pioneering Famine scholar Cecil Woodham-Smith donated this only known painting of the blight to the National Folklore Commission.

Macdonald sometimes succeeded in making the local epic. The idyllic landscape in *Irish Peasant Children* is reminiscent of the classical serenity of a Claude, but, in Romantic mode, the swirling mist and gathering storm represent the national tragedy in train. To paint a subject as troubling as the Great Irish Famine for British audiences was a challenge. Macdonald was adept at insinuating nuanced narratives into the salons of Britain. The seductive beauty of a painting such as this would have made it palatable to audiences normally hostile to Irish material of this nature. It is interesting, therefore, that the painting was owned by the family of the revolutionary republican Constance Gore-Booth (later Countess Markievicz), a painter herself and whose discerning eye would not have been blind to strains of both beauty and terror in the Irish landscape.

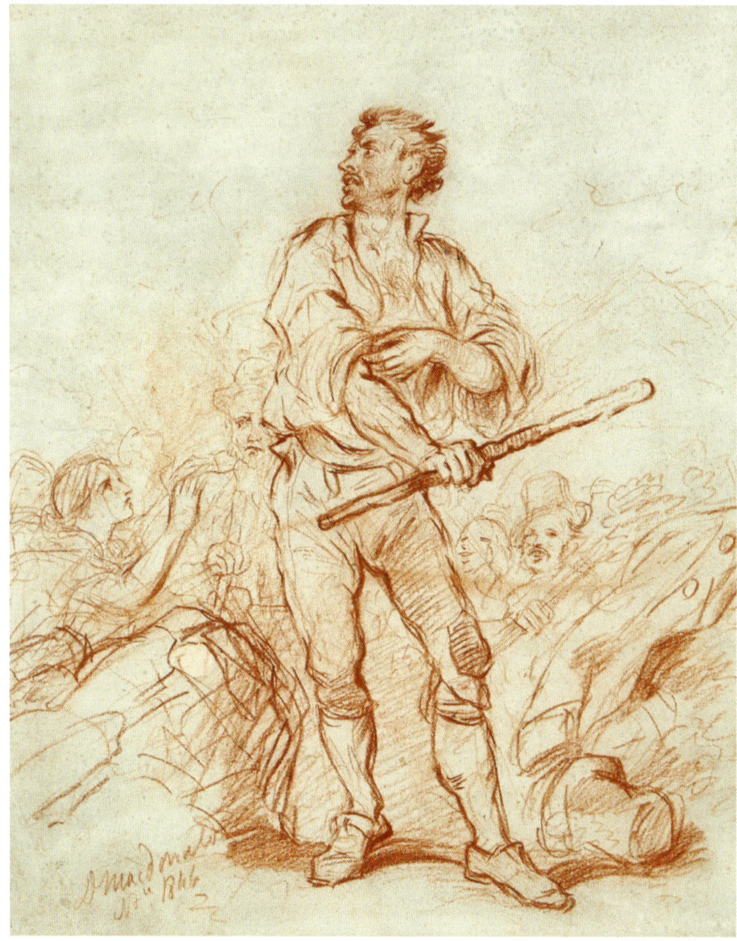

The Irish Faction Leader (preparatory sketch), 1844
Red chalk on paper, 18 x 14 in (45.72 x 35.56 cm)

Irish Peasant Children, 1846
Oil on canvas, 24 x 20 in (61 x 50.8 cm)

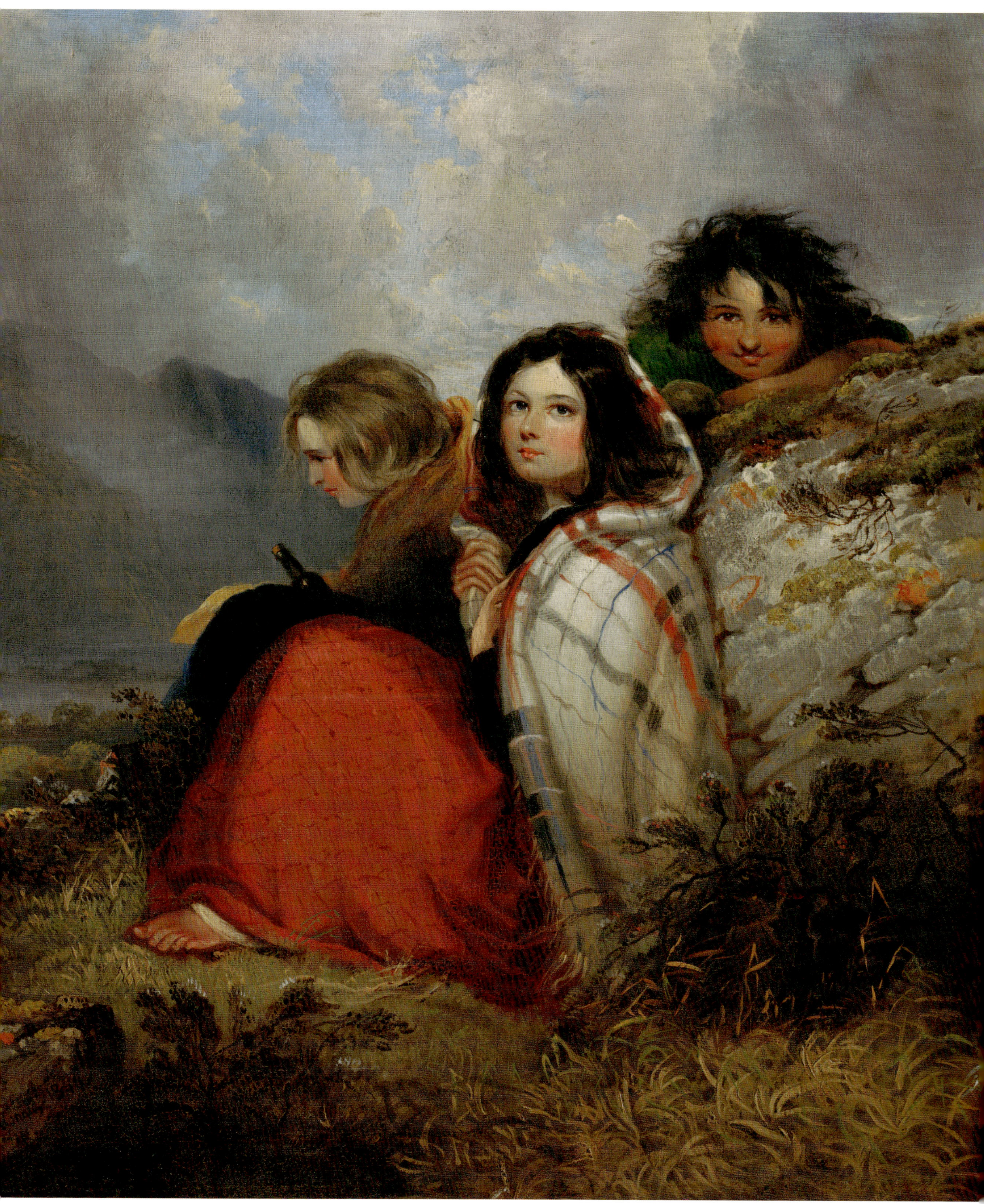

Magrath, William

(1838–1918)

In 1904 Magrath's tribute to Thomas Moore, *The Harp That Once Through Tara's Halls*, was exhibited in the National Academy in New York. The *Daily Tribune* described a "huge, overcrowded and very poorly painted composition" (January 2, 1904), but it was ecstatically received in Ireland, where, it was argued, it should "adorn a historic building in the event of the realisation of national aspirations".[129] The lost painting took four years to complete, and was considered "accurate in every detail".[130]

Having attended the Cork School of Art, Magrath emigrated in 1855 as a seventeen-year-old stowaway. He worked as a sign painter in New York, became a night porter at a hotel, and enrolled in the National Academy's antique class in 1865. Soon he had a studio and was specializing in sentimental scenes of Irish rural life, although he also painted classical subjects à la Alma-Tadema.

Magrath was a member of the American Watercolor Society from 1868, exhibited at the National Academy of Design, and was elected an academician in 1876, becoming chairman of the academy's hanging committee in 1878, when, according to the *New York Herald Tribune*, he kept up "the good old tradition by which hanging committees, since time began, have thrown delicacy to the winds and looked out unblushingly for number one" (February 2, 1878).

Although occasionally faulted for "want of vigour", the American critic Samuel Benjamin flatteringly – if somewhat inflatedly – compared Magrath to William Mount and Jean-François Millet, seeing "inimitable humanity" as his subject. Benjamin observed that his compositions "command sincere attention ... we see him [as] one of the strongest artists in genre on this side of the Atlantic".[131] His fashionably sentimental paintings of Irish peasants, *Paddy's Honeymoon* (1879), *Ah Rory, Be Aisey, Don't Tease Me No More* (*c.* 1865) (from Samuel Lover's *Rory O'Moore*), and *On the Old Sod* (1879, Metropolitan Museum of Art) charmed many. However, instead of being patronized by the wealthy Irish in America, Magrath

found, to his disgust, that our "nouveaux riches" of Hibernian extraction are extremely sensitive on the score of their humble antecedents, and some who really enjoyed his cleverly depicted scenes of cabin-life were afraid to hang them in their homes, lest their fashionable friends might take them to be family souvenirs.[132]

Magrath lived a peripatetic existence. He traveled around Europe, painting in Belgium, Holland, and Italy. From 1879 to 1883 he was in London and exhibited at the RA, the Royal Institute of Painters in Water Colours, and Manchester City Art Gallery. Over the next two decades he moved between Washington DC, New York, Ireland and England. He returned to Ireland regularly. He exhibited three pictures in the 1883 Cork Industrial Exhibition: *Thinking it Over (The Land Question)*, *The Green Fields of Erin*, and *The Seaweed Girl*, indicative of his ongoing interest in broader Irish political and social issues. There was complexity to Magrath's intentions, if not his execution. The description of his work as "racy of the soil" invokes the epigraph for the *Nation,* signaling that newspaper's support for the struggle for the land that marked every aspect of life in Ireland in the nineteenth century.[133]

According to *Munsey's Magazine* (July 1894),[134] following the Phoenix Park murders in 1882 he was "so deeply moved by what he regarded as a stain upon the fair name of his native island, that he resolved thenceforth to find other subjects for his brush" (a promise he did not keep). Just quite how "moved" is unknown, but during the 1880s he was under surveillance for the explosions in London carried out by Irish and Irish-American militants. Moreover, while living at Bedford Gardens artists' studios he was named in association with the Whitechapel murders in the chief constable's Special Branch Register as a possible "undesirable":

McGrath, William - suspicious Irishman at 57 Bedford Gardens

McGrath, William - said to be connected to Whitechapel murders.[135]

To complicate matters, Magrath met the Russian occultist and spirit medium Madame Blavatsky, and became involved with the Theosophists.

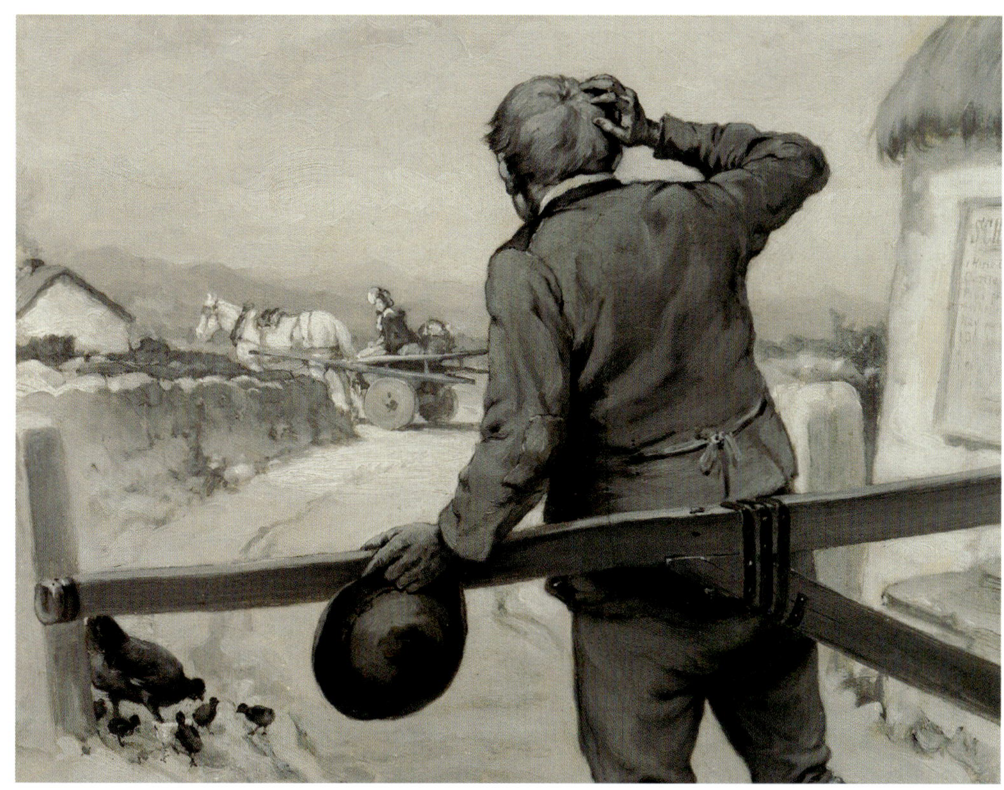

The Farewell, n.d.
Oil on canvas, 11.25 x 13.25 in (28.5 x 33.5 cm)

Maguire, Brian

(b. 1951)

Maguire's early work focused on the male figure, often himself, alone, anxious, alienated. He is one of the group of Irish New Expressionists that emerged in the mid-1980s, and which was denounced by *Irish Times* critics Brian Fallon and Desmond MacAvock. The former condemned "the excretion of enormous amounts of loose paint ... applied to canvases the size of cricket pitches in brash, slovenly ... and distinctly unappealing ways" (October 17, 1984), while the latter descried the "slap-dash figure drawing masquerading as angst but only succeeding as turgid banality" (October 24, 1984) – appraisals that Maguire and friends rejected as the "wilful complicity with those arbiters of art in Ireland whose personal (not to mention economic) interests lies in the malodorous influence of the post-academic art world of the Fifties and Sixties and its present day practitioners" (*Irish Times*, November 7, 1984).

Now acknowledged as an artist of international stature, he is motivated by social issues of injustice and exclusion. Maguire's lineage – historic, aesthetic, political – includes Edvard Munch and Vincent Van Gogh, George Grosz and Francis Bacon, Joseph Beuys and Leon Golub. In its earlier guise expressionism was denounced by the Nazis as degenerate, at least, as Donald Kuspit puts it, "by the standards of ordinary pictorial propriety". In Maguire's hands it is "crude and violent, and even ugly". That such an expressionism "is still viable, indicates that the storm-and-stress mentality inseparable from it – an art expressive of rage and determined by outrage – still makes socio-emotional sense at this time in Western history ... [and] signals that the century's inhumane reality can still arouse apocalyptic emotions".[136]

Maguire's paintings emanate violence, intensity, unhappiness; the pigment is applied thickly, coarsely, viscerally; the gesturing is aggressive, paranoid, savage; the effect is overpowering, unpredictable, provocative; the physicality is animated, painterly, primeval. In *The World Is Full of Murder,* reds, blacks, and browns are smeared, splattered, and striated. The body parts are splayed, foreshortened, and fragmented. "What interested me at the time", he says, "was the physicality rather than the spirituality of the deaths."[137] It shows a bunch of bodies "mangled – murdered – by their own pathos" beside and on top of each other in a ditch.[138] The absence of a horizon reduces depth, so that the figures seem close to the viewer. The painting has its origins in newsreel footage of Nazi atrocities that he saw as a twelve-year-old at his local cinema. Having dodged the censor's age restriction and played truant from school, he couldn't admit to what he saw at home, making the impact all the more traumatic. The painting was also based on a photograph of people who died from starvation in Eastern Europe in the 1940s, and was dedicated to the essayist Hubert Butler, whose *Children of Drancy* (1988) inspired Maguire to follow in his footsteps through Eastern Europe, evoking the 4,051 Jewish children deported from Drancy and murdered in Auschwitz. The title is from a Hitler Youth marching song in which young Nazis anticipate their own glorious deaths: "Oh restless journeyer, beware, beware, the world is full of murder!" This resonated with Maguire as the killings in Northern Ireland continued in the 1980s.

The painting functions on several levels: personal, political, historical. Kuspit suggests that Maguire's gesturalism

has much to do with the Irish situation, in which the normal human condition of inner conflict between the instincts and the superego has been exacerbated by a prolonged battle for self-determination and self-expression against various oppressive authority systems and institutions, whether from the colonial past or the Catholic present.[139]

Maguire says the painting is

pertinent to the Irish Famine, as deaths from hunger in a world with excess food supplies is murder. Food was exported from Ireland during the Great Hunger. There was enough food available then (and now) to feed everyone but its availability to the poor (and to poor countries) is determined by factors other than hunger and need. In my view, where death from hunger exists in the world in the 21st century it is a crime committed by all of us who are in secure situations. The Irish experience is mirrored today in the famine experience of the poorest countries. It is the collective memory of the 1847 famine that enables us to hold this gaze on contemporary famine.

For Maguire the Irish Famine is thus linked across time and around the globe. He had previously explored the theme in *Child Looking for Six Grains of Rice in Uganda* (1982, Ed and Nancy Kiehholz Collection). As a committed artist and visual commentator, he believes in the capacity of art to express political, social, and humanitarian concerns. He identifies with the outsider, and engages with the poor and dispossessed, representing them and facilitating their representation of themselves. Since 1987 he has worked as artist-in-residence in jails in Portlaoise, Spike Island, Matsqui in Vancouver, and Bayview in New York. In the case of adult criminals, Maguire sees his work with them as re-humanizing. He had a residency in Long Kesh/Maze during the implementation of the Good Friday Agreement, painting portraits of members of the Ulster Defence Association, the Irish Republican Army, the Ulster Volunteer Force, and the Irish National Liberation Army alike.

He exhibited his own work alongside that of prisoners at the White Box Gallery, New York, at the same time as a billboard in Manhattan depicted portraits of a number of female prisoners, liberating the art from the citadel of the cultural world. He was invited to represent Ireland at the XXIV São Paulo Biennial in 1998, where he had a residency in a shantytown. Here, in the Centro Cultural Vila Prudente, founded by Irishman Pat Clarke, a Holy Ghost priest who works with the Movement for the Defence of Favela Residents, Maguire worked with some forty-five children. He combined portraits of them with portraits based on newspaper photographs of convicts. Thomas McEvilly says, "As his commitment to both streams of portraits intensified, it became a private performance which he carried out with virtually religious fervor; he would sometimes work for several days on one of the newspaper based pictures, remaining very isolated, talking to no one."[140] His exhibition for the biennial included images of their impoverished homes, in which the portrait was an unusual feature, making the connection between their young lives and the lives of their older neighbors in prison. Maguire understands crime as the product of poverty. In Brazil innocent children brutalized by poverty become criminals; then, as convicts, they are murdered by the forces of order, images of their corpses emblazoned across newspapers. Drawing them "is an act of love", he says.

To "be authentically – existentially – individual in Ireland today", Kuspit suggests,

one must rebel against it in spirit the way it once politically rebelled against England. The spiritual revolt which Maguire's paintings represent can be read as an aesthetic – political rebellion ... Maguire's angry Expressionist paintings give the lie to the happiness of Irish life and betray the fabled Irish Romanticism. In this, they are violently adversarial.[141]

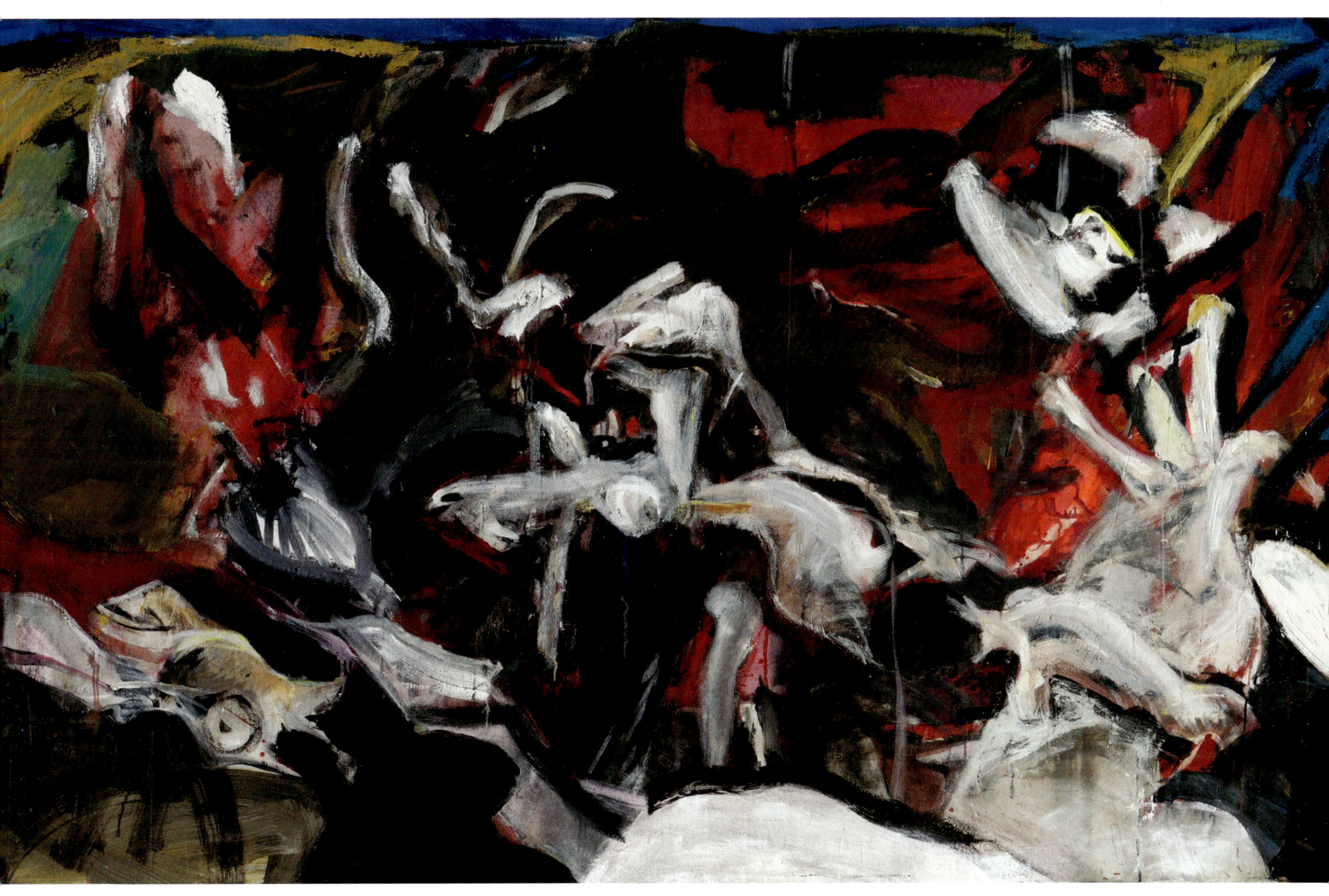

The World Is Full of Murder, 1985
Acrylic on canvas, 53 x 87 in (134.62 x 221 cm)

Mahony, James

ARHA (*c.* 1810–59)

Attempts to disentangle the artist James Mahony (*c.* 1810–59) from the artist James Mahoney (1847–79) (note different spellings of their surnames), both watercolorists and illustrators, have hitherto been inconclusive. If not one and the same, it has been suggested that they may have been father and son. Mahony, the Cork artist - it has been said - moved to London in 1859, where he became a prominent illustrator of magazines and Charles Dickens's work, and died in 1879. However, Dickens's illustrator was categorically *not* the Cork artist, but an uneducated London waif who became a draughtsman, and the Dickens illustrations were produced after Mahony's death in 1859. The confusion continues to cause misattribution in the case of their respective paintings.

Mahoney's work displays an awareness of social realism, but tends towards sentimentality, and, as Reid puts it, "bad drawing and debased faces were regarded by Mahoney as amusing". Not, then, to be confused with the Cork Mahony - a different proposition. In the 1880s Vincent Van Gogh purchased some illustrations. In a letter to his brother Theo (September 9, 1882), he described them as by James Mahoney, an "excellent draughtsman" who illustrated Dickens's *The Adventures of Oliver Twist, Little Dorrit* and *Our Mutual Friend* (Household edition, 1871), and, in another letter (October 22, 1882), he told Anton Van Rappard that these illustrations were "very beautiful". Although these were by Mahoney, coincidentally the purchase also included a sheet by Mahony, *Sketches in the West of Ireland* (for the *ILN*, February 20, 1847).

Friend of Maclise, Hogan, Brown, Frith, and other Victorian greats, the Cork Mahony was a regular at the levees at Dublin Castle, a guest of fashionable houses and diplomatic circles, and honorary consul in Uruguay and Honduras.[142] Mahony was friendly with Captain G.A. Taylor, who purchased many of his paintings and bequeathed a sum of £400 for the purchase of more of his work, to be executed in Spain (duly delivered to Taylor's trustees and now in the NGI).

Following several years traveling in Europe, in 1841 he returned home. He and fellow artist Samuel Skillen established the Cork Art Union for the purposes of annual exhibitions and the awarding and presentation of prizes.

Mahony painted church and literary subjects, genre paintings, and panoramic city and country scenes. His impressive watercolors include *Queen Victoria and Prince Albert in the Paintings and Sculpture Hall of the Irish Industrial Exhibition, Dublin* (*c.* 1853, NGI) and *Dublin from the Spire of Saint George's Church, Hardwicke Place* (1854, NGI). Among his oil paintings are two magnificent church interiors: *The Church of St. Roch, Paris* (RHA, 1844) and *St. Mary's, Pope's Quay, Cork*.

Notwithstanding his Castle contacts, Mahony was firmly on the side of Repeal. On June 9, 1845, at a demonstration of some 500,000 people in Cork in support of the Liberator, Mahony designed the spectacle. O'Connell's chair, a most elaborate affair, was surmounted by a canopy painted by Mahony representing Justice, Truth, Fortitude, and Prudence. On the car he painted an allegorical painting. And a "splendid" banner designed by the artist was held aloft and carried by the Reformed Corporation of Carpenters, with the motto "Be Just and Fear Not" and in a gold square the word "Repeal". The mass meeting "Declaring for Nationality" was "magnificent in its pomp and circumstances", in effect "testifying" to the world that the Irish were "resolved on having liberty and self-government".[143]

It was Mahony who provided the elaborate and moving images of O'Connell's obsequies in 1847. From 1846 to 1853 he was employed as an illustrator and reporter for the *Illustrated London News*. His illustrations broke the cycle of condemnatory commentary on an Irish peasantry believed to be in the grip of savagery and primitivism, and presented to the world a people devastated by poverty and hunger.

During the Famine, while hundreds of thousands were dying, almost 4,000 British vessels sailed out of Ireland laden with foodstuffs for British consumers. At the same time American vessels were sailing into Ireland carrying food that saved many lives. News of conditions in Ireland led to Captain Robert Bennet Forbes sailing from Boston to Cork in March 1847 with 800 tons of foodstuff and twenty-eight barrels of clothing. There, Forbes was presented with an engraved salver and a lithograph, the *U.S. Sloop of War Jamestown* by George Mounsey Wheatley Atkinson, a copy of which was entrusted to Forbes for presentation to the president of the United States. In addition, a banner designed by Mahony was given to Forbes for presentation to the city of Boston. Featuring the American eagle supporting a wreath of shamrocks interspersed with silver stars, in the center of which was the Irish harp in a sunburst, painted on white silk, it was duly presented to Josiah Quincy, mayor of Boston, in gratitude for the "munificent aid to this wretched country, for centuries struggling against indifference, neglect, and oppression, and now visited with the terrible scourges of famine and pestilence".[144]

Mahony's commitment to Cork was unwavering. The French Dominican order was established there in the thirteenth century. Following the dissolution of the monasteries and the confiscation of their property by Henry VIII in 1536, the Dominicans settled near Shandon. As the Penal Laws that prohibited Catholics

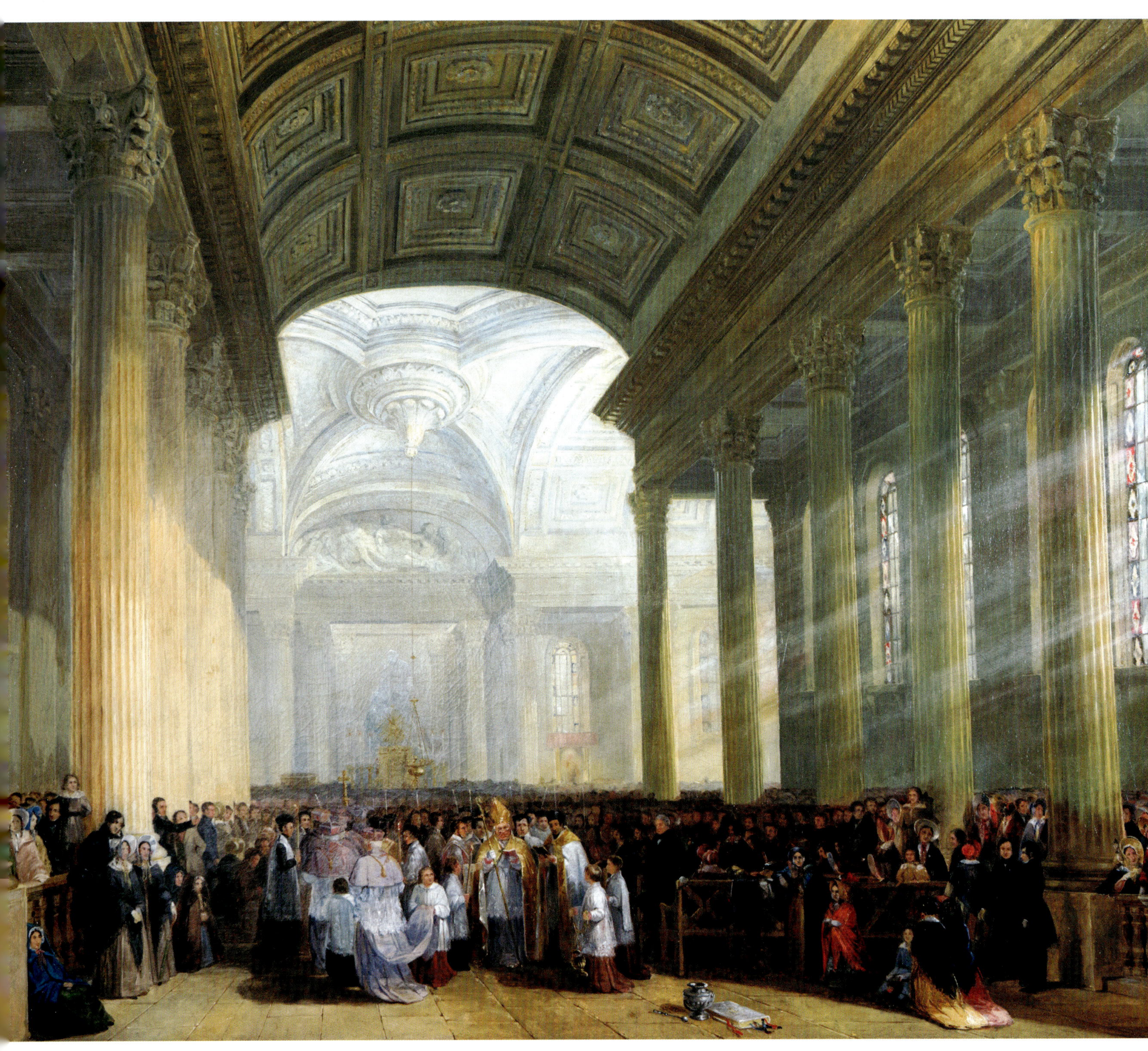

The Consecration of the Roman Catholic Church of St. Mary's, Pope's Quay, Cork, c. 1841
Oil on canvas, 37 x 43 in (95.25 x 109.22 cm)

from practicing were relaxed, and with the granting of Emancipation in 1829, the eruption of church building was a material manifestation of Catholic rights – a second Counter-Reformation. The consecration of St Mary's was an early sign of a resurgent, if not triumphant, Church.

The painting shows the consecration on October 20, 1839. Funding was provided by public subscription, by the Dominicans, and by the brewing firms Beamish & Crawford and Murphy's. It was designed by the Cork Protestant architect Kearns Deane, who gave his services free of charge. At this time, Edward McParland argues, architectural precedents were needed to create a distinctly Catholic building typology, and Paris provided good models: Deane would appear to have been influenced by Saint-Vincent-de-Paul and Ste-Geneviève (the Panthéon).[145] Monsignor James O'Brien believes this is the only depiction of a church consecration in Ireland.[146]

The impressive interior, with its Corinthian columns, elaborate stucco work, and coffered rose ceiling was executed by local craftsmen. Mahony clearly had an interest in ecclesiastical architecture and design, and was an adept at their depiction; indeed, an intriguing letter to the *Southern Reporter* from "an admirer of the arts" attests to Mahony's own involvement in its construction.

I presume you will not deny me the gratification of drawing public attention to a specimen of Architecture, executed by a fellow-citizen, which for elegance of design and exquisiteness of workmanship, would be highly creditable to the first masters of the Italian, I allude to a massive composition column of the Corinthian order, recently erected by Mr. Mahony, in the new Dominican on Pope's Quay. The composition the sole invention of the artist, which, for the splendour of its tone of colour and the durability of its material – surpassing even the purest Portland stone – I conceive unequalled.[147]

The original architecture and interior were important for their date, and the painting shows how the church looked prior to structural and decorative changes in the late 1860s. But, above all, what it says of Catholic Emancipation makes this a painting of great historical significance. Daniel O'Connell, founder in 1823 of the Catholic Association, forged the nexus between Irish identity and Roman Catholicism that remained indivisible well into independence. The Church played an important role in forging the unity necessary for nationalism to play its part in bringing colonialism to an end in Ireland.

Mahony excelled at crowd scenes, and, although executed veduta-style following his sojourn in Rome, the architect himself (Kearns Deane), the archbishop of Armagh and primate of all Ireland, Dr Crolly, and Daniel O'Connell are identifiable. The painting was exhibited at the Cork Art Union in 1841 and the RHA in 1842 (and presented to Kearns Deane in its magnificent frame).

The consecration was in accordance with the *Pontificale Romanum* published by Clement VIII. A change from purple to gold vestments takes place at the beginning of the procession of relics into the church, as we see in the painting. The *Southern Reporter* visited Mahony's studio, and published an article on May 26, 1840:

The action shows the procession on the middle aisle, bending towards the high altar. To the left are seen the Roman Catholic hierarchy of Ireland in pontificalibus, *with the exception of their mitres; they are accompanied by their attendant Priests, Deacons, Acholytes and Train and Torch bearers – the backs only of the individuals who form this portion of the procession are presented to view. The succeeding part of the procession is seen moving onwards towards the front, in the centre of the picture. The most prominent figures in the foreground are the officiating Prelate, the Right Reverend Doctor Murphy, arrayed in splendid pontificals, with his mitre, crozier, and richly-wrought episcopal mantle, resplendent with gold and embroidery, and the Very Rev. Archdeacon O'Keefe – both these figures have breviaries [*Liber Usualis*] in their hands, and are reading the service: they are followed by a long train of Priests and Acholytes, bearing lighted waxen flambeaux, chaunting the service. Directly in front, this group is skilfully broken and relieved by the introduction of boys in white surplices, one of them bearing a censer. The rest of the foreground is filled up with the congregation, amongst whom the portraits of many well-known persons are indiscriminately scattered. To the right of the canvas, in front, is introduced the figure of Mr. Kearns Deane, the architect of this classic edifice; it is a striking likeness of our talented fellow-citizen. ... The colouring of the sun-beams glancing among the columns through the stained windows, and diffusing through the aisles their dim, religious light, is executed in a style indicative of the taste and acumen of the artist.*

For its part, the *Cork Examiner* (December 3, 1841) described the young artist as "a man of decided talent", but, not for the first time, regretted Mahony's faces as "unpleasingly similar". Nevertheless, he is thought here to have resisted "the hateful trammels of the rule system", and "sketched from living nature". The reviewer concluded: "There are some exquisite 'bits' in the foreground, which would of themselves make sweet pictures."

Mulvany, Thomas James

RHA (attributed) (1779–1845)

Strickland declared Mulvany a man of cultivated taste, with a considerable knowledge of the history of art and a brilliant conversationalist, but dismissed his disquisitions in the *Citizen* as "long-winded and wearying".[148] Mulvany advocated a charter of incorporation for Irish artists, and when, in 1823, the Royal Hibernian Academy was founded, he was appointed keeper.

Killarney became a tourist destination in the eighteenth century. Between the upper and lower lakes – a spectacular beauty spot – the 1,700-foot-high Eagle's Nest housed an eyrie of birds. Here, Mulvany shows the Eagle's Nest and Long Range River, with the McGillycuddy's Reeks and Purple Mountain to the north-west.

Viscount Kenmare would hide cannons at strategic spots on the shore, where they could be heard but not seen, and engaged local buglers to draw out the echoes that reverberated from the mountain as if "the emanation of some celestial organ".[149] William Ockenden described the experience:

... suddenly, to our inexpressible amazement, we were surprised with music sweeter than any I had ever heard before ... breaking upon us in short melodious strains, fill[ing] the very soul with transport [until an explosion] rent the mountain with its roar and filled us with the apprehension of being instantly buried in a chaos of hill, wood, and water; but the horror was suddenly dissipated by the return of the same soothing strains which had before enchanted us ...[150]

While there were plenty of poor musicians who marred the experience, Mr and Mrs Samuel Carter Hall described the spellbinding melodies of Spillane:

First he played a single note – it was caught up and repeated, loudly, softly, again loudly, again softly, and then as if by a hundred instruments, each a thousand times more musical that that which gave its rivals both twirling and twisting around the mountain, running up from its foot to its summit, then rolling over it, and at length dying away in the distance until it was heard as a mere whisper, barely audible, far away. Then he blew a few notes – ti-ra-la-ti-ra-la: a multitude of choices, seemingly from a multitude of hills, at once sent forth a reply; sometimes pausing for a second, as if waiting for some tardy comrade to join in the marvelous chorus, then mingling together in a strain of sublime grandeur, and delicate sweetness, utterly indescribable.

The Halls went on to describe the firing of the cannon:

... the match was applied. In an instant every mountain for miles around seemed instinct with angry life, and replied in voices of thunder to the insignificant and miserable sound that had roused them from the slumbers. The imagination was excited to absolute terror ... The sound was multiplied a thousand-fold, and with infinite variety; at first it was repeated with a terrific growl, then a fearful crash; both were caught up and returned by the surrounding hills; mingling together, now in perfect harmony, now in utter discordance; awhile those that were nearest became silent, awaiting the oncoming of those that were distant; then joining together in one mighty sound ... that would seem to have been heard hundreds of miles away.[151]

For over a century and a half, artists such as Jonathan Fisher, William Sadler, George Petrie, Bartholomew Colles Watkins, and Daniel Macdonald attempted a visual articulation of the experience. John Urry's concept of "sacralization" – a process that transforms an object or place of tourist interest to a level of sacredness – is apposite here.[152]

Engulfed, the lingering cadences of both the man-made and natural sounds led Lord Manners to describe how he "listened in a sort of dreamy ecstasy to the wild and mournful notes as they lingered in the air" before coming to his senses and realizing that the whole thing was really a form of social contamination and more suited to the "lower" sort. And, of course, such tourist traps spawned much "fakelore". The "natives" competed to sell "mountain dew", goat's milk, bog oak, and even homespun stockings to the bemused tourists, and enterprising peasants became, if not adept at guiding, adept at importuning – as many as six or eight might attach themselves to a group, causing much annoyance to the conflicted tourists, who grappled with the crowds, swatting away peasants, in search of a pure experience. Killarney thus fueled both the prejudices of critics and assuaged the expectations of reforming thinkers, both reinforcing stereotypes about the Irish and dispelling them.[153]

The growth of a tourist industry, the beginnings of modernization, a dawning recognition of the potency of the place, and the resourcefulness of the people were abruptly ruptured with the Famine. Mulvany captures both Killarney's grandeur and serenity just before.

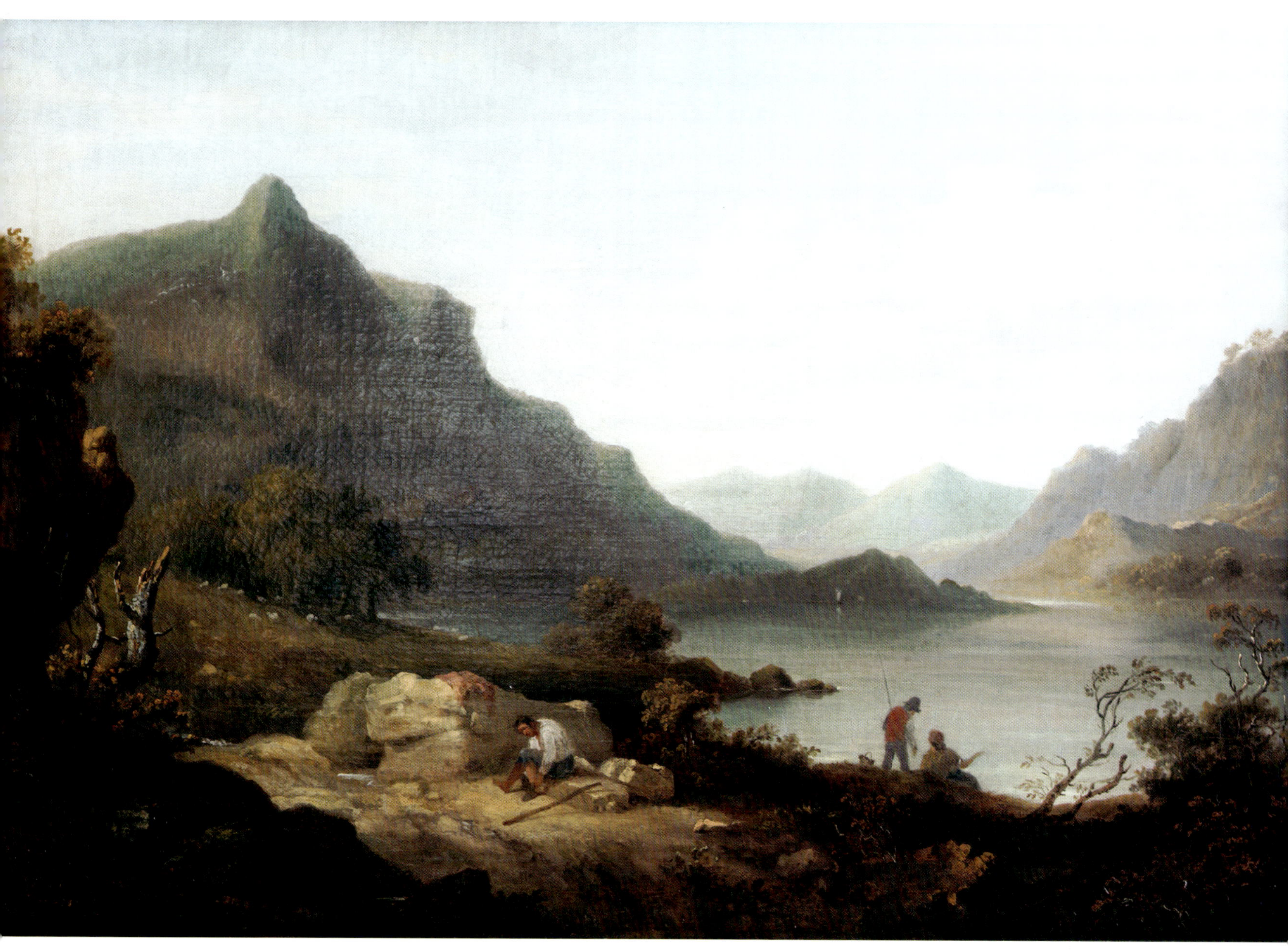

The Eagle's Nest, Killarney, c. 1840
Oil on canvas, 18 x 26.5 in (46 x 67 cm)

Nicol, Erskine

RSA, ARA (1825–1904)

Scottish born, Nicol came to Ireland in 1846 and stayed for four years. He taught in Dublin during the Famine years, and observed deteriorating conditions in both the city and the country. He returned to Scotland, but continued to paint Irish subject matter. In 1862 he moved to London, but in the same year set up a studio on Clonave Island, Lough Derravaragh, County Westmeath, to which he returned regularly.

One of the most prolific painters of the Irish poor, Nicol painted almost 100 Irish subjects. Forelock touching, aggressive, or buffoonish, opinion is divided as to the malevolence of his characterizations: personal bias, commercial imperatives, or comedic pandering to Victorian prejudice? But while racially derogatory images of drinking and dancing, courting and fighting abound, others, such as *The 'Merican Difficulty* (1862, Ulster Museum) (showing an elderly woman seeking a report about the American Civil War for news of her emigrated children) or *An Ejected Family* (1853, NGI) (showing three generations cast out onto the side of the road by a heartless landlord) evince sympathy for those who, at other times, he depicted as benighted.

The Tenant, Castle Rackrent – for all that it is but a single figure in a compressed space – is one of Nicol's more complex paintings.[154] Sitting in front of a map of a landlord's demesne is a farmer, waiting to pay his rent. As Maria Edgeworth's 1800 novel *Castle Rackrent* suggests, the tenant may occupy his meager home at the mercy of his landlord, but this tenant's eye contact asserts his moral and historical rights vis-à-vis the "legal" right of his landlord. Between them is the blunderbuss on the wall, instrument of coercion on the one hand, and potential weapon of liberation on the other.

Nicol's work was widely disseminated in various media. The lithographs *Outward Bound* and *Homeward Bound* portray pre-emigration poverty and post-emigration wealth, suggesting an unlikely eventuality – the simianized emigrant returning home a successful and civilized man. His work was reproduced in the *Art Journal*, published by Samuel Carter Hall, through whom he met Hall's wife, Anna Maria; in

1909 Mrs Hall's *Tales of Irish Life and Character* (1910) was illustrated by sixteen reproductions of Nicol's paintings.[155]

In *A Knotty Point* we see a small community turn an eviction (see the "tumbled" roof in the background) into a jolly picnic. Tables, chairs, and tablecloth (unlikely possessions) have been installed outdoors. The three standing "gents" are barely human and among the worst of caricatures, even by Nicol's standards. The rest, although uncouth, are accorded some redeeming features. As well as commenting on the supposed Irish ability to transcend adversity, Nicol concedes their literacy. Notwithstanding assertions of backwardness, pre-Famine literacy, at twenty-eight per cent in 1841, was comparatively high. By 1851 there were sixty-five provincial newspapers around the country, sustained by mounting levels of literacy due to the operation, since 1831, of the National school system (of which there was no equivalent in England until 1870). Fifty-three per cent of the population was now recorded as literate, with all that that implies in terms of awareness and functioning. In Famine terms, the literate at least knew what relief was available, and even how to emigrate; illiterates and monoglots fared less well.

The well-padded and "tanned' peasants suggest a combination of well-fed-ness, indolence, and lack of hygiene. But for those afflicted by famine conditions, as described by Dr Daniel Donovan, the first person to appraise scientifically the effect of hunger on the human body,

... the face and limbs become frightfully emaciated; the eyes acquire a most peculiar stare; the skin exhaled a peculiar and offensive foetor, and was covered with a brownish filthy-looking coating, almost as indelible as varnish. This I was at first inclined to regard as encrusted filth, but further experience has convinced me that this is a secretion poured out from the exhalants on the surface of the body.[156]

The snub nose, prognathous jaw, and short forehead signaled an "individual of little worth and of low social order", and caused much mirth.[157] However, the *Art Journal* (edited by an Irishman) noted that "the sons and daughters of the Emerald Isle should dislike seeing the grosser features of their poverty and wit turned by Art into subjects of laughter for the amusement of others more socially fortunate" (1861).[158] Even if, as Brendan Rooney says, Nicol was merely conforming to "the current and modish perceptions of particular physical and physiognomic types", does indulging in such stereotypes not confirm his own prejudices?[159] Artists studied the pseudoscience of phrenology in the belief that it would assist in the illustration of the psychology of their characters. Theories of "temperament" at the time described the Celtic race as "prolix", "playful in humours", "credulous in trade", "despairing in danger", and "furious in warfare". Camper's study of the connections between anatomy and art was used to explain how the shape of the skull indicated the degree of evolution of the person, leading to a hierarchy of races and a view that the Irish were low on the evolutionary scale (perhaps even the "missing link").[160] From there Thomas Carlyle saw the Irishman, in his "squalid apehood", become "the sorest evil this country has to strive with. In his rags and laughing savagery, he is there to undertake all work that can be done by mere strength of hand and back; for wages that will purchase him potatoes."[161] Charles Kingsley (responsible for what Joseph Valente called the "most notorious of the simianizing blood libels upon the Irish"),[162] professed to being "haunted by the human chimpanzees" he saw while visiting Ireland in 1860; "to see white chimpanzees is dreadful; if they were black, one would not feel it so much, but their skins, except where tanned by exposure, are as white as ours", he shuddered.[163]

Nicol modified his titles to suit his audiences. His RHA paintings tended to feature more neutral titles, such as *Awarding Prizes in a Village School*, as opposed to more suggestive, phonetic titles – such as *Hould Me or I'll Fight!!!* (RSA, 1852) – that fed anti-Irish prejudice. *Both Puzzled* (1866), for example, features a "carroty-pated youngster, and his no less bamboozled teacher", who, the *Evening Gazette* opined, was no wiser than the child (October 11, 1870). The mimicking legend – "If wanst nought be nothin', then twice nought must be somethin', for it's double what wanst nought is" – was good for a laugh, leading the *Daily Gazette* to declare the master "wonderfully wooden headed" (November 8, 1876). Revisionist appraisals suggest that Nicol has been "misunderstood", but while not all his paintings are offensive, many are.[164] The paunchiness of the *Knotty Point* protagonists and their cheery demeanor belie the reality of a residualized peasantry. Nevertheless, the concession to peasant literacy is not nothing, to coin a Nicolesque phrase.

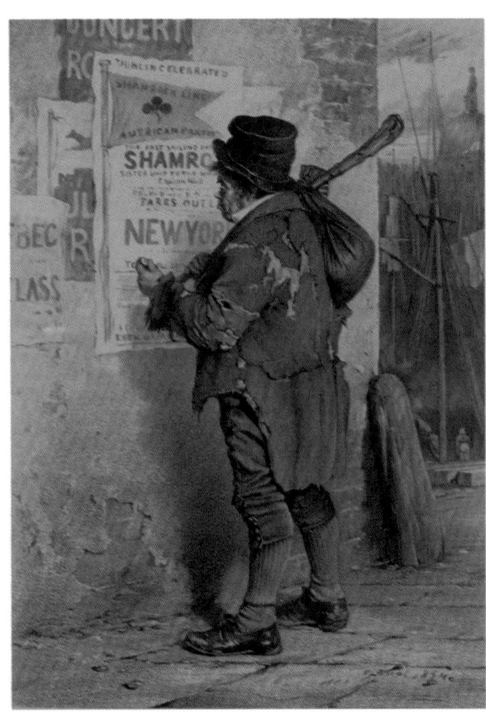

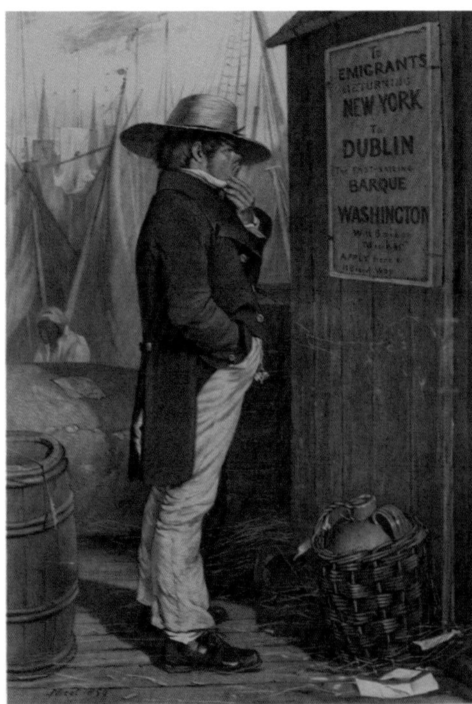

Outward Bound: The Quay of Dublin, 1854
Lithograph, 13 x 9.5 in (33.02 x 24.13 cm)

Homeward Bound: The Quay of New York, 1854
Lithograph, 13 x 9.5 in (33.02 x 24.13 cm)

A Knotty Point, 1853
Oil on board, 11 x 14.25 in (27.94 x 36.19 cm)

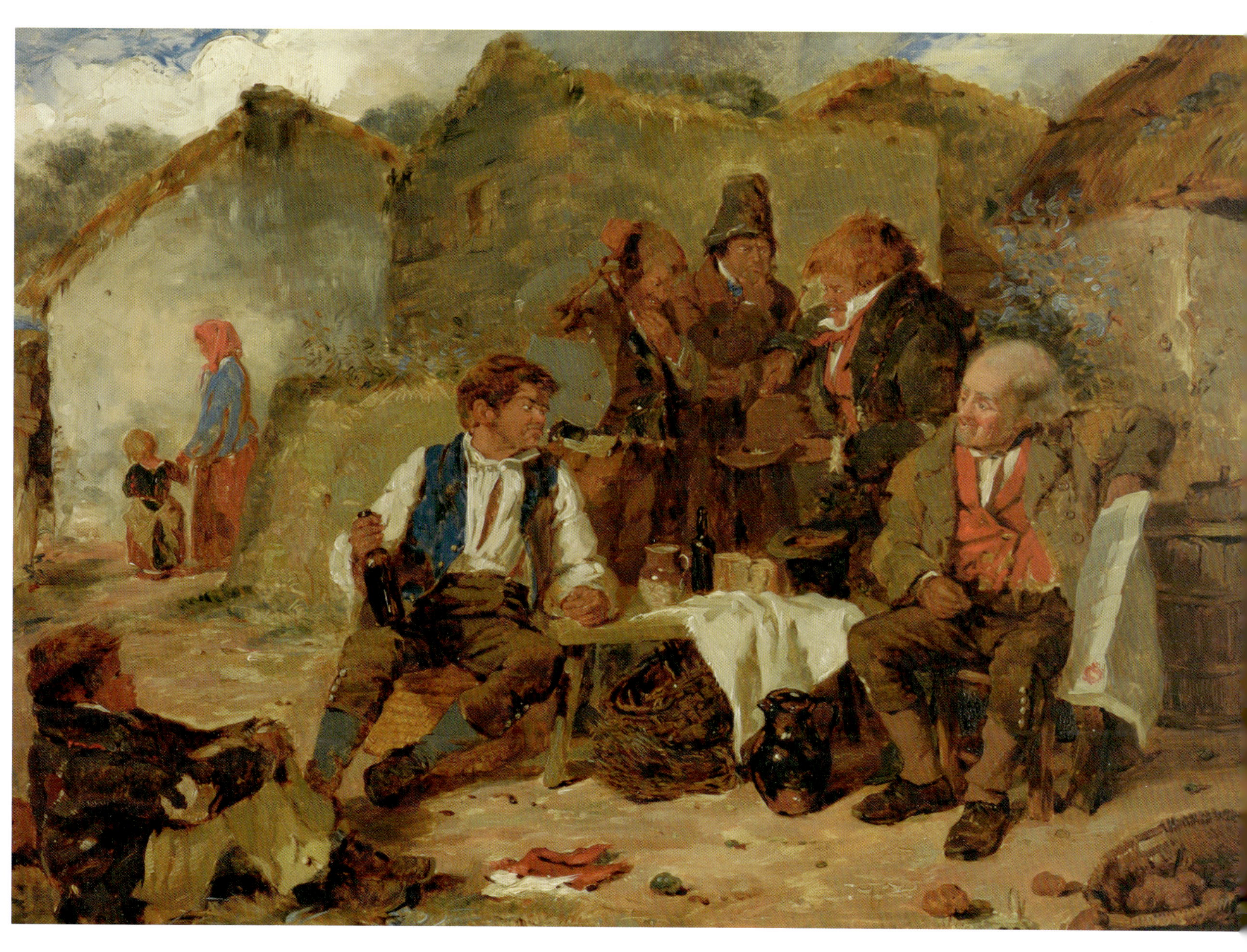

O'Connor, James Arthur

(1792-1841)

Son of an engraver and print seller, O'Connor learnt art at his father's side; he may also have studied with William Sadler II. He went to London in 1813, intending to settle there, but returned to Ireland in 1818, and executed a number of topographical commissions in the tradition of William Ashford, painting the demesnes of the Marquis of Sligo, Westport, County Mayo; the Earl of Clanricarde, Galway; and Lord Lorton, Rockingham, County Roscommon. By 1822 he was back in London, exhibiting Irish views at the RA and the British Institution.

Eighteenth and nineteenth-century paintings of landed estates show Irish demesnes organized along English and Continental park lines. Aristocratic aestheticization of the land eliminated the traces of those who also lived on the land and worked it: "constructing impressive vistas and pleasure grounds generated significant social costs for the tenants displaced in the process".[165] Vera Kreilkamp notes that O'Connor's estate paintings are "silent ... about the most dramatic changes in the landscape, changes that were to figure in catastrophe within three decades and transform Mayo into a center of resistance to Ascendancy land policies".[166] O'Connor's estate portraits, such as *Pleasure Grounds, Ballinrobe, Co Mayo* (1818, NGI), may have airbrushed peasant poverty out of the picture, but they still merit nuanced reading.[167]

There is some evidence that in 1828 O'Connor made a trip home. If so, this was one of the comparatively few landscapes he painted in Ireland, imbuing it with added authenticity. An 1828 view of Connemara – probably this – was exhibited in the centenary exhibition held at the Hugh Lane Municipal Gallery of Modern Art, Dublin in 1941. And in 1830, on his second return, O'Connor wrote to the artist Francis Danby, "I am going to the wild and beautiful scenery of my native country to refresh my memory and get some studies to help me in future exertion in my profession", adding "I know that I will be benefited by a sight of the grand ... scenery I will meet in Ireland, and hope to show it on canvas."[168]

O'Connor employed classical compositional devices: golden light, figures on desolated paths receding into the distance, the use of rocks and trees to create depth. He was an adept at small-scale paintings with diminutive figures set in large landscapes. And he used impasto to heighten the immediacy, as we see here in his trademark red-coated figure in the middle distance.

The Burkean concept of the sublime established in eighteenth-century aesthetics had been overtaken by the development of Romantic landscape painting in which human beings, rather than the landscape itself, became the focus of the picture. O'Connor's early landscapes were inspired by the new concept of the picturesque, his later work became increasingly Romantic.

O'Connor may have avoided representing the harsh realities of life for the peasant, but in painting the landscape of Connemara he presented a benign view of a region that was heavily stigmatized by the Cromwellian edict "To hell or to Connacht", and was thus pioneering. In 1832, only four years after he painted this scene, the *Dublin Penny Journal* wrote of the virtually unknown land behind the natural barrier of lakes and mountains:

Cunnemara [bays of the sea] is a word which to English, and even to Irish ears, is expressive of nothing but the ultima Thule *of barbarism … the inland country, [is] wild, mountainous, and ill cultivated, and so little known and visited, that its name is a proverb … [T]he traveller who ventures to enjoy its romantic and picturesque scenery, and who, from natural or acquired taste, can relish the "lone majesty of untamed nature", may here have his feelings gratified to the full.*

It conceded that its inhabitants are "behind the rest of Ireland in knowledge and civilization", but insisted "if the reader understands by this, that they are *barbarians*, and destitute of the feelings of humanity, he commits a very great mistake. Our Irish highlanders are a warm-hearted generous people, attached to their wild mountains and romantic glens, and, considering the few advantages which they enjoy, a lively, intelligent race."

In earlier times, the journal noted, Connemara "was the retreat of those daring spirits who scorned to submit to the yoke of an invader; and here, preferring poverty and freedom to restraint and submission, they found a shelter".[169]

Marjorie Howes and Kevin O'Neill argue that

this land did not simply mark the low social status of the native Irish; it also functioned as symbolic and material resource in their struggles for repossession. Irish rebels, certainly absent from landscapes commissioned for aristocratic patrons, often hid in remote, uncultivated areas, exploiting their superior knowledge of that terrain … Secret agrarian societies like the Whiteboys of the eighteenth century, as well as the Rockites, Terry Alts, and Molly Maguires of the nineteenth century, were vivid reminders of an alternative notion of landscape – one that did not deny the existence of ownership, but which insisted upon the rights of the occupier.[170]

John Hutchinson, O'Connor's biographer, describes the artist as conservative, and believes that his popular reputation is based largely on his "pleasant picturesque rural scenes", such as this, while his more ambitious topographical landscapes have been neglected because they are "redolent of an Ascendancy ethos", and his Romantic landscapes are "too broody and disconcerting".[171] In response, it should be noted that O'Connor not only painted in counties Dublin and Wicklow but also further afield, in the south-west and west of Ireland, making him quite the pioneer. In this respect his "valiant stand ... in perceiving beauty where others had only seen desolation, makes this exquisite small painting an important document in the development of Irish landscape painting and, more generally, our appreciation of the West".[172] The *Penny Journal* concluded its article on the isolation of the west with the empty comfort that "when in Cunnemarra one is in the 'nearest *parish* to America'!"; from here emigration remained a dream, people being too poor even to pay the seventy-shilling fare to America.[173]

Scene in Connemara, 1828
Oil on canvas, 12 x 14 in (30.48 x 35.56 cm)

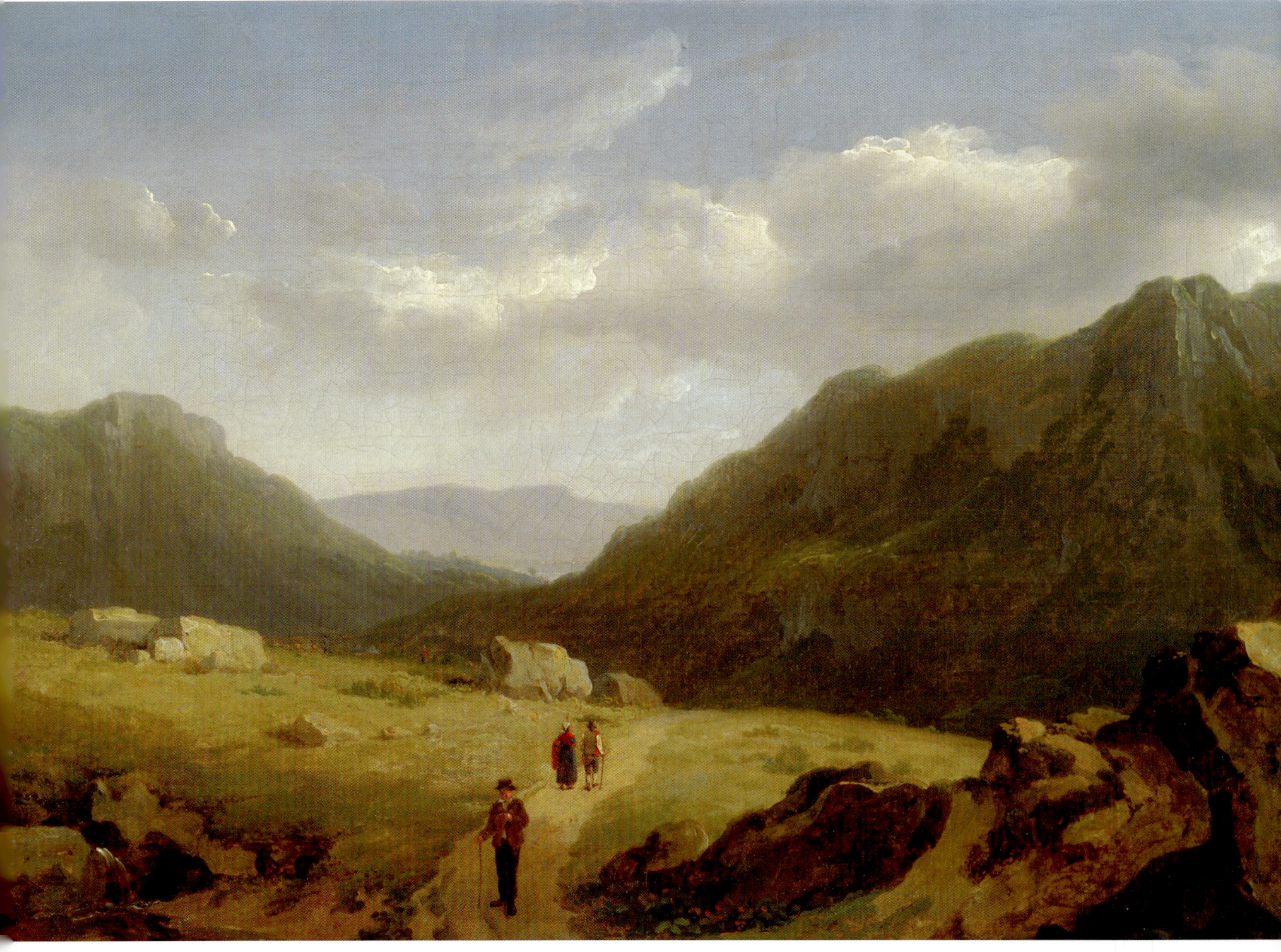

O'Donoghue, Hughie

(b. 1953)

The scale and breadth of O'Donoghue's work lends itself to the sublime beauty of parts of north-west County Mayo on the one hand, and the unparalleled destitution during the Famine on the other. There are few artists who could do justice to the epic nature of scene and circumstance that was Mayo during the Great Hunger. There is no more visually eloquent proponent than O'Donoghue, whose DNA is there and who has the skills to articulate it.

O'Donoghue was born in Manchester to Irish immigrants. He is known for his interest in history. And he has a deep connection to the art of the past: Titian and El Greco, Rembrandt and Poussin, Bacon and Rothko. From a synthesis of these sources he explores his ancestry, and he expects his viewers to bring their own experiences to the work, too. Memory - personal and collective - is the subject of his art. "Its subjectivity is illuminating and tells us something about ourselves, something about who we think we are. There is a relationship between the things we remember or choose to remember and those which we forget", he says.[174]

The archaeology of memory led him to recover stories of supernatural occurrences around Irish bogs and lakes. Erris in north-west Mayo, where his mother was from, is bounded by the Atlantic on two sides. Inland are swathes of bog and lake. Since the early 1980s the human figure swimming in water, walking in the landscape, or entombed in the earth recurs in O'Donoghue's work. The figures reveal themselves, evoking Tollund Man or Grauballe Man emanating from the bog. Technically, rather than being "observed", they materialize through scumble, glaze, and incision.

James Hack Tuke - a prominent member of the Society of Friends chiefly remembered for his philanthropic work - inspected the area in 1847, and wrote of unparalleled Irish poverty:

I have visited the wasted remnants of the once noble Red Man on his reservation grounds in North America, and explored the "negro quarter" of the degraded and

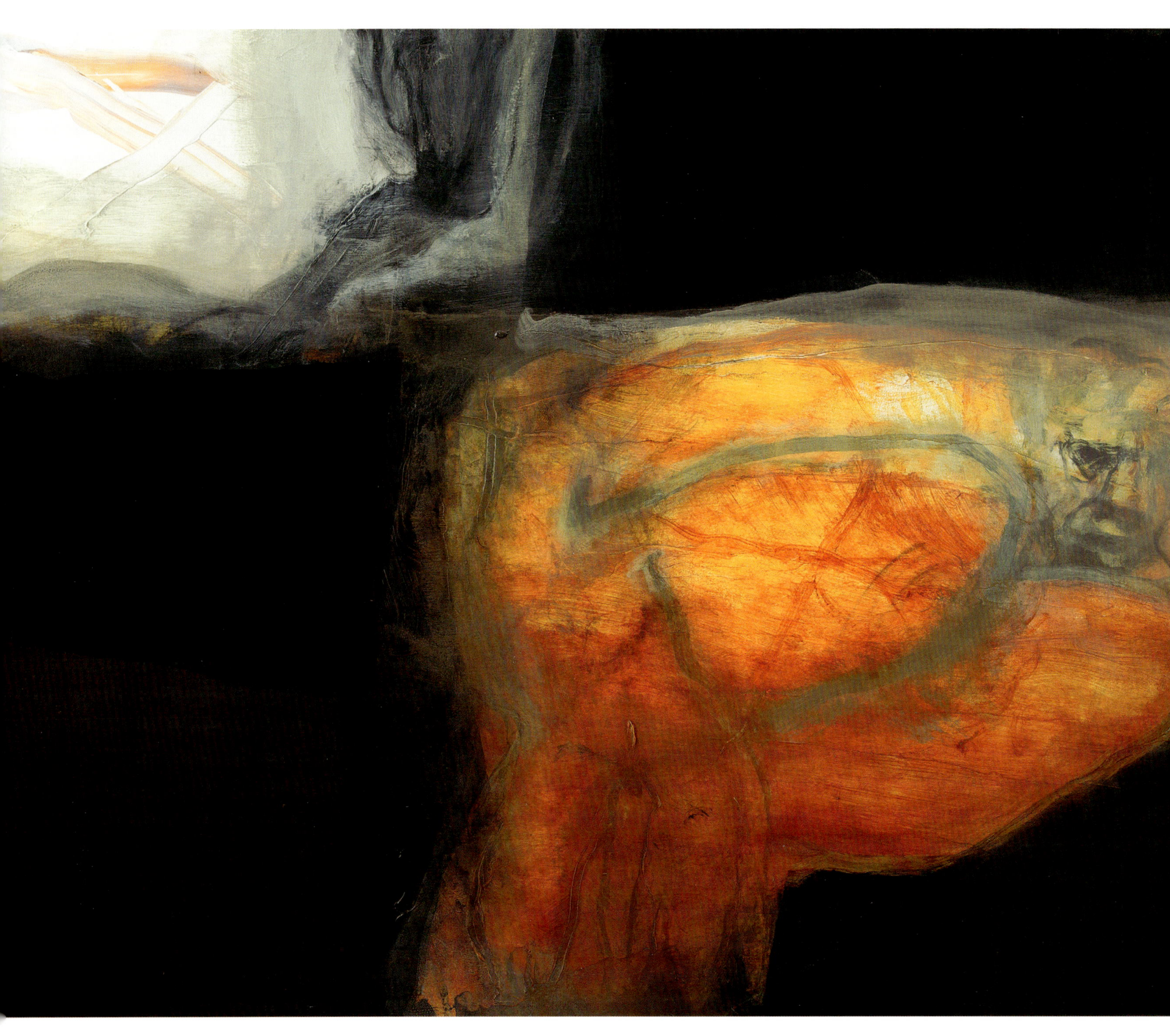

On Our Knees, 1996–97
Acrylic on canvas, 48 x 60 in (121.92 x 152.4 cm)

enslaved African, but never have I seen misery so intense, or physical *degradation so complete, as among the dwellers in the bog-holes of Erris.*[175]

The Famine brought many inversions of the natural order of life. The *Mayo Constitution*, for instance, reported how those who "died from starvation and cold", instead of being provided with coffins, would be "thrown into a mountain slough, with a few sods thrown over them" (May 17, 1849). Tuke found "swarms of human dwellings" there in which the roof on one side met the ground:

Window there is none, chimneys are not known; an aperture in front, some three or four feet in height ... smoke, pigs, and children, all pass in and out of this aperture ... it is perhaps safest to enter on all-fours ... the darkness and stifling turf-smoke for awhile prevent the use of the eyes [until] you are able to discern the size of this human burrow; and in a space from seven to ten feet square (I have measured them even less) you may find a family of six or eight persons, men, women, and children, in this filthy stinking hole, kneeling or squatting round the peat-fire, or lying on the damp ground. As for furniture, there is none; one or two broken stools and the "boiling-pot," and in some, a slightly raised space, upon which is spread a little damp dirty straw, oftener upon the cold ground, and a ragged coverlid, constitute, in many cases, the whole ... rags and tatters are their only garments, and nakedness even is the portion of some, who are [thus] obliged to remain in-doors.[176]

In 1848 Castlehill landlord John Walsh evicted 140 families - between 600 and 700 persons - in the depths of winter, without food or shelter. Some struggled to the workhouse forty miles away but were denied entry because the landlords of Erris had not paid their poor rates. With roofs "tumbled" to prevent reoccupation, there was nothing for it but to move from above ground to below, initially to scalpeens (dwellings roofed with turf and sticks thrown up after the bailiffs had gone) and then to scalps (holes dug in the earth) - human burrows in which people lived. Things were so bad that the inhabitant of the scalp, "like a fox, or some other vermin ... expect[ed] to be unearthed, and left even without the shelter of what may be called a preparatory grave" (*ILN*, December 15, 1849). A comparable sense of emanation, as he goes beneath the surface and draws his figures out, is prevalent in O'Donoghue's work.

The Famine looms large in paintings such as *A Pathway for Ghosts* (2011), which exposes the bleak but beautiful landscape of the plains of Erris. This and similar paintings feature figures crouched foetal-like or sheltering in the landscape. "On our knees", an expression his mother used, relates to a series of paintings around Loch Carrowmore and Erris, where she was born in 1914 and to which he returns still. "There was a pervasive melancholy that coloured her memories of her home, it had to do with poverty and hardship, the bleakness and the beauty of the landscape, its history and memory of the Famine years and the fact that leaving it in 1937 had been a necessity as opposed to an option.[177]

The humiliation of grinding poverty, the deprivations of his forebears, were, according to James Hamilton, "cut into the family's collective consciousness".[178] His mother's father died in 1920 when she was six years old; his grandmother then raised seven children on a poor farm with no assistance of any kind. O'Donoghue's grandfather had been born in Doolough in 1850, just a year after one of the most tragic episodes of the Famine. Two officials from the Westport Poor Law Union arrived in Louisburgh to inspect paupers claiming relief there. Instead of offering compassion, they demonstrated remarkable cruelty. From Louisburgh the inspectors set off for Delphi Lodge, twelve miles away, leaving instructions that the poor should assemble there for inspection the next morning. The already half-starved made their way south. Many had already walked miles to reach Louisburgh, as far as twenty-eight miles there and back. Clad in rags, these human skeletons – some sources estimate as many as 600 – struggled against the rain and sleet, and walked through the night. Those that made it were required to wait until the inspectors finished lunch. They left with nothing. Reports that up to 400 depleted people perished on the return were exaggerated, but many were blown into the lake, and corpses were found on the lakeshore, some with grass in their mouths – their last meal.

From a population of 28,000 in the barony of Erris, 2,000 emigrated and 6,000 died of starvation and famine fever. Tuke observed that half of those left were, "strictly speaking, on the verge of starvation", yet "within forty-eight-hours' journey of the metropolis of the world, living, or rather starving, upon turnip-tops, sand-eels, and sea-weed, a diet which no one in England would consider fit for the meanest animal which he keeps".[179] Mahatma Gandhi asked, "How can men feel themselves honoured by the humiliation of their fellow beings?"; his question is inscribed on the memorial to the Doolough dead.

While O'Donoghue's Famine work zooms in on the personal and the local, his strength lies in his ability to universalize. At his core O'Donoghue is a monumental painter who addresses the great themes of art – spiritual, historical, mythical – and who demonstrates masterful command of his medium – the breadth of a Michelangelo, the color of a Titian, the passion of a Goya – to communicate emotions at the heart of the human condition: anguish, atonement, hope.

O'Kelly, Alanna

(b. 1955)

No Colouring Can Deepen the Darkness of Truth (1992) is part of a trilogy of performances and installations, *The Country Blooms, a Garden and a Grave* (1992–95), that won for O'Kelly the first IMMA/Glen Dimplex Artists Award (1994).[180] This series is the only work by O'Kelly on permanent display, and constitutes one of the most sustained bodies of contemporary work relating to the Famine.

O'Kelly emerged as one of Ireland's most experimental artists in the 1970s. She works in a wide variety of media: video, film, sound, projection, photomontage, and text. She has performed throughout Europe and North and South America, including Lapland, where she designed and built a snow house in which she lived for a time. During her early career O'Kelly explored universal forms, using organic materials sited in natural habitats. Fusing the ritual and the radical, like many women artists she turned to performance art in the 1980s.

In 1984 she went to England to support women living outside the security cordon of the United States Air Force base at Greenham Common, who were trying to prevent the establishment of a cruise-missile base there. In *Chant Down Greenham* she performed traditional Irish keening (the wordless dirge for the dead). Jean Fisher described this as "a tone poem" in which she pitches her voice, her own weapon, against the whirring of helicopters, the sound of war - paralleling the conflict between human and technological values through "the socially unifying function of communal chanting". O'Kelly's sonorous keening, Fisher argues, "liberates the voice from the specular body and reinvents it as political agency, alluding, among other things, to a refusal of the pacification of Irish identities effected through English colonialism".[181]

O'Kelly has an acute sense of history. In the early 1990s, with the one-hundred-and-fiftieth anniversary of the Great Famine - a then neglected narrative - there was an eruption of memorials erected around Ireland and wherever in the world its emigrants settled: bronze sculptures of "coffin ships" or emaciated specters on quaysides in Ireland waiting to board, or, for those who survived, disembark on quaysides in America, Britain, or Australia. O'Kelly's response to the death and displacement was unique.

Undoubtedly her time in Britain in the 1980s sensitized her to the emigrant experience in the context of complex British/Irish relations.[182] Around this time she generated a cluster of artworks on the topic. Niamh Ann Kelly argues, that in confronting the discomfort that was felt about the subject, her "chosen form of mediation [was] not through words ... to conjure a visual description, but rather through a series of sounds that coalesce to produce a sense of immediacy".[183] Moreover, Catherine Marshall believes that "O'Kelly understood what official attempts to commemorate the Famine a few years later did not; that no amount of bronze monuments could ever assuage those emotions until the nation had first acknowledged the scale of the trauma and had mourned its dead, and the damage to its culture".[184]

O'Kelly's six-panel *A Kind of Quietism* comprises views of Achill Island and Belmullet, County Mayo; Black Head, County Clare; Connemara; and the Rock of Gibraltar. The overlaid text from contemporary historical sources, personal narratives, and accounts by witnesses provides a harrowing insight into the Famine. Her related video *No Colouring ...* is utterly immersive. Through an alchemy of sound and image, in Irish and English, O'Kelly performs a catharsis: sighing and singing, panting and chanting, praying and keening, as she scours the landscape for traces of a traumatized past and signs of rebirth and renewal. Conscious of the trans-generational impact of the Famine, she focuses not only on the loss of life and the guilt of the survivors but also on the erosions of language and culture, the scarring of the landscape, and the warping of memory. O'Kelly believes that we need to acknowledge, understand, and let go.

Her interest in the Great Hunger was provoked by images of famines accompanying civil unrest around the world in the early 1990s. She recalls a starving Kurdish mother among a group of refugees in the mountains telling an Irish reporter, "You tell the world I hold my dead baby in my arms because my breasts have dried up." At the time O'Kelly was feeding her eldest child, and had been reading about an Irish Famine family that was too unwell to carry out relief work - breaking stones or building walls. To enable the fourteen-year-old son to work for them all, he suckled at his mother's breast. And so the trope of the continuous flowing milk in *No Colouring ...* was born, and is core to the piece.

The work commences with an intimate close-up of milk flowing from a breast underwater. This is echoed by the ebb and flow of water lapping around the mound at Louisburgh in County Mayo - the Famine grave where bodies were dragged to die (it was once an early Christian site and graveyard, Teampall Duach Mór). As women did then, she keens - harrowing, sonorous sounds for the dead. The lament intermingles with voices murmuring the names of places stricken by the Famine, visceral sounds of birth, and the plaintive, lonely sound of the curlew. By using ancient sounds from around the world, such as the abstracted sound of the didgeridoo, she invokes places in Africa, Asia, and India, where famine exists today, reminding us that Ireland's experience was not unique, and that we have responsibilities, not just to make reparation for the past but to address the sufferings of the present. So much of our Famine was about complicity - something we must guard against in ourselves today, she believes.

Sound and visuals of a primeval pulsating jellyfish, a sighing belly, a newborn baby's breathing insist on the primacy of life, and grab aural as well as visual attention. "The place names are quiet at first: linear vocal, refrains - sung like a prayer - that rise on each line, higher and louder." She had been working on this in her studio with Donal Lunny, but was about to give birth to her second child and became breathless. She called on Maighread Ní Dhomhnaill, who did the sound with her at the very end, pulling everything together. O'Kelly recalls strong tides that year throwing up long-buried bones, teeth, and human skulls. "It seemed right for me not to touch anything, but to witness it, and record it as it was uncovering its dead", she said.[185] Uncannily, shortly after there was a huge storm and the remains of the mound were swept away. Were it not for *No Colouring Can Deepen the Darkness of Truth*, it would be no more.

A Kind of Quietism, 1990
Photo text, 3 panels, 19.7 x 29.5 in (50 cm x 75 cm),
3 panels, 19.7 x 14.6 in (50 cm x 37 cm)

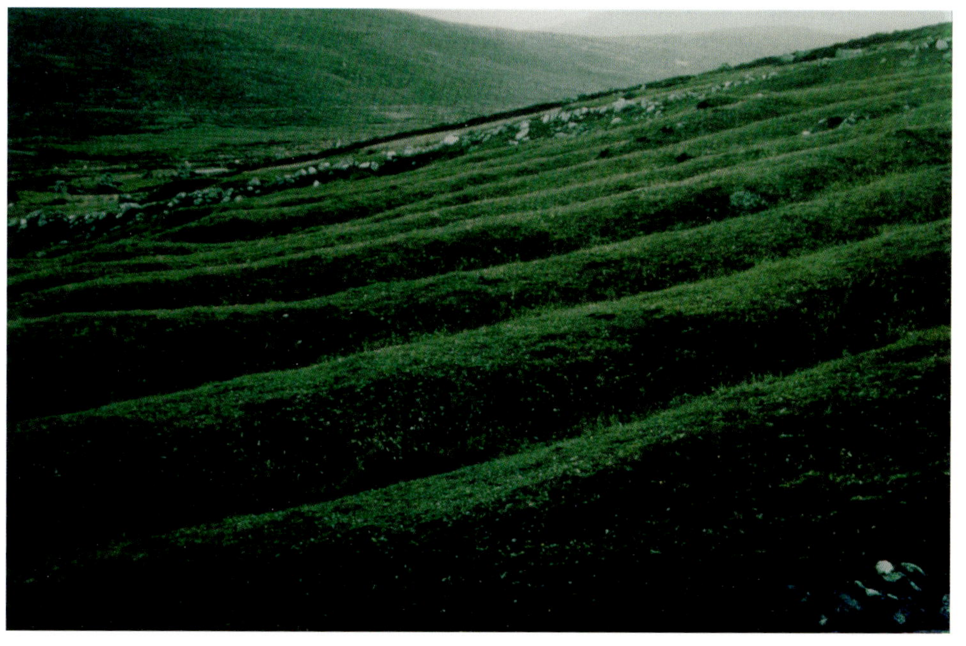

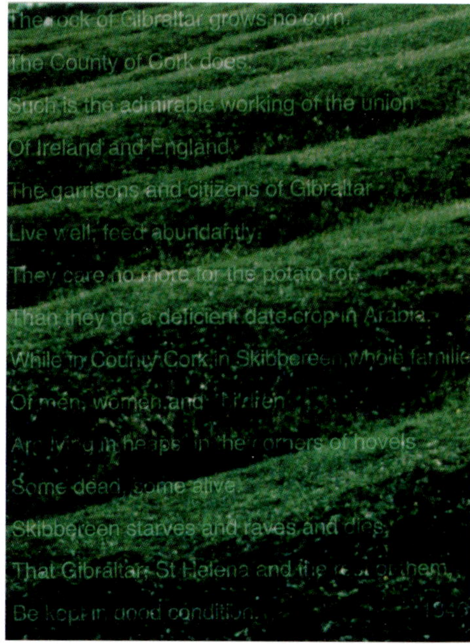
The rock of Gibraltar grows no corn.
The County of Cork does.
Such is the admirable working of the union
Of Ireland and England.
The garrisons and citizens of Gibraltar
Live well, feed abundantly.
They care no more for the potato rot
Than they do a deficient date-crop in Arabia.
Some dead, some alive.
Be kept in good condition.

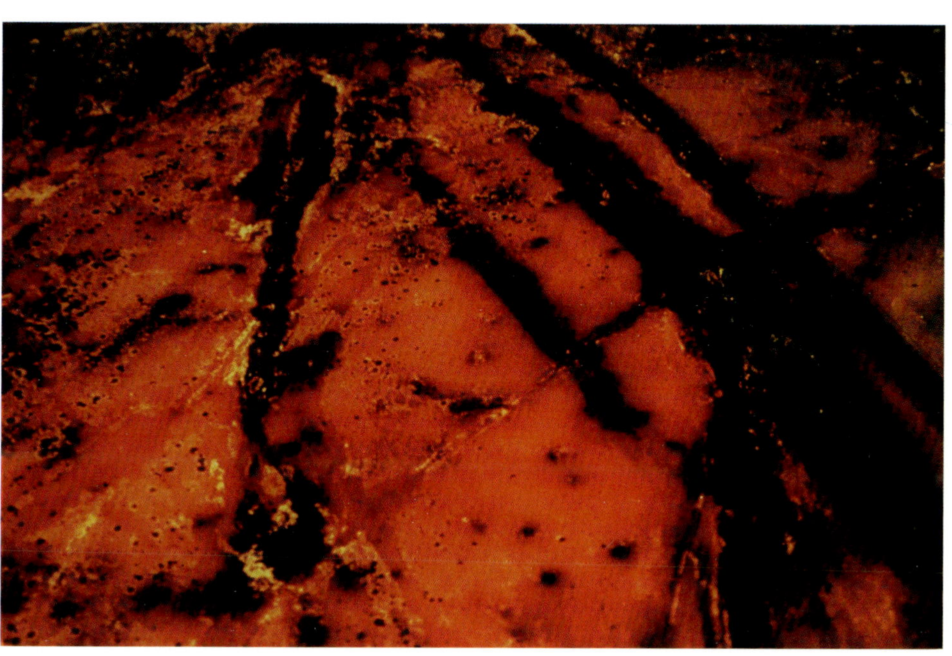

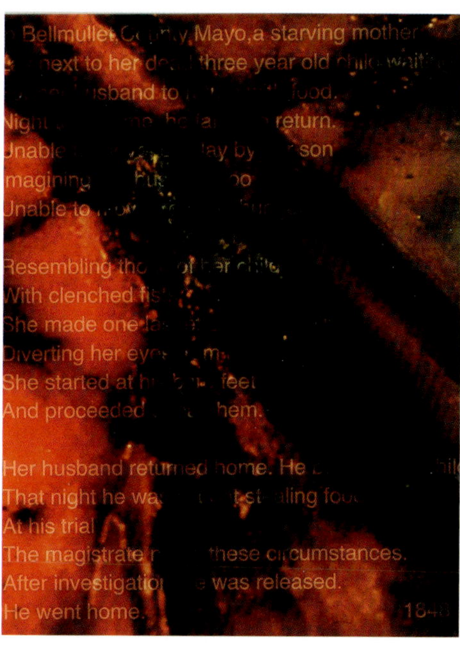
Bellmullet, County Mayo, a starving mother
Her husband returned home.
At his trial
He went home.

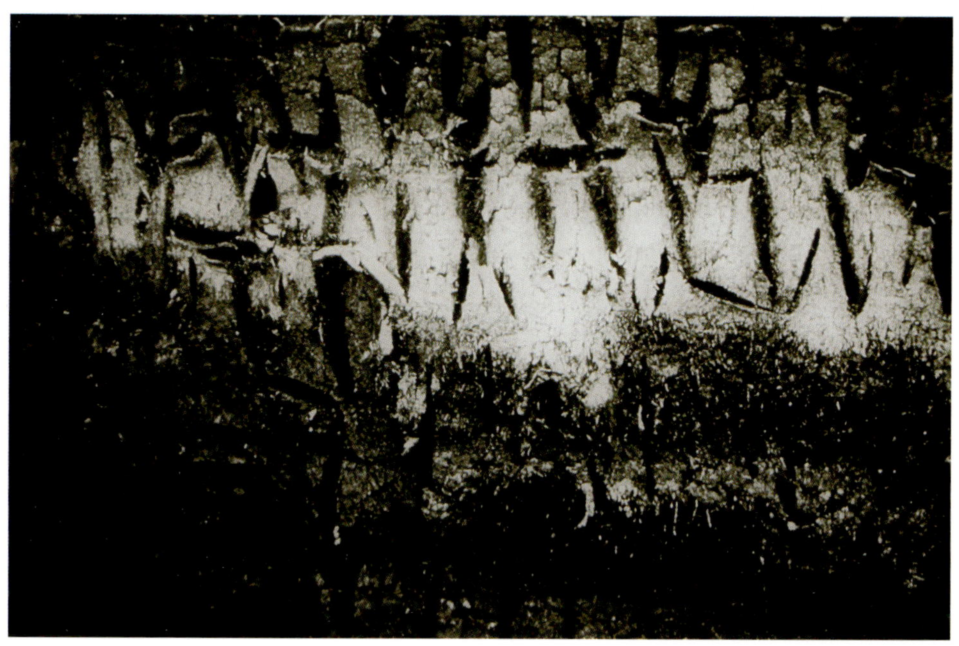

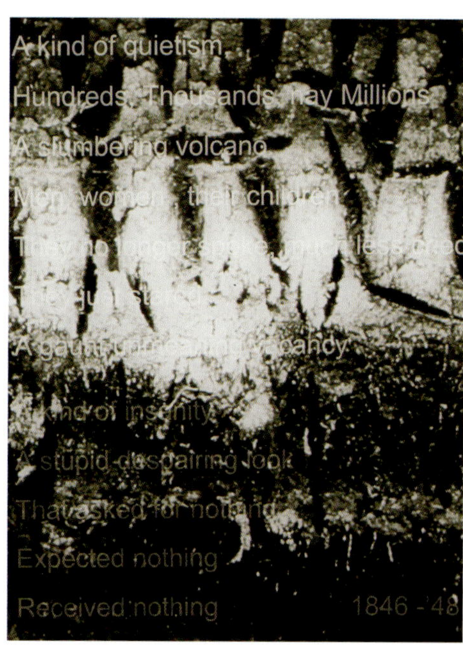
A kind of quietism
A slumbering volcano
A kind of insanity
A stupid despairing look
That asked for nothing
Expected nothing
Received nothing
1846 - '48

Oliver (Williams), William

(attributed) (1823–1901)

The Irish Piper, 1874
Oil on canvas, 30 x 25 in (76.2 x 63.5 cm)

There were three William Olivers who painted in or around the same time (1804–53, 1823–1901, 1837–1927), none of whom are known to have visited Ireland. Although William Oliver the Elder exhibited in the RHA from 1843 until his death, none of the paintings are of Irish subject matter. And although each Oliver has his distinguishing features, there are enough similarities (not least in the signatures of the 1804–53 and 1823–1901 Olivers) that misattributions occur, exacerbating difficulties in differentiating one from another. But from the accuracy and detail of this painting, and its impressive standard of authenticity, whichever Oliver, he certainly visited Ireland.

With his Welsh background it would seem as if William Oliver Williams, known professionally as "William Oliver" – who exhibited at the British Institution and the Royal Academy (from which he won a medal in 1851 for the best drawing from the antique) – is a likely candidate. This Oliver, born in Worcester, lived in Wales and then London with his nine children and three servants; in 1863 he was declared bankrupt. He was known for his paintings of winsome young women, like this coquettish redhead. The barrel on the right and the bottles of beer and jugs on the little hanging dresser suggest a shebeen in the west of Ireland. Here, above the floor-level turf fire, hang hooks and crooks for cooking, a bastable pot for boiling potatoes and stews, and, not unusually, a hens' nest. The girl is well dressed, and the strewn potatoes suggest good times, but above the doorway to the curtained enclave on the left is an emigrant's chest – a reminder of the ongoing legacy of the Famine. The poor *uilleann* piper – felt hat, torn breeches, unraveling stockings, and battered hobnailed boots – shows the artist's more robust painterly skills. Foreign artists in Ireland relished such detail.

Music is generally considered the foremost art form in Ireland, with the harp being the national emblem. Foreign commentators identified the pipes as the martial instrument of the Irish. But the first reference to the *uilleann* pipes was cultural – in a *dinnseanchas* (a topographical poem), "Aonach Carman", in the Book of Leinster (*c.* 1160) – while the earliest visual representations – seen on high crosses dating to the ninth century – were religious. Known for their haunting sweetness of tone, the present form of *uilleann* pipes (meaning "pipes of the

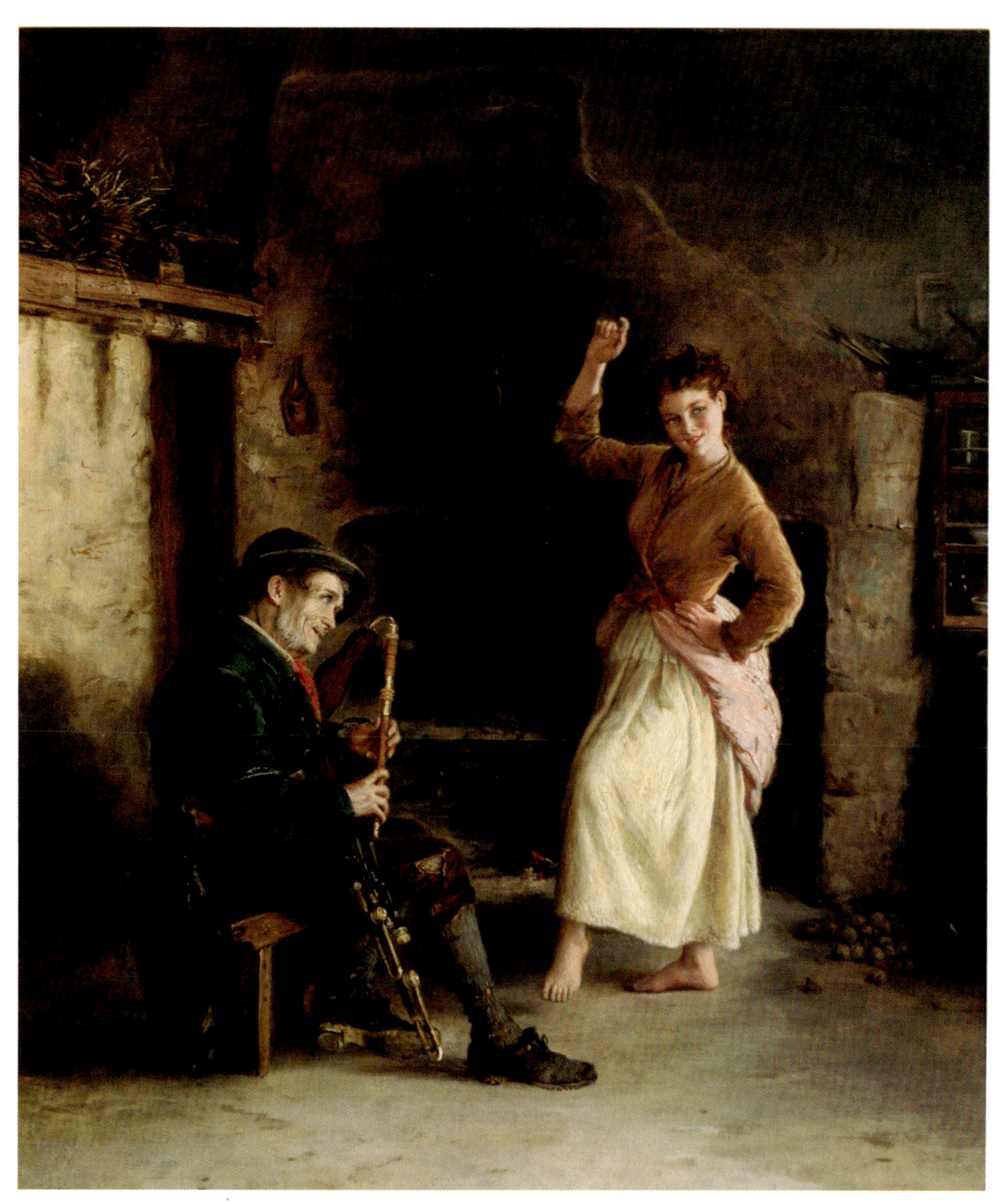

elbow", because of their pump-operated bellows) emerged in the early eighteenth century, comprising bag, bellows, chanter, three drones, and three regulators, and takes years to master. Terry Moylan, archivist with Na Píobairí Uilleann, says this piper conforms to the trope of the "aged bard" or "wandering minstrel". He plays a full set of pipes, and his seat and fingering are accurately observed. Joseph Haverty's *Blind Piper* (1844, NGI) was the iconographic model for piper paintings.

Notwithstanding hardship, the joyful side of Irish life was irrepressible: whatever the occasion, there were music and dancing. According to the antiquary Thomas Crofton Croker, the lower orders were "immoderately attached" to dancing. Everyone learned. The dancing master, usually itinerant, would be accompanied by a fiddler or piper (often blind). Croker recounts having seen a piper play without a moment's pause and given alcoholic sustenance by another holding the jug of porter to his lips to maintain the flow, so to speak.[186]

In peasant dwellings the lack of furniture allowed floor space for *céilithe*. Tables would be folded up flat against the wall, and beds folded away for dancing.[187] Although dancers achieved greater syncopation by dancing on an unhinged door, this lass dances daintily on the rough, earthen floor. She glances to her left, indicating an appreciative audience beyond the frame.

Dancing was a vernacular art, a cultural expression of vitality. As Kevin Whelan puts it:

The accomplished traditional dancer rode the rhythm, consummately mastering the movement. But s/he also oscillated along the porous boundary between the respect for tradition and an assertive individuality. For the spectator, the attraction was the expressive tension between tradition and the individual talent; the dancer bound to the strictly prescribed music, could also innovate within and against it. When male and female danced together, there was also sexual theatre – expressed through the heavier "hit" of the male dancer (culminating in the "batter", heavy rhythmic drumming with the full foot), counterpoised against the quicker buoyant step of the female performer.[188]

The Church, of course, took issue with dancing as providing sexualized contact, and, as it was usually fueled by alcohol, it was heavily condemned.

Apart from natural pleasure, Irish dancing and music – requiring "discipline, control and coordination" – were ideologically charged and "facilitated the shaping, sensing and experiencing of Irish culture and identity".[189] In furtherance of this, nationalist ideologists invented traditions – "a process of formalization and ritualization, characterized by reference to the past, if only by imposing repetition"; in this, music and dancing played their part.[190] After the Famine the old dances were replaced with sets and half-sets, and the pipes were superseded by melodeon and concertina, but in this painting Oliver anticipates the national revival towards the end of the nineteenth century, when the Gaelic League set out to restore "lost" culture.

O'Reilly, Geraldine

(b. 1956)

In 1989 O'Reilly was awarded a Fulbright Scholarship to the United States, resulting in the exhibition *Journal* (1990) based on emigration during the Great Famine. Arising then from a residency at the Heinrich Boll House, Achill Island, O'Reilly created a series of photo etchings conceived in association with the poem "Slievemore: The Abandoned Village" by John F. Deane (a native of Achill) and an excerpt from Eavan Boland's essay "Outside history" (1990).

The village of Slievemore dates to about 1750. Comprising up to a hundred tiny stone dwellings in which families of ten or more lived, it stretched for one mile, with potato ridges - lazy beds - rising up the mountain behind. It lost approximately a third of its population during the Famine, the rest leaving in the 1850s. Slievemore is one of the last places in Ireland where transhumance was practiced, with inhabitants tending cattle during the summer months on the mountainside, then returning to the villages of Pollagh and Dooagh for the winter. In the 1920s, booleying, as it was called, ceased, and the village returned to a state of nature.

Eavan Boland describes how, as a young woman, she met an old woman who remembered those during the Famine who abandoned their homes in Keel, where "the cliffs of Minaun rose sheer out of the water", and moved closer to the sea, "the better to eat the seaweed". But, as Boland observes, "[m]emory is treacherous. It confers meanings which are not apparent at the time". She says, "I knew without having words for it that she came from a past that affected me", as it did O'Reilly, who went to the deserted village to create work that would resonate with the present. Against the backdrop of the property crash, the present-day ghost estates seem to echo the derelict village stretched out along the mountainside.

In Deane's poem, the graveyard dominates the now deserted village:

... in the wind-swept ravenous
mountainside of grief, this is the long tilted
valley where famine
came like an old and infamous flood
from the afflicting hand of God. Beyond all
understanding. Inarticulate. And pleading.

The poem and text contextualize the images, albeit they are less about the Great Hunger per se than its aftermath – how the landscape holds the memory of the Famine in the crumbling walls of the village. In keeping, the images are printed without color. The first is the view of the mountain and graveyard seen from the distance, coinciding with the imagery in the poem. The final image is the view of Minaun Heights and the sea, where the villagers moved to get food.

In writing of O'Reilly's work, Luke Gibbons invokes Susan Sontag when observing that "[a] photograph is like the delayed rays of a star; the object may have disappeared long ago but the light lives on in the present". In O'Reilly's photo etchings of the deserted village,

light itself is defined by the shadows acast on the landscape since the nineteenth century. Grass-stubbled roads cannot find their way home. Abandoned gable walls loom like headstones and, from a distance, the originals in graveyards suggest they have more in common with other rocks, than with the people they left behind.[191]

The photo etchings have a timeless, haunted quality.

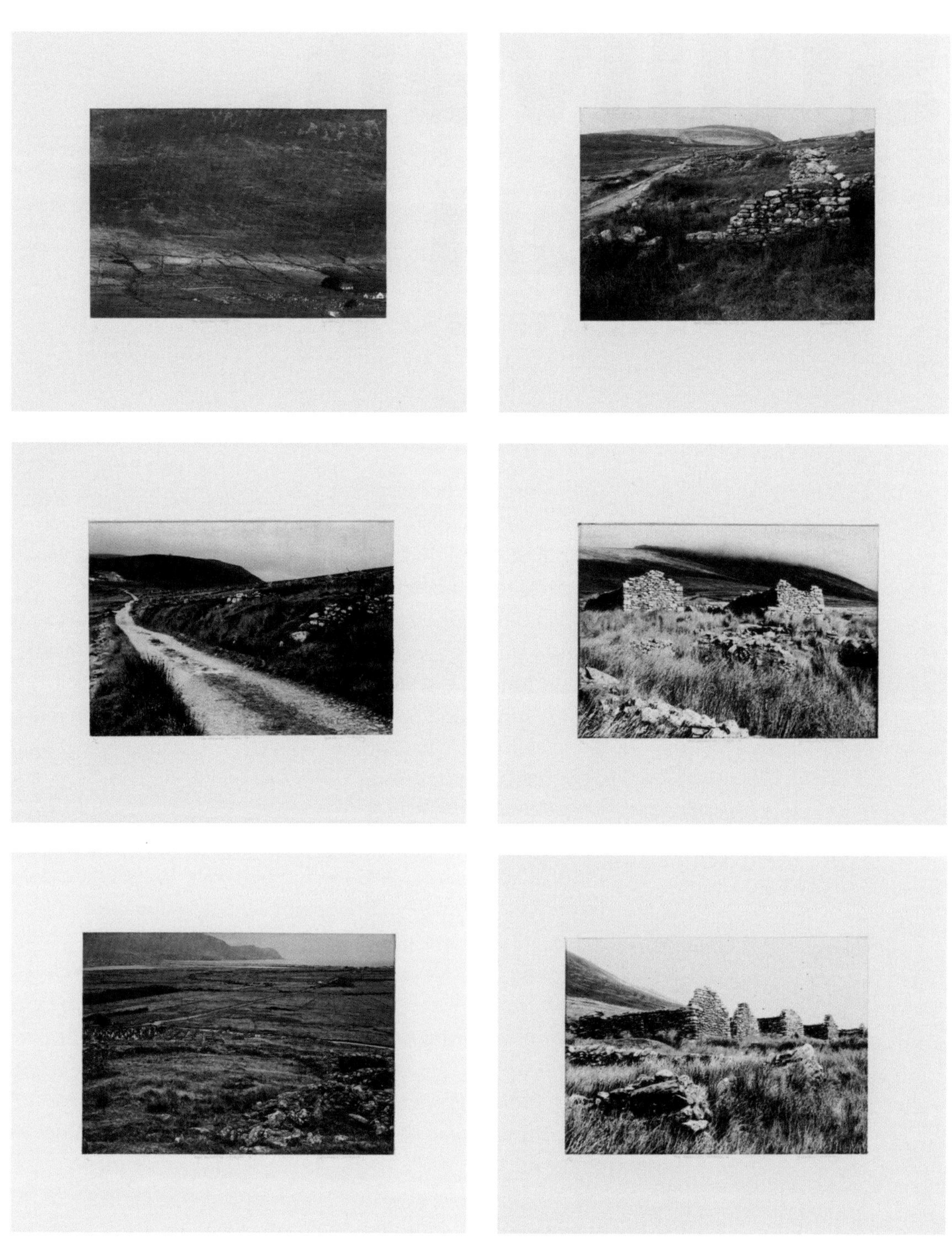

Deserted Village, Achill Island, 2012
Photo etchings, 14 x 16.5 in (35.56 x 41.91 cm)

O'Sullivan, Seán

RHA (1906-64)

Seán O'Sullivan studied drawing at the Dublin Metropolitan School of Art. His teacher, Seán Keating, became a lifelong friend. O'Sullivan won a scholarship to the Central School of Arts and Crafts in London, where he met his wife, the artist Rene Mouw. Together they went to Paris to study at the Académie Colarossi (where the renowned Irish designer Eileen Gray studied)[192] and at the Académie de la Grande Chaumière, schools that were less hidebound than the École des Beaux-Arts. In Paris O'Sullivan was friends with Samuel Beckett, James Joyce, and Thomas MacGreevy, as well as the French painter Georges Rouault. Back in Dublin he associated with Patrick Tuohy, Maurice MacGonigal, Harry Kernoff, and Nano Reid. He was an excellent linguist and raconteur.

He exhibited at the RHA, Oireachtas exhibitions, the Victor Waddington Gallery, Dublin, and the Helen Hackett Gallery, New York. In 1955 he held an exhibition of work - his only solo show - in Philadelphia; it was considered a major success.

In 1928 he was appointed an associate of the RHA, the youngest ever, and in 1931 a full member. He executed religious paintings, interiors, and landscapes, but was primarily known as a portrait painter. He painted prominent politicians, actors, revolutionaries, artists, and writers, such as Maud Gonne MacBride, Jack B. Yeats, James Joyce, Patrick Kavanagh, and James Larkin. His *Portrait of Éamon de Valera* (Áras an Uachtaráin) was hailed as a "tour de force of painting, drawing and psychology".[193]

In *Connemara Woman with Red Skirt*, O'Sullivan portrays a rosy-cheeked woman from the west of Ireland wearing traditional dress. Head covered, arms folded, she stands full square in front of a lovely landscape. Cottages are sparsely spread throughout the stony land. The low horizon allows for an expansive cloudy sky above the mountains, which are saturated with iridescent light.

With colonialism and plantation came the consignment of the dispossessed Irish to the west, which became increasingly differentiated from the rest of the country.

Marked by its poverty, isolated culturally, and geographically inaccessible, the west came to be seen as the "real" Ireland, the repository of Gaelic culture, language, and religion, giving rise to an iconography of its own in which the association of women with nature is an important trope. The red skirts of the women, for example, can be understood "in the context of the cultural and biological role which was afforded to women in the West", where women functioned as personifications of wholesomeness, domesticity, and authenticity.[194]

O'Sullivan had a studio at 20 Molesworth Street, Dublin, today home to the Gorry Gallery. A respected academic artist who maintained a conservative course in the face of encroaching modernism, Éimear O'Connor maintains that he

could turn his hand to any form of visual art production: from book covers, to advertisements; from lithographs to large-scale commissioned portraits; from caricatures to religious commissions and personal reflections. He possessed an extraordinary talent, one that should be fully and properly evaluated in the context of the history of twentieth-century Irish art.[195]

His untimely death was not due to sobriety, but on hearing of it the then president of the RHA, Maurice MacGonigal, noted that "one of the defects of mankind is its failure to recognise genius until it has been removed".[196]

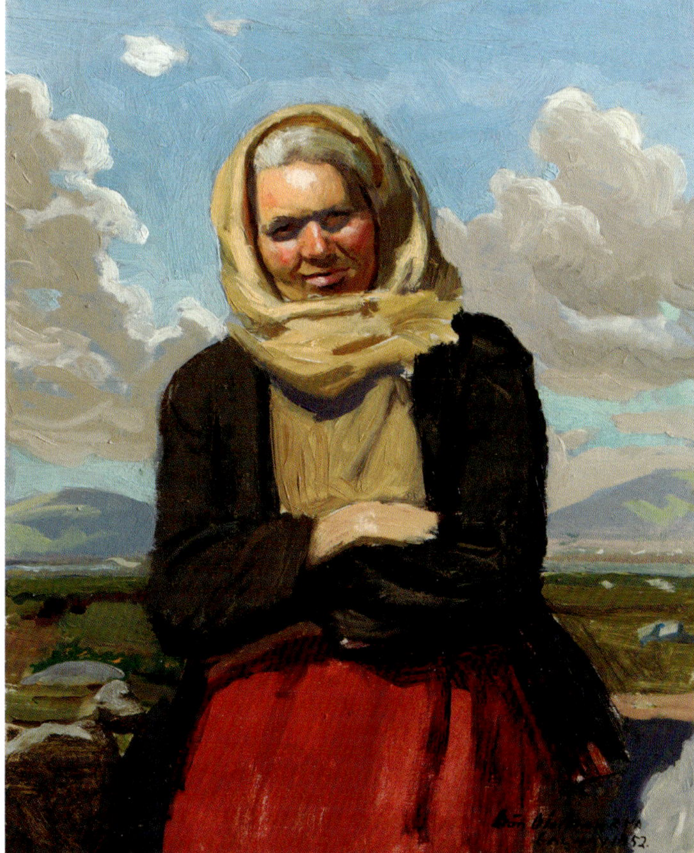

Connemara Woman with Red Skirt, 1952
Oil on board, 16.5 x 13 in (41.91 x 33 cm)

Reaney, Pádraic

(b. 1952)

Although the native language had been declining in the pre-Famine period, the Famine accentuated the process. Death and emigration exerted a heavy toll, bringing with them the silence of mourning, a loss of voice, the rupture of social relations, sundering of family ties, and fissures in cultural production and transmission that endure to the present day.

Like Máirtín Ó Cadhain, Pádraic Reaney was born in, and lives and works in, Connemara. He studied at Regional Technical College Galway, and exhibits regularly at the Kenny Gallery, Galway. In some respects Reaney's images could function as the tragedy version of Ó Cadhain's comedy *Cré na Cille* (1949), in which the Connemara dead took their grievances with them to the grave. In the case of the Famine victims, not even Caitríona Paudeen's greatest humiliation, the paltry ten-shilling plot, was accorded to these poor people. Notwithstanding the black comedy of the novel, the language of both the living and the dead mattered to Ó Cadhain, who considered the threat to the language from the marginalization of Gaelic in Penal times, the loss of so many speakers through emigration, and the subsequent neglect by government as an existential crisis in Irish identity: "If we lose the Irish language ... We'll be finished as a people. The vision that every generation of Irish people had will be at an end."[197]

In *Departure* a family has been evicted, in *The Last Visit 1* people pay their last respects to their dead before they emigrate. There is nothing left for them in their own country. Walking single file through the night, they tread over the unmarked graves of their kin to face the treacherous crossing to America. Given such spectral images, it is not hard to understand how for so long memories were buried inexpressibly in the mind as well as in the ground. Given the severity of the Famine in Connemara, the scars on the landscape continue to be apparent to those who live there. In this painting the high horizon extends the visual narrative below, reminding us that traces of the atrocity remain to this day, congealed in the blood-red soil.

Reaney's dead are isolated, one from the other, deep in the soil, for notwithstanding the reality (and indignity) of mass graves, the sequestration of each figure suggests they are denied even the comfort of a communal end, their last consolation. In folklore there are many tales of hearing voices underfoot - the victims of the Great Hunger who cannot rest - and, metaphorically, if the eye is attuned to history it can also pick up on these resonances.

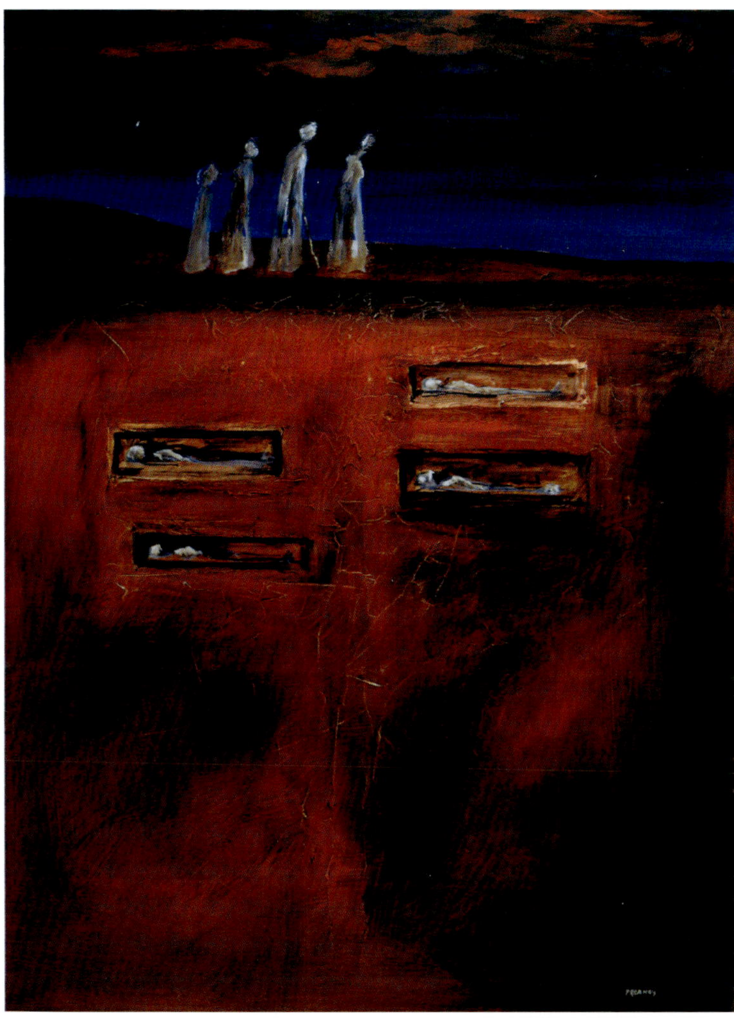

Departure, 1995
Oil on masonite, 30 x 21 in (76.2 x 53.34 cm)

The Last Visit 1, n.d.
Oil on masonite, 30 x 24 in (76.2 x 61 cm)

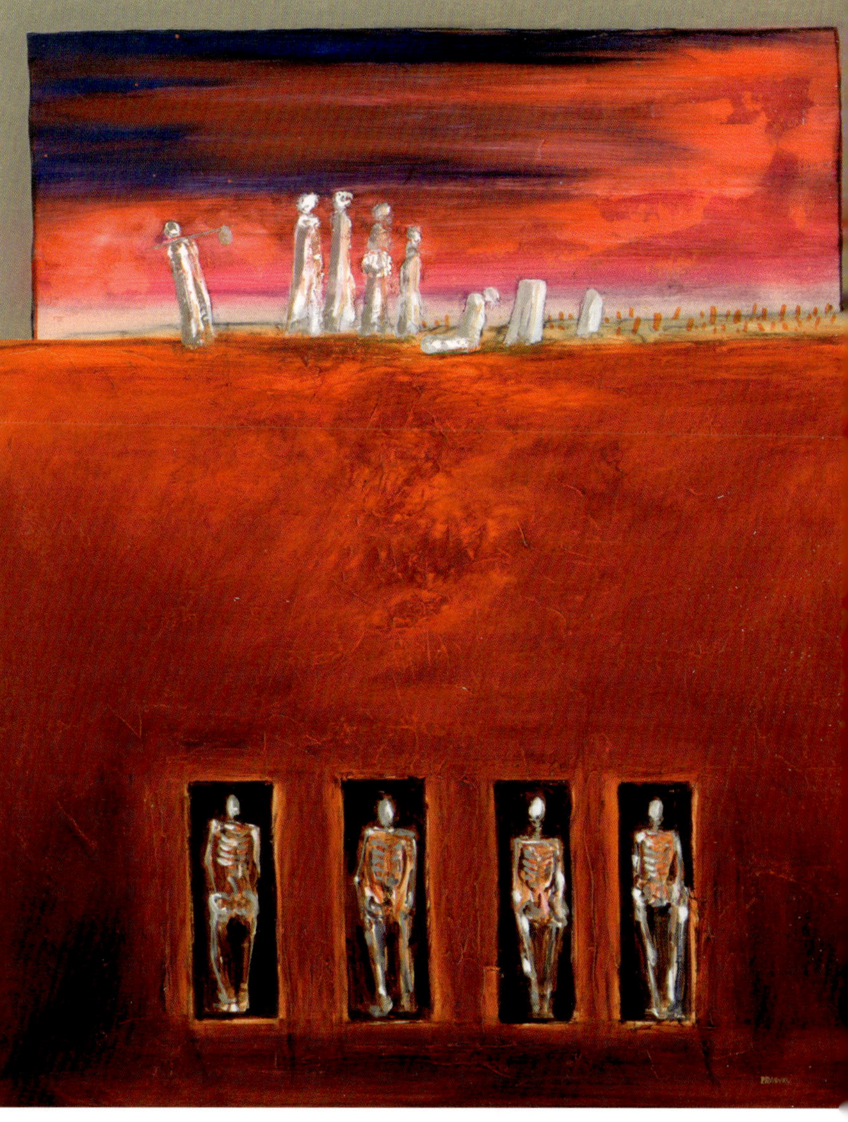

Topham, Francis William

(1808–77)

Topham was born in Leeds. From an apprenticeship printing letterheads, business cards, and coffin plates, he moved to London, where he first worked as a heraldic engraver. His earliest painting, *The Rustic's Meal*, was shown at the RA in 1832. He became a member of the Artists' Society for the Study of Historical, Poetical and Rustic Figures (Clipstone Street), founded by John Prescot Knight in 1838. John Tenniel, Charles Keene, Thomas Seddon, Albert Moore, Frank Dicksee, as well as the Dalziels and *Punch* illustrators Phil May and W.S. Gilbert were members. These early realist artists brought in – and further roughened or rusticated from an extensive wardrobe and props room – real beggars whom they posed in their stable yard. They took it in turns to nab a beggar for the study of the "living clothed figure".[198] The society also provided nude models (unusual at the time). Here, surgeon J. Henry Rogers taught anatomy using recent dissections and living models, and lectures were held on contemporary matters such as the chemical properties of pigments, perspective, and phrenology. Although conservative stylistically, the outlook of many of the society's artists was radical. Seen as bohemian, the society was described as "a vigorous, if somewhat casual and promiscuous, centre of artistic life in London".[199]

The Vigil
Watercolor and graphite on paper, 15 x 21.5 in (38 x 54.61 cm)

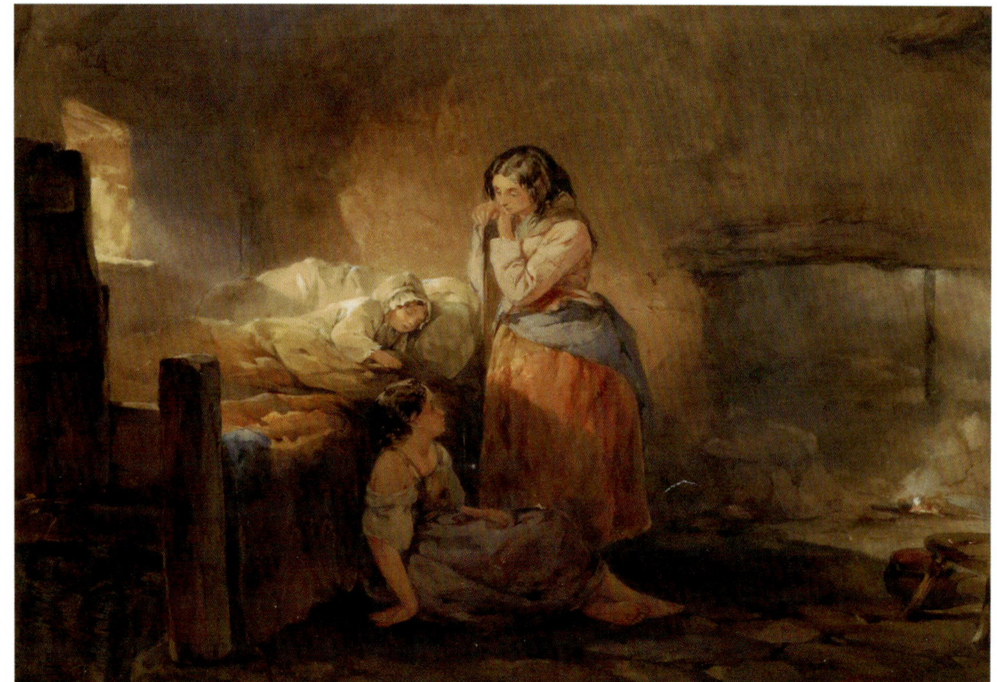

When Topham first accompanied Frederick Goodall, Alfred Fripp, and (Henry) Mark Anthony to Ireland in 1844, he found extremes of poverty and deprivation that exceeded anything staged in Clipstone Street.[200] But, however devoted he was to the "study of veritable rustic figures from the life", even by the standards of the day, Topham, a father of twelve, tended towards the tender rather than gritty, especially in painting women and children.[201]

Distinctive similarities in style and subject matter are to be found in the work of the society's members: mending nets and homely scenes of domesticity set in desperately poor cabins made of mud and shored up with driftwood. Notwithstanding a tendency towards sentimentality, their paintings tend to be closely observed and informative of living conditions and customs in Ireland at this time. Topham's paintings are important visual documents of impoverished dwellings, household chores, and objects of material culture from this period, and exude ethnographic empathy.

Real-life conditions in the Claddagh, Galway and around Connemara led to the production of a number of fascinating works – including *Gossips at a Well* (Guildhall Art Gallery, London), *Saturday Evening in Connemara* (1848, Sheffield Museum), *At the Holy Well* (Glasgow Museums), and *The Irish Pattern* (Walker Art Gallery, Liverpool) – that lend themselves to the study of ethnography in nineteenth-century Ireland. Somewhat hyperbolically, the art critic James Dafforne declared *Pilgrims to the Holy Well* as "classed among the most brilliant achievements of British Art".[202] *Feeding Chickens* features the same humble dwelling seen in the exuberant *Saturday Evening in Connemara* and *Cabin on the Moor*, and the same girl features in *Chick! Chicks* (illustrated in the *Art Journal*, February 1880). Dafforne perceived "nothing vulgar nor unpleasant in the poverty it depicts – it rather suggests the simplicity of lowly rural life than suffering or want".[203] And so it is: the poverty is picturesque, the tumbled village kept to the background, the evicted out of sight.

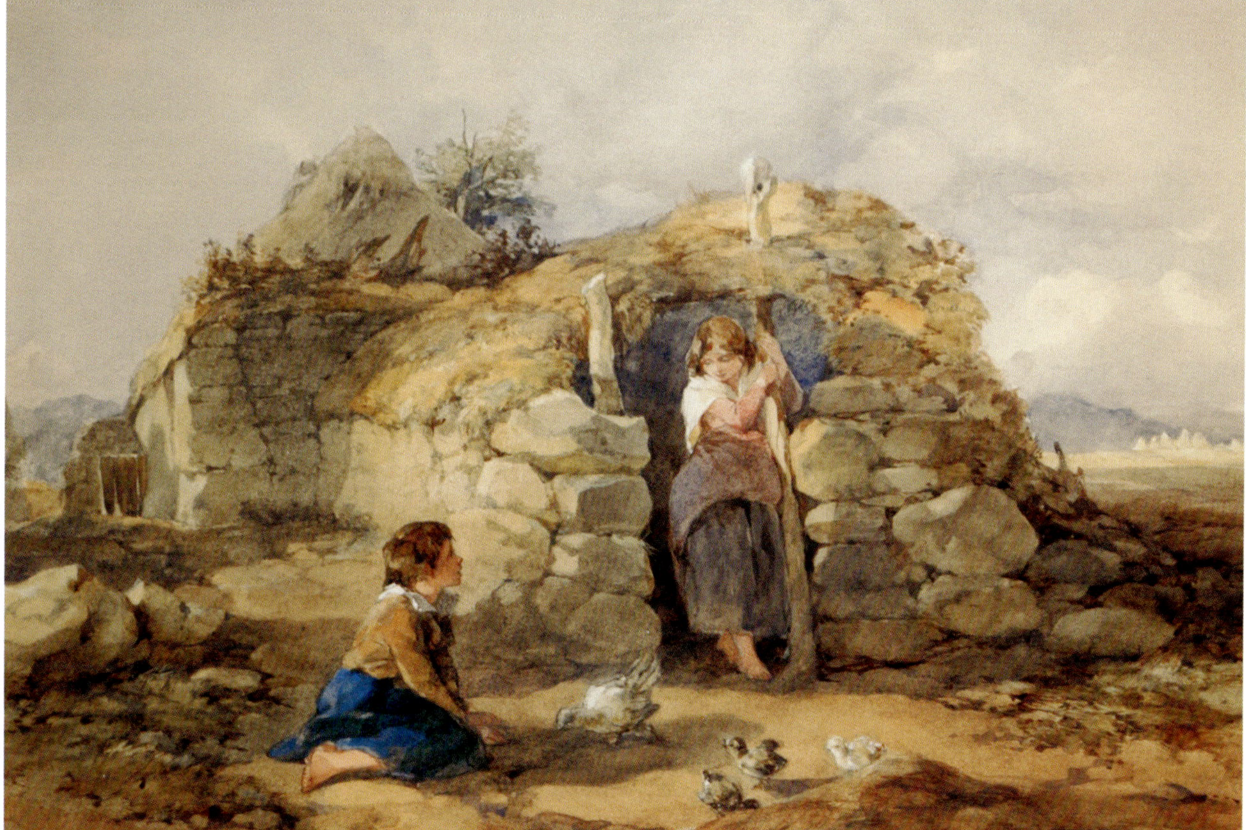

Feeding Chickens, 1848
Watercolor, 11.42 x 15.75 in
(29 x 40 cm)

Tuohy, Kieran

(b. 1953)

Thank You to the Choctaw, 2005
Bog oak, 52.5 in (133.35 cm)

The symbolism of both giving and receiving feature in Famine commemorations. The Choctaw tribe – with its own long history, rich culture, and troubled past – took the sufferings of an unknown people, the Irish, onto themselves. In 1847 the tribe raised and sent more than $170 – a huge amount given their own needs – for the relief of famine in Ireland. Only sixteen years before, President Andrew Jackson (whose parents were from Antrim) seized the fertile lands of the Choctaw in Mississippi, and forced them to undertake the 500-mile trek to Oklahoma. Of the 21,000 who embarked on the Trail of Tears, more than half died from exposure, hunger, and disease. The Choctaw thus identified with the Irish as victims of cultural suppression, dispossession, and exile. Tuohy parallels a totem-pole-style storytelling with the intricacies of a Celtic way of narrative.

A carpenter who trained with Israeli artist Yoram Drori, Tuohy began by carving designs from the Book of Kells in mahogany. From his studio in Kilcolgan, County Galway, he now uses hard black oak, a primordial material and a difficult medium in which to work. The acidic conditions of the peat bog help preserve giant trees that formed the great oak forests of Ireland. The bogs formed as rotting vegetation collected in swamps, where it was broken down by microorganisms. Timber that fell into the swamps sank slowly, and gradually was buried beneath semi-solid layers of peat. The low pH levels acted as a preservative. As the bogs are reclaimed for agriculture or fuel, huge trees, perfectly preserved, are thrown up, having been buried for thousands of years. The Palaeoecology Centre, Queen's University, Belfast has dated this piece as between 1705 and 1389 BC.

Bog oak is steeped in folklore and history. Seasoned, collective memories – traces of our ancestors – reside within. Tuohy uses oak and yew to tell stories of the mythic and distant past, as well as the Famine, from which, he believes, Ireland has never fully recovered.

In *Surplus People* Tuohy works through a range of emotions associated with hunger: terror, grief, helplessness, anger, loneliness, and despair. They have not done this to themselves, but they are surplus to requirements. Many landlords saw in the Famine the opportunity to curb the population – evicting tenants so they could turn their land to greater profit, and shifting to open grazing for cattle, which could be sold to feed the growing industrial cities of Britain.

The surplus people have nowhere to live, no one to turn to, and by their isolation it would appear that they are beyond turning to each other – and yet we glimpse a remnant of tenderness as the mother whispers her last words to her dying baby.

Every year a walk takes place from Doolough to Louisburgh in memory of the Irish Famine and of the long and arduous walk undertaken by those about to board ships and emigrate. Sometimes the walk is joined by someone from the Choctaw Nation in memory of its extraordinary generosity at that time.

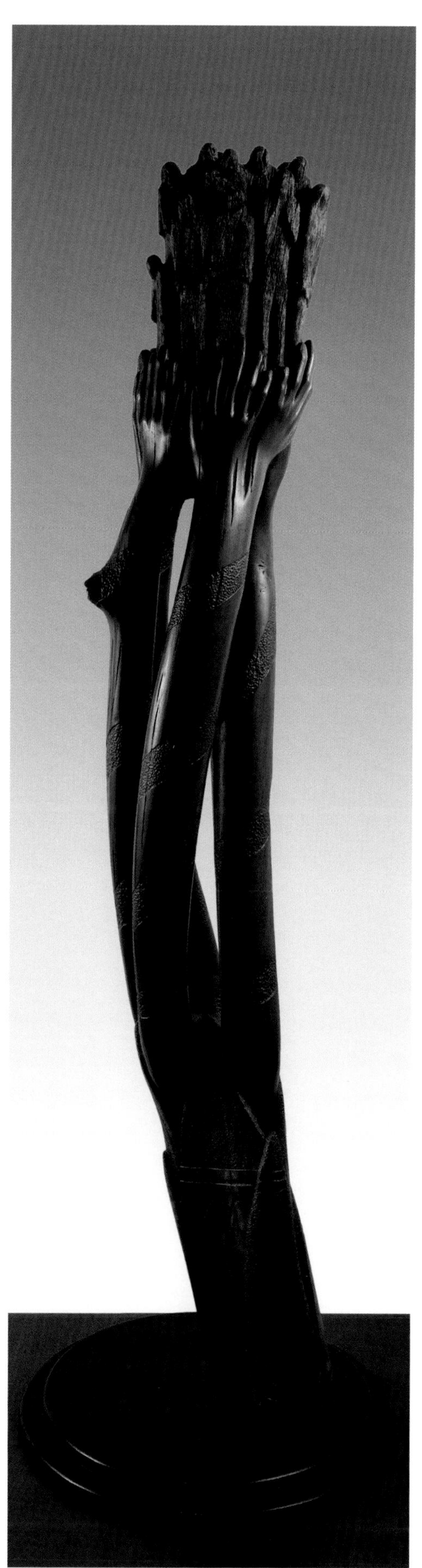

Williams, Alexander

RHA (1846–1930)

An accomplished marine, landscape, and cityscape painter, Alexander Williams traveled around Ireland, England, and Scotland, and was especially drawn to Achill Island, County Mayo.[204]

Alongside the family business as hatters, the Williams brothers were taxidermists of international stature. Alexander was also an ornithologist – of the shooting, skinning, and stuffing variety; a significant proportion of the avifauna and small-mammal collection in the Natural History Museum, Dublin and the Ulster Museum, Belfast came from the Williamses' studio. Alexander was also an alto at Her Majesty's Chapel Royal, Dublin Castle, performing on Sundays for the Lord Lieutenant. And as a prodigious diary and letter writer, an unusual amount of material on his life is extant.[205]

In 1873 Williams was one of the first artists to go to the remote island of Achill, an arduous journey that in the 1840s was recorded as taking three days. There he "found a part of Ireland where there was an immense field for the activities of an artist", and where he intended "to make it peculiarly my own and devote myself to making its wonderful scenery known".[206] Although outgoing himself, his art, not unlike the place, exudes melancholy and isolation.

Achill – a small land mass of fifty-seven square kilometers – is Ireland's largest island, and is among Europe's most westerly islands; it is separated from the mainland by a narrow sound. Inhabited for some 5,000 years, it is rich in prehistoric monuments. However, comprising two thirds peat bog, its infertile soil was inimical to feeding a population that expanded in the late seventeenth century when the Cromwellian plantations consigned the Irish "to hell or to Connacht". There they eked out a miserable existence (the landlord even charging a tax on seaweed collected as fertilizer). By 1841 the population was almost 5,000; post-famine it was closer to 4,000.

In 1883 Samuel Carter Hall reminisced:

This is the sight I see: a growth of diseased vegetation covers the thatched roof (a roof of slate distinguished the houses of the doctor, the landlord, and the priest); a cess pool of stagnant water oozes from the dung-heap, at either side of the door; a big slab of flat stone forms a sort of bridge across it; the mud walls have given way in parts, and there is a gradual sinking of the fabric; the door is hanging by broken hinges; two holes indicate windows; into one of them, if the weather be damp, the tenant's top-coat is thrust to keep out the cold ... Generally the rain finds its way through some part of the roof and there is a consequent puddle on the floor. The pig goes in and out as he pleases; there is a constant "hurrish" to drive him from the "pratee" [potato] corner ... as a rule there is but one [room], in which a whole family live and sleep ... as many as eight or ten human beings of all ages and sexes, will be crowded into this one miserable room. Water is seldom used for any purpose, personal or domestic.

While this account describes Williams's cottage, the artist himself thought Achill "inexpressibly wild and romantic".[207] In fact, Williams's depictions of Achill were the first many saw of the on-going deprivation in the west.

This painting evokes terrible memories of terrible times, when poor, starving people were evicted from their homes during the Great Hunger. Not for Williams the sanitized whitewashed cottages of Paul Henry; this cottage may look derelict but the spectral figure of a man – as if a ghost from the past – can be discerned in the doorway.

The granting of Catholic Emancipation in 1829 provoked a surge in Protestant missionary activity in Ireland, and the Famine provided the opportunity for retaliation: food in exchange for conversion. Evangelical Protestants believed that the idolatrous cult of Catholicism was at the root of Irish economic backwardness, lawlessness, superstition, and antipathy to their colonial masters. In 1831 Edward Nangle went to Achill and founded a Protestant colony near the village of Dugort, beneath Slievemore (seen in the background of the painting). Slievemore comprised some 100 windowless, dry-stone cottages; the single room was kitchen, living room, bedroom, and even stable. While some had a small outhouse, as depicted here, most families lived with their livestock, which would be brought into the house at night and tethered. Most had opposing doorways: the cow was taken in one door, milked, and put out the opposite door. Inside, a shallow channel in the floor led into a manure pit outside the building.

Nangle established schools, a church, a hotel, and a printing press to counter native "savagery". But, according to his biographer, Rev. Henry Seddal, he was "headstrong in forming his opinions, stubborn in holding them, and harsh in giving them expression".[208] The Catholic archbishop of Tuam, John McHale, retaliated by inciting his priests against such "venomous fanatics". In *A Tour in Connaught*, Caesar Otway recounted a sermon preached against the mission by Fr Dwyer:

Have nothing to do with these heretics - curse them, hoot at them, spit in their faces - cut the sign of the cross in the air when you meet them, as you would against devils - throw stones at them - pitch them, when you have opportunity, into the bog holes - nay more than that, do injury to yourselves in order to injure them - don't work for them, though they pay in ready money - nay, don't take any medicine from their heretic doctor, rather die first.[209]

The Great Famine hit Achill hard. Nangle declared it God's judgement for Ireland's sins. He believed that it was not coincidental that the British government's support in 1847 for the Catholic seminary at Maynooth - "the fountain-head of Popery in Ireland" - was committed the very same month that "famine begins, and is followed by plague, pestilence, blood!" (Incidentally, the Williams family supplied the top hats for Maynooth College!)[210] Initially, Nangle required conversion to Protestantism in exchange for food, earning him the sobriquet "souper" and "black Protestant". But that year, out of Achill's total population of 7,000, some 5,000 were receiving relief; without the mission, thousands more would have starved to death.

In 1850 the mission purchased three fifths of the island; the remaining land was purchased by Archbishop McHale and his nephew, instigating a Catholic "Counter-Reformation" with a papal diktat to bring the mission to an end. By the 1880s the mission colony was dead.

Additional to sectarian divisions were class antipathies. Unusually, Williams managed to get on with landlord and tenant, Catholic and Protestant. He held his first solo exhibition in 1884, concerning which the *Irish Times* noted that "dramatic and technical excellence ... bring him into the front rank of Irish painters" (November 18, 1884). He commanded substantial figures for his paintings. His solo exhibitions were favored by successive Lords Lieutenant and what was known as the "Castle Set", attendances mounting to a thousand or more. His work was also shown in Switzerland, Canada, and America (at the World Fair, Chicago (1893), and the St Louis World Fair (1904), at which the brothers also exhibited a taxidermy collection of birds). Much praised for revealing the beauties of Ireland, the *Irish Times* declared that through his art "he has done the nation service" (January 21, 1901).

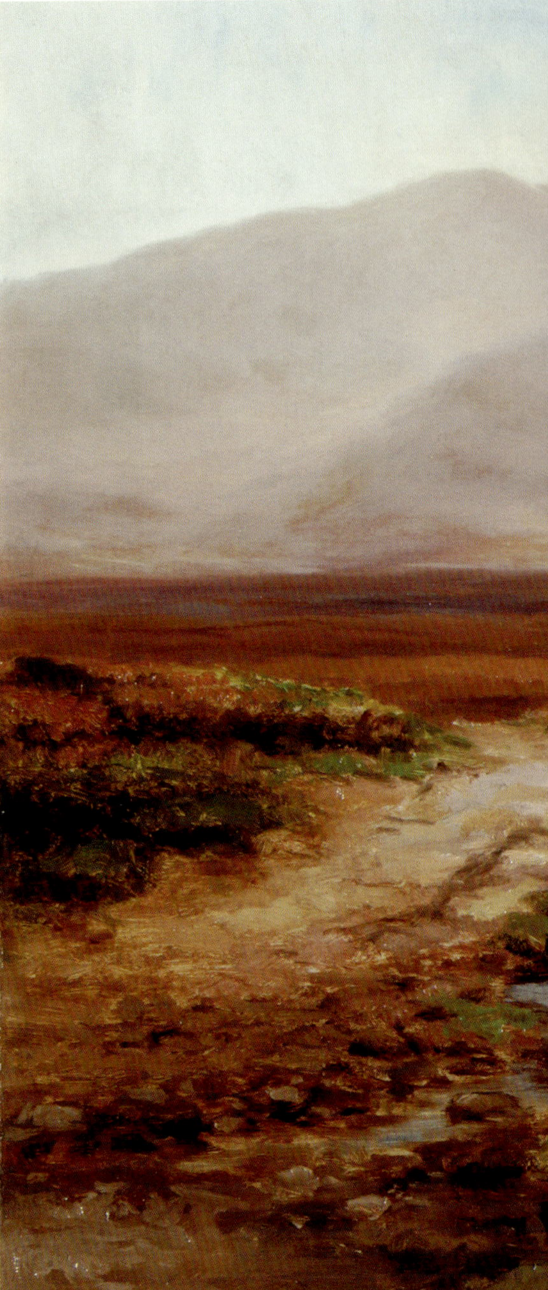

Cottage, Achill Island
Oil on canvas, 24 x 42 in (61 x 106.68 cm)

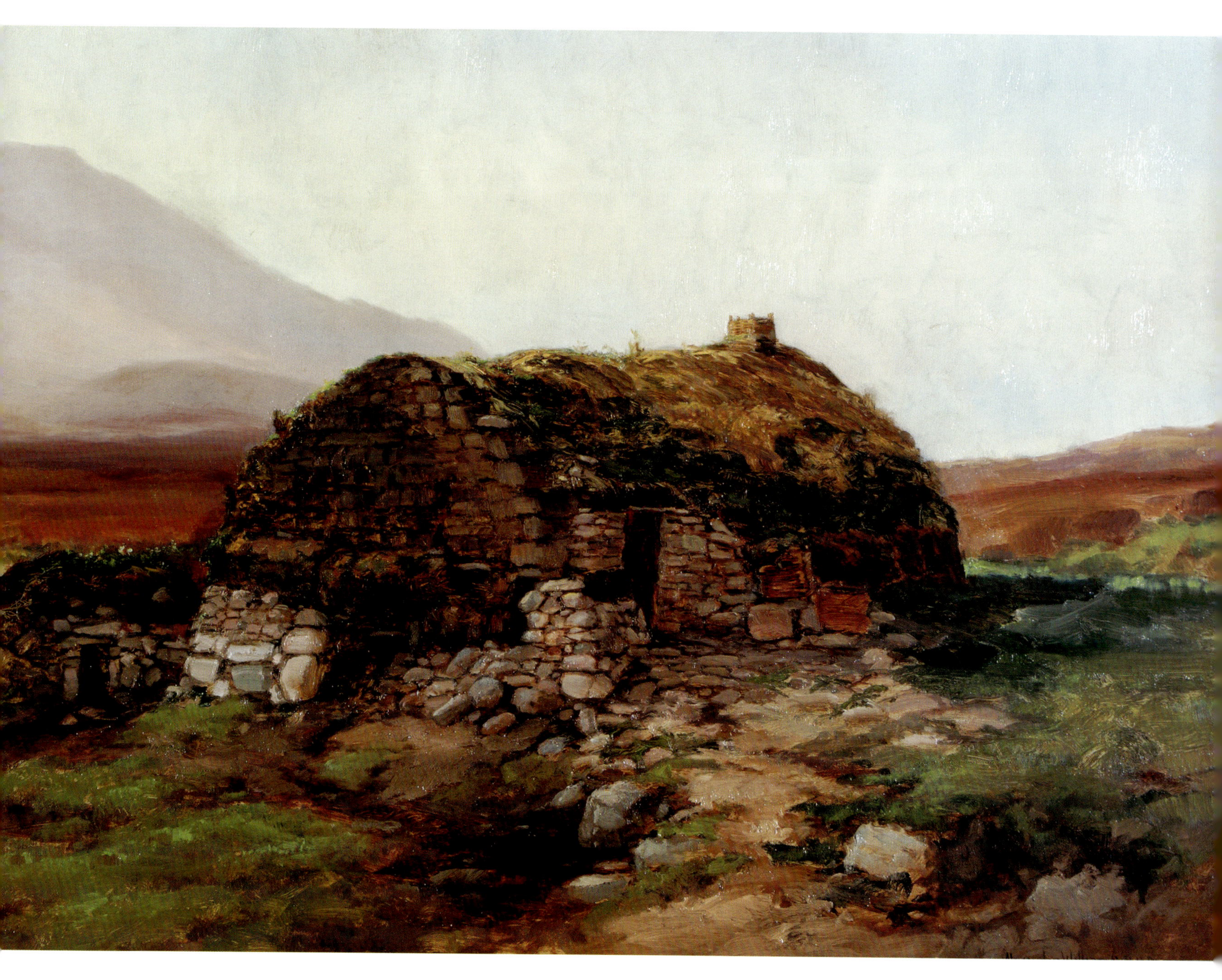

Yeats, Jack B.

RHA (1871–1957)

Derrynane, 1927
Oil on canvas, 24 x 36 in (61 x 91.44 cm)

Yeats was born into a brilliantly gifted family: Jack, William, Lily, and Lolly – the children of John Butler Yeats and Susan Pollexfen – were outstanding artists, designers, and writers. Their father trained as a barrister but followed a more impecunious career as an artist. Jack spent lengthy periods of time with his Pollexfen grandparents. As he said himself, he rarely painted a picture "without a bit of Sligo in it".

The Sligo of Yeats's childhood was deeply scarred by the not-so-distant Great Hunger, and more recently mired in the Land War of the late nineteenth century. The 1860s saw the highest emigration figures since the Famine. In 1867 William Pollexfen had witnessed the arrival from America of *Erin's Hope* laden with Fenian arms but which was refused entry to Sligo Bay and returned to New York. These were the stories the seafaring grandfather told his grandchildren, and Jack was receptive to their contemporary resonance.

His romantic and often symbolic images of Irish people and landscape encouraged many to see him as *the* national painter. Yeats was a humanist, yet he followed political affairs closely. The turmoil of the War of Independence, the Treaty, the civil war, and the bitterness of the early 1920s informed his work. "When painting takes its rightful place it will be in a free nation, for though pictures speak all languages the roots of every art must be the country of the artist, and no man can have two countries", he declared in 1922.[211] Yet, in an important caveat, he insisted that "a painting is not a vehicle for anything except itself" (*Daily Express*, October 12, 1929). Initially, he applied the paint in broad, flat strokes, but by the mid-1920s was painting with brushes, fingers, and palette knife directly from the tube. By the late 1920s the work had become bold. Finally, from 1940 color took over and became, at times, the subject of the painting. Late works, such as *Men of Destiny* (1946) and *Grief* (1951), show evidence of extraordinary power and experimentation. Hilary Pyle, Yeats's biographer, believes that the emotional pitch of these late works are indicative of his detachment from politics following the death of his wife and siblings, leading to a growing subjectivity and spirituality. He now revisited themes from his early work, reconfigured to suggest what Róisín Kennedy calls "nostalgia, dislocation or euphoria".[212]

Kennedy notes that "by a primitive handling of form, which accentuates the exotic nature of Irish rural life ... Yeats's novel depiction of the Irish peasant as stalwart, humorous and exuberant was based on scenes witnessed on his visits to the west of Ireland and recorded in his sketchbooks".[213] His deep pool of memories, personal and collective, allowed him to produce work that was at once uncompromisingly Irish and insistently international. He had many connections with avant-garde artists and writers, notably Oskar Kokoschaka. Closer to home he was championed by Thomas McGreevy and Samuel Beckett. Beckett ranked Yeats alongside Kandinsky, Braque, and Klee, while James Joyce believed that he and Yeats shared a "method". All owned works by Yeats.

In 1945 a retrospective of his career showing 179 works was held in the National College of Art, Dublin, and attended by some 20,000 people. The catalogue essay was written by Ernie O'Malley (1897–1957), who had risen to leadership ranks in the republican movement during the Irish War of Independence (1919–21) and the civil war (1922–23).[214] According to Luke Gibbons, O'Malley had "developed a keen awareness of the imprint of history on the Irish countryside discerning its inner histories", and O'Malley himself described Yeats's painting as being at one with the landscape, climate, and vernacular culture.[215] "The new Ireland", he wrote, "still fluid politically and socially, has found in Jack Yeats a painter of major rank."[216] With his "hawk's swift eye", as O'Malley put it, Yeats painted more than 1,100 works in oils alone.[217] And he segued from one art form to the other: the poetic is evident in his paintings, the visual in his writings.

O'Malley owned *Derrynane* (exhibited at the NCA; Aonach Tailteann (1932); and the International Exhibition, Carnegie Institute, Pittsburgh (1938)), thus taking its place in the Yeats canon. Painted from memory, it is described by Hilary Pyle as "the most important landscape painting of Yeats's middle period".[218] Arguably, Yeats was at his best when painting from memory (he mined his sketchbooks for material throughout his career; several sketches in the NGI anticipate this oil). As a seascape it is representational with identifiable topographical features, but leans towards the semi-abstract in its emphasis on the materiality of the ultramarine, blue, yellow, and crimson.

Yeats visited Kerry in 1905 with his friend the playwright J.M. Synge, returned in 1913 to learn Irish, and visited again in 1925, when he executed a number of sketches of the O'Connell estate. But when Yeats stood in front of his easel to paint *Derrynane* – home to the Liberator Daniel O'Connell – he knew this was no ordinary place but a landscape riven with history.

In the distance is Skellig Michael. Atop a vertiginous rock, 230 meters above sea level, one of the most daring architectural manifestations of monasticism was constructed. During the medieval period the site was renowned throughout Europe as a place of pilgrimage and mysticism.

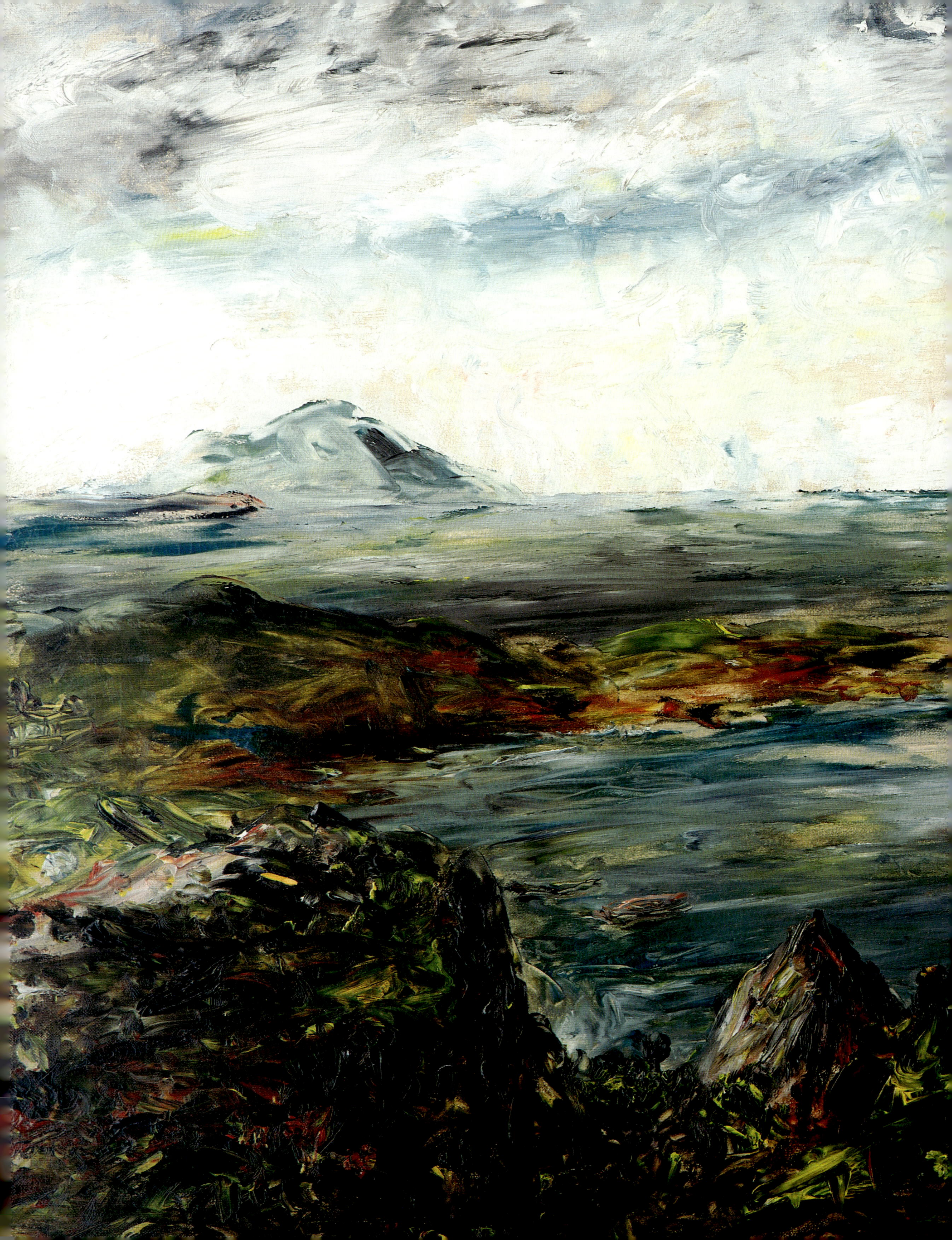

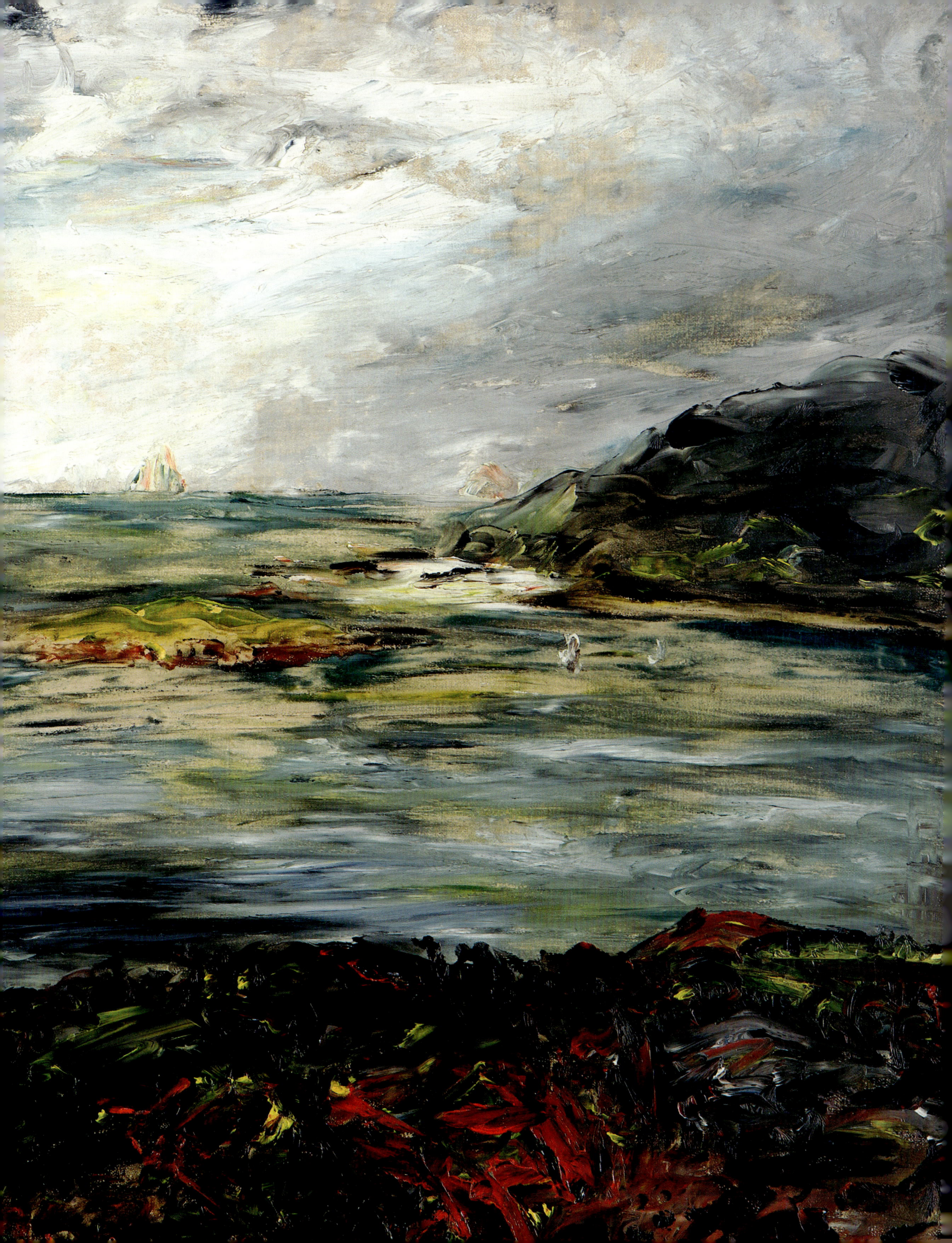

Daniel O'Connell (1775–1847), barrister, politician, and nationalist leader, was born in Carhen, on the Iveragh Peninsula. The O'Connells were Catholic landholders of old Gaelic stock, who, despite plantation and Penal Laws, managed to hold onto their land. Derrynane House was owned by O'Connell's uncle, Maurice (1728–1825), alias Hunting Cap; following his death, Daniel inherited the property and lived there for half the year.

Yeats admired O'Connell, not least as "King of the Beggars" (the Yeats family cat was called Daniel O'Connell!). Like Yeats, O'Connell loved the sea. Recalling a visit to Kerry, the Victorian reformer Harriet Martineau remarked on O'Connell's yacht "riding in the sound" – the surest reminder of "enterprises that were conducted by night"; smuggling was "considered rather an act of patriotism than an offence", as "disaffected" Kerrymen "amazingly enjoyed depriving England ... of the produce of the Customs".[219] Yeats's love of the sea is tangible in the gestural and expressive manner in which he painted this panoramic seascape.

Repulsed by the French Revolution that erupted while he was studying in France, and the bloodshed of the 1798 Rebellion in Ireland, O'Connell was nevertheless opposed to the enactment of the Act of Union. In May 1823 the Catholic Association was formed, and, with O'Connell as leader, developed as a formidable mass movement. In 1828 O'Connell was prevailed upon to stand for election though, as a Catholic, he would have been unable to take his seat. He won, bringing matters to a head: Catholic Emancipation followed in 1829.

O'Connell may have been "the greatest innovator in modern democratic politics", but his subsequent efforts at the Repeal of the Union were vehemently

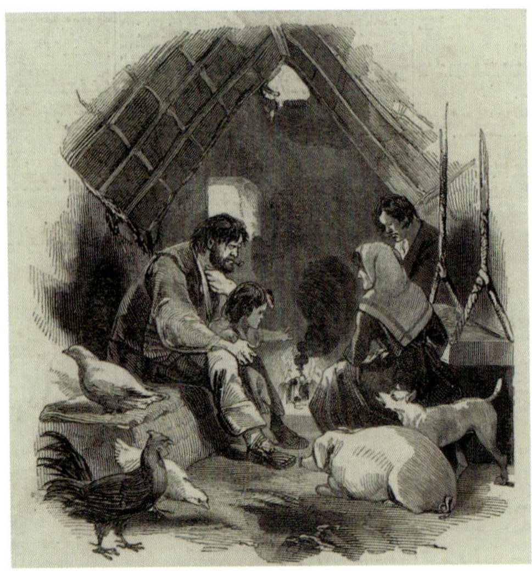

"Ardcara – Cabin of J. Donoghue"
Pictorial Times (February 7, 1846)

opposed.[220] His "monster meetings" kept the people keyed for the final push for Repeal, but when the government proscribed the 1843 meeting in Clontarf, O'Connell faltered. The Young Ireland movement denounced his disavowal of violence as cowardice. With the onset of the Famine the movement fell into disarray. O'Connell urged the government to import food, but, while sympathetic to his own tenants, employed a kinsman whose severity as an agent did untold damage to his reputation, occasioning many journalists and illustrators to visit Derrynane to ascertain the truth. "*The Times* Commissioner", Thomas Campbell Foster, wrote that O'Connell would be remembered "among the most neglectful landlords who are a curse to Ireland". He observed "the lowest degree of squalid poverty" on his estate:

There is not a pane of glass in the parish, nor a window of any kind in half the cottages, some have got a hole in the wall for light, with a board to stop it up. In not one in a dozen is there a chair to sit upon, or anything whatever in the cottages beyond an iron pot and a rude bedstead with some straw on it; and not always that.[221]

There was outcry. Beset by deteriorating health, financial problems, and the reported state of his tenantry, O'Connell died in March 1847. Sixty years later, Yeats's glorious landscape must have reawakened both inspirational and distressing memories for many.

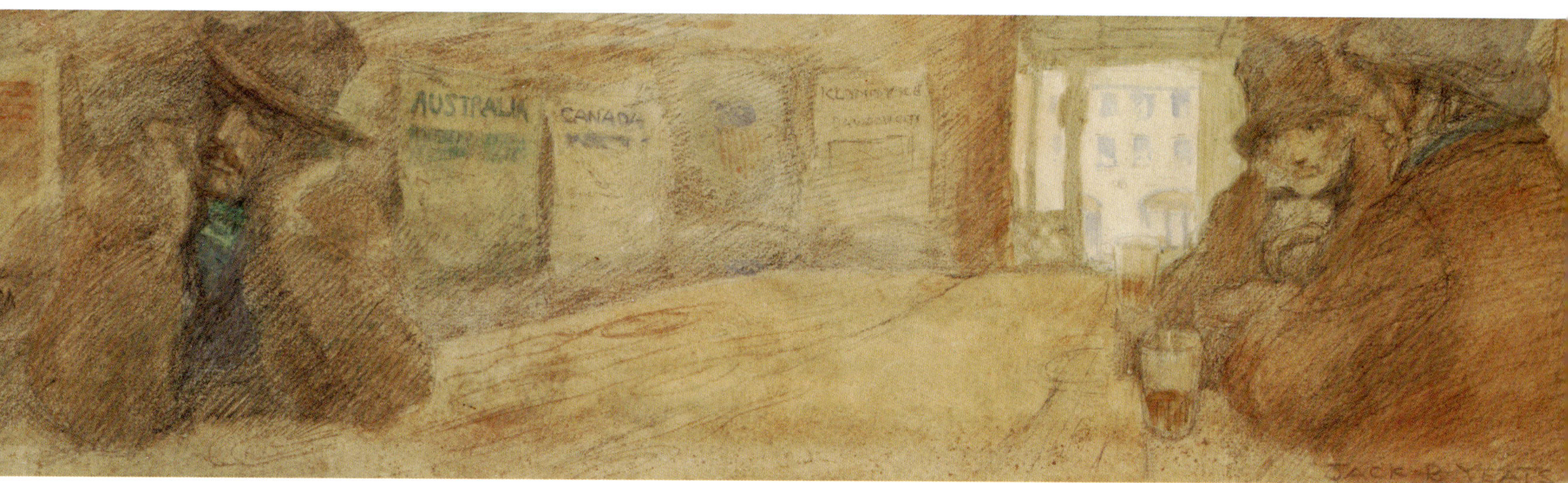

A Young Man's Troubles, 1900
Watercolor, pastel and pencil on paper,
6 x 18 in (15.24 x 45.72 cm)

Endnotes:

Niamh O'Sullivan: "In the land of the dead": Art & the Great Hunger

1 Thomas Davis, "The state of the peasantry", in idem, *Literary and Historical Essays* (Dublin: James Duffy, 1865), p. 341.
2 Ibid.
3 Richard Lovell Edgeworth and Maria Edgeworth, *Memoirs*, vol. 2 (London: R. Hunter & Baldwin, Cradock & Joy, 1821), p. 350.
4 Quoted in Max Wyman, *The Defiant Imagination: Why Culture Matters* (Vancouver: Douglas & McIntyre, 2004), p. 85.
5 David Rieff, *In Praise of Forgetting: Historical Memory and its Ironies* (New Haven, CT and London: Yale University Press, 2016), p. 28.
6 Primo Levi, *The Drowned and the Saved* [1986] (New York: Simon & Schuster, 1989), p. 8.
7 John Bigelow (ed.), *The Life of Benjamin Franklin, Written by Himself*, vol. 2 (Cambridge: Cambridge University Press, 2011), p. 98.
8 Arthur Young, *A Tour in Ireland, 1776–1779*, vol. 2 (London: Cadell, 1780), pp. 127–8.
9 Frederick Douglass [letter], Montrose [Scotland], Feb. 26, 1846 to William Lloyd Garrison, in Philip Foner (ed.), *Life and Writings of Frederick Douglass* (New York: International Publishers, 1950), vol. i, p. 138.
10 Quoted in Leslie A. Williams, *Daniel O'Connell: The British Press and the Irish Famine: Killing Remarks* (Farnham, Surrey: Ashgate, 2003), p. 155.
11 For further commentary on Macdonald's work, see Niamh O'Sullivan, *In the Lion's Den: Daniel Macdonald, Ireland and Empire* (Hamden, CT: Quinnipiac University Press/Ireland's Great Hunger Museum, 2016).
12 Davis,"State of the peasantry", p. 342. The antiquary Thomas Crofton Croker described the banshee as "a small and shrivelled old woman with long white hair, supposed to be peculiarly attached to old houses or families, and to announce the approaching dissolution of any members by mournful lamentations"; Thomas Crofton Croker, *Researches in the South of Ireland* [1824] (Dublin: Irish Academic Press, 1981), p. 91.
13 Justin Carville, *Photography and Ireland* (London: Reaktion, 2011), p. 66.
14 For fuller discussion, see Niamh O'Sullivan, *The Tombs of a Departed Race: Illustrations of Ireland's Great Hunger* (Hamden, CT: Quinnipiac University Press/ Ireland's Great Hunger Museum, 2014).
15 For fuller discussion, see Michael Foley, *Death in Every Paragraph: Journalism and the Great Irish Famine* (Hamden, CT: Quinnipiac University Press/Ireland's Great Hunger Museum, 2015).
16 Daniel Donovan, "Observations on the peculiar diseases to which the famine of the last year gave origin and on the morbid effects of insufficient nourishment", *Medical Examiner: A Monthly Record of Medical Science*, vol. 4, June 1848, p. 382; see also Breandán MacSuibhne, *The End of Outrage: Post-Famine Adjustment in Rural Ireland* (London and New York: Oxford University Press, 2017) for an incisive study not only of what the poor did *for* but *to* each other.
17 Ireland's Great Hunger Museum has an extensive searchable database (over 1,500 images) of news-paper reportage and illustrations from the period; https://repository.quinnipiac.edu/collections/home.do
18 Susan Sontag, *Regarding the Pain of Others* (New York: Picador, 2003), p. 60.
19 See Luke Gibbons, *Limits of the Visible: Representing the Great Hunger* (Hamden, CT: Quinnipiac University Press/Ireland's Great Hunger Museum, 2014), p. 23.
20 Elihu Burritt, *A Journal of a Visit of Three Days to Skibbereen and its Neighbourhood* (London: Charles Gilpin, 1847).
21 Thomas Armstrong, *My Life in Connaught* (London: Elliott Stock, 1906), p. 13.
22 Alfred Swaine Taylor, *Medical Jurisprudence* (Philadelphia: 1853), p. 549.
23 Fintan Cullen, *Visual Politics: The Representation of Ireland, 1750–1930* (Cork: Cork University Press, 1997), p. 116.
24 Nicholas Tromans, *David Wilkie: The People's Painter* (Oxford, 2007), p. 190.
25 "These little pictures constitute a strong argument in favour of emigration. Pat goes out a beggar. He returns a gentleman ... How soon the Irish question would be solved if people were all like Erskine Nicol's sample"; *Manchester Courier and Lancashire General Advertiser*, May 10, 1887.
26 Donovan, "Observations on the peculiar diseases", p. 382.
27 Kevin Whelan, "Immoral economy: interpreting Erskine's Nicol's *The Tenant*", in Adele M. Dalsimer and Vera Kreilkamp (eds), *America's Eye: Irish Paintings from the Collecton of Brian P. Burns* (Boston: Boston College Museum of Art, 1996), p. 64.
28 See L. Perry Curtis Jr., *Apes and Angels: The Irishman in Victorian Caricature* (Washington DC: Smithsonian Institution Press, 1997).
29 Mary Howitt, *Howitt's Journal of Literature and Popular Progress*, vol. 2 (1847), p. 10.
30 For detailed analyses of cabin interiors, see Claudia Kinmonth, *Irish Rural Interiors in Art* (New Haven, CT and London: Yale University Press, 2006).
31 David Lloyd, "The memory of loss", in David L. Eng and David Kazanjian (eds), *Loss: The Politics of Mourning* (Berkeley: University of California Press, 2003), p. 218.
32 See Paschal Mahoney, *Grim Bastilles of Despair: The Poor Law Union Workhouses in Ireland* (Hamden, CT: Quinnipiac University Press/Ireland's Great Hunger Museum, 2016).
33 See *Frederick William Burton: For the Love of Art* (Dublin: National Gallery of Ireland, 2017).
34 See Angela Bourke, *Voices Underfoot: Memory, Forgetting, and Oral Verbal Art* (Hamden, CT: Quinnipiac University Press/Ireland's Great Hunger Museum, 2016); and Niamh Ann Kelly, *Ultimate Witnesses: The Visual Culture of Death, Burial and Mourning in Famine Ireland* (Hamden, CT: Quinnipiac University Press/Ireland's Great Hunger Museum, 2017).
35 Thomas Crofton Croker, *Researches in the South of Ireland, Illustrative of the Scenery, Architectural Remains, and the Manners and Superstitions of the Peasantry* (London: J. Murray, 1824), p. 172.
36 Laurence Geary, "Epidemic diseases of the Great Famine", *History Ireland*, vol. 4, no. 1 (spring 1996), pp. 27–32: p. 29.
37 Charles E. Trevelyan, "The Irish crisis", *Edinburgh* Review, no. clxxv, reprinted 1848, p. 1.
38 Quoted in Jennifer Hart, "Sir Charles Trevelyan at the Treasury", *English Historical Review*, vol. lxxv, no. 294 (1960), pp. 92–109: p. 99.
39 Quoted in Christine Kinealy, "How politics fed the Famine", *Magazine of the American Museum of Natural History*, vol. 105, no. 1 (1996), pp. 34–5.
40 John Mitchel, *The Last Conquest of Ireland (Perhaps)* (Glasgow: Washbourne, 1862), p. 139; for a fuller discussion, see Tadhg Foley, *Death by Discourse? Political Economy and the Great Irish Famine* (Hamden, CT: Quinnipiac University Press/Ireland's Great Hunger Museum, 2016).
41 Mitchel, *Last Conquest of Ireland*, p. 112.
42 Quoted in Cecil Woodham-Smith, *The Great Hunger: Ireland 1845–1849* (London: Hamish Hamilton, 1962), p. 376.

43 See Mary Jane Boland, "Creating order? Painting the crowd in nineteenth-century Ireland", in Brendan Rooney (ed.), *Creating History: Stories of Ireland in Art* (Dublin: Irish Academic Press, 2016), pp. 105–10, 119.
44 Previously called *The Fighter*, the recent acquisition by the IGHM of an inscribed preliminary sketch confirms the title of the oil as *The Irish Faction Leader.*
45 Patrick Butler, for example, notes of the immediate pre- and post-Famine period in relation to Tipperary that it was "badly affected by agrarian agitation and faction fighting, more so than any other, but also by the Famine, a combination of which led to high incidents of transportation"; Patrick Butler, "The transportation of convicts from County Tipperary to Australia, 1836–1853", unpublished MA thesis (NUI Maynooth, 2005), p. iii.
46 See L. Perry Curtis Jr., *Depiction of Eviction in Ireland: 1845–1910* (Dublin: University College Dublin Press, 2011).
47 See Fintan Cullen, "Displaying distress", in idem, *Ireland on Show: Art Union and Nationhood* (Farnham, Surrey: Ashgate, 2012), pp. 87–124.
48 Emily Mark-Fitzgerald, "Photography and the visual legacy of the Famine", in Oonagh Frawley (ed.), *Memory Ireland, Volume 3: The Famine and the Troubles* (New York: Syracuse University Press, 2014), p. 127.
49 M.S. Watts, *George Frederic Watts, Volume 1: The Annals of an Artist's Life* (London: Macmillan & Co.), pp. 108–9; and Wilfrid Philip Ward, *Aubrey de Vere: A Memoir* (London: Longmans, Green, & Co.; New York: Longmans, 1904), p. 164; see also Wilfred Blunt, *"England's Michaelangelo": A Biography of George Frederic Watts, O.M., R.A.* (London: Hamish Hamilton, 1975), pp. 47, 55–6, 211, 220.
50 Walter Strickland, *A Dictionary of Irish Artists, Vol. 1* (Dublin: Maunsel, 1913), p. 573.
51 Catherine Marshall, "Painting Irish history: the Famine," *History Ireland*, vol. 4, no. 3 (autumn 1996), pp. 48–9: p. 47.
52 Quoted in Kerby A Miller, *Emigrants and Exiles: Ireland and the Irish Exodus to North America* (New York: Oxford University Press, 1985), pp. 4–7.
53 Crookshank and Glin, for example, credit the Willes's painting as one of the most interesting Famine paintings, effectively visualizing the tragedy of emigration; Anne Crookshank and the Knight of Glin, *Ireland's Painters, 1600–1940* (New Haven, CT and London: Yale University Press, 2002), p. 231; see also William Laffan, "William Willes' *The Mock Funeral*", in Brendan Rooney (ed.), *A Time and a Place: Two Centuries of Irish Social Life* (Dublin: National Gallery of Ireland, 2007), pp. 85–6; and Brendan Rooney, "William Willes", in Nicola Figgis (ed.), *Art and Architecture of Ireland, Volume II: Painting 1600–1900* (London and New Haven, CT: Yale University Press, 2014), p. 506.
54 See Fintan Cullen, "Representing the Irish emigrant: humour to pathos?", *Visual Culture in Britain*, vol. 18, no. 2 (2017), DOI: 10.1080/14714787.2017.1328987.
55 See Mick Moloney, *Across the Western Ocean: Songs of Leaving and Arriving* (Hamden, CT: Quinnipiac University Press/Ireland's Great Hunger Museum, 2016).
56 The Grey Nuns are the subject of a touring exhibition, *Saving the Famine Irish: the Grey Nuns and the Great Hunger Exhibition*, organized by Ireland's Great Hunger Institute; see Jason King, "The Famine Irish, the Grey Nuns, and the fever sheds of Montreal: prostitution and female religious institution building", in Christine Kinealy, Jason King, and Ciarán Reilly (eds), *Women and the Great Hunger* (Quinnipiac, CT and Cork: Quinnipiac University Press/Ireland's Great Hunger Museum and Cork University Press, 2016).
57 Linda Nochlin, "The imaginary Orient", *Art in America*, vol. ixxi, no. 5 (1983), pp. 118–31.
58 William Robert Wilde, *Irish Popular Superstitions* (Dublin: McGlashan, 1852), p. 10.
59 Cited in Margaret Ward, *Maud Gonne: Ireland's Joan of Arc* (London: Pandora, 1990), p. 49.
60 See for example Marshall, "Painting Irish history", pp. 47–9; Marshall, *Monuments and Memorials of the Great Famine* (Hamden, CT: Quinnipiac University Press/Ireland's Great Hunger Museum, 2014); Emily Mark-Fitzgerald, *Commemorating the Irish Famine: Memory and the Monument* (Liverpool: Liverpool University Press, 2013); and, forthcoming, Niamh Ann Kelly, *Imaging the Great Irish Famine: Representing Dispossession in Visual Culture* (London: I.B. Tauris, 2018); and Emily Mark Fitzgerald, Oona Frawley, and Marguérite Corporaal (eds), *The Great Irish Famine and its Impacts: Visual and Material Cultures* (Liverpool: Liverpool University Press, 2018).
61 See, notably, Nicola Figgis (ed.), *Art and Architecture of Ireland, Volume II: Painting 1600–1900* (London and New Haven, CT: Yale University Press, 2014); Catherine Marshall and Peter Murray (eds), *Art and Architecture of Ireland, Volume V: Twentieth Century* (London and New Haven, CT: Yale University Press, 2014); and Paula Murphy (ed.), *Art and Architecture of Ireland, Volume III: Sculpture* (London and New Haven, CT: Yale University Press, 2014); John Crowley, William J. Smyth, and Mike Murphy (eds), *Atlas of the Great Irish Famine* (Cork: Cork University Press, 2012).
62 Luke Gibbons, "Words upon the windowpane: image, text, and Irish culture", in James Elkins (ed.), *Visual Cultures* (Chicago: University of Chicago Press, 2010), p. 44.
63 Paul Ricœur, "Memory and forgetting", in Richard Kearney and Mark Dooley (eds), *Questioning Ethics: Contemporary Debates in Philosopy* (London: Routledge, 1999), pp. 12–17: p. 8.

Ciarán Reilly: Feasting in a Time of Famine: Dublin Castle & the Great Hunger

1 Denis McCarthy, *Dublin Castle at the Heart of Irish History* (Dublin: Government Stationery Office, 2004), p. 12.
2 Eilís O'Sullivan, *Ascendancy Women and Elementary Education in Ireland: Educational Provision for Poor Children, 1788–1848* (London: Palgrave Macmillan, 2017), p. 30.
3 Mike Cronin and Daryl Adair, *The Wearing of the Green: A History of St Patrick's Day* (London: Psychology Press, 2006), p. 27.
4 Ibid. p. 4.
5 Ibid. p. 5.
6 Ibid. p. 6.
7 See for example *Freeman's Journal*, Mar. 15, 1851.
8 See *Dublin Evening Post*, Feb. 10, 1849.
9 *Belfast Newsletter*, Jan. 9, 1849.
10 *The Advocate, or Irish Industrial Journal*, Mar. 6, 1849.
11 For reports of distress, see the voluminous Relief Commission Papers held in the National Archives of Ireland.
12 See for example *Pilot*, Mar. 27, 1846.
13 *Dublin Evening Packet and Correspondent*, Mar. 19, 1846.
14 *Freeman's Journal*, Jan. 24, 1846.
15 See for example *Dublin Evening Packet and Correspondent*, Mar. 19, 1846.
16 Ibid. Mar. 28, 1846.
17 See for example *Freeman's Journal*, Sept. 26, 1846.
18 *Dublin Evening Mail*, June 4, 1847.
19 *Kerry Evening Post*, June 19, 1847.
20 *Illustrated London News*, Mar. 25, 1848.
21 *Newry Examiner and Louth Advertiser*, Apr. 5, 1848.
22 *Nation*, May 6, 1848.
23 *The Advocate, or Irish Industrial Journal*, Feb. 28, 1849.
24 Ibid. Mar. 6, 1849.
25 *Dublin Evening Post*, Feb. 10, 1849.
26 *Belfast Newsletter*, Feb. 13, 1849.
27 *Dublin Evening Post*, Feb. 10, 1849.
28 Cecil Woodham-Smith, *The Great Hunger* (London: Hamish Hamilton, 1962), p. 40.
29 "Queen Victoria's Journal, 8 Aug. 1849" (Royal Archives, London), quoted in James H. Murphy, *Abject Loyalty: Nationalism and Monarchy in Ireland During the Reign of Queen Victoria* (Washington DC: Catholic University of America Press, 2001), p. 94.
30 Ibid.
31 See A.C. Benson and Viscount Escher (eds), *The Letters Of Queen Victoria, 1844–1853*, 5 vols, vol. ii (London, 1907), pp. 225–6. See also Murphy, *Abject Loyalty*, pp. 94–5.
32 *Roscommon Messenger*, Aug. 11, 1849.
33 *Freeman's Journal*, June 29, 1849.
34 Bewley's advertisements appeared on a weekly basis in national and provincial papers; see for example *Freeman's Journal*, Mar. 27, 1846.
35 Ibid.
36 Ibid. June 27, 1845.
37 See for example Henry Brett, OPW county surveyor in Mayo, to Lord Lieutenant, Dublin Castle, reporting the continued advance of the potato disease in storage pits and in the soil, Nov 29, 1845, National Archives of Ireland, Relief Commission Papers, 2/Z17412.
38 See for example Duke of Leinster to Relief Commissioners, Dublin Castle, Dec. 7, 1845, National Archives of Ireland, Relief Commission Papers, 2/Z17412.
39 Nicholas Sadlier to James Sadlier, Nov. 12, 1845 (in private possession).
40 *Nation*, Apr. 25, 1846.
41 For an example of this, see Ciarán Reilly, *John Plunket Joly and the Great Famine in King's County* (Dublin: Four Courts Press, 2012).
42 Petition sent to T. Lucas Clements, Feb. 11, 1846, Lucas-Clements Papers, Maynooth University. I am grateful to Professor Terence Dooley for allowing me access to these papers.
43 James Roberts to T. Lucas Clements, Oct. 15, 1846, Lucas-Clements Papers, Maynooth University.
44 Letter to T. Lucas Clements, unsigned, Jan. 17, 1847, Lucas-Clements Papers, Maynooth University.
45 In April the committee hastily prepared a tender to provide coffins. Fifty handbills were printed calling for tenders and posted throughout the barony. For more, see Lucas-Clements Papers, Maynooth University.
46 A. Armstrong, Cavan to T. Lucas Clements, Jan. 11, 1847, Lucas-Clements Papers, Maynooth University.
47 Robert Bannon to T. Lucas Clements, n.d. but 1847, Lucas-Clements Papers, Maynooth University.
48 For a commentary on this, see various issues of *Punch*, July–Dec. 1848.
49 See for example *Anglo Celt*, May 28, 1847.
50 *Nation*, Aug. 28, 1847.
51 Minute book of the Rathkenny Relief Committee, Lucas-Clements Papers, Maynooth University.
52 *Dublin Evening Post*, Sept. 23, 1847.

53 See for example Robert Graham to T. Lucas-Clements, Dec. 1, 1846, Lucas-Clements Papers, Maynooth University.
54 *Nation*, Aug. 28, 1847.
55 Ibid.
56 *Extract of a Report of the Commissioners of Inquiry into Matters Connected with the Failure of the Potato Crop*, Jan. 20, 1846, p. 33.
57 Cited in *Eclectic Review*, vol. 22 (Jan.–Dec. 1847), p. 329.
58 Report on the sanitary convenience of Dublin Castle, 12 Nov 1845, National Archives of Ireland, Relief Commission Papers.
59 Quoted in Cormac Ó Gráda, *Black '47 and Beyond: The Great Famine in History, Economy and Memory* (Princeton, NJ: Princeton University Press, 1999), p. 160.
60 Ibid. p. 173.
61 *Freeman's Journal*, 4 Jan., 1847.
62 *Kerry Evening Post*, Oct. 20, 1849.
63 *Kerry News*, Feb. 11, 1914.

Laurence Geary: "Frightful and fearful is the havoc around": The Great Famine in Cork City & County

1 *Cork Constitution*, Feb. 7, 1847, Rev. Dr Robert Traill, rector of Schull, to the editor dated Feb. 5, 1847.
2 Margaret Crawford, "The Great Irish Famine 1845–9: image versus reality", in Brian P. Kennedy and Raymond Gillespie (eds), *Ireland: Art into History* (Dublin: Town House, 1994), pp. 75–88.
3 James S. Donnelly Jr., *The Land and the People of Nineteenth-century Cork: The Rural Economy and the Land Question* (London and Boston: Routledge & Kegan Paul, 1975), p. 73.
4 James S. Donnelly Jr., *The Great Irish Potato Famine* (Stroud: Sutton, 2001), p. 57, Fr Theobald Mathew to Charles Trevelyan, permanent secretary at the Treasury, Aug. 7, 1846.
5 *Cork Constitution*, Apr. 24, 1847, quoted in Donnelly, *The Land and the People*, pp. 86–7.
6 *Dublin Quarterly Journal of Medical Science*, no. 8 (1849), p. 279.
7 Ibid. p. 270.
8 R.B. Forbes, *The Voyage of the Jamestown on Her Errand of Mercy* (Boston, 1847), pp. 22–3; *Cork Examiner*, Apr. 14, 1847. See also Forbes to Elihu Burritt, Apr. 20, 1847, in which he described Cork and its neighborhood as a charnel house; Forbes, *The Voyage of the Jamestown*, appendix 83, pp. cxii–cxiii. For the *Jamestown* relief mission, see Laurence M. Geary, "'The noblest offering that nation ever made to nation': American philanthropy and the Great Famine in Ireland", *Éire-Ireland*, vol. 48, nos 3–4 (fall/winter 2013), pp. 103–28.
9 Chief Secretary's Office Registered Papers (hereafter CSORP) 1847 H5408, National Archives of Ireland (hereafter NAI), Dublin. See also Colman O'Mahony, *In the Shadows: Life in Cork 1750–1939* (Cork: Tower Books, 1997), pp. 164–6; Donnelly, *The land and the people*, p. 87.
10 Fr Mathew to the under secretary, Dublin Castle, June 4, 1847, CSORP 1847 H 6843, NAI.
11 *Distress in Ireland. Extracts From Correspondence Published by the Central Relief Committee of the Society of Friends, No. 1* (Dublin, 1847), pp. 20–2.
12 See in particular Peter Gray, *Famine, Land, and Politics: British Government and Irish Society, 1843–1850* (Dublin: Irish Academic Press, 1999).
13 *Distress in Ireland. Extracts From Correspondence Published by the Central Relief Committee of the Society of Friends, No. 2* (Dublin, 1847), p. 7.
14 *Southern Reporter* (hereafter *SR*), Mar. 4, 1847, cited in Patrick Hickey, "Famine, mortality and emigration: a profile of six parishes in the Poor Law union of Skibbereen, 1846–7", in Patrick O'Flanagan and Cornelius G. Buttimer (eds), *Cork: History and Society. Interdisciplinary Essays on the History of an Irish County* (Dublin: Geography Publications, 1993), p. 873.
15 For Traill, see Patrick Hickey, "Some Famine letters of Dr Robert Traill, rector of Schull (1830–47)", *Mizen Journal* (1995), pp. 11–19; for Donovan, see obituary in *West Cork Eagle and County Advertiser*, Oct. 6, 1877.
16 See, for instance, Fr John Fitzpatrick's acknowledgement of the role of publicity and the power of the press at a public meeting in Skibbereen Courthouse on Jan. 16, 1847, *Cork Examiner* (hereafter *CE*), Jan. 18, 1847. See also, *CE*, Jan. 8, 1847, publicity trip to England by two local Church of Ireland clergymen, Richard Boyle Townsend and C. Caulfield.
17 Joseph Kidd, "On the fever and dysentery of Ireland in 1847", in Francis Treuherz (ed.), *Homoeopathy in the Irish Potato Famine* (London: Samuel Press, 1995), pp. 76–102: pp. 77–8; originally published in *British Journal of Homoeopathy*, no. 6 (Jan. 1848), pp. 85–109.
18 *Correspondence from January to March, 1847, Relating to the Measures Adopted for the Relief of Distress in Ireland. Commissariat Series [Second Part]*, British Parliamentary Papers (hereafter BPP) 1847 [796] lii, pp. 162–4, Commander Caffin to Captain Hamilton, Febuary 15, 1847.
19 F.F. Trench, "Letters concerning the Famine in Schull", in W. Steuart Trench, *Realities of Irish Life* (London: Longmans, Green, & Co., 1868), pp. 388–407. For a more complete account of the issues referred to in this paragraph, see Laurence M. Geary, "'The living were out of their feeling': a socio-cultural analysis of the Great Famine in Ireland", in Breandán Ó Conaire (ed.), *The Famine Lectures: Léachtaí an Ghorta* (Boyle: Roscommon Herald, 2000), pp. 308–28.
20 Trench, "Letters concerning the Famine in Schull", pp. 404–5, Richard Chenevix Trench to F.F. Trench.
21 Richard Chenevix Trench, "Three days of the Famine at Schull", *Fraser's Magazine for Town and Country*, no. 36 (July 1847), pp. 1–13.
22 Charles Northend (ed.), *Elihu Burritt; a Memorial Volume Containing a Sketch of His Life and Labors, with Selections from His Writings and Lectures, and Extracts from His Private Journals in Europe and America* (New York: D. Appleton & Company, 1879), pp. 34–5, pp. 217–34; Elihu Burritt, *A Journal of a Visit of Three Days to Skibbereen, and its Neighbourhood* (London and Birmingham, 1847).
23 Daniel Donovan, "Observations on the peculiar diseases to which the Famine of last year gave origin, and on the morbid effects of insufficient nourishment", *Dublin Medical Press*, Feb. 2, 1848, pp. 67–8, Mar. 1, 1848, pp. 129–32, May 3, 1848, pp. 275–78.
24 Laurence M. Geary, *Medicine and Charity in Ireland, 1718–1851* (Dublin: UCD Press, 2004), pp. 182–3.
25 CSORP 1847 H 1198; CSORP 1847 H 4454, NAI. See also *CE*, Jan. 11, 1847.
26 *SR*, Mar. 18, 1847, T. McCarthy Downing to editor, Mar. 14, 1847.
27 CSORP 1847 H 5209, NAI.
28 "Cork union. Report from Dr Stephens to the Board of Health, on the Cork workhouse", Feb. 17, 1847, "Second report from Dr Stephens to the Board of Health, on the Cork workhouse", Feb, 18, 1847, in *Workhouses (Ireland). A Copy of the Reports Made to the Board of Health in Dublin, by the Medical Officers Sent to Inquire into the State of the Workhouses in Cork, Bantry, and Lurgan*, BPP 1847, lv.11, pp. 1–6; "Observations by the Board of Health on the Cork Union, 20 February 1847", CSORP 1847 H 6048, NAI.
29 CSORP 1847 H 1704, 6048, NAI; O Mahony, *In the shadows*, pp. 157–8.
30 "Bantry union. Report from Dr Stephens to the Board of Health, on the Bantry workhouse", Feb. 20, 1847, in *Workhouses (Ireland)*, pp. 7–10; "Observations by the Board of Health on the Bantry Union, 8 March 1847", CSORP 1847 H 6048, NAI.
31 *CE*, Dec. 18, 1846.
32 Ibid. Dec. 21, 1846.
33 *Transactions of the Central Relief Committee of the Society of Friends During the Famine in Ireland, in 1846 and 1847* (Dublin, 1852), p. 191.
34 See, for instance, CSORP 1847 H 650, NAI.
35 *Freeman's Journal*, Jan. 9, Feb, 6, 7, 17, 1847.
36 Denis Chas. O'Connor, *Seventeen Years' Experience of Workhouse Life: With Suggestions for Reforming the Poor Law and its Administration* (Dublin: McGlashan & Gill, 1861), pp. 32, 48.
37 *Distress in Ireland. Extracts from Correspondence, No. 2*, pp. 26–7.
38 CSORP 1847 H 650, 1532 and 2026, NAI.
39 CSORP 1847 H 3506, NAI.
40 Trench, "Famine in Schull", p. 245.
41 *Transactions of the Central Relief Committee of the Society of Friends*, pp. 201–2.
42 Trench, "Famine in Schull", pp. 244–6; *Transactions of the Central Relief Committee of the Society of Friends*, p. 155; *FJ*, 17 Feb. 1847, Fitzpatrick to Miley, 6 Feb. 1847 and to Mrs B., 7 Feb. 1847.
43 Donnelly, *The land and the People*, p. 120.

Breandán Mac Suibhne: Entering the Gray Zone: Hugh Dorian & "the years of famine"

1 All details from the General Registrar 's Office's (GRO) Indices of Births, Deaths and Marriages, and National Archives of Ireland, Census 1901 and Census 1911. Dorian's age at death is calculated from census returns, which he completed; his son underestimated his age as seventy-six when registering his death. The GRO entry for Ellen's marriage in 1899 returns Hugh as a laborer.
2 Hugh Dorian, *The Outer Edge of Ulster: A Memoir of Social Life in Nineteenth-century Donegal*, eds Breandán Mac Suibhne and David Dickson (Dublin: Lilliput Press, 2000), pp. 216–17.
3 Ibid. p. 223.
4 Ibid. p. 227.
5 Cormac Ó Gráda, *Black '47 and Beyond: The Great Irish Famine in History, Economy, and Memory* (Princeton: Princeton University Press, 1999), pp. 194–225.
6 Dorian, *Outer Edge of Ulster*, pp. 191–2, 227–9, 239–40, 255–6.
7 Ibid. pp. 211, 215, 248, 255.
8 Primo Levi, *The Drowned and the Saved* (1986), pp. 20, 36–69.
9 Dorian, *Outer Edge of Ulster*, p. 230.
10 Ibid. p. 215.
11 Ibid. p. 323.
12 On reduction, see my *Subjects Lacking Words? The Gray Zone of the Great Famine* (Hamden, CT: Quinnipiac University Press, 2017). On images of famine, see Luke Gibbons, *Limits of the Visible* (Hamden, CT: Quinnipiac University Press, 2014).

13 Ireland's Great Hunger Museum, http://ighm.org/irish-peasant-children (accessed Dec. 19, 2017); Niamh O'Sullivan, *In the Lion's Den: Daniel Macdonald, Ireland and Empire* (Hamden, CT: Quinnipiac University Press/Ireland's Great Hunger Museum, 2016).
14 Dorian, *Outer Edge of Ulster*, p. 191.
15 *Londonderry Journal*, July 24, 1861.
16 Seán Ó Faoláin [Sean O'Faolain], *Vive Moi! An Autobiography* [1963] (London: Hart-David, 1965), p. 145.
17 John Berger, *Pig Earth* [1979] (New York: Vintage, 1992), p. xxiv.
18 On Dorian's career, see idem, *Outer Edge of Ulster*, pp. 27–43; and Raymond Blair, "The Dorian Letters, Fanad", *Donegal Annual*, no. 67 (2015), pp. 49–52. The population of Fánaid had stood at 10,344 in 1841, suggesting that it was close to 11,000 when the blight came in 1845; there were only 8,244 persons left in Fánaid in 1851.
19 For these letters, see Leitrim Papers MS 5,178, National Library of Ireland.
20 For a period Dorian taught shorthand for the Phonetic Society; see *Londonderry Sentinel*, Apr. 27, 1876; thanks to Raymond Blair for this reference.
21 *Derry Journal*, Jan. 29, 1899.
22 Ibid. Aug. 23, 1901.
23 Ibid. Sept. 6, 1901. James may not have accompanied the other Dorians when, in 1903, they moved to Nelson Street; certainly, in 1911 he was living in a boarding house on Bridge Street.
24 Ibid. Dec. 17, 1897.
25 *Judicial Statistics, Ireland, 1899, Part I* ..., HC 1900, Cd.313, vol. 104, p. 17.
26 Dorian, *Outer Edge of Ulster*, pp. 323–34.
27 Ibid. pp. 43–5.
28 *Belfast Newsletter*, Feb. 15, 1889.
29 Dorian, *Outer Edge of Ulster*, pp. 61–2 n. 4.
30 Ibid. p. 227.
31 Ibid. pp. 217–18.
32 Ibid. p. 227.
33 Ibid. p. 223.
34 Ibid. pp. 214–15.
35 Ibid. p. 230.
36 Ibid. pp. 191–2.
37 Ibid. pp. 224–7.
38 Ibid. pp. 218–19.
39 Ibid. p. 223.
40 Ibid. p. 222.

Niamh O'Sullivan: *Coming Home: Art & the Great Hunger* Exhibition Catalogue

1 See Jeanne Sheehy, "The Irish at Antwerp", *Irish Arts Review Yearbook*, vol. 10 (1994), pp. 163–6.
2 Julian Campbell, "Henry Allan", *Irish Arts Review*, vol. 29, no. 2 (summer 2012), pp. 94–7: p. 97.
3 *Harper's Weekly*, Sept. 13, 1873.
4 Jacob Riis, *How the Other Half Lives: Studies Among the Tenements of New York* (New York: Charles Scribner, 1890), p. 23.
5 See Niamh O'Sullivan and Claudia Kinmonth, *An Exhibition of 18th–20th Century Irish Paintings* (Dublin: Gorry Gallery, 2008), pp. 46–8.
6 See Niamh O'Sullivan, *Aloysius O'Kelly: Art, Nation, Empire* (Dublin: Field Day Publications, 2010).
7 Philip Bagenal, *The American Irish and Their Influence on Irish Politics* (London: 1882), p. 201.
8 "Dynamiters in Paris", *The Gentleman's Magazine and Historical Chronicle* (London: 1886), p. 370.
9 *William Holman Hunt and His Works: A Memoir of the Artist's Life with Description of His Pictures* (London: James Nisbet, 1860), p. 11.
10 Ford Madox Brown, *The Diary of Ford Madox Brown*, ed. Virginia Surtees (New Haven, CT and London: Yale University Press/Mellon Centre for Studies in British Art, 1981), p.132; William Michael Rossetti, *Pre-Raphaelite Diaries and Letters* (London: Hurst & Blackett, 1900), p. 176; Ian Fleming-Williams and Leslie Parris, *The Discovery of Constable* (London: Hamish Hamilton, 1984); Allen Staley, *The Pre-Raphaelite Landscape* (Oxford: Clarendon Press, 1973), p. 179.
11 See *Hereford Times*, Dec. 24, 1859.
12 *Athenaeum*, Dec. 11, 1886, p. 790.
13 William Michael Rossetti, "Art news from London", *Crayon*, no. 1, Apr. 25, 1855, pp. 263–5.
14 William Michael Rossetti, *Some Reminiscences of William Michael Rossetti* (New York: Charles Scribner; London: Brown, Langham, 1906).
15 Kieran Flanagan, *Sociological Noir: Irruptions and the Darkness of Modernity* (Abingdon: Routledge, 2017).
16 Deborah Kennedy, "The ruined abbey in the eighteenth century", *Philological Quarterly*, vol. 80, no. 4 (2001), pp. 501–23.
17 Flanagan, *Sociological Noir*, p. 135.
18 Quoted in Mr and Mrs S.C. Hall, *Ireland: its Scenery, Character &c.* (London: Hall, Virtue & Co., *c.* 1841), vol. 1, p. 101.
19 Ibid. pp. 101–2.
20 *Dublin University Magazine*, vol. 14, no. 84 (Dec. 1839); *Irish Penny Journal*, vol. 1, no. 7, Aug. 15, 1840; William Stokes, *The Life and Labours in Art and Archaeology of G. Petrie* (London: Longmans, Green, & Co., 1868), p. 73.
21 Brian McAvera, *Irish Arts Review*, autumn 2006, p. 71.
22 Patrick Murphy, *Robert Ballagh – Artist and Designer: A Retrospective*, catalogue of exhibition at the RHA/Gallagher Gallery, 2006, Introduction.
23 Brian O'Doherty, *Portrait of the Artist Micheal Farrell and Other Works by Robert Ballagh* (Cork: Crawford Art Gallery, 2003), n.p.
24 John Berger, *Ways of Seeing* (UK: BBC and Penguin Books, 1972).
25 For example, Émile Mâle, *The Gothic Image: Religious Art in France of the Thirteenth Century* (London: Dent, 1913); Erwin Panofsky, *Gothic Architecture and Scholasticism* (Latrobe, PA: Archabbey Press, 1951); Lawrence G. Duggan, "Was art really the "Book of the Illiterate"", *Word and Image*, vol. 5, no. 3 (July–Sept. 1989), pp. 227–51.
26 Catherine Marshall, *The Face of Revolution: Robert Ballagh – A Centennial Reflection* (2016).
27 Catherine Marshall, "Choosing the battleground: Robert Ballagh's paintings", *Irish Arts Review Yearbook*, vol. 12 (1996), pp. 147–55: p. 148.
28 In correspondence with author.
29 *Irish Times*, Feb. 6, 2008.
30 Brian Fallon, *John Behan, Sculpture 1960–1994* (Galway: Galway Arts Festival, 1994), p. 5.
31 Ibid.
32 Adrian Frazier, *John Behan: The Bull from Sheriff Street* (Dublin: Lilliput Press, 2015), p. 18.
33 Behan archive, Kenny Gallery, Galway.
34 Hilary Pyle, "John Behan", *Circa*, vol. 71 (spring 1995), p. 72.
35 Frazier, *John Behan*, p. 98.
36 Ibid. p. 19.
37 Ibid. p. 106.
38 William Laffan, "James Brenan", in Nicola Figgis (ed.), *Art and Architecture of Ireland, Volume II: Painting 1600–1900* (Dublin and New Haven, CT: 2014), pp. 183–4.
39 Descriptions of work derive from correspondence with author.
40 *Hansard's Parliamentary Debates*, vol. civ (London: 1849), p. 103.
41 Asenath Nicholson, *Annals of the Famine in Ireland*, ed. Maureen Murphy (Dublin: Lilliput Press, 1998), pp. 117–18.
42 David Lloyd, "The indigent sublime: specters of Irish Hunger." *Representations*, vol. 92, no. 1 (fall 2005), pp. 152–85: p. 156.
43 Robin Lydenberg, *Dorothy Cross and the Ethics of Touch*, published in conjunction with the Dorothy Cross exhibition, *Connemara* (Dublin: Royal Hibernian Academy, 2014), pp. 6–13: p. 6.
44 Dorothy Cross, *Fountainstown* (Connemara: Occasional Press and Ballynahinch Castle, 2012), n.p.; and idem, *Montenotte* (Connemara: Occasional Press and Ballynahinch Castle, 2012), n.p.
45 Hal Foster, *Compulsive Beauty* (Cambridge, MA: MIT Press, 1993), p. 166.
46 James Hack Tuke, *Report of the Society of Friends on Distress in Ireland*, NLI, Ms Ir. 9410859.
47 Hal Foster, *Compulsive Beauty* (Cambridge, MA: MIT Press, 1993), quoted in Robin Lyndenberg, *GONE: Site-specific Works by Dorothy Cross* (Boston: McMullen Museum and University of Chicago Press, 2005), p. 19.
48 Aidan Dunne, "Dorothy Cross: life, death and magic on the Connemara coast", *Irish Times*, Mar. 27, 2014.
49 Quoted in Ian Kirkwood, *Artlog*, no. 5 (Winchester, 1976), n.p.
50 Katharine Crouan *William Crozier: Rainbow's End* (Hamden, CT: Quinnipiac University Press/Ireland's Great Hunger Museum, 2016), p. 3.
51 See Katharine Crouan and Seán Kissane (eds), *William Crozier: The Edge of the Landscape* (Skibbereen: Uillinn: West Cork Arts Centre; Dublin: Irish Museum of Modern Art, 2017).
52 Ibid. p. 107.
53 Crouan *William Crozier: Rainbow's End*, p. 3; and idem, *William Crozier, Recent Paintings*, exhibition catalogue (London: Arthur Tooth & Sons, 1964).
54 Crouan, *William Crozier: Rainbow's End*, p. 4.
55 Crouan (ed.), *William Crozier* (Aldershot and London: Lund Humphries, 2007), p. 15.
56 Crouan, *William Crozier: Rainbow's End*, p. 7.
57 Philip Vann, "A man of imagination", in Katharine Crouan (ed.), *William Crozier*, p. 41.
58 Quoted in Crouan and Kissane (eds), *William Crozier: The Edge of the Landscape*, p. 81.
59 Quoted in Crouan (ed.), *William Crozier* (Aldershot and London: Lund Humphries 2007), p. 158.
60 Edmund Burke, *A Philosophical Enquiry into the Origin of Our Ideas of the Sublime and Beautiful* [1756], section vii.
61 See Muiris O'Sullivan and Liam Downey, "Children's burial grounds", *Archaeology Ireland*, vol. 27, no. 3 (autumn 2013), pp. 22–5; and Eileen M. Murphy, "Children's burial grounds in Ireland (cillíní) and parental emotions toward infant death", *International Journal of Historical Archaeology*, vol. 15, no. 3 (Sept. 2011), pp. 409–28.
62 Katherine Cahill, "In the mainstream of Irish naturalism: the art of Lilian Lucy Davidson, 1879–1954", *Irish Arts Review Yearbook*, vol. 15 (1999), pp. 35–45.
63 *Bell*, vol. 5, no. 1 (Oct. 1942), pp. 42–8.
64 *Irish Arts Review*, vol. 23, no. 3 (autumn 2006), p. 136.
65 Aidan Dunne, *Micheal Farrell* (Kinsale: Gandon, 1998), p. 7.
66 Cyril Barrett, *Micheall Farrell* (Dublin: Douglas Hyde Gallery, 1979), p. 10.

67 Micheal Farrell, interview with Maev Kennedy, *Irish Times*, Aug. 16, 1977.
68 *Irish Times*, Aug. 21, 1969.
69 David Farrell, *Micheal Farrell: The Life and Work of an Irish Artist* (Dublin: Liffey Press, 2006), p. 81.
70 See Alyce Mahon, "The body", in Catherine Marshall and Peter Murray (eds), *Art and Architecture of Ireland Volume V: Twentieth Century* (Dublin and New Haven, CT: Royal Irish Academy and Yale University Press, 2015), p. 48.
71 Dunne, *Micheal Farrell*, p. 8.
72 Quoted in Jennifer Hart, "Sir Charles Trevelyan at the Treasury", *English Historical Review*, no. ixxv (1960), pp. 92–110: p. 94; John Mitchel, *The Last Conquest of Ireland (Perhaps)*, ed. and intro. Patrick Maume [1862] (Dublin, 2005), p. 219.
73 Tom Verde, "An Irish tale of hunger and the Sultan", *Aramco World*, Jan./Feb. 2015.
74 Farrell, *Micheal Farrell*, pp. 160–1.
75 *Magazine of Art*, 1895, p. 472.
76 Frederick Goodall, *The Reminiscences of Frederick Goodall, RA* (London: Walter Scott, 1902), pp. 28–31.
77 Quoted in Marion McEnroy,"'Joannes Clericus': the life and work of the Revd John Rooney", *Irish Arts Review Yearbook*, vol. 17 (2001), pp. 122–6; and J. Mitchell, "The Rev. John Rooney", *Journal of Galway Archaeological and Historical Society*, vol. 33 (1972–73), pp. 76–7; Duffy's *Irish Catholic Magazine*, vol. 1 (Dublin, 1848), pp. 149–51.
78 *Howitt's Journal of Literature and Popular Progress*, vol. 2 (1847), p. 10.
79 In correspondence with author.
80 Kathryn Stephenson, "The Quarantine War: the burning of the New York Marine Hospital in 1858", *Public Health Reports*, vol. 119, Jan.–Feb. 2004, pp. 79–92.
81 In conversation with artist.
82 Quoted in Roger Kohn, *Rowan Gillespie: Looking for Orion* (Dublin: O'Brien Press, 2007).
83 Yael Merkin, "Playing with fire: the Staten Island Quarantine Riots of 1858", unpublished thesis (Columbia University, 2007), p. 6.
84 "The Staten Island War: further arrests," *New York Times*, Sept. 7, 1858.
85 Quoted in Edward Jonas, "Dimensional compositions: an interview with Glenna Goodacre, NA", *Art of the Portrait Newsletter*, first quarter, 2002.
86 Ibid.
87 Julian Hawthorne, *Shapes that Pass: Memories of Old Days* (Boston and New York: Houghton Mifflin Company, 1928), p. 119.
88 Clarence Cook, "An American Wilkie", *Quarterly Illustrator*, vol. 2, no. 8 (Oct.–Dec. 1894), pp. 357–60: pp. 358–9.
89 Claudia Kinmonth "Rags and rushes: art and the Irish artefact, c. 1900", *Journal of Design History*, vol. 14, no. 3 (2001), pp. 167–85: p. 179.
90 Quoted in Cecil Woodham-Smith, *The Great Hunger* (London: Hamish Hamilton, 1962), p. 291.
91 Barbara H. Weinberg, *The Lure of Paris: Nineteenth-century Painters and Their French Teachers* (New York: Abbeville Press, 1991), p. 138.
92 Katherine Tynan, "Irish types & traits", *Magazine of Art*, vol. 11 (1888), pp. 19–25, 127–35: p. 132.
93 Ibid.
94 Cook, "An American Wilkie", pp. 357–60.
95 "The drift of the day", *Collector*, vol. 3, no. 9 (Mar. 1892), pp. 129–30.
96 Ibid.
97 Cook, "An American Wilkie", pp. 357–60.
98 *The Paintings of Paul Henry and Grace Henry* (Hugh Lane Municipal Gallery (now Dublin City Gallery The Hugh Lane), 1991).
99 J.G. Cruickshank, *Grace Henry: The Person and Artist* (Dublin: Jorgensen Fine Art and Designroom, 2010); and "Grace Henry", *Irish Arts Review Yearbook*, vol. 9 (1993), pp. 174–8.
100 Anon., "Nationality in art: the work of Paul and Grace Henry", *Colour* (London, 1918), pp. 52–6.
101 See Eamonn Mallie (ed.), *One Hundred Years of Irish Art* (privately printed, 2000), p. 143.
102 Thomas MacGreevy, *Studio*, Sept. 1939, pp. 125–7: p. 125.
103 Thomas MacGreevy, *Irish Times*, Apr. 2, 1943.
104 In 1939 Henry accompanied Seán Ó Faoláin around Ireland. He illustrated Ó Faoláin's *An Irish Journey* (London: Longmans, Green, & Co., 1947), and Ó Faoláin provided the foreword to Henry's *An Irish Portrait* (London: Batsford, 1951), p. 50.
105 S.B. Kennedy, *Paul Henry: with a Catalogue of the Paintings, Drawings, Illustrations* (New Haven, CT and London: Yale University Press, 2007), catalogue nos 240, 689 (see also nos 622, 637, 638, 642, 643 and 822). I am grateful to Brian (S.B.) Kennedy for his assistance.
106 Henry, *An Irish Portrait*, p. 25.
107 Ibid. p. 17.
108 Quoted in Kennedy, *Paul Henry*, p. 33.
109 Henry, *An Irish Portrait*, p. 3.
110 Ibid. pp. 60–1.
111 Seán O'Faoláin [Sean O'Faolain], *An Irish Journey* (London: Longmans, Green, & Co., 1947), pp. 173–4.
112 Henry, *An Irish Portrait*, pp. vi–viii.
113 Ibid. p. 22.
114 Rosa Mulholland, "Irish painters in the present year", *Irish Monthly*, Sept. 17, 1889, p. 484.
115 Henry, *An Irish Portrait*, p. 48.
116 Ibid. p. 108.
117 Ó Faoláin, *An Irish Journey*, p. 186.
118 *Freeman's Journal*, Aug. 6, 1920.
119 Thomas Bodkin, *Twelve Irish Artists* (Dublin: Victor Waddington, 1940), p. 6.
120 See Kennedy, *Paul Henry*, p. 51.
121 Claudia Kinmonth, "The Connemara spinner", Gorry Gallery catalogue (Dublin, 2016), p. 5.
122 James Johnson, *A Tour of Ireland with Meditations and Reflections* (London: Highley, 1844), p. 294.
123 Kinmonth, "The Connemara spinner", p. 5.
124 See Margaret MacCurtain, "The real Molly Macree", in Adele Dalsimer (ed.), *Visualizing Ireland: National Identity and the Pictorial Tradition* (London: Faber & Faber, 1993), pp. 9–21.
125 Barbara O'Connor, "Colleens and comely maidens: representing and performing Irish femininity in the nineteenth and twentieth centuries", in Eoin Flannery and Michael Griffin (eds), *Ireland in Focus: Film, Photography, and Popular Culture* (New York: Syracuse University Press, 2009).
126 Walter Strickland, *A Dictionary of Irish Artists*, 2 vols (Dublin: Maunsel, 1913).
127 Sir William Wilde [William Robert Wilde], "Irish popular superstitions", in idem, *Ireland: Her Wit, Peculiarities, and Popular Superstitions* (Dublin: McGlashan & Gill, 1852), p. 11.
128 See Niamh O'Sullivan, *In the Lion's Den: Daniel Macdonald, Ireland and Empire* (Hamden, CT: Quinnipiac University Press/Ireland's Great Hunger Museum, 2016).
129 M.H., "Necrology: William Magrath", *Journal of the Cork Historical and Archaeological Society*, ser. 2, vol. 24, no. 117 (1918), pp. 45–7.
130 Ibid.
131 *Putnam's Magazine* (New York, 1869), p. 378; Samuel Greene Wheeler Benjamin, *Art in America: A Critical and Historical Sketch* (1880), pp. 117–18.
132 Anon., "Gallery and studio", *Art Amateur*, Sept. 1882, p. 70.
133 John Gilbert, "A record of authors, artists and musical composers born in the County of Cork", *Journal of the Cork Historical and Archaeological Society*, ser. 2, vol. xix (1913), pp. 168–81.
134 *Munsey's Magazine*, vol. 11, July 1894, p. 346.
135 Lyndsay Clutterbuck, "An accident of history? The evolution of counter terrorism methodology in the Metropolitan Police from 1829–1901", unpublished PhD thesis (University of Portsmouth, 2002). Whistler and Sickert also came to police attention; see Spiro Dimolianis, *Jack the Ripper and Black Magic: Victorian Conspiracy Theories, Secret Societies and the Supernatural Mystique of the Whitechapel Murders* (North Carolina and London: Jefferson, 2011), p. 219.
136 Donald Kuspit, *Brian Maguire, Paintings 1982–1987* (Dublin: Douglas Hyde Gallery; and Derry: Orchard Gallery, 1988), p. 6.
137 In correspondence with author.
138 Kuspit, *Brian Maguire*, p. 14.
139 Ibid. p. 7.
140 Thomas McEvilley, 'Brian Maguire at White Box', *Art in America*, no. 5 (May 2003); Thomas McEvilley, "Brian Maguire at the XXIV São Paulo Bienal, 3 October to 13 December, 1998", http://www.gogobrazil.com/maguire.html (accessed July 4, 2017).
141 Kuspit, *Brian Maguire*, n.p.
142 See Anon., "Obituaries", *Southern Reporter*, Nov. 19, 1859, *Cork Examiner*, Nov. 23, 1859, and *Weekly Freeman's Journal*, Apr. 11, 1857.
143 *Cork Examiner*, June 9, 1855.
144 Ibid. Apr. 23, 1847.
145 Br James Alphonsus Dwyer, *The Dominicans of Cork City and County* (Cork: Guy, 1896); Edward McParland, "Chapel or church? The Case of St Mary's, Pope's Quay, Cork", in Raymond Gillespie and R.F. Foster (eds), *Irish Provincial Cultures in the Long Eighteenth Century* (Dublin: Four Courts Press, 2012), p. 231; Gorry Gallery catalogue, Dublin (Dublin, 2013), p. 9.
146 I am grateful to Msgr James O'Brien for details of the rite of consecration.
147 *Southern Reporter and Cork Commercial Courier*, Dec. 24, 1835.
148 Walter Strickland, *Dictionary of Irish Artists*, 1913.
149 Quoted in William Williams, *Creating Irish Tourism: The First Century, 1750–1850* (London, 2010), pp. 139–40.
150 William Ockenden, *Letters Describing the Lakes of Killarney and Muckross Gardens* (c. 1760), pp. 134–5.
151 Hall and Hall, *Ireland: Its Scenery, Character, &c.*, pp. 210–11.
152 Williams, p. 138.
153 See ibid. pp. 129–50.
154 See Kevin Whelan, "Immoral economy: interpreting Erskine Nicol's The Tenant", in Adele M. Dalsimer and Vera Kreilkamp (eds), *America's Eye: Irish Paintings from the Collection of Brian P. Burns* (Boston: Boston College, Museum of Art, 1996), pp. 57–67.
155 Amélie Dochy, "Standing at cultural crossroads: Erskine Nicol's representations of Ireland", *Anglophonia/Caliban*, no. 33 (2013), pp. 41–58; idem, "Representing Irishness in words and images: Erskine Nicol's illustrations of *Tales of Irish Life and Character*", *Revue LISA E-journal* (online), vol. xii, no. 3 (2014).
156 Daniel Donovan, "Observations on the peculiar diseases to which the Famine of last year gave origin", *Dublin Medical Press*, no. 19 (1848), p. 67.
157 Mary Cowling, *The Artist as Anthropologist: The*

Representation of Type and Character in Victorian Art (Cambridge: Cambridge University Press, 1989), p. 150; see also L. Perry Curtis, *Apes and Angels: The Irishman in Victorian Caricature* (Washington DC: Smithsonian Institution Press, 1997).
158 *Art Journal*, vol. 7 (1861), p. 172.
159 Brendan Rooney (ed.), *A Time and a Place: Two Centuries of Irish Social Life* (Dublin: NGI, 2006), p. 143.
160 Pieter Camper, *The Works of the Late Prof. Camper, on the Connexion Between the Science of Anatomy and the Arts of Drawing, Painting, Statuary, etc.*, ed. T. Cogan (London: C. Dilly, 1794).
161 Thomas Carlyle, "Chartism", in idem, *The Works of Thomas Carlyle* [1839] (Cambridge: Cambridge University Press, 2010), vol. 4, p. 138.
162 Joseph Valente, *The Myth of Manliness in Irish National Culture, 1880–1922* (Illinois: University of Illinois Press, 2011), p. 15.
163 *Charles Kingsley: His Letters and Memories of His Life*, vol. 2, ed. Frances Eliza Kingsley [1877] (Cambridge: Cambridge University Press, 2011), p. 107.
164 See for example Emily D. Mark, "Pathos and Paddywhackery: Erskine Nicol and the painting of the Irish Famine", in Shane Alcobia-Murphy, Johanna Archbold, John Gibney and Carole Jones (eds), *Beyond the Anchoring Grounds: More Cross-currents in Irish and Scottish Studies* (Belfast: University of Aberdeen/Queen's University, 2005), pp. 184–96; and Fintan Cullen, "Representing the Irish emigrant: humour to pathos?", *Visual Culture in Britain*, vol. 18, no. 2 (2017), DOI: 10.1080/14714787.2017.1328987 (accessed July 10, 2017).
165 Marjorie Howes and Kevin O'Neill, "Toward a history of the Irish landscape", in Vera Kreilkamp (ed.), *Éire/Land* (Boston: McMullen Museum of Art, 2003), p. 18.
166 Vera Kreilkamp (ed.), "Painting Mayo's landscape: the Big House, the pleasure grounds, and the mills", in idem, *Éire/Land* (Boston: McMullen Museum of Art, 2003), p. 75.
167 Ibid. pp. 71–8.
168 Quoted in John Hutchinson, *James Arthur O'Connor* (Dublin: NGI, 1985), p. 151.
169 *Dublin Penny Journal*, vol. 1, no. 4, July 21, 1832.
170 Howes and O'Neill, "Toward a history of the Irish landscape", p. 18.
171 Hutchinson, *James Arthur O'Connor*, p. 11.
172 "James Arthur O'Connor", Gorry Gallery catalogue (Dublin, 2011), p. 19.
173 *Dublin Penny Journal*, vol. 1, no. 4, July 21, 1832.
174 Anon., *Naming the Fields: Hughie O'Donoghue: New Painting* (Dublin: Rubicon Gallery, 2001), p. 6.
175 James Hack Tuke, *A Visit to Connaught in the Autumn of 1847* (London: Charles Gilpin, 1848), pp. 26–7.
176 Ibid. pp. 21–2.
177 Anon., *Naming the Fields*, p. 10.
178 James Hamilton, *Painting, Memory, Myth* (London: Merrell, 2003), p. 15.
179 Tuke, *A Visit to Connaught*, p. 55.
180 Of this trilogy, IMMA purchased *Sanctuary Wasteland*; editions of her photographic montages with text, *A Kind of Quietism*, were acquired by the Crawford Art Gallery and the IGHM; an edition of *No Colouring Can Deepen the Darkness of Truth* (1992) was installed in the Workhouse Famine Museum in Carrick-on-Shannon in 2008, and another in the IGHM in 2012. A related work, *Á Beathú*, was shown when she represented Ireland at the São Paolo Bienal in 1996.
181 Jean Fisher, *Signs of the Times: A Decade of Video, Film and Slide-tape Installations in Britain, 1980–1990* (Oxford: Museum of Modern Art, 1990), pp. 60–7.
182 Fionna Barber, *Art in Ireland Since 1910* (London: Reaktion Books, 2013), pp. 223–4, 240.
183 Niamh Ann Kelly, "Transgressing time: imagining an exhibition of works by Alanna O'Kelly and Phil Collins", in Mieke Bal and Miguel Á. Hernández-Navarro (eds), *Art and Visibility in Migratory Culture: Conflict, Resistance, and Agency* (Amsterdam and New York: Rodopi, 2011), p. 166.
184 Catherine Marshall, "Alanna O'Kelly", in Catherine Marshall and Peter Murray (eds), *Art and Architecture of Ireland Volume V: Twentieth Century* (Dublin and New Haven, CT: Royal Irish Academy and Yale University Press, 2015), pp. 330–1.
185 Alanna O'Kelly in conversation with Catherine Marshall and Niamh O'Sullivan, Apr. 2012.
186 Thomas Crofton Croker, *Researches in the South of Ireland* [1824] (Dublin: Irish Academic Press, 1981), pp. 280–1.
187 Claudia Kinmonth, Gorry Gallery catalogue (Dublin, 2014), p. 19.
188 Kevin Whelan, 'The cultural effects of the Famine', in Joe Cleary and Clare Connolly (eds), *The Cambridge Companion to Modern Irish Culture* (Cambridge: Cambridge University Press, 2005), pp. 137–54: p. 143.
189 Catherine E. Foley, *Step Dancing in Ireland: Culture and History* [2013] (London: Routledge, 2016), p. 136.
190 Eric Hobsbawn and Terence Ranger, *The Invention of Tradition* (Cambridge: Cambridge University Press, 1983), p. 4.
191 Luke Gibbons, "Field of vision", essay accompanying *Of Space and Place* exhibition (Dublin: The Lab, 2014).
192 The school closed in the 1930s when Madame Colarossi burned the archives in revenge for her husband's philandering.
193 *Dublin Magazine*, July–Sept. 1943.
194 Catherine Nash, "Remapping and renaming: new cartographies of identity, gender and landscape in Ireland," *Feminist Review*, no. 44 (summer 1993), pp. 39–57: p. 45.
195 Éimear O'Connor, *Seán O'Sullivan RHA (1906–1964): An Extraordinary Talent* (Dublin: Adam's Auctioneers, 2012), p. 10.
196 Theo Snoddy, *Dictionary of Irish Artists, 20th Century* (Dublin: Merlin, 1996), p. 385.
197 Quoted in William Brennan, "The Irish novel that's so good people were scared to translate it", *New Yorker*, Mar. 17, 2016.
198 *New Monthly Magazine and Literary Journal*, vol. 48 (1836), p. 109.
199 Quoted in Roger Simpson, *Sir John Tenniel: Aspects of His Work* (Cranbury, NJ: Associated University Presses, 1994), p. 16.
200 Claudia Kinmonth, *Irish Rural Interiors in Art* (New Haven, CT: Yale University Press, 2006), p. 18.
201 Tom Pocock, *Topham and Son: A Family of Artists* (London: Burgh House Museum, 1985), p. 4.
202 James Dafforne, "British painters – Francis William Topham", *Art Journal*, vol. 6 (Feb. 1880), p. 34.
203 Ibid. pp. 33–5.
204 Williams produced a small illustrated booklet, *Something About Achill* (Dublin: Williams, B.B. & Robinson. 1897).
205 His daughter Alice, notwithstanding her own penurious old age, held onto thirty-five volumes of her father's papers; see Gordon T. Ledbetter, *Privilege and Poverty: The Life and Times of Irish Painter and Naturalist, Alexander Williams RHA, 1846–1930* (Cork: Collins Press, 2010).
206 Alexander Williams, *Memoirs of Alexander Williams*, unpublished MS, 2 vols, vol. 1 (1911), p. 132.
207 Ibid. p. 131.
208 Henry Sedall, *Edward Nangle: The Apostle of Achill: A Memoir and a History* (London: Hatchards, 1884), p. xv.
209 Caesar Otway, *A Tour in Connaught* (Dublin: William Curry, 1839), p. 364.
210 Sedall, *Edward Nangle*, p. 242.
211 Yvonne Scott (ed.), *Jack B. Yeats: Old and New Departures* (Dublin, 2008), p. 34.
212 Róisín Kennedy, "Jack B. Yeats", in Catherine Marshall and Peter Murray (eds), *Art and Architecture of Ireland, Volume V: Twentieth Century* (Dublin and New Haven, CT: Royal Irish Academy and Yale University Press, 2015), p. 499.
213 Ibid. p. 498.
214 Earnán O'Malley, *Jack B. Yeats: National Loan Exhibition, June–July* (Dublin, 1945).
215 Luke Gibbons, "Ernie O'Malley", in Niamh O'Sullivan, *The Bigger Picture: Jack. B. Yeats' "Derrynane"* (Hamden, CT: Ireland's Great Hunger Museum, Quinnipiac University Press, 2014), p. 14.
216 O'Malley, *Jack B. Yeats*, p. 16.
217 Ibid. p. 10.
218 *Jack B. Yeats: A Catalogue Raisonné of the Oil Paintings*, vol. 1 (London, 1992), p. 305.
219 Deborah Anna Logan (ed.), *Harriet Martineau and the Irish Question: Condition of Post-Famine Ireland* (Bethlehem: Lehigh University Press, 2012), p. 166.
220 Oliver MacDonagh, *The Emancipist: Daniel O'Connell, 1830–1847* (London, 1989), p. x.
221 Thomas Campbell Foster, *Letters on the Condition of the People of Ireland* (London: Chapman & Hall, 1846), pp. 396–7.

Works Cited:

Adair, Daryl and Mike Cronin, *The Wearing of the Green: A History of St Patrick's Day* (London: Psychology Press, 2006)

Advocate, or Irish Industrial Journal, Feb. 28, 1849; Mar. 6, 1849

Anglo Celt, May 28, 1847

Anon., *Distress in Ireland. Extracts From Correspondence Published by the Central Relief Committee of the Society of Friends, No. 1* (Dublin, 1847)

_____, *Distress in Ireland. Extracts From Correspondence Published by the Central Relief Committee of the Society of Friends, No. 2* (Dublin, 1847)

_____, *Frederick William Burton: For the Love of Art* (Dublin: National Gallery of Ireland, 2017)

_____, "Gallery and studio: William Magrath", *Art Amateur*, vol. 7, no. 4 (Sept. 1882)

_____, "Irish peasant children", Ireland's Great Hunger Museum, https://www.ighm.org/irish-peasant-children/ (accessed Dec. 19, 2017)

_____, "James Arthur O'Connor", in *An Exhibition of 17th-20th Century Irish Paintings* (Dublin: Gorry Gallery, 2011)

_____, letter to T. Lucas Clements, unsigned, Jan. 17, 1847, Lucas-Clements Papers, Maynooth University

_____, *Naming the Fields: Hughie O'Donoghue: New Painting* (Dublin: Rubicon Gallery, 2001)

_____,"Nationality in art: the work of Paul and Grace Henry", *Colour* (London, 1918)

_____, "Obituaries", *Southern Reporter* (Scotland), Nov. 19, 1859

_____, petition to T. Lucas Clements, Feb. 11, 1846, Lucas-Clements Papers, Maynooth University

_____, "Remains at Monasterboice, County Louth", *Irish Penny Journal*, vol. 1, no 7 (Aug. 15, 1840)

_____, "The Irish highlands", *Dublin Penny Journal*, vol. 1, no. 4 (July 21, 1832)

_____, "The Staten Island war: further arrests", *New York Times*, Sept. 7, 1858

_____, unsigned letter to T. Lucas Clements, Jan. 17, 1847, Lucas-Clements Papers, Maynooth University

"Anonymous ("An admirer of the arts")", *Southern Reporter and Cork Commercial Courier*, Dec. 24, 1835

Armstrong, A., Cavan, letter to T. Lucas Clements, Jan. 11, 1847, Lucas-Clements Papers, Maynooth University

Armstrong, Thomas, *My Life in Connaught: With Sketches of Mission Work in the West* (London: Elliott Stock, 1906)

Athenaeum, Dec. 11, 1886

Bagenal, Philip, *The American Irish and Their Influence on Irish Politics* (London: Kegan Paul, Trench & Co., 1882)

Ballagh, Robert and Brian McAvera, "Style and substance", *Irish Arts Review*, vol. 23, no. 3 (autumn 2006)

Bannon, Robert, letter to T. Lucas Clements, 1847, Lucas-Clements Papers, Maynooth University

"Bantry union. Report from Dr Stephens to the Board of Health, on the Bantry workhouse", Feb. 20, 1847, in *Workhouses (Ireland)*

Barber, Fionna, *Art in Ireland Since 1910* (London: Reaktion Books, 2013)

Barrett, Cyril, *Micheal Farrell* (Dublin: Douglas Hyde Gallery, 1979)

Belfast Newsletter, Jan. 9, Feb. 13, 15, 1849; Feb. 15, 1889

Benjamin, S.G.W., *Art in America: A Critical and Historical Sketch* (New York: Harper & Brothers, 1880)

Benson, A.C. and Viscount Escher (eds), *The Letters of Queen Victoria, 1844–1853*, vol. 2 (London: J. Murray, 1907)

Berger, John, *Pig Earth* [1979] (New York: Vintage, 1992)

_____, *Ways of Seeing* (UK: BBC and Penguin Books, 1972)

Bigelow, John (ed.), *The Life of Benjamin Franklin, Written by Himself*, vol. 2 [1874] (Cambridge: Cambridge University Press, 2011)

Brett, Henry, OPW county surveyor in Mayo, to Lord Lieutenant, Dublin Castle, reporting the continued advance of the potato disease in storage pits and in the soil, Nov 29, 1845, National Archives of Ireland, Relief Commission Papers, 2/Z17412

Blair, Raymond, "The Dorian letters, Fanad", *Donegal Annual*, vol. 67 (2015)

Blunt, Wilfred, *"England's Michaelangelo": A Biography of George Frederic Watts, O.M., R.A.* (London: Hamish Hamilton, 1975)

Bodkin, Thomas, *Twelve Irish Artists* (Dublin: Victor Waddington, 1940)

Boland, Mary Jane, "Creating order? Painting the crowd in nineteenth-century Ireland", in Brendan Rooney (ed.), *Creating History: Stories of Ireland in Art* (Dublin: Irish Academic Press, 2016)

Bourke, Angela, *Voices Underfoot: Memory, Forgetting, and Oral Verbal Art* (Hamden, CT: Quinnipiac University Press/ Ireland's Great Hunger Museum, 2016)

Bourke, Brian, "Micheal Farrell: the life and work of an Irish artist", *Irish Arts Review*, vol. 23, no. 3 (autumn, 2006)

Brennan, William, "The Irish novel that's so good people were scared to translate it", *New Yorker*, Mar. 17, 2016

Brett, Henry, letter to Lord Lieutenant, Nov. 29, 1845, Relief Commission Papers, National Archives of Ireland (2/Z17412)

Brown, Ford Madox, *The Diary of Ford Madox Brown*, ed. Virginia Surtees (New Haven and London: Yale University Press/Mellon Centre for Studies in British Art, 1981)

Burke, Edmund, *A Philosophical Enquiry into the Origin of Our Ideas of the Sublime and Beautiful*, section VII [1756] (New York: Harper & Brothers, 1856)

Burke, Ulick (Lilian Lucy Davidson), "Her only son", *Bell*, vol. 5, no. 1 (Oct. 1942)

Burritt, Elihu, *A Journal of a Visit of Three Days to Skibbereen and its Neighbourhood* (London: Charles Gilpin, 1847; Birmingham: John Whitehouse Showell, 1847)

Butler, Patrick, "The transportation of convicts from County Tipperary to Australia, 1836–1853", unpublished MA thesis (NUI Maynooth, 2005)

Cahill, Katherine, "In the mainstream of Irish naturalism: the art of Lilian Lucy Davidson, 1879–1954", *Irish Arts Review Yearbook*, vol. 15 (1999)

Campbell, Julian, "Henry Allan", *Irish Arts Review*, vol. 29, no. 2 (summer 2012)

_____, "Mahony, James", in Nicola Figgis (ed.), *Art and Architecture of Ireland, Volume II: Painting 1600–1900* (Dublin and New Haven, CT: Yale University Press, 2014)

_____, "Separating Mahony and Mahoney", *Irish Arts Review* (summer 2011)

Camper, Pieter, *The Works of the Late Prof. Camper, on the Connexion Between the Science of Anatomy and the Arts of Drawing, Painting, Statuary, etc.*, ed. T. Cogan (London: C. Dilly, 1794)

Carlyle, Thomas, "Chartism", in idem, *The Works of Thomas Carlyle* [1839], vol. 4 (Cambridge: Cambridge University Press, 2010)

Carville, Justin, *Photography and Ireland* (London: Reaktion, 2011)

Census of Ireland, 1901, National Archives of Ireland

Census of Ireland, 1911, National Archives of Ireland

Chief Secretary's Office Registered Papers, National Archives of Ireland, 1847 H5408; 1847 H 1198; 1847 H 4454; 1847 H 1704, 6048; 1847 H 3506; 1847 H 5209; 1847 H 650, 1532, 2026

Clutterbuck, Lyndsay, "An accident of history? The evolution of counter terrorism methodology in the Metropolitan Police from 1829–1901", unpublished PhD thesis (University of Portsmouth, 2002)

Cook, Clarence, "An American Wilkie", *Quarterly Illustrator*, vol. 2, no. 8 (Oct.–Dec. 1894)

Cork Constitution, Feb. 7, Apr. 24, 1847

Cork Examiner, Dec. 18, 1846; Jan. 8, 11, 18, Apr. 14, 23, 1847; June 9, 1855; Nov. 23, 1859

Cowling, Mary, *The Artist as Anthropologist: The Representation of Type and Character in Victorian Art* (Cambridge: Cambridge University Press, 1989)

Crawford, Margaret, "The Great Irish Famine 1845–9: image versus reality", in Brian P. Kennedy and Raymond Gillespie (eds), *Ireland: Art into History* (Dublin: Town House, 1994)

Cronin, Mike and Daryl Adair, *The Wearing of the Green: A History of St Patrick's Day* (London: Psychology Press, 2006)

Croker, Thomas Crofton, *Researches in the South of Ireland: Illustrative of the Scenery, Architectural Remains, and the Manners and Superstitions of the Peasantry* [1824] (Dublin: Irish Academic Press, 1981)
Crookshank, Anne, *The Watercolours of Ireland* (London: Barrie & Jenkins, 1994)
____ and the Knight of Glin, *Ireland's Painters, 1600–1940* (New Haven and London: Yale University Press, 2002)
____ and the Knight of Glin, *Painters of Ireland, c. 1660–1920* (London: Barrie & Jenkins, 1978)
Crowley, John, William J. Smyth, and Mike Murphy (eds), *Atlas of the Great Irish Famine* (Cork: Cork University Press, 2012)
Cross, Dorothy, *Fountainstown* (Connemara: Occasional Press and Ballynahinch Castle, 2012)
____, *Montenotte* (Connemara: Occasional Press and Ballynahinch Castle, 2012)
Crouan, Katharine (ed.), *William Crozier* (Aldershot and London: Lund Humphries, 2007)
____, *William Crozier: Rainbow's End* (Hamden, CT: Quinnipiac University Press/Ireland's Great Hunger Museum, 2016)
____, *William Crozier, Recent Paintings* (London: Arthur Tooth & Sons, 1964)
____ and Seán Kissane (eds), *William Crozier: The Edge of the Landscape* (Skibbereen: Uillinn: West Cork Arts Centre; Dublin: Irish Museum of Modern Art, 2017)
Cruickshank, J.G., *Grace Henry: The Person and Artist* (Dublin: Jorgensen Fine Art and Designroom, 2010)
____, "Grace Henry", *Irish Arts Review Yearbook*, vol. 9 (1993)
Cullen, Fintan, "Displaying distress", in *Ireland on Show: Art Union and Nationhood* (Surrey: Ashgate, 2012)
____, "Representing the Irish emigrant: humour to pathos?", *Visual Culture in Britain*, vol. 18, no. 2 (2017), DOI: 10.1080/14714787.2017.1328987
____, *Visual Politics: The Representation of Ireland, 1750–1930* (Cork: Cork University Press, 1997), p. 116
Curtis, L. Perry Jr., *Apes and Angels: The Irishman in Victorian Caricature* (Washington DC: Smithsonian Institution Press, 1997)
____, *Depiction of Eviction in Ireland: 1845–1910* (Dublin: University College Dublin Press, 2011)
Dafforne, James, "British painters – Francis William Topham", *Art Journal*, vol. 6 (Feb. 1880)
Davis, Thomas, "The state of the peasantry", in idem, *Literary and Historical Essays*, ed. Charles Gavan Duffy (Dublin: James Duffy, 1865)
Derry Journal, Dec. 17, 1897; Jan. 29, 1899; Aug. 23, Sept. 6, 1901
Dimolianis, Spiro, *Jack the Ripper and Black Magic: Victorian Conspiracy Theories, Secret and the Supernatural Mystique of the Whitechapel Murders* (Jefferson, NC and London: McFarland & Co., 2011)
Dochy, Amélie, "Representing Irishness in words and images; Erskine Nicol's illustrations of *Tales of Irish Life and Character*", *Revue LISA/LISA e-journal* (online), vol. xii, no. 3 (2014)
Dochy, Amélie, "Standing at cultural crossroads: Erskine Nicol's representations of Ireland", *Anglophonia/Caliban*, vol. 33 (2013)
Donnelly Jr., James S., *The Great Irish Potato Famine* (Stroud: Sutton, 2001)
____, *The Land and the People of Nineteenth-century Cork: The Rural Economy and the Land Question* (London and Boston: Routledge & Kegan Paul, 1975)
Donovan, Daniel, "Observations on the peculiar diseases to which the famine of last year gave origin, and on the morbid effects of insufficient nourishment", *Dublin Medical Press* (Feb. 2, 1848)
____, "Observations on the peculiar diseases to which the famine of last year gave origin, and on the morbid effects of insufficient nourishment", *Dublin Medical Press* (Mar. 1, 1848)
____, "Observations on the peculiar diseases to which the famine of last year gave origin, and on the morbid effects of insufficient nourishment", *Dublin Medical Press* (May 3, 1848)
____, "Observations on the peculiar diseases to which the famine of the last year gave origin and on the morbid effects of insufficient nourishment", *Medical Examiner: A Monthly Record of Medical Science*, vol. 4 (June 1848)
Dorian, Hugh, *The Outer Edge of Ulster: A Memoir of Social Life in Nineteenth-century Donegal*, eds Breandán Mac Suibhne and David Dickson (Dublin: Lilliput Press, 2000)
Douglass, Frederick, [letter], Montrose [Scotland], Feb. 26, 1846 to William Lloyd Garrison, in idem, *Life and Writings of Frederick Douglass*, ed. Philip Foner, vol. 1 (New York: International Publishers, 1950)
Downey, Liam and Muiris O'Sullivan, "Children's burial grounds", *Archaeology Ireland*, vol. 27, no. 3 (autumn 2013)
Dublin Evening Mail, June 4, 1847
Dublin Evening Packet and Correspondent, Mar. 19, 1846
Dublin Evening Post, Sept. 23, 1847; Feb. 10, 1849
Dublin Quarterly Journal of Medical Science, no. 8 (1849)
Duffy, James, *Duffy's Irish Catholic Magazine*, vol. 1 (Dublin: James Duffy, 1848)
Duggan, Lawrence G., "Was art really the 'book of the illiterate'?", *Word and Image*, vol. 5, no. 3 (July–Sept. 1989)
Dunne, Aidan, "Between the lines", *Irish Times*, Aug. 25, 2011
____, "Dorothy Cross: life, death and magic on the Connemara coast", *Irish Times*, Mar. 27, 2014
____, *Micheal Farrell* (Kinsale: Gandon, 1998)
____, "Rare encounter with sculpture in the spotlight", *Irish Times*, Feb. 6, 2008
Dwyer, Br James Alphonsus, *The Dominicans of Cork City and County* (Cork: Guy, 1896)
Eclectic Review, vol. 22 (Jan.–Dec. 1847)
Edgeworth, Richard Lovell and Maria Edgeworth, *Memoirs*, vol. 2 (London: R. Hunter & Baldwin, Cradock & Joy, 1820)
Extract of a Report of the Commissioners of Inquiry into Matters Connected with the Failure of the Potato Crop, Jan. 20, 1846
Fallon, Brian, *John Behan, Sculpture 1960–1994* (Galway: Galway Arts Festival, 1994)
Farrell, David, *Micheal Farrell: The Life and Work of an Irish Artist* (Dublin: Liffey Press, 2006)
Figgis, Nicola (ed.), *Art and Architecture of Ireland, Volume II: Painting 1600–1900* (London and New Haven, CT: Yale University Press, 2014)
"Fine Arts", *New Monthly Magazine and Literary Journal*, vol. 48 (1836)
____, *Putnam's Magazine*, New York (1869)
Fisher, Jean, *Signs of the Times: A Decade of Video, Film and Slide-tape Installations in Britain 1980–1990* (Oxford: Museum of Modern Art, 1990)
Fitzgerald, Emily Mark, *Commemorating the Irish Famine: Memory and the Monument* (Liverpool: Liverpool University Press, 2013)
____,"Eamonn O'Doherty", in Paula Murphy (ed.), *Art and Architecture of Ireland, Volume III: Sculpture 1600–2000* (London and New Haven, CT: Yale University Press, 2014)
____, Oona Frawley and Marguérite Corporaal (eds), *The Great Irish Famine and its Impacts – Visual and Material Cultures* (Liverpool: Liverpool University Press, 2018)
____, "Photography and the visual legacy of the Famine", in Oonagh Frawley (ed.), *Memory Ireland, Volume 3: The Famine and the Troubles* (New York: Syracuse University Press, 2014)
Fitzpatrick, Fr John, letter to Miley, *Freeman's Journal*, Feb. 17, 1847
____, letter to Mrs B, *Freeman's Journal*, Feb. 17, 1847
Flanagan, Kieran, *Sociological Noir: Irruptions and the Darkness of Modernity* (Abingdon: Routledge, 2017)
Fleming-Williams, Ian and Leslie Parris, *The Discovery of Constable* (London: Hamish Hamilton, 1984)
Foley, Catherine E., *Step Dancing in Ireland: Culture and History* (London: Routledge, 2016)
Foley, Michael, *Death in Every Paragraph: Journalism and the Great Irish Famine* (Hamden, CT: Quinnipiac University Press/Ireland's Great Hunger Museum, 2015)
Foley, Tadhg, *Death by Discourse? Political Economy and the Great Irish Famine* (Hamden, CT: Quinnipiac University Press/Ireland's Great Hunger Museum, 2016)
Forbes, R.B., *The Voyage of the Jamestown on Her Errand of Mercy* (Boston, 1847)
Foster, Thomas Campbell, *Letters on the Condition of the People of Ireland* (London: Chapman & Hall, 1846)
Frazier, Adrian, *John Behan: The Bull from Sheriff Street* (Dublin: Lilliput Press, 2015)
Freeman's Journal, June 27, 1845; Jan. 24, Mar. 27, 28, 26 Sept., 1846; Jan. 4, 9, Feb, 6, 7, 17, 1847; June 29, 1849; Mar. 15, 1851; Apr. 11, 1857; Aug. 6, 1920
Geary, Laurence [M.], "Epidemic diseases of the Great Famine", *History Ireland*, vol. 4, no. 1 (spring 1996)
____, *Medicine and Charity in Ireland, 1718–1851* (Dublin: UCD Press, 2004)
____, "'The living were out of their feeling': a socio-cultural analysis of the Great Famine in Ireland", in Breandán Ó Conaire (ed.), *The Famine Lectures: Léachtaí an Ghorta* (Boyle: Roscommon Herald, 2000)
____, "'The noblest offering that nation ever made to nation': American philanthropy and the Great Famine in Ireland", *Éire-Ireland*, vol. 48, nos 3–4 (fall/winter 2013)
Gibbons, Luke, "Ernie O'Malley", in Niamh O'Sullivan, *The Bigger Picture: Jack. B. Yeats' "Derrynane"* (Hamden, CT: Ireland's Great Hunger Museum, Quinnipiac University Press, 2014)
____, "Field of vision", essay accompanying *Of Space and Place* exhibition (Dublin: The Lab, 2014)
____, *Limits of the Visible: Representing the Great Hunger* (Hamden, CT: Quinnipiac University Press/Ireland's Great Hunger Museum, 2014)
____, "Words upon the windowpane: image, text, and Irish culture", in James Elkins (ed.), *Visual Cultures* (Chicago: University of Chicago Press, 2010)
Gilbert, John, "A record of authors, artists and musical composers born in the County of Cork", *Journal of the Cork Historical and Archaeological Society*, ser. 2, vol. xix (1913)
Goodall, Frederick, *The Reminiscences of Frederick Goodall, R.A.* (London: Walter Scott, 1902)
Graham, Robert, letter to T. Lucas-Clements, Dec. 1, 1846, Lucas-Clements Papers, Maynooth University
Gray, Peter, *Famine, Land, and Politics: British Government and Irish Society, 1843–1850* (Dublin: Irish Academic Press, 1999)
Hall, Mr and Mrs S.C., *Ireland: Its Scenery, Character, &c.*, vol. 1 (London: Hall, Virtue & Co., c. 1841)
Hall, S.C., *Retrospect of a Long Life: From 1815–1883* (London: R. Bentley; New York: Appleton, 1883)
Hamilton, James, *Hughie O'Donoghue: Painting, Memory, Myth* (London: Merrell, 2003)
Hansard's Parliamentary Debates, vol. civ (London: Cornelius Buck, 1849)
Hart, Jennifer, "Sir Charles Trevelyan at the Treasury", *English Historical Review*, vol. 75 (1960)
Hawthorne, Julian, *Shapes that Pass: Memories of Old Days* (Boston and New York: Houghton Mifflin Company, 1928)
Henry, Paul, *An Irish Portrait* (London: Batsford, 1951)
Hereford Times, Dec. 24, 1859
Hickey, Patrick, "Famine, mortality and emigration: a profile of six parishes in the Poor Law union of Skibbereen, 1846–7", in Patrick O'Flanagan and Cornelius G. Buttimer (eds), *Cork: History and Society. Interdisciplinary Essays on the History of an Irish County* (Dublin: Geography Publications, 1993)

____, "Some Famine letters of Dr Robert Traill, rector of Schull (1830–47)", *Mizen Journal* (1995)
Hobsbawn, Eric and Terence Ranger, *The Invention of Tradition* (Cambridge: Cambridge University Press, 1983)
Howes, Marjorie and Kevin O'Neill, "Toward a history of the Irish landscape", in Vera Kreilkamp (ed.), *Éire/Land* (Boston: McMullen Museum of Art, 2003)
Howitt, Mary, *Howitt's Journal of Literature and Popular Progress*, vol. 2 (London: W. Lovett, 1847)
Hutchinson, John, *James Arthur O'Connor* (Dublin: National Gallery of Ireland, 1985)
Illustrated London News, Mar. 25, 1848
Indices of Births, Deaths and Marriages, Office of the General Registrar, Dublin, Ireland
Irish Times, Nov. 18, 1884; Apr. 2, 1943; Aug. 21, 1969; Aug. 16, 1977; Feb. 6, 2008; Aug. 25, 2011; Mar. 27, 2014
Johnson, James, *A Tour in Ireland with Meditations and Reflections* (London: S. Highley, 1844)
Jonas, Edward, "Dimensional compositions: an interview with Glenna Goodacre, NA", *Art of the Portrait Newsletter* (first quarter, 2002)
Judicial Statistics, Ireland, 1899, Part I ..., HM Stationery Office, HC 1900, Cd.313, vol. 104
Kelly, Niamh Ann, *Imaging the Great Irish Famine: Representing Dispossession in Visual Culture* (London: I.B. Tauris, 2018)
____, "Transgressing time: imagining an exhibition of works by Alanna O'Kelly and Phil Collins", in Mieke Bal and Miguel Á. Hernández-Navarro (eds), *Art and Visibility in Migratory Culture: Conflict, Resistance, and Agency* (Amsterdam and New York: Rodopi, 2011)
____, *Ultimate Witnesses: The Visual Culture of Death, Burial and Mourning in Famine Ireland* (Hamden, CT: Quinnipiac University Press/Ireland's Great Hunger Museum, 2017)
Kennedy, Deborah, "The ruined abbey in the eighteenth century", *Philological Quarterly*, vol. 80 no. 4 (fall 2001)
Kennedy, Maev, interview with Micheal Farrell, *Irish Times*, Aug. 16, 1977
Kennedy, Róisín, "Jack B. Yeats", in Catherine Marshall and Peter Murray (eds), *Art and Architecture of Ireland, Volume V: Twentieth Century* (Dublin and New Haven, CT: Royal Irish Academy and Yale University Press, 2015)
Kennedy, S.B., *Paul Henry: With a Catalogue of the Paintings, Drawings, Illustrations* (New Haven and London: Yale University Press, 2007), catalogue nos 240, 622, 637, 638, 642, 643, 689, 822
Kerry Evening Post, June 19, 1847; Oct. 20, 1849; Feb. 11, 1914
Kidd, Joseph "On the fever and dysentery of Ireland in 1847', in Francis Treuherz (ed.), *Homoeopathy in the Irish Potato Famine* (London: Samuel Press, 1995), originally published in *British Journal of Homoeopathy*, no. 6 (Jan. 1848)
Kinealy, Christine, "How politics fed the Famine", *Magazine of the American Museum of Natural History*, vol. 105, no. 1 (1996)
Kingsley, Charles, *Charles Kingsley: His Letters and Memories of His Life*, vol. 2, ed. Frances Eliza Kingsley [1877] (Cambridge: Cambridge University Press, 2011)
Kinmonth, Claudia, *An Exhibition of 18th-21st Century Irish Paintings* (Dublin: Gorry Gallery, 2014)
____, "The Connemara spinner", in idem, *An Exhibition of 18th-21st Century Irish Paintings* (Dublin: Gorry Gallery, 2016)
____, *Irish Rural Interiors in Art* (New Haven and London: Yale University Press, 2006)
____, "Rags and rushes: art and the Irish artefact, c. 1900", *Journal of Design History*, vol. 14, no. 3 (2001)
____ and Niamh O'Sullivan, *An Exhibition of 18th-20th Century Irish Paintings* (Dublin: Gorry Gallery, 2008)
Kirkwood, Ian, interview with William Crozier, *Artlog*, no. 5 (1976)
Kohn, Roger, *Rowan Gillespie: Looking for Orion* (Dublin: O'Brien Press, 2007)
Kreilkamp, Vera, "Painting Mayo's landscape: the Big House, the pleasure grounds, and the mills", in idem (ed.), *Éire/Land* (Boston: McMullen Museum of Art, 2003)
____ (ed.), *Éire/Land* (Boston: McMullen Museum of Art, 2003)
Kuspit, Donald, *Brian Maguire, Paintings 1982–1987* (Dublin: Douglas Hyde Gallery; Derry: Orchard Gallery, 1988)
Laffan, William, "James Brenan", in Nicola Figgis (ed.), *Art and Architecture of Ireland, Volume II: Painting 1600–1900* (Dublin and New Haven, CT: Yale University Press, 2014)
____, "William Willes' *The Mock Funeral*", in Brendan Rooney (ed.), *A Time and a Place: Two Centuries of Irish Social Life* (Dublin: National Gallery of Ireland, 2007)
Ledbetter, Gordon T., *Privilege and Poverty: The Life and Times of Irish Painter and Naturalist, Alexander Williams RHA, 1846–1930* (Cork: Collins Press, 2010)
Leinster, Duke of, letter to Relief Commissioners, Dublin Castle, Dec. 7, 1845, Relief Commission Papers, National Archives of Ireland (2/Z17412)
Leitrim Papers, National Library of Ireland (MS 5, 178)
Leventhal, A.J., "Royal Hibernian Academy of Arts Exhibition", *Dublin Magazine*, vol. xviii, no. 3 (July–Sept. 1943)
Levi, Primo, *The Drowned and the Saved* [1986] (New York: Simon & Schuster, 1989)
Lloyd, David, "The indigent sublime: specters of Irish hunger", *Representations*, vol. 92, no. 1 (fall 2005)
____, "The memory of loss", in David L. Eng and David Kazanjian (eds), *Loss: The Politics of Mourning* (Berkeley: University of California Press, 2003)
Logan, Deborah A. (ed.), *Harriet Martineau and the Irish Question: Condition of Post-Famine Ireland* (Bethlehem, PA: Lehigh University Press, 2012)
Londonderry Sentinel, July 24, 1861; Apr. 27, 1876
Lucas-Clements Papers, Maynooth University
Lydenberg, Robin, *Dorothy Cross and the Ethics of Touch*, published in conjunction with the Dorothy Cross exhibition *Connemara* (Dublin: Royal Hibernian Academy, 2014),
____, *GONE: Site-specific Works by Dorothy Cross* (Boston: McMullen Museum; Chicago: University of Chicago Press, 2005)
Lynch, Brian, "Eamonn O'Doherty: Genius Loci", *Irish Arts Review*, vol. 25, no. 1 (spring 2008)
MacCurtain, Margaret, "The real Molly Macree", in Adele Dalsimer (ed.), *Visualizing Ireland: National Identity and the Pictorial Tradition* (London: Faber & Faber, 1993)
MacDonagh, Oliver, *The Emancipist: Daniel O'Connell, 1830–1847* (London: Palgrave Macmillan, 1989)
MacGreevy, Thomas, "Grace Henry's art: an enchanting exhibition", *Irish Times*, Apr. 2, 1943
____, "In the world's art centres: London", *Studio* (Sept. 1939)
Mac Suibhne, Breandán, *Subjects Lacking Words? The Gray Zone of the Great Famine* (Hamden: Quinnipiac University Press, 2017)
____, *The End of Outrage: Post-Famine Adjustment in Rural Ireland* (London and New York: Oxford University Press, 2017)
Mahon, Alyce, "The body", in Catherine Marshall and Peter Murray (eds), *Art and Architecture of Ireland, Volume V: Twentieth Century* (Dublin and New Haven, CT: Royal Irish Academy and Yale University Press, 2015)
Mahoney, Paschal, *Grim Bastilles of Despair: The Poor Law Union Workhouses in Ireland* (Hamden, CT: Quinnipiac University Press/Ireland's Great Hunger Museum, 2016)
Mâle, Émile, *The Gothic Image: Religious Art in France of the Thirteenth Century* (London: Dent, 1913)
Mallie, Eamonn (ed.), *One Hundred Years of Irish Art* (privately printed, 2000)
Mark, Emily D., "Pathos and Paddywhackery: Erskine Nicol and the painting of the Irish Famine", in Shane Alcobia-Murphy, Johanna Archbold, John Gibney, and Carole Jones (eds), *Beyond the Anchoring Grounds: More Cross-currents in Irish and Scottish Studies* (Belfast: University of Aberdeen/Queen's University, 2005)
Marshall, Catherine, "Alanna O'Kelly", in idem and Peter Murray (eds), *Art and Architecture of Ireland, Volume V: Twentieth Century* (Dublin and New Haven, CT: Yale University Press and Royal Irish Academy, 2014)
____, "Choosing the battleground: Robert Ballagh's paintings", *Irish Arts Review Yearbook*, vol. 12 (1996)
____, *The Face of Revolution: Robert Ballagh – A Centennial Reflection* (2016)
____, *Monuments and Memorials of the Great Famine* (Hamden, CT: Quinnipiac University Press/Ireland's Great Hunger Museum, 2014)
____, "Painting Irish history: the Famine", *History Ireland*, vol. 4, no. 3 (autumn 1996)
____ and Peter Murray (eds), *Art and Architecture of Ireland, Volume V: Twentieth Century* (Dublin: Royal Irish Academy, 2015)
Mathew, Fr, to the under secretary, Dublin Castle, June 4, 1847, CSORP 1847 H 6843, National Archives of Ireland
McCarthy, Denis, *Dublin Castle at the Heart of Irish History* (Dublin: Government Stationery Office, 2004)
McEnroy, Marion, "'Joannes Clericus': the life and work of the Revd John Rooney", *Irish Arts Review Yearbook*, vol. 17 (2001)
McEvilley, Thomas, "Brian Maguire at White Box", *Art in America*, no. 5 (May 2003)
McParland, Edward, "Chapel or church? The case of St Mary's, Pope's Quay, Cork", in Raymond Gillespie and R.F. Foster (eds), *Irish Provincial Cultures in the Long Eighteenth Century* (Dublin: Four Courts Press, 2012)
Meason, Malcolm Laing, "The Irish dynamiters in Paris", in Sylvanus Urban (ed.), *The Gentleman's Magazine and Historical Chronicle* (London: Spottiswoode & Co., 1886)
Merkin, Yael, "Playing with fire: the Staten Island Quarantine Riots of 1858", unpublished thesis (Columbia University, 2007)
M.H., "Necrology: William Magrath", *Journal of the Cork Historical and Archaeological Society*, ser. 2, vol. 24, no. 117 (1918)
Miller, Kerby A., *Emigrants and Exiles: Ireland and the Irish Exodus to North America* (New York: Oxford University Press, 1985)
Minute book of the Rathkenny Relief Committee, Lucas-Clements Papers, Maynooth University
Mitchel, John, *The Last Conquest of Ireland (Perhaps)* (Glasgow: R. & T. Washbourne, 1861)
Mitchell, J., "The Rev. John Rooney", *Journal of Galway Archaeological and Historical Society*, vol. 33 (1972–73)
Moloney, Mick, *Across the Western Ocean: Songs of Leaving and Arriving* (Hamden, CT: Quinnipiac University Press/Ireland's Great Hunger Museum, 2016)
Mulholland, Rosa, "Irish painters in the present year", *Irish Monthly* (Sept. 17, 1889)
Murphy, Antoinette (ed.), *The Paintings of Paul Henry and Grace Henry* (Dublin: Hugh Lane Municipal Gallery (now Dublin City Gallery The Hugh Lane), 1991)
Murphy, Eileen M., "Children's burial grounds in Ireland (cillíní) and parental emotions toward infant death", *International Journal of Historical Archaeology*, vol. 15, no. 3 (Sept. 2011)
Murphy, James H., *Abject Loyalty: Nationalism and Monarchy in Ireland During the Reign of Queen Victoria* (Washington DC: Catholic University of America Press, 2001)
Murphy, Patrick, *Robert Ballagh – Artist and Designer, A Retrospective* (Dublin: RHA/Gallagher Gallery, 2006)

Murphy, Paula (ed.), *Art and Architecture of Ireland, Volume III, Sculpture 1600–2000* (London and New Haven, CT: Yale University Press, 2014)
Nash, Catherine "Remapping and renaming: new cartographies of identity, gender and landscape in Ireland", *Feminist Review*, vol. 44 (summer 1993)
Nation, Apr. 25, 1846; Aug. 28, 1847; May 6, 1848
Newry Examiner and Louth Advertiser, Apr. 5, 1848
Nicholson, Asenath, *Annals of the Famine in Ireland*, ed. Maureen Murphy (Dublin: Lilliput Press, 1998)
Nochlin, Linda, "The imaginary Orient", *Art in America*, vol. ixxi, no. 5 (1983)
Observations by the Board of Health on the Cork Union, 20 February 1847", CSORP 1847 H 6048, National Archives of Ireland
Ockenden, William, *Letters Describing the Lakes of Killarney and Muckross Gardens (c. 1760)* (Cork: J. Connor, 1800)
O'Connor, Barbara, "Colleens and comely maidens: representing and performing Irish femininity in the nineteenth and twentieth centuries", in Eoin Flannery and Michael Griffin (eds), *Ireland in Focus: Film, Photography, and Popular Culture* (New York: Syracuse University Press, 2009)
O'Connor, Denis Chas., *Seventeen Years' Experience of Workhouse Life: With Suggestions for Reforming the Poor Law and its Administration* (Dublin: McGlashan & Gill, 1861)
O'Connor, Éimear, *Seán O'Sullivan RHA (1906–1964): An Extraordinary Talent* (Dublin: Adam's Auctioneers, 2012)
O'Doherty, Brian, *Portrait of the Artist Micheal Farrell and Other Works by Robert Ballagh* (Cork: Crawford Art Gallery, 2003)
Ó Faoláin, Seán [Sean O'Faolain], *An Irish Journey* (London: Longmans, Green, & Co., 1947)
____, *Vive Moi! An Autobiography* [1963] (London: Hart-David, 1965)
Ó Gráda, Cormac, *Black '47 and Beyond: The Great Irish Famine in History, Economy, and Memory* (Princeton, NJ: Princeton University Press, 1999)
O'Malley, Earnán, *Jack B. Yeats: National Loan Exhibition, June–July* (Dublin: National College of Art, 1945)
O'Mahony, Colman, *In the Shadows: Life in Cork 1750–1939* (Cork: Tower Books, 1997)
O'Sullivan, Eilís, *Ascendancy Women and Elementary Education in Ireland: Educational Provision for Poor Children, 1788–1848* (London: Palgrave Macmillan, 2017)
O'Sullivan, Niamh, *Aloysius O'Kelly: Art, Nation, Empire* (Dublin: Field Day Publications, 2010)
____, *In the Lion's Den: Daniel Macdonald, Ireland and Empire* (Hamden, CT: Quinnipiac University Press/Ireland's Great Hunger Museum, 2016)
____, *The Tombs of a Departed Race: Illustrations of Ireland's Great Hunger* (Hamden, CT: Quinnipiac University Press/Ireland's Great Hunger Museum, 2014)
Otway, Caesar, *A Tour in Connaught* (Dublin: William Curry, 1839)
Panofsky, Erwin, *Gothic Architecture and Scholasticism* (Latrobe, PA: Archabbey Press, 1951)
Petrie, George, "An essay on the round towers of Ireland", *Dublin University Magazine*, vol. 14, no. 84 (Dec. 1839)
Pilot, Mar. 27, 1846
Pocock, Tom, *Topham and Son: A Family of Artists* (London: Burgh House Museum, 1985)
Punch, July–Dec. 1848
Pyle, Hilary, *Jack B. Yeats: A Catalogue Raisonné of the Oil Paintings*, vol. 1 (London: André Deutsch, 1992),
____, "John Behan", *Circa*, nos 71–2 (spring 1995)
"Queen Victoria's journal, 8 Aug. 1849", Royal Archives, London
Reilly, Ciarán, *John Plunket Joly and the Great Famine in King's County* (Dublin: Four Courts Press, 2012)
Relief Commission Papers, National Archives of Ireland
Report on the Sanitary Convenience of Dublin Castle, Nov. 12, 1845, Relief Commission Papers, National Archives of Ireland
Ricœur, Paul, "Memory and forgetting", in Richard Kearney and Mark Dooley (eds), *Questioning Ethics: Contemporary Debates in Philosophy* (London: Routledge, 1999)
Rieff, David, *In Praise of Forgetting: Historical Memory and its Ironies* (New Haven and London: Yale University Press, 2016)
Riis, Jacob, *How the Other Half Lives: Studies Among the Tenements of New York* (New York: Charles Scribner, 1890)
Roberts, James, letter to T. Lucas Clements, Oct. 15, 1846, Lucas-Clements Papers, Maynooth University
Rooney, Brendan, "William Willes", in Nicola Figgis (ed.), *Art and Architecture of Ireland, Volume II: Painting 1600–1900* (London and New Haven, CT: Yale University Press, 2014)
Roscommon Messenger, Aug. 11, 1849
Rossetti, William Michael, "Art news from London", *Crayon*, no. 1 (Apr. 25, 1855)
____ (ed.), *Pre-Raphaelite Diaries and Letters* (London: Hurst & Blackett, 1900)
____, *Some Reminiscences of William Michael Rossetti* (New York: Charles Scribner; London: Brown, Langham, 1906)
Sadlier, Nicholas, letter to James Sadlier, Nov. 12, 1845 (private collection)
Scott, Yvonne (ed.), *Jack B. Yeats: Old and New Departures* (Dublin: Four Courts Press, 2008)
Sedall, Henry, *Edward Nangle: The Apostle of Achill: A Memoir and a History* (London: Hatchards, 1884)
Sheehy, Jeanne, "The Irish at Antwerp", *Irish Arts Review Yearbook*, vol. 10 (1994)
Simpson, Roger, *Sir John Tenniel: Aspects of His Work* (Cranbury, NJ: Associated University Presses, 1994)
Snoddy, Theo, *Dictionary of Irish Artists, 20th Century* (Dublin: Wolfhound Press, 1996)
Sontag, Susan, *Regarding the Pain of Others* (New York: Picador, 2003)
Southern Reporter, Mar. 4 18, 1847
Staley, Allen, *The Pre-Raphaelite Landscape* (Oxford: Clarendon Press, 1973)
Stephens, Dr, "Cork union. Report from Dr Stephens to the Board of Health, on the Cork workhouse", Feb. 17, 1847, in *Workhouses (Ireland). A Copy of the Reports Made to the Board of Health in Dublin, by the Medical Officers Sent to Inquire into the State of the Workhouses in Cork, Bantry, and Lurgan*, BPP 1847, lv.11
____, "Second report from Dr Stephens to the Board of Health, on the Cork workhouse", Feb, 18, 1847, in *Workhouses (Ireland). A Copy of the Reports Made to the Board of Health in Dublin, by the Medical Officers Sent to Inquire into the State of the Workhouses in Cork, Bantry, and Lurgan*, BPP 1847, lv.11
Stephens, F.G. "The late Alfred Downing Fripp", *Magazine of Art*, vol. 18 (1895)
____, *William Holman Hunt and His Works: A Memoir of the Artist's Life with Description of His Pictures* (London: James Nisbet, 1861)
Stephenson, Kathryn, "The quarantine war: the burning of the New York Marine Hospital in 1858", *Public Health Reports*, vol. 119 (Jan.–Feb. 2004)
Stokes, William, *The Life and Labours in Art and Archaeology of G. Petrie* (London: Longmans, Green, & Co., 1868)
Strickland, Walter, *A Dictionary of Irish Artists*, 2 vols (Dublin: Maunsel & Co., 1913)
Taylor, Alfred Swaine, *Medical Jurisprudence* (Philadelphia: Blanchard & Lea, 1853)
Transactions of the Central Relief Committee of the Society of Friends
Transactions of the Central Relief Committee of the Society of Friends, p. 155;
Transactions of the Central Relief Committee of the Society of Friends During the Famine in Ireland, in 1846 and 1847 (Dublin, 1852)
Trench, F.F., "Letters concerning the Famine in Schull", in W. Steuart Trench, *Realities of Irish Life* (London: Longmans, Green, & Co., 1868)
Trench, Richard Chenevix, "Three days of the Famine at Schull", *Fraser's Magazine for Town and Country*, no. 36 (July 1847)
Trevelyan, Charles E.,"The Irish crisis", *Edinburgh Review*, no. clxxv (Edinburgh: Longmans, Brown, Green, & Co.; London: Longmans, 1848)
Tromans, Nicholas, *David Wilkie: The People's Painter* (Edinburgh: Edinburgh University Press, 2007)
Trumble, Alfred (ed.),"The drift of the day", *Collector*, vol. 3, no. 9 (Mar. 1, 1892)
Tuke, James H. *A Visit to Connaught in the Autumn of 1847* (London: Charles Gilpin, 1848)
____, *Report of the Society of Friends on Distress in Ireland*, National Library of Ireland, Ms Ir. 9410859
Tynan, Katherine, "Irish types & traits", *Magazine of Art*, vol. 11 (1888)
Valente, Joseph, *The Myth of Manliness in Irish National Culture, 1880–1922* (University of Illinois Press, 2011)
Vanderhoof, Charles A., "A tenement house in Mulberry street", *Harper's Weekly*, Sept. 13, 1873
Vann, Philip, "A man of imagination", in Katharine Crouan (ed.), *William Crozier* (Aldershot and London: Lund Humphries, 2007)
Verde, Tom, "An Irish tale of hunger and the Sultan", *Aramco World* (Jan./Feb. 2015)
Ward, Margaret, *Maud Gonne: Ireland's Joan of Arc* (London: Pandora Press, 1990)
Ward, Wilfrid Philip, *Aubrey de Vere: A Memoir* (New York: Longmans, Brown, Green, & Co.; London: Longmans, 1904)
Watts, M.S., *George Frederic Watts, Volume 1: The Annals of an Artist's Life* (London: Macmillan & Co., 1912)
Weinberg, Barbara H., *The Lure of Paris: Nineteenth-century Painters and Their French Teachers* (New York: Abbeville Press, 1991)
West Cork Eagle and County Advertiser, Oct. 6, 1877
Whelan, Kevin, "Immoral economy: interpreting Erskine Nicol's *The Tenant*", in Adele M. Dalsimer and Vera Kreilkamp (eds), *America's Eye: Irish Paintings from the Collection of Brian P. Burns* (Boston: Boston College Museum of Art, 1996)
____, "The cultural effects of the Famine", in Joe Cleary and Clare Connolly (eds), *The Cambridge Companion to Modern Irish Culture* (Cambridge: Cambridge University Press, 2005)
Wilde, Sir William [William Robert Wilde], "Irish popular superstitions", in idem, *Ireland: Her Wit, Peculiarities, and Popular Superstitions* (Dublin: McGlashan & Gill, 1852)
Williams, Alexander, *Memoirs of Alexander Williams*, unpublished MS, vol. 1 (1911)
____, *Something About Achill* (Dublin: Williams, B.B. & Robinson, 1897)
Williams, Leslie A., *Daniel O'Connell: The British Press and the Irish Famine: Killing Remarks* (London: Ashgate, 2003)
Williams, William, *Creating Irish Tourism: The First Century, 1750–1850* (London: Anthem Press, 2010)
Woodham-Smith, Cecil, *The Great Hunger: Ireland 1845–1849* (London: Hamish Hamilton, 1962)
Wyman, Max, *The Defiant Imagination: Why Culture Matters* (Vancouver: Douglas & McIntyre, 2004)
Young, Arthur, *A Tour in Ireland, 1776–1779*, vol. 2 (London: Cadell, 1780)

Abbreviations:

IGHM	Ireland's Great Hunger Museum
ILN	*Illustrated London News*
IMMA	Irish Museum of Modern Art
NCA/NCAD	National College of Art (and Design)
NFC	National Folklore Collection
NGI	National Gallery of Ireland
NGS	National Galleries of Scotland
PRHA	President of the Royal Hibernian Academy
PT	*Pictorial Times*
RA	Royal Academy
RHA	Royal Hibernian Academy
RSA	Royal Scottish Academy
UCD	University College, Dublin

Copyright:

Index:

Image Credits:

Cover
William Crozier (1930–2011)
Rainbow's End, 1970
Oil on canvas, 71.7 x 47.8 in (182 x 121.5 cm)
© Estate of William Crozier

Figure 1
(Henry) Mark Anthony (1817–86)
Sunset (also known as *Rock of Cashel)*,
c. 1847
Oil on canvas, 45 x 45 in (114 x 114 cm)
© Ireland's Great Hunger Museum

Figure 2
James Mahony,
"The Hut or Watch-house in the
Old Chapel Yard"
(*Illustrated London News*, February 13, 1847)

Figure 3
James Mahony, "Boy and Girl at Cahera"
(*Illustrated London News*, February 20, 1847)

Figure 4
James Mahony,
"Woman Begging at Clonakilty"
(*Illustrated London News,* February 13, 1847)

Figure 5
"Bridget O'Donnel and Children"
(*Illustrated London News*, December 22,
1849)

Figure 6
"Attack on a Potatoe [*sic*] Store"
(*Illustrated London News*, June 25, 1842)

Figure 7
James Mahony, "The Village of Mienies"
(*Illustrated London News*, February 20, 1847)

Figure 8
Gustave Courbet (1819–77)
Burial at Ornans, France, 1849
Oil on canvas, 124 x 263 in (315 x 668 cm)
Erich Lessing/Art Resource, NY

Figure 9
Francisco De Goya (1746–1828)
No hay quien los socorra
(Nobody can help them), *c*. 1812
Etching and aquatint with burin and
burnishing, printed in brown, on laid paper,
9.25 x 9.18 in (23.5 x 23.2 cm)
Courtesy National Gallery of Art Washington

Figure 10
Théodore Géricault (1791–1824)
Raft of the Medusa, 1819
Oil on canvas, 193 x 282 in (491 x 716 cm)
© Art Resource

Figure 11
Sir David Wilkie (1785–1841)
The Peep-o'-Day Boys' Cabin
in the West of Ireland
1835–36
Oil on canvas, 49.5 x 69 in (125.7 x 175.3 cm)
© Tate, London 2017

Figure 12
Erskine Nicol (1825-1904)
A Knotty Point, 1853
Oil on canvas, 11 x 14.25 in (27.94 x 36.19 cm)
© Ireland's Great Hunger Museum

Figure 13
Thomas Nast, "St. Patrick's Day, 1867
– 'The day we celebrate'"
(*Harper's Weekly*, April 6, 1867)

Figure 14
Kenny Meadows, "The Irish Frankenstein"
(*Punch, or The London Charivari*, 1843)

Figure 15
"Irish Physiognomy"
(*Illustrated London News*, October 7, 1843)

Figure 16
"Idiot and Mother"
(*Illustrated London News,* August 12, 1843)

Figure 17
Frederick Goodall, "Fairy Struck, or,
the Dying Child"
(*People's Journal*, January 9, 1847)

Figure 18
"M. Soyer's Model Soup Kitchen"
(*Illustrated London News*, April 17, 1847)

Figure 19
"Miss Kennedy Distributing Clothing
at Kilrush"
(*Illustrated London News*, December 22,
1849)

Figure 20
George M.W. Atkinson (*c*. 1806–84)
U.S. Sloop of War Jamestown, 1847
Lithograph, 16.53 x 20.47 in (42 x 52 cm)
Courtesy of American Antiquarian Society

Figure 21
Frederic William Burton (1816–1900)
Aran Fisherman's Drowned Child, 1841
Watercolor on paper, 34.8 x 30.9 in
(88.4 x 78.5 cm)
National Gallery of Ireland Collection,
NGI.6048
Photo © National Gallery of Ireland

Figure 22
Nathaniel Gorgan (1740–1807)
The Wake, c. early 19th century
Oil on panel, 18.5 x 24.5 in (47 x 62.2 cm)
Gift of the Martin I. and Margaret J. Zankel Revocable Trust and of the West Family Trust to the Fine Arts Museums Foundation
Image provided by the Fine Arts Museums of San Francisco

Figure 23
H. Smith, "The Famine in Ireland - Funeral at Skibbereen"
(*Illustrated London News*, January 30, 1847)

Figure 24
"Sketch in a House at Fahey's Quay, Ennis - The Widow Connor and her Dying Child"
(*Illustrated London News*, January 5, 1850)

Figure 25
James Mahony, "Mullins's Hut at Scull"
(*Illustrated London News*, February 20, 1847)

Figure 26
"Forging Pikes – a Recent Scene in Ireland"
(*Illustrated London News*, August 5, 1848)

Figure 27
"The Affray at the Widow McCormack's House, on Boulagh Common"
(*Illustrated London News*, August 12, 1848)

Figure 28
Joseph Patrick Haverty (1794–1864)
The Monster Meeting at Clifden in 1843, 1844
Oil on canvas, 43.3 x 72 in (110 x 183 cm)
Photo © National Gallery of Ireland

Figure 29
Daniel Macdonald (1820–53)
The Irish Faction Leader, 1844
Oil on canvas, 50 x 40 in (128.3 x 102.2 cm)
Collection of Sir Michael Smurfit
Image courtesy of Sir Michael Smurfit

The Irish Faction Leader, 1844
Red chalk on paper, 17.25 x 13.75 in (43.82 x 34.9 cm)
© Ireland's Great Hunger Museum

Figure 30
Fitzpatrick, "Ejectment of Irish Tenantry"
(*Illustrated London News*, December 16, 1848)

Figure 31
Fitzpatrick, "The Day After the Ejectment"
(*Illustrated London News*, December 16, 1848)

Figure 32
"Village of Moveen"
(*Illustrated London News*, December 22, 1849)

Figure 33
Erskine Nicol (1825–1904)
An Ejected Family, 1853
Oil on canvas, 19.7 x 32.3 in (50 x 82 cm)
National Gallery of Ireland Collection, NGI 4577
Photo © National Gallery of Ireland

Figure 34
Daniel Macdonald (1820–53)
Eviction, c. 1850
Oil on canvas, 25 x 29 in (63 x 75 cm)
Image courtesy of Crawford Art Gallery, Cork

Figure 35
Robert George Kelly (1822–1910)
An Ejectment in Ireland (A Tear and a Prayer for Erin), 1848–51
From the collection of Anthony J. Mourek
Image provided by *Irish Arts Review*

Figure 36
Lady Elizabeth Butler (1846–1933)
Evicted, 1890
Oil on canvas, 51.57 x 76.37 in (131 x 194 cm)
National Folklore Collection, University College Dublin

Figure 37
William Willes (c. 1785–1851)
Mock Funeral, 1851
Oil on canvas, 40.1 x 50 in. (101.9 x 127 cm)
Image courtesy of William Laffan

Figure 38
Erskine Nicol (1825–1904)
An Irish Emigrant Landing in Liverpool (Jim Blake landing in Liverpool), 1871
Oil on canvas, 56 x 39.76 in (142 x 101 cm)
National Galleries of Scotland
Presented by Sir A. Oliver Riddell 1905

Figure 39
James Glen Wilson (1827–63)
Emigrant Ship Leaving Belfast, 1852
Oil on canvas, 28.11 x 35.94 in (71.4 x 91.3 cm)
© National Museum NI
Collection Ulster Museum, BELUM.U178

Figure 40
George Catlin (1796–1872)
Five Points, 1827, 1859
Hand colored lithograph, 7 x 11.9 in (17.78 x 30.23 cm)
McSpedon & Baker/Museum of the City of New York, 97.227.3

Figure 41
Samuel Bell Waugh (1814–85)
Immigrants Disembarking at the Battery, Castle Garden (also known as *The Bay and Harbor of New York*), 1847
Oil on canvas, 99 x 198 in (251.46 x 502.92 cm)
Museum of the City of New York, 33.169.1

Figure 42
John Joseph Barker (1824–1904)
Irish Immigrants, c. 1847
Oil on canvas, 100.4 x 72.9 in (255 x 185.2 cm)
Victoria Art Gallery, Bath and North East Somerset Council/Bridgeman Images

Figure 43
F.J. Davis
The State Ballroom, St. Patrick's Hall, Dublin Castle
c. 1845–50
Oil on wood panel, 37.5 x 51.5 in (95.25 x 130.81 cm)
The Irish Art Collection of Brian P. Burns

Figure 44
Daniel Macdonald (1820–53)
An Irish Peasant Family Discovering the Blight of Their Store, 1847
Oil on canvas, 33 x 41 in (84 x 104 cm)
National Folklore Collection, University College Dublin

Figure 45
Hugh Dorian manuscript
Courtesy of Hugh Casey

Acknowledgments:

Coming Home: Art and the Great Hunger is a collaboration between Ireland's Great Hunger Museum and the Coach House, Dublin Castle, Uillinn: West Cork Arts Centre, and Cultúrlann Uí Chanáin, Derry. We thank their directors and boards, in particular Mary Heffernan, Joanne Bannon, Ann Davoren, Cyril Thornton, Declan Tiernan, Dan Reilly, Gearóid Ó hEára, Eibhlín Ní Dhochartaigh, and their colleagues. We also thank Cork City Council and Cork County Council, and the many Cork cultural and historical organizations that have welcomed this initiative, in particular Terri Kearney and Philip O'Regan of the Skibbereen Heritage Centre, and Dr Siobhán Burke.

At Quinnipiac University we have had the support of the Office of Public Affairs, especially Jim Ryan, Christine Smith, Peter Gallay and the entire Integrated Marketing Communications office, and from Don Weinbach, head of development, and Rick Ryan, director of corporate relations. Also, Lucille Marottolo, Jan Headley, Greg Garvey, and Jonah Warren.

The exhibition is accompanied by an exciting contextual program, and we thank Seán Kissane, curator Irish Museum of Modern Art, Kevin Whelan, director Keough Naughton Institute, University of Notre Dame, Sheila Pratschke, Arts Council, Ruth Hegarty, Royal Irish Academy, and Karen Walshe, St Patrick's Festival. We have benefitted from the support of the International Literature Festival, Dublin, University College, Cork, National University of Ireland, Maynooth, University College, Dublin, Trinity College, Dublin, National University of Ireland, Galway, the Chester Beatty Library, Strokestown Park and Famine Museum, Fáilte Ireland, and the Arts Council/An Chomhairle Ealaíon.

The design work for this exhibition was undertaken by the award-winning designer Rachel Foley, whose creativity and skill animates so many of the publications emanating from the museum. We warmly thank Dominic Carroll for his skillful copy-editing and meticulous attention to detail in the production of this catalogue. And for the ongoing support of Cork University Press we express our gratitude.

Following the groundwork undertaken by Conor Kenny of Kenny's of Galway, the collection has been expanded with the assistance of dealers and auctioneers: in Ireland James Adam's, Whyte's, de Vere's, Shepherd's, Morgan O'Driscoll, and the Taylor Gallery; in London Piano Nobile and the Frith Street Gallery. We thank Susan Mulhall, who has restored many of the period frames of paintings to their current pristine state. The museum is particularly indebted to James and the late, much-loved Thérèse Gorry of the Gorry Gallery, Dublin for their exceptionally generous and unstinting support of the museum.

Since its foundation, many friends and colleagues have advised on the development of the museum, without whom this exhibition would never have come about. I value this opportunity to thank Angela Bourke, Mary Broderick, Marguérite Corporaal, Marion Casey, Katharine Crouan, Fintan Cullen, Ciarán Deane, Nicola Figgis, Oona Frawley, Anne Hodge, Terri Kearney, Brian S.B. Kennedy, Joe Lee, Breandán Mac Suibhne, Maurice Manning, Eddie McParland, Amy Meyers, Margaret Kelleher, Claudia Kinmonth, Elizabeth Kirwan, Vera Kreilkamp, Críostóir Mac Cárthaigh, Emily Mark-Fitzgerald, William Laffan, Niamh McNally, Donal Maguire, Mick Moloney, Lucy Masterson, Alan Moore, Paula Murphy, Peter Murray, Maureen O'Connor, Cormac Ó Gráda, Cormac O'Malley, Philip O'Regan, Brendan Rooney, and Nick Tromans.

Our film, *The Hunger Times*, was commissioned to help us tell the story of the Famine to children. We deeply appreciate the dedication of our producer Tony Tracy; the Tile Media team, Dave Farrell, Keith Farrell, Colin Farrell, and Hannah Salt; and Fran Keaveney. The film was funded by The Ireland Funds, and we thank them for their generous sponsorship. Our program includes related film events, for which we thank Ross Keane and Sunniva O'Flynn of the Irish Film Institute, and Patrick O'Neill at Wildcard Distribution.

I wish to express my gratitude to Perry Curtis, who has inspired so much scholarship in the field of representations of the Irish, and who has taken a big interest in our museum. I thank Catherine Marshall for her helpful comments on parts of this text, and her ongoing advice on aspects of the museum. And, as ever, I owe a huge debt to Luke Gibbons; I have benefitted enormously from his knowledge and I thank him for his reading of my essay in this catalogue, and his invaluable advice and comments.

Without Claire Puzarne's management of the project, this exhibition would not have seen the light of day. An exhibition of this scale, emanating from a small university museum but six years old, is an enormous undertaking. As assistant director, Claire has handled it with consummate skill. The *Coming Home* project was initiated under the directorship of Grace Brady, who was recently replaced by Ryan Mahoney, who is working on future exhibitions, and is assisted by museum personnel Kate Sweeney, Margaret Vaughan, and Frank McCarthy.

The contemporary artists in the collection have worked with us in establishing the reputation of the museum: John Behan, Meg Chamberlain, John Coll, Dorothy Cross, Rowan Gillespie, Glenna Goodacre, Charlotte Kelly, Brian Maguire, Hughie O'Donoghue, Alanna O'Kelly, Geraldine O'Reilly, Pádraic Reaney, and Kieran Tuohy. The museum takes great pride in the generosity of Robert Ballagh, who donated a painting specifically executed to mark this exhibition.

We have worked with the Department of Education, Patrick Coffey, Scoilnet, school inspectors Frances Moss and Kevin McCarthy, and teachers Anne-Marie Ryan and Dave O'Mahony in the generation of educational materials as part of the museum's commitment to making its collection accessible to audiences of all ages.

Stillwater Communications, Cilian Fennell, Niamh Mongey, and Rebecca Bury have supported and guided the promotional, press, and public-relations aspects of the exhibition. We are very grateful to them for their energy and vision in bringing it to public awareness.

The museum's publications program ensures that audiences have access to the latest scholarship as it pertains to both the historical and contemporary dimensions of the collection. Our *Famine Folios* demonstrate the vitality of Famine scholarship in history, art history, cultural theory, media history, political economy, literature, and music across interdisciplinary lines, with essays by Angela Bourke, L. Perry Curtis Jr., Michael Foley, Tadhg Foley, Christine Kinealy, Luke Gibbons, Richard Kearney and Sheila Gallagher, Niamh Ann Kelly, Gearóid Ó Tuathaigh, Paschal Mahoney, Breandán Mac Suibhne, Catherine Marshall, Mick Moloney, Robert Smart and Vincent Woods.

The catalogue for *Coming Home: Art and the Great Hunger* includes a preface by President Michael D. Higgins and essays by Laurence Geary, Breandán Mac Suibhne and Ciarán Reilly – cogent, provocative, and insightful contributions to Famine scholarship. In the museum we draw on Christine Kinealy's scholarship, and, of course, the board of the museum, President John L. Lahey and vice-presidents Jean Husted, Lynn Bushnell, Pat Healy, and Mark Varholak have supported bringing this exhibition to Ireland, I thank them warmly. Ireland's Great Hunger Museum is as yet small, but, as its collection demonstrates, is committed to the best. And in this museum, in this, the year of his retirement, President John Lahey's legacy lies.

The Famine has become part of the fabric of my family. To Deirdre, Fiona, Kevin, Derval and Eavan, John, Ger, Paul, and Conor I express my appreciation for them having shared their expertise and contacts, for offering valued advice, and for many acts of practical assistance. As ever, Mick has done so much more than provide encouragement: his invaluable media advice and connections, in both Ireland and the United States, have enhanced the development and profile of the museum internationally. My daughter Rachel (our designer), son Luke, and son and daughter-in-law Paul and Meg have been so supportive. My personal dedication is to their children, my grandchildren, Ben, Luke, and Nicholas, that they may know their story.

Niamh O'Sullivan

Contributors:

Laurence Geary has held teaching and research appointments at the Australian National University, Canberra, the University of Melbourne, the University of Edinburgh, and the Royal College of Surgeons in Ireland. He recently retired as senior lecturer in history from University College, Cork. He has published extensively on the social, political, and medical history of nineteenth-century Ireland, and on the history of the Irish in Australia. He is the author of *The Plan of Campaign, 1886–1891* (Cork: Cork University Press, 1986) and *Medicine and Charity in Ireland, 1718–1851* (Dublin: University College Dublin Press, 2004), and joint editor of *Philanthropy in Nineteenth-century Ireland* (Dublin: Four Courts Press, 2015).

Breandán Mac Suibhne is the author of *The End of Outrage* (Oxford: Oxford University Press, 2017), a study of post-Famine adjustment in rural Ireland. He is editor of two annotated editions: John Gamble's *Society and Manners in Early-nineteenth-century Ireland* (Dublin: Field Day, 2011), and, with David Dickson, Hugh Dorian's *The Outer Edge of Ulster* (Dublin: Lilliput, 2000), the longest lower-class account of the Famine. He was a founding editor, with critic Seamus Deane, of *Field Day Review* (2005–), and, with Enda Delaney, edited *Ireland's Great Famine and Popular Politics* (Abingdon: Routledge, 2016). He teaches in Centenary University, New Jersey.

Niamh O'Sullivan is professor emerita of visual culture (National College of Art and Design), and curator and board member of Ireland's Great Hunger Museum, Quinnipiac University. She curated the retrospective exhibition of Aloysius O'Kelly (Dublin City Gallery, The Hugh Lane, 1999–2000) and Daniel Macdonald (Ireland's Great Hunger Museum, 2016). She contributed to, and served on, the advisory committee for the Royal Irish Academy's *Irish Art and Architecture* (2014). Her publications include *Aloysius O'Kelly: Art, Nation, Empire* (Dublin: Field Day Publications, 2010), *The Tombs of a Departed Race: Illustrations of Ireland's Great Hunger* (Hamden, CT: Quinnipiac University Press/Ireland's Great Hunger Museum, 2014), and *In the Lion's Den: Daniel Macdonald, Ireland and Empire* (Hamden, CT: Quinnipiac University Press/Ireland's Great Hunger Museum, 2016).

Ciarán Reilly is a historian of nineteenth and twentieth-century Irish history, specialising in the Great Famine, Irish country houses and landed estates. He is author of *The Irish Land Agent, 1830–60* (Dublin: Four Courts Press, 2014), *Strokestown and the Great Irish Famine* (Dublin: Four Courts Press, 2014), and *John Plunket Joly and the Great Famine in King's County* (Dublin: Four Courts Press, 2012).

Sponsors:

The following sponsors have contributed to the publication of this catalogue or the *Coming Home* exhibition. We thank them for their support.

Department of Foreign Affairs and Trade

Department of Culture, Heritage and the Gaeltacht

The Ireland Funds

FIP Construction

RTÉ: Supporting the Arts

Morgan O'Driscoll

Additional support was provided by:

Jacqueline A., Bailey N., and Barry L. Bestle

Ms Lynn Bushnell

Ms Janet Claire Corcoran and Mr Francis John Dwyer III

Mr George Dunn

Ms Loretta Glucksman

Mr and Mrs Pat Healey

Kenny Gallery

Dr and Mrs John L. Lahey

Mr Douglas James and Ms Kay Mollick

The Merrion Hotel

Lev and Ivan Nussberg

The O'Herron Family Foundation

Mr and Mrs Alan Puzarne

The Ryan Family

Ms Patricia Vitanza

Mr George Waldron

Whyte's

And various other donors

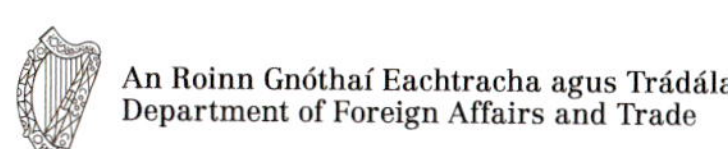

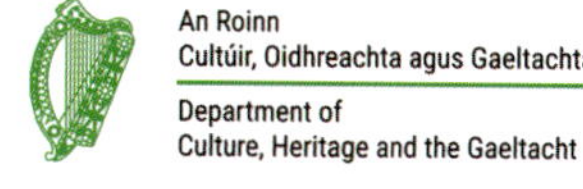

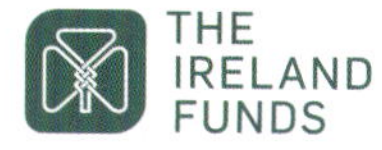

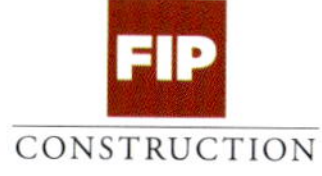

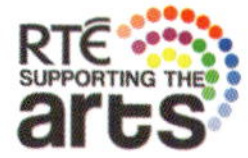

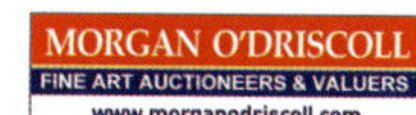

EDITOR
Niamh O'Sullivan

PROJECT MANAGER & PICTURE EDITOR
Claire Puzarne

EDITORIAL ASSISTANT
Kathryn Sweeney

COPY-EDITOR
Dominic Carroll

DESIGN
Rachel Foley
rachelfoleydesigns.com

PRINTING
GRAPHYCEMS

ISBN 978-0-9978374-8-3

Ireland's Great Hunger Museum
Quinnipiac University
3011 Whitney Avenue
Hamden, CT 06518-1908
203-582-6500
www.ighm.org